The Construction of Profess

LANGUAGE IN SOCIAL LIFE SERIES

Series Editor: Professor Christopher N. Candlin

Language and power
Norman Fairclough

Discourse and the translator
Basil Hatim and Ian Mason

Planning language, planning inequality
James W. Tollefson

Language and ideology in children's fiction
John Stephens

Linguistics and aphasia
Ruth Lesser and Lesley Milroy

Language and the law
John Gibbons

Literacy practices: investigating literacy in social contexts
Mike Baynham

The cultural politics of English as an international language
Alastair Pennycook

Fictions at work: language and social practice in fiction
Mary Talbot

Critical discourse analysis: the critical study of language
Norman Fairclough

Knowledge machines: language and information in a technological society
Denise E. Murray

Achieving understanding: discourse in intercultural encounters
Katharina Bremer, Celia Roberts, Marie-Thérèse Vasseur, Margaret Simonot and Peter Broeder

The construction of professional discourse
Britt-Louise Gunnarsson, Per Linell and Bengt Nordberg

The Construction of Professional Discourse

Edited by
Britt-Louise Gunnarsson,
Per Linell and
Bengt Nordberg

LONGMAN
London and New York

Addison Wesley Longman Limited
Edinburgh Gate
Harlow, Essex CM20 2JE
United Kingdom
and Associated Companies throughout the world

*Published in the United States of America
by Addison Wesley Longman, New York*

First published 1997

ISBN 0 582 25942 8 Csd
ISBN 0 582 25941 X Ppr

British Library Cataloguing-in-Publication Data

A catalogue record for this book is
available from the British Library

Library of Congress Cataloging-in-Publication Data

The construction of professional discourse / edited by Britt-Louise Gunnarsson, Per Linell, and Bengt Nordberg.
p. cm. – (Language in social life series)
Includes bibliographical references and index.
ISBN 0-582-25941-X (pbk.) – ISBN 0-582-25942-8 (cased)
1. Discourse analysis. I. Gunnarsson, Britt-Louise. II. Linell, Per, 1944- . III. Nordberg, Bengt. IV. Series.
P302.C6217 1997
401'.41–dc21 96-46802
CIP

Transferred to digital print on demand 2001

Printed and bound by Antony Rowe Ltd, Eastbourne

Contents

Contributors

Jan Anward, Associate Professor of Linguistics, Stockholm University, Sweden

Charles Bazerman, Professor of English, University of California, Santa Barbara, USA

Christopher N. Candlin, Executive Director, National Centre for English Language Teaching and Research, Macquarie University, Sydney, Australia

Brenda Danet, Professor of Sociology and Communication, Hebrew University of Jerusalem, Israel

Charles Goodwin, Professor in the Department of Applied Linguistics, University of California, Los Angeles, USA

Marjorie Harness Goodwin, Professor in the Department of Anthropology, University of California, Los Angeles, USA

Christopher Hall, Doctor of Philosophy, University of Bristol, England

Lars-Christer Hyden, Associate Professor in the Department of Social Work, Stockholm University, Sweden

Charlotte Linde, Senior Research Scientist in the Institute for Research on Learning, Menlo Park, California, USA

Yon Maley, Senior Research Associate, Macquarie University, Sydney, Australia

Elliot G. Mishler, Professor of Social Psychology, Harvard Medical School, USA

Srikant Sarangi, Lecturer in the Centre for Language and Communication Research, University of Wales, Cardiff, Wales

Stefaan Slembrouck, Lecturer in the Department of English, University of Gent, Belgium

Anna Trosborg, Associate Professor of English, Aarhus School of Business, Denmark

Ellen Valle, Senior Lecturer in English, University of Turku, Finland

Ruth Wodak, Professor of Applied Linguistics, University of Vienna, Austria

General Editor's Preface

I would like in the Preface to this most recent contribution to the *Language in Social Life Series* to highlight a number of key constructs, approaches to methodology, and contributions to our understanding of discursive and social practices, that characterise both this rich and persuasive collection and the study of language in social life more generally. It is important to widen the perspective beyond the book itself, not least because its diversity of reference to institutional and professional practice, and its making concrete of some of the ways that linguists and discourse analysts may engage with institutional and professional members, makes it more than usually emblematic of the purposes and scope of the *Language in Social Life Series* as a whole.

'Discourse' is often used to refer to connected language in general, a generalization or an abstraction which is realized in specific pieces of connected and coherent language, or texts. Discourse in this sense is no more than stretches of connected spoken or written language, but since any interpretation of their meaning necessarily implies that such analysis depends on the context or social situation in which they occur and on which any interpretation of their meaning depends, then more commonly discourse refers to language in use, as a process which is socially situated. However, as here in this book, and without any sense of conflict with this view, we may go on to stress the constructive and dynamic role of either spoken or written discourse in structuring areas of knowledge and the social and institutional practices which are associated with them. In this sense, discourse is a means of talking and writing about and acting upon worlds, a means which both constructs and is constructed by a set of social practices within these worlds, and in so doing both reproduces and constructs afresh particular social-discursive practices, constrained or encouraged by more macro movements in the overarching social formation. Moreover, because it is individuals who use and create discourse, (which is not to say that discourse is individualistic), discourse analysis may explore ways in which the lexico-grammatical, the semantic and the textual-discursive (in the sense of creating and packaging coherent discourse) options available to and chosen by such individuals can be interpreted as serving to construct, reinforce, and critique social roles, social behaviours and social practices. Further, describing and interpreting discourses in this way at the same time involves also our hypothesising the linguistic, semantic and pragmatic exclusions, the meanings that are unwelcome and non-functional in given contexts. These exclusions are part of a system of constraints, extra-linguistic, social motivations for selecting or rejecting linguistic formulations or discursive patterns in the construction of a given discourse. Since discourses are inherently part of social behaviour, on either interpretation, they are also inherently cultural.

It is this exercise of creativity and problem-framing that discources typically complexify as they draw on and frequently contend with the resources of other discourses associated with other social practices. This complexification is especially likely to occur at times when as Foucault suggests, functional correlations across discourses motivate the value of incorporating linguistic elements of various kinds from one text type to another, or from one socially situated discourse to another. Discourses are thus made internally variable by the incorporation of such intertextual and interdiscursive elements. Such evolving and hybridised discourses are thus intertextual in that they manifest a plurality of text sources. However, insofar as any characteristic text evokes particular discoursal values (in our second sense above), in that it imbricates some institutional and social meanings, such discourses are at the same time interdiscursive.

In saying this I am also pointing to the argument that all texts are in some sense intertextual, all discourses interdiscursive, requiring a Foucaultian archaeology to uncover and explicate how it is that they are multiply formed. On Fairclough's argument, such analysis is important for the understanding of social change, in particular revelatory of how in institutions where orders of discourse are unstable, consisting of internally heterogeneous discursive practices whose boundaries are in flux, such productive and innovative interdiscursivity permits a parallel exploration of heterogeneity and potential innovation in social and institutional practices. New and newly integrated voices revalue the old, creatively evidencing as a novel resource the emergence of new orders of discourse which may then be taken as partial evidence for social and institutional change. We should, however, be clear that the relationships entered into by discourses in such a process of interdiscursivity may not always be harmonious. Frequently, discourses may be in relationships of opposition as they jockey for positional advantage in the arena of pragmatic and social space.

All the above constitutes a backdrop, then, against which one may embark on reading this book edited by Gunnarsson, Linell and Nordberg. There are, however, other constructs which are implied and which deserve identification. The first, inherent in the foregoing, is that to which Scollon refers to in his writings as *communities of practice,* the processes, objectives, modes of working, mediated interactions, of particular groupings of members in certain locations and at historically situated moments which allow them to be recognised, to themselves and for outsiders, as sharing belonging. To this construct we may conveniently add Swales' notion of *discourse communities,* emphasising thereby the discursive (re)construction of such communities, much as is heralded above. In identifying this collectivity, however, it is important not to homogenise diversity and lose the characteristic interdiscursivity emphasised by Bourdieu, one, by the way, which is not only interpersonal within the community but intrapersonal within the ideological constitution of the individual. To a degree that recognition of diversity can be guaranteed by adopting another of Scollon's constructs, that of the *sites of engagement* within the practices of the community. To do so is not only important as a warrant for discourse analysts who need a focused purchase on texts, but also conveniently underpins the diversity represented by the chapters in this book. They are all sites of engagement. More than merely being *sites*, however, (and remembering here Gumperz's construct of *crucial* sites), they are the settings for what I have called elsewhere *critical moments*, where personal and community matters of concern are critically evidenced and in play, typically matters surrounding issues of rights, powers, claims and responsibilities, which set at question who the framers and gatekeepers of such issues are, and who the respondent followers. Critical moments, moreover, where discursive (in)competence is at a premium. The contributions here all offer evidence of such sites and such moments, and do so not in some vacuum but always as appropriately historically, institutionally and above all, contingently and locally constructed.

What then of the participants themselves? Two perspectives are worth highlighting, both relating to the construct of *identity*, itself not explicitly foregrounded in the title of the book (though it might well have been), but present throughout in the chapters and in the editors' own introductory remarks. As Rodney Jones points out in a recent paper in the new *Journal of Sociolinguistics* concerned with the representation of persons living with AIDS, the topic of individual and collective identity is central to the intellectual debates of modern and post-modern writers on the social condition. Such debates are everywhere concretised but perhaps especially so in multilingual and multicultural societies like my own Australia. Here, individual and societal notions of identity (racial, ethnic, social, professional, institutional) under the pressures of dynamic change and the diversity I spoke of earlier, and in the light of considerable transformation of the social fabric, in homes, workplaces, the academy, and against a re-evaluation of beliefs and traditions, can no longer find firm purchase, given the polyphony of claimed representative voices and the polyvalence of participant roles. *Identity* thus not only resists easy definition but is itself a crucial site, and one which houses a multitude of critical moments whose characteristics are that it is just in such moments that the definitions are being proposed, struggled with and over, resisted and collaboratively negotiated. Not that the responsibility for *identification* lies only with the participants; after all, we might say from reading these chapters and our own experiences, people far more often have their identities authored for them than authoring them themselves. So, not only are selves and persons at odds, but the signalling of identity itself is problematised in the midst of such empowered diversity, a diversity which is not only characterised by knowledge distribution – which knowledge which identities can acquire – but by process access – which means are open and available to which identities.

So, if *identity* is the construct that is not explicitly named, (yet is consistently invoked indirectly), what of *professional* which is? Here the book offers us an opportunity of making a useful distinction, one which many chapters implicitly at least highlight, between the profession and the institution. In keeping with the notion of interdiscursivity I emphasised earlier, we can not only point to an intrinsic interdiscursivity within a given profession but also an interdiscursivity between profession and institution in which the former represents the achievement of licensed belonging, as it were, on the basis of accredited skill and knowledge, and the latter the potential exercise of authority, and gatekeeping, by virtue of that license. Of course, and inherently so, the practices of the profession cannot be de-institutionalised, one always empowers or disempowers by what one does and how one acts. This is of course exactly what Foucault's and Fairclough's *orders of discourse* are all about, and not only, it should be remembered, in terms of what and how people say and write what they do, but even more significantly, because equally ideologically naturalised yet not open to inspection, how and what they think.

The discussion so far has been focused on the social, discursive and philosophical constructs underlying the study of the situated encounter. There has been no especial reference to methodological issues, equally central to evaluating the contribution of this book. In one of his papers, Cicourel calls for 'ecologically valid' discourse-based research. How would such a methodology be characterised? What emerges is a requirement for a parallel and complex interdiscursivity of analysis, matching the interplay between the macro and the micro, the actual and the historical, the ethnographic and the ethnomethodological, the interactively sociolinguistic and the discoursal and above all acknowledging the need to offer explanations of *why* rather than merely descriptions of *how*. The issue then immediately arises of how to capture these distinctive methodological discourses in a workable program of research, not merely harmonising the different discourses but actively making use of their distinct epistemologies and modes of practice to enrich and expand a grounded analysis. The chapters in this book, taken together, provide one resource for establishing such an interdiscursive methodology, and imply a 'rational' research program, in Fairclough's terms, which resists some arbitrary sampling of what Haberland and Mey call 'objects trouves'.

How could such a research methodology be captured? One view from the contributions represented in this collection is that an appropriate model might be one which permitted the multiple relevance and engagement of a variety of different analytical discourses in the search for that ecological validity to discourse-based research I mention earlier. Such a model would begin from the position that social institutions and their associated 'professional' memberships (using *profession* not in any sense of select group but workers more generally) occupy a pivotal position linking the macro and the micro worlds, and that they are most illuminatingly seen as cultures characterised by negotiated practices among their participant members. This suggests that field research and naturalistic data collection need to be informed by a critical historical and structural exploration of the tenets, ideologies, and variably understood and announced purposes of the cultures of the institution in question in terms of their variant constituent social and discursive practices. This requirement in turn calls for processes of researcher triangulation of the analysed data with the participating sources of that data. Not that this elevates such a reflexive methodology to the point that it necessarily affords greater access to 'reality', simply that it affords an additional set of potentially corroborative or disturbing data, another set of discourses, in fact, to be accommodated and integrated into the research. Of course, such a methodology raises practical constraints of an ethical, practical and ideologically-invested kind that may work against a full achievement of the validity Cicourel seeks. It is for this reason that it is imperative that a research alliance be forged between the analyst and the 'professional', much in the manner illustrated in many of the papers in this book. Overall, the assumption is that different kinds of data and different methodological procedures and perspectives will produce differing kinds of results, and that similar patterns of textual realisation and discursive structures will have varying significance according to the varied social practices of the institutions and professions under focus, and, equally, will receive variable attention according to the professional affiliations and purposes of the analyst. This assumption is very well brought out in the chapters in this book.

What should be said here, of course, is that the commitment to an explanatory as well as descriptive and interpretive account is not a matter of researcher commitment only; in the experience of many of the authors represented here, it is regularly required by professional groups themselves. So for example, any discourse analytical perspective on the encounters between, say, lawyers and clients, or doctors and patients, or media makers and their subjects, ought not to escape some explanation of social relationships between such participants in their respective social institutions. For the professionals, in my experience, description is a necessary but not sufficient component. Indeed, one issue that regularly concerns such professionals is how the detail of the interaction may be shown, in an institutional sense now, to reflect and sustain shifting and unequal relationships of power, how their institutions do feed into and reinforce existing social and professional roles, how, in short, the orders of discourse of the institution stack up in interaction, and how access to knowledge *what* and knowledge *how* constrain (at least) the capacity of the institution to change and develop. Nowhere is this more sharply revealed in professional training and development, nowhere more likely to evidence the critical moments in what is itself, characteristically, a crucial site. Such a multi-perspectived approach often uncomfortably reveals ways in which the dynamic and emergent discourses themselves reflect parallel, yet unrecognised, dynamism and change throughout the fabric of the institutions themselves. The dialogue between researchers and researched must necessarily be collaborative if it is to achieve that reflexivity. More than that, however, such an approach needs to present its data and its 'results' not as *faits accomplis,* but as critical texts for explanatory analysis. In short, to formulate them as a set of sources for hypotheses about action which do not follow axiomatically, but which require the readers/actors to infer from them what interpretations (and what further data) would be necessary to verify the hypotheses, the candidate explanations, and to test them against both what they 'knew' to be the case, and, very importantly, against what might under certain circumstances *be* the case. From that comparison might arise the domains, the targets, and the discursively mediated means of change. There remain two caveats: the first is the question of the perspective that is taken in the research, whether from the institution 'downwards' as it were, or from the participating 'subjects', 'upwards'. Even if both directionalities are taken into account, the potential for analyst distortion has to be recognised since both involve reductionist dangers, both run the risk of assuming a greater centrality and importance of discourse as means and cause where, frankly, more bald-on-record inequities and summary injustices are patently to be countered. The second, more simply put, is our capacity to explain our findings in ways that our partners can find tractable, engaging and ultimately, convincing.

Christopher N. Candlin
Centre for Language in Social Life,
Macquarie University, Sydney

Editors' acknowledgements

Most of the chapters in this volume are based on papers given at the international conference *Discourse and the Professions* held in Uppsala, Sweden on 26–29 August 1992. The conference was organized by the three of us and held under the auspices of ASLA, the Swedish Association for Applied Linguistics. In this volume the four plenary lectures together with a selection of other papers around the theme of the construction of professional discourse are brought together.

Two publications appear as a result of the conference. Besides the present volume, the following anthology has been published: *Text and Talk in Professional Contexts.* Selected Papers from the International Conference 'Discourse and the Professions', Uppsala, 26–29 August 1992. Britt-Louise Gunnarsson, Per Linell and Bengt Nordberg (eds). (ASLA:s skriftserie nr 6.) ASLA, The Swedish Association of Applied Linguistics, Uppsala 1994. It can be obtained from ASLA, c/o FUMS, Box 1834, S-751 48 Uppsala, Sweden.

We gratefully acknowledge the financial support that the conference and thus also the editing of this book received from Marcus Wallenberg Foundation for International Cooperation in Science, the Swedish Council for Social Research (SFR), the Ministry of Education and Science, and Uppsala University.

We would also like to thank Christopher Candlin for his initiative to consider the book for the Longman series *Language in Social Life* and for his continuous support during the editorial process.

Britt-Louise Gunnarsson
Per Linell
Bengt Nordberg
Uppsala and Linköping
November 1996

Publisher's acknowledgements

The Publishers are grateful to the following to reproduce copyright material:

George Holliday for three half-tone photographs from "George Holliday's videotape of the Rodney King Beating" © 1991; Elsevier Science, Amsterdam for permission to reproduce parts of the paper 'Statutes and Contracts: An Analysis of Legal Speech Acts in the English Language of the Law' by Dr. Anna Trosborg in a special issue of *Journal of Pragmatics* 23 (31–5), a preliminary version of this paper was published in *Hermes* 6 (65–90).

ONE

Introduction

Britt-Louise Gunnarsson, Per Linell and Bengt Nordberg

The important role played by discourse within the construction and reconstruction of the professions is undeniable. Written texts, spoken discourse and various forms of non-verbal communication have all played essential parts in the historical creation of professional practices, and they continuously contribute to the gradual reproduction and reshaping of these practices. Though the processes are as old as the professions, the interest in the understanding of the dynamics of professional discourse is quite new and growing among researchers as well as practitioners. The research interest relates not only to the understanding of contemporary processes but also to the understanding of their historical roots.

Probably due to the ongoing differentiation and specialization of professions, more and more people are becoming aware of the importance of effective communication among organizations and individuals in business and government. Not only do the old academic professions, such as lawyers and doctors, rely heavily on writing and speaking skills, but language has become one of the most important tools of many new professions where oral and written contact with the general public forms the core of professional work. Telephone calls, meetings, negotiations and conferences have become the cornerstones of professional contacts. Many experts – business people, lawyers, health care personnel, street-level bureaucrats – spend a lot of their working hours in talk with clients, colleagues and other professionals. In the majority of cases, these spoken events are intertwined with, preceded and followed by writing practices, leading to an abundant production of memos, reports, contracts, proceedings, etc. Efficient communication – in speech and writing – not only within the professional group, but also between different specialist groups and between experts and laymen, is absolutely vital for society to function properly. At the same time, the development of new communication technology has created new forms for professional interaction. Many people's professional work consists of an intricate interaction between people and advanced technical equipment and systems.

The growing interest among practitioners in communication is reflected in an increase in scientific studies within this area. Within a multidisciplinary framework, linguists, sociologists, psychologists, communication scientists and anthropologists are analysing the historical evolution of professional genres and the contemporary social practice within different professional settings. In a society where change is taking place at an increasing pace, the need not only to grasp the contemporary practices, but also to understand these in the light of history is becoming more and more central.

As the title of this volume indicates, a key term for the chapters is 'construction', and in various degrees they relate to and depend on the general theoretical paradigm known as social constructivism (or constructionism). This theoretical perspective has traditionally been associated with the sociology of knowledge, where Berger and Luckmann's (1967) seminal work, with its telling title *The Social Construction of Reality*, has become quite influential. Social constructivism has since been adopted in other fields of sociology, and now increasingly within other scholarly disciplines dealing with language, discourse and culture. Its basic tenet is that cultural knowledge and representations of reality are interactionally constructed, socially transmitted, historically sedimented and often institutionally congealed, and finally communicatively reproduced *in situ*. There are many varieties of social constructivism. In some fields, e.g. certain approaches to social problems theory, quite radical versions have sometimes appeared, virtually claiming that social realities are to be explained entirely as sociocultural constructs. Other more 'contextual' varieties of constructivism take caution to secure a social place for subjective agency and stress the dependence on material conditions (e.g. Holstein and Miller 1993).

One controversy within social constructivism concerns how to strike a balance between the reproduction of culturally well-established patterns and the production of new social and communicative meaning in situated action and language use. Though the individual chapters of this volume have different foci, most of them reflect a combination of perspectives, i.e. they point to knowledge systems and interactional routines that have been socially (communicatively) constructed through cultural history rather than on the spot, and yet such structures and routines are all the time actively and productively re-created in situated practices. Accordingly, this book covers different aspects of how professional language and discourse have been developed historically as part of social activities, how the use of language and discourse in the professions shapes social reality, and reproduces and maintains social activities and relations, how its genres and patterns are sustained by social institutions, and how discourse enters into the continuing process of negotiations that produces novel arrangements for our social future.

From the viewpoint of linguistics this is something new and quite different from the studies of vocabulary, syntax and stylistic patterns carried out within the traditional field of language for specific purposes with purposes directed towards text typology and applications such as plain language and standardization of terminology. The constructivist approach of this volume also differs from that of the traditional field of discourse analysis in that it goes beyond the atomistic understanding of discourse strategies in a contextual vacuum, and insists on an analysis in terms of sociocultural and situational contexts.

The construction of professional discourse can thus be located and studied both in a long-term and a short-term perspective. The continuity of professional practices extends over long periods. At the same time, they are made manifest only under historically situated, concrete circumstances. The professional genres have been constructed over the years in relation to cognitive and social demands of the field and the professional group, and to those of society. They are a reflection of the political ideologies and power structures within the studied society as well as of the actual knowledge level of the field and of the social patterns of the professional group.

Genres are continuously being renewed due to changes in political ideologies, power structures, knowledge levels and social patterns. To understand professional discourse as it is, we must view it in its historical framework. We must then ask ourselves not only how professional genres have been constructed but also for whom, for what needs and why they have been formed the way they are. We must also analyse the continuous construction and reconstruction processes taking place in the various social practices *in situ*. The historical and situated contemporary construction processes are mutually constitutive. It is the repeated social practices that form the genre, and it is within the historically created genre – and due to the demands of this – that the everyday professional discourse takes place. Our task as scholars is not only to describe this relationship but also to be open for a critical analysis of these social practices and of the professional genres and ask ourselves whether these are maximally functional, in whose interests they are formed and whether there are alternative models for various professional practices. Here a deeper understanding of the historical background to the existing discourse patterns – comprising an analysis of not only how but also for whom and for which purposes these patterns have been formed – opens up new vistas on the contemporary which can facilitate such a critical and constructive analysis of the current professional practices.

The understanding of the construction of professional discourse is dependent on the empirical study both of written and spoken discourse and of non-verbal communication. Due to disciplinary traditions, research has come to reinforce boundaries between these media. These boundaries, however, are artificial, badly reflecting what has taken place and what is taking place in real-life communication (Gunnarsson 1995). We can see how, during the course of history, the spoken and written media replace each other, and how non-verbal language, due to the development of new technology, gets a new role, partly replacing the traditional verbal communication (see Danet, this volume). In real-life situations, various verbal and non-verbal resources are used interchangeably (see Goodwin and Goodwin, this volume).

This volume brings together research on different media and on the interplay between them. It places side by side studies carried out within different research traditions: conversation analysis, critical discourse analysis, narratology, sociology of science, pragmatics, text linguistics and genre studies to name a few of the traditions. A unification like this is still quite unique, surprisingly enough. Our claim, however, is that it is not only natural, considering what takes place in real-life communication, but it also enriches our understanding of professional discourse. By viewing the historical and contemporary aspects, continuity and change, from a similar perspective, we can get insights into the interplay of the now and then and the interdependencies between different media. Spoken as well as written genres have been created as answers to cognitive, social and societal needs, and they are continuously renewed and recreated in the professional practice due to the same needs. The abandoning of old genres and the creation of new ones certainly are a social act with a social meaning.

With regard to professional domains the book includes studies on legal, medical, social welfare and educational as well as scientific discourse. In certain respects each professional area is unique with a unique set of cognitive needs, social conditions and relationships with society at large, and for each area the roles of language and discourse vary. The main purpose of this volume, however, is not to present results on communication within these domains specifically, but to enlarge our understanding of the various processes involved in the construction of professional discourse.

On the whole, the remaining thirteen chapters of the book are arranged thematically, beginning with studies of the evolution and contemporary functions of professional text genres. The second part of the book – starting with Anward's chapter – consists of studies of present-day professional discourse and interaction.

The first chapter, written by Brenda Danet, opens with a broad overview of the origins, evolution and future of the performativity of language. The constitutive function of performativity is traced back to the symbolic activities of the Neanderthal people and to the social construction of performativity in the rituals of non-literate societies. With various examples, Danet analyses the transfer of performativity from speech to writing in periods when writing is in the process of becoming institutionalized. Legal documents from Ancient Mesopotamia, for instance, are found to reveal a latent struggle to transfer performativity to the new written medium. The transition stage to literacy is further discussed in relation to Old English. Basing her discussion on a case study of Anglo-Saxon wills, Danet shows how these old legal texts reflect a symbiotic relationship with the oral ceremonies which preceded them and at the same time a struggle to transfer performativity to documents. A striking feature of these documents is also their context-dependence, that is, their reliance on shared knowledge. Danet contrasts this old practice with the modern legal practice, where decontextualization is the rule. In the last part of her chapter, Danet speculates about the future of performativity in the era of the new electronic media. She claims that the processes of decontextualization of the verbal content of written texts have so much been in focus of our attention that we have ignored the function of the text-as-object. Gradually our experience of the materiality of texts has become undermined by the new technologies, which, for instance, could open up a future replacement of the written will by video films of oral ceremonies.

Performatives are also dealt with in the theoretical chapter by Charles Bazerman. With a particular focus on patents at the time of the famous inventor Thomas Edison, he discusses the history and function of performatives constituting value. The patent grants legal status and also economic value to the work of inventors, thereby translating the professional work of inventors to a valued commodity within corporations and financial networks. Status and value, however, are granted only if certain discursive actions are carried out, and it is these discursive practices which are the subject of Bazerman's analysis. Viewing the history and function of patents through both speech-act theory and sociological theory, he is able to reveal the achievements accomplished by these documents, standing at the intersection of three professional systems: technology, law and finance.

The aspect of legal language as social action, expressed by explicit or implicit performatives, is also the theme of the contribution by Anna Trosborg. The focus here is on the linguistic realization of contemporary regulative acts in simple contracts within the field of English contract law which is contrasted with the corresponding acts in law texts and in everyday conversation. Trosborg's analysis is based on politeness theory and Searlian speech-act theory and concentrates on the balancing between the needs for face redress and for clarity of the directive intent in the three contrasted genres. Both frequencies and rhetorical realizations of directive acts, such as obligation, prohibition, permission, and of constitutives and commissives are studied. One salient difference between the genres is that in law texts and contracts there is a marked predominance of direct strategies as far as statements of obligation and prohibition are concerned whereas in conversational English conventionally indirect strategies are favoured. It is argued that the cause for this difference is to be sought in the external factors of the social situation, notably the relationship between sender and receiver (e.g. contracting parties, lawyers) and not in the media (written vs. spoken language).

The evolution of scientific discourse is dealt with in two chapters. In a text rhetorical tradition, Ellen Valle traces the historical emergence of the English scientific article genre. Analysing a large corpus of articles published in the *Philosophical Transactions of the*

Royal Society of London from 1711 to 1870, she looks at the way the discourse community is represented in the texts during these 160 years. During the studied period, the life sciences (biology, medicine and natural history) evolved from a relative lack of separate identity into a cluster of autonomous disciplines. Valle's study shows how this gradual emergence of a separate disciplinary identity is reflected in the texts in relation to different textual features: the subject matter of the texts and their general rhetorical structure, the implicit or explicit 'recipient' or addressee of the text, and the presence or absence of an explicit text 'motivation', e.g. statement of purpose.

The sociohistorical construction of scientific discourse in a broader perspective is the topic of Britt-Louise Gunnarsson's contribution. Using a model developed for quantitative analysis of the cognitive content of texts, she discusses the evolving scientificality in Swedish economic articles from 1730 to 1980. The texts were classified in terms of 'cognitive world' (scientific, practical, object, private, external), 'cognitive aspect' (theory, classification, experiment within scientific world, etc.) and 'cognitive dimension' (cause, phenomenon, process, result). The historical growth of scientificality is traced in the texts, e.g. as an increase in the proportion of the scientific world and a decrease as to the external world. This historical variation is discussed in relation to the situation within the scientific community and society at different periods. From a sociohistorical viewpoint, she distinguishes three stages: a pre-establishment stage, where the scientist acts mainly within society, an establishing stage, where the scientist acts within the scientific community as well as within society, and a specialized stage, where the scientist acts mainly within the scientific community.

A major type of professional discourse is involved in what has been known as institutional discourse (Agar 1985), i.e. talk between an expert representing some authority and a layman. This type of discourse displays several common features that set it off from everyday conversation and warrant its status as a genre of its own. A further subdivision of the genre has usually been based on the contents of the conversation, the professional roles of the participants and the aim of the interaction, e.g. doctor–patient conversations, job interviews, trials. In Jan Anward's chapter it is argued that the different subgenres of institutional discourse could be distinguished by the varying patterns of the division of saying that obtains between participants and is linked to the functions of utterances as 'activity talk', 'topic talk' and 'text talk'. Extending Goffman's concept of principal to mean the one answerable for the adequacy of an utterance, Anward demonstrates how now the professional, now the layman is principal of activity, of topic and of text. He argues that the different divisions of saying are direct expressions of the social activities in which they operate. Each of these activities is cast in a particular format describable by a specific combination of values on a common set of parameters. According to Anward, these activity formats are normative, something participants strive to maintain, and thus have a great impact on the construction of professional discourse.

If Anward attempts a general framework for classifying types of professional discourse activity, Charlotte Linde provides an empirical study in some detail of one activity type, i.e. evaluation, as an example of a linguistic and social phenomenon connecting, in Linde's terms, linguistic structure and social practice. Linde studies evaluation at 'the topic level' in cases where a major purpose of the discourse is to arrive at evaluations, rather than just provide incidental assessments in discourse. Her data are drawn from two work sites in which collaborators are involved in jointly learning a new communications technology. In such cases, when professionals are trying out new equipment, evaluation is a recurrent feature of their discourse. Evaluation is pervasive in mundane conversation too, e.g. in dialogical story-telling, but in Linde's data we can see it invading varieties of professional talk, where it takes the form of a specific minor genre (or 'activity format' in Anward's terms).

As pointed out earlier, we as scholars cannot content ourselves with just describing professional discourse and the social practices of which it is a part and which has formed the various genres. We should also evaluate its functionality and its capability of promoting optimal social and personal satisfaction to the parties engaged. Ruth Wodak's study of the linguistic and non-linguistic interaction in an Austrian out-patients' ward is an example of such critical discourse analysis. She demonstrates how an understanding of the verbal and non-verbal interaction must be based on a minute analysis of the context, the routines and the organization of work. The discourse reflects and consolidates the hierarchical structure of the ward and it is also a product of the specific organization and rules of work at the clinic. A particular source of irritation and discontent, both on the part of personnel and patients, is the clash between the real situation at the ward and the different myths that flourish about hospitals and doctors. Wodak argues that if physicians and patients were made more aware of the true nature of these myths, e.g. the infallibility of doctors and the efficient organization of the work at the clinic, the quality of doctoring would rise considerably. The major contribution to this would be given by a change in attitude and communicative strategies of the doctors.

Christopher Candlin and Yon Maley discuss the emergence of a new genre of professional discourse – mediation as an alternative type of dispute resolution. Their data are derived from sessions in divorce and custody matters in Australia. When discourse genres are re-created in the continuity of practices, people make use of both intertextual and interdiscursive links to other texts (or discourses) and discourse types (using a distinction between intertextuality and interdiscursivity due to Fairclough 1992). Such processes may lead to new hybrid discourses (or discourse types), where elements from different social and linguistic, professional and everyday practices combine. In the mediation discourse described by Candlin and Maley, mediators try to facilitate processes in which parties themselves provide mutually agreeable solutions, i.e. mediators are not supposed to render decisions or enforce agreements. The authors demonstrate that this discourse is a mix drawing upon, to varying extents, features of two competing sets of professional practices and ideologies, i.e. law vs. social work (counselling and therapy).

A very illustrative example of the significance of interactional work for shaping professional discourse, in this case even a genre that has traditionally been regarded as the prototypical monologue, the narrative, is given in the chapter by Elliot Mishler. Using material from two clinical encounters and one research interview focusing on the life history of a woman potter, he demonstrates how this work of story production is done through the ways that physicians and researchers question, listen and respond to what their interlocutors say and on how, in response, the latter clarify, develop and change their stories over its course. In examining this process, the author makes problematic some of the assumptions of earlier text-based models, e.g. that the story which is told is the singular possession of the story-teller and not the result of a dynamic interactional process.

Narratives are also the subject of the contribution by Lars-Christer Hydén, but in this case the narratives constitute the written reports produced in modern bureaucratic institutions by social workers concerning child neglect and abuse and by psychiatrists concerning the involuntary commitment of patients. Hydén claims that these institutional narratives can be read as ancient tragedies with a fixed set of characters. Of these, the institutional representative invariably plays the role of the good saviour – although he/she constantly and tragically fails in his/her mission – and, in a broader perspective, the upholder of social and moral order. Hydén demonstrates how the main function of the narratives is to justify the actions and decisions of the authority and to contribute to the self-understanding of the professionals and to the meaning of their work. The narrative in a way structures the institutional reality, and objectifies and preserves the doings and motives of the actors. Hydén's examples also show how the impression of objectivity and impersonal professionalism is created by a number of stylistic devices. Thus, these narratives are easily seen as the true and objective rendering of events and characters although each of the narratives is only one story to the exclusion of other potential stories. The perspective of the institution becomes the official legally valid version.

In their chapter, Christopher Hall, Srikant Sarangi and Stefaan Slembrouck analyse an interview with a social worker on a case of suspected child abuse or neglect. Their analysis provides evidence of how narratives are used in a particular institution, that of public welfare agencies, to establish and re-establish professional legitimation and control, and, at the same time, to reconstruct one form of professional discourse. The social worker uses narrative techniques to bring in different institutional voices – e.g. those of medical professionals, welfare workers and the police – to endorse a version of the case, a version that justifies institutional intervention. Like Hydén, these authors show that social work discourse is replete with moral implications, in this case in categorizing the mother's character and behaviour and in justifying intervention. The authors argue that the story-tellings in social work are strongly constrained by discourse practices that have been developed in the history of the profession. In addition, particular case stories gain institutional credibility, authority and robustness through a series of inter-institutional re-tellings. The production and reproduction of professional discourse can be seen in the long time-span as establishing the discourse types of the profession, over a series of re-tellings of the same case story across institutional contexts, and finally in the individual discourse token, such as one single interview with its many voices and facets.

Finally, Charles and Marjorie Harness Goodwin widen the scope of our outlook on professional discourse in several ways. Drawing their empirical data from the well-known 1992 Californian trial about four white policemen's beating of the black motorist Rodney King, the Goodwins deal with professionals' visions, i.e. practices used to call attention to particular features in the perceptual field, or rather to use such features to construct phenomenal objects around which discourse can be organized. For example, what may have seemed to be a brutal beating of a helpless man lying on the ground could be discursively constructed by the defense in the court trial as a careful police response to a dangerous individual controlling the situation. This became possible by the use of specific conceptual schemes for coding features on the video-tape, and of various tools for manipulating the images, and thereby highlighting particular details. The Goodwins demonstrate how discourse often encompasses more than talk; gestures, non-verbal activities, and the use of tools and graphic representations (such as graphs and photographs). By such means experts establish intersubjectivity in ways of perceptually and cognitively organizing parts of the world, e.g. highlighting certain features that are particularly important precisely, and maybe only, within the specific professional activities. Goodwin and Goodwin conclude that such visions and practices belong to the experts' professions, the historically constructed ways of cognizing the world, and should not be seen as abilities lodged in individual minds. When experts voice their versions, the dialogue may become asymmetrical in the sense that those unacquainted with these professionally crafted visions will get marginalized. Goodwins' chapter therefore ties back to several themes in the volume.

By focusing on the professional integration of other discursive means than talk and text, the Goodwins provide another perspective on problems taken up in Danet's chapter, thus closing the thematic circle of the book. In our view, the volume has, as a whole, indicated not only the diversity of perspectives on professional discourse but also the opportunities for fruitful integration that could form the backdrop of future research in this interdisciplinary field.

REFERENCES

Agar, Michael (1985) 'Institutional discourse', *Text* **5**, 147–68.

Berger, Peter and Luckmann, Thomas (1967) *The Social Construction of Reality.* Harmondsworth: Penguin.

Fairclough, Norman (1992) *Discourse and Social Change.* Cambridge: Polity Press.

Gunnarsson, Britt-Louise (1995) 'Studies of language for specific purposes: a biased view of a rich reality', *International Journal of Applied Linguistics* **5**, 111–34.

Holstein, James and Miller, Gale (eds) (1993) *Reconsidering Social Constructionism. Debates in Social Problems Theory.* New York: Aldine de Gruyter.

TWO

Speech, writing and performativity: an evolutionary view of the history of constitutive ritual

Brenda Danet

INTRODUCTION

One of the most prominent universal functions of language in all societies is to provide recipes for the constitution of new social relationships and social arrangements, and for transformations of the status of individuals or groups. In preliterate societies these recipes are the verbal formulas which lie at the heart of many kinds of ritual, from initiation rites to peace treaties between warring tribes. In modern life, in contrast, many, if not most, of our constitutive rituals are routinely performed in writing. Thus, legislators debate prospective laws orally, but their official enactment occurs in writing. In private transactions, written documents are generally involved whenever we apply for a loan at the bank, buy or sell a house, make a will, or rent a car. Even in private sales, buyers and sellers frequently say, 'Let's put it into writing'.

Of interest are not those documents, or functions of documents, which merely certify that something is the case (e.g. results of a medical test as court evidence), or which simply identify a person, such as an identity or membership card, but those which relate some change in status of the individual or individuals involved. Thus, the transfer of a diploma during a graduation ceremony should be distinguished, analytically, from the later function of the same diploma as testifying to one's being a graduate, when applying for a job. Similarly, when presented at a national border, a passport identifies the person as someone eligible to enter a country; however, when originally issued, it confers upon the recipient a general right to leave the country.

The use of documents of all kinds is so taken for granted that we rarely ask how and why this practice developed. We are so deeply rooted in literate culture that we can hardly imagine how the business of society could be conducted without the written word. Yet, societies without writing manage their affairs perfectly well without it (Ong 1982). Many of the social acts performed in constitutive ceremonies, whether written or oral, are treated by members of these societies as legally binding. In modern societies a person who violates a contract can be sued by the other party in a formal legal suit. I shall use the term 'legal' in the broadest sense, so as to include societies without courts, formally enacted laws, or specially designated legal personnel such as judges or lawyers (Roberts 1979). These acts are considered legal in preliterate societies in the sense that the rights and obligations so created are potentially backed by force, or at least by informal sanctions such as ostracism, ridicule, avoidance, or a denial of favours.

It is useful to make a distinction between sacred and secular ritual. The latter concept was introduced by Moore and Myerhoff (1977) to refer to ritual in industrial societies. A typical anthropological definition of ritual, composed with sub-Saharan African societies in mind, is: 'a stereotyped sequence of activities involving gestures, words, and objects, performed in a sequestered place, and designed to influence preternatural entities or forces on behalf of the actors' goals and interests' (Turner 1977: 183). Influenced by Durkheim, anthropological studies of ritual in societies without writing have also emphasized 'the manner in which a particular rite states, reiterates, or reinforces social ties, or expresses social conflicts, or delineates social roles' (Moore and Myerhoff 1977: 5). Ritual may not only mirror existing social arrangements and existing modes of thought. It may reorganize them or even help to create them. This is particularly striking in the secular ceremonies of our own day, which are often performed precisely for that purpose (Moore and Myerhoff 1977: 5).

In this chapter the terms 'constitutive ritual' and 'performativity' will be used more or less interchangeably, although, strictly speaking, they are not synonymous. Performativity is a feature of language-in-use, while 'ritual' refers to events in which this feature is given expression. My research interest has been primarily in *the transfer of performativity from speech to writing*, in periods when writing is becoming institutionalized.

Even after many constitutive uses of language have been shifted from speech to writing, oral formulas may continue to predominate in certain settings. Ordinarily, one cannot legally get married solely by filling out a written form or by writing out a private agreement. Similarly, swearing-in ceremonies for presidents, prime ministers, judges, and members of parliaments continue to be oral. Also, oral and written modes of constituting relationships are sometimes combined in intriguing ways. Thus, in Jewish tradition, the actual wedding ceremony is performed orally. However, the groom must also have prepared and signed beforehand a written marriage contract called a *ketuba*. In orthodox Jewish law, it is the *ketuba* which gives legitimacy to the couple's cohabitation (Ungerleider-Meyerson 1986: 43).

In July 1992 a new Israeli Knesset, or parliament, and government were installed. The text of the oath for Knesset members was read aloud, and members were asked to rise individually and to say the Hebrew words *mitxayev ani* ('I commit myself'). The oath was as follows: 'I swear to remain loyal to the State of Israel and to fulfil my mission in the Knesset in good faith.' The names of the Knesset members were read aloud, one by one, from an alphabetized list; each in turn rose and uttered these words. Alphabetization is, of course, itself a device of literate culture (Daly 1967). Not only the list, but the text of the formula had been prepared in written form. Unlike the formulas of oral culture, in literate culture we tend not to know these formulas by heart, and therefore we often need written scripts as props.

In this chapter, I will speculate briefly on the origins and evolution of this constitutive function of language. Secondly, I will suggest that almost from the beginning of the history of writing in ancient times, legal documents contain evidence of a latent struggle to transfer performativity from speech to writing. Thirdly, I will summarize results of a case study of the transition to literacy in medieval England, arguing that the language of documents reflects their symbiotic relationship with the oral ceremonies which preceded them, and, at the same time, reveals evidence of a struggle to transfer performativity to documents. Finally, I will speculate on the future of performativity in the era of the new electronic media – electronic mail, fax, video and virtual reality.

CONSTITUTIVE SPEECH ACTS

Oral ritual is extremely rich in communicational components. In addition to verbal formulas, often involving archaic, esoteric or very formal language (Rappaport 1971; Tambiah 1968, 1985), we often find special stylized gestures and ceremonial objects (Hibbitts

1992, 1995), ceremonial dress and body adornment, special food and drink, decoration of the setting and other forms of rich appeal to the senses, organized in a manner which conveys complex messages (Leach 1976; Turner 1977; Murray 1977; Myerhoff 1977).

Austin's notion of performativity

Marriage ceremonies, coronations and initiation rites are all acts in which saying the words does not merely describe an existing state of things, but rather, creates a new relationship, social arrangement or entitlement. In speech-act terms, these are instances when *saying is doing*. J. L. Austin, the founder of speech-act theory, proposed to call this class of communicative acts 'performative utterances' (Austin 1970a). He later gave up this expression, preferring to speak, instead, of the illocutionary force of an utterance (Austin 1970b), or the intention of the speaker in uttering the words in a particular context.

Searle's typology of speech acts

Searle (1976, 1979) revised Austin's preliminary typology of speech acts, suggesting five major categories: (i) assertives; (ii) directives; (iii) expressives; (iv) declarations; and (v) commissives. There is a sixth, hybrid category in Searle's typology, representative declarations. The pronouncement 'guilty' by a judge or jury is a declaration – it is consequential for the defendant. However, it is also a representative or assertive, since it asserts that a certain state of things is so.

Of Searle's five main categories, declarations and commissives are pertinent here. Declarations are unilateral acts backed by the institutional authority of the person making them. This category includes nominations, declarations of war, peace treaties and wedding ceremonies. 'With this ring I thee wed' is a declaration, while the question 'Do you promise to love, honour and obey?' elicits a commissive utterance. Searle notes that declarations involve an extra-linguistic institution, a system of constitutive rules in addition to the constitutive rules of language, in order that the declaration may successfully be performed. Mastery of the rules which constitute linguistic competence by the speaker and hearer is not in general sufficient for the performance of a declaration. In addition, there must exist an extra-linguistic institution, and the speaker and hearer must occupy places within this institution. It is only given such institutions as the Church, the law, private property, the state and a special position of the speaker and hearer within them that one can excommunicate, appoint, give and bequeath one's possessions,or declare war (Searle 1976: 14).

The formulaic language of constitutive rituals

The verbal means to constitute new relationships and statuses in oral ceremonies tend to be highly formulaic (Ong 1982). Often it is the indexicality of the formula which provides the missing links to the participants (Murray 1977: 199–201). Thus, one can only know the referents of a given performance of the formula 'With this ring I thee wed' by being present and seeing the couple. In contrast, documents like contracts and wills must make explicit who the referents are, so that those not present at the signing of the document will be able to identify the parties and, if needed, take steps to execute or enforce their terms.

A related feature of formulaic language is that deviation from the formula is not usually tolerated. Consider the following hilarious sequence from a British trial:

CLERK: Do you plead guilty or not guilty.
DEFENDANT: Yes, I did it. I said I did it.
CLERK: No. Do you plead guilty or not guilty.
DEFENDANT: Yes, I did it. I just want to get it over.
MAGISTRATE: (to probation officer) Can you be of help here?

(The probation officer goes over to the defendant and eventually goes out of court with her. Later in the morning the case is 'called on' again.)

MAGISTRATE: Do you plead guilty or not guilty?
DEFENDANT: Yes, I did it.
MAGISTRATE: No, I'm asking you whether you plead guilty or not guilty. You must use either the words 'not guilty' or 'guilty'.
DEFENDANT: (looking toward probation officer) She said, 'Say guilty'.
MAGISTRATE: No, you must say what you want to say.
DEFENDANT: Yes, I'll say what you like. I did it.
MAGISTRATE: No. You must use the language of the court. (To probation officer) Did she understand?
PROBATION OFFICER: Yes, she understood.

(Carlen 1976: 110–11)

Only after the probation officer whispered to the defendant what words to say did she finally pronounce the word 'guilty'.

Two aspects of the installation of Israel's current Knesset and government, described briefly above, provide illuminating material about social attitudes towards formulaic language. In the swearing-in ceremony for Knesset members, they were instructed not to add any words to those required – *mitxayev ani* ('I commit myself') for a man, and *mitxyevet ani* for a woman. This meta-comment is rare, explicit evidence of the special nature of constitutive language. To modify the formula is potentially to harm the efficacy of the constitutive act. This formula (literally, 'commit myself I') also illustrates yet another important point about formulaic language, that it is often cast in a very high, formal register. The unmarked, everyday, conversational order of the words would be *ani mitxayev*, with the first person pronoun occurring first. Although the reversed order sounds peculiar in English, it is not unusual in the formal register of Hebrew.

When ministers of the new government were later installed, the reappointed Minister of the Interior failed to perform the entire formula, even adding some words of his own. A few days later, a lawyer filed a petition in the High Court of Justice requesting that he be prevented from serving as Minister, on the grounds that he had not yet sworn allegiance to the State as a member of the government, as required by law. Initially, the Minister had said aloud only the first of three components of the following formula, adding the words 'with the help of God', on his own initiative:

> I swear as a member of the government (1) to remain loyal to the State of Israel and to its laws [with the help of God], (2) to fulfil faithfully my role as a member of the government and (3) to uphold the decisions of the Knesset (my translation).

Only after the Secretary of the Knesset called the omission to his attention, did he utter the second component, and he failed altogether to utter the third, 'to uphold the decisions of the Knesset'. The petitioner argued that by omitting the second and third parts, and by adding the words 'with the help of God', which are not part of the official formula, the Minister, associated with an orthodox religious party, conveyed that his first loyalty is to Jewish religious law and only then to secular law.

The need for a historical perspective

Searle's theory of speech acts presupposes that the institutional arrangements which are preconditions for the successful performance of declarations are already in place. This assumption is legitimate and necessary in a general theory of speech acts. However, in periods of transition from one communication medium to another, the institutional arrangements to which Searle refers are most definitely *not yet in place*. On the contrary, they are in a state of flux.

How then does the transfer of performativity to a new medium come about? Surely, it cannot simply be that one day the law is changed from above, making documents constitutive rather than supplementary. Members of the society must come to realize the potential of the new medium to serve the same functions as the old one, as well as, perhaps, to fulfil new ones. They must learn to trust the new medium (Clanchy 1979: chapter 9), and to develop formulas for the constitution of relationships in writing. And of course the law must also eventually be changed to make the new medium the official way to constitute new relationships. All of these developments take time and are likely to involve a struggle. I do not, of course, mean to imply that there is a necessary sequence in these developments, which may occur more or less simultaneously within any given society.

THE ORIGINS AND EVOLUTION OF CONSTITUTIVE RITUAL

The beginnings of symbolic activity

A fascinating but enormously difficult question is: how did this constitutive function of language come about? Is its development tied to the emergence of speech? Or was it a later development, after certain critical features of language were already in place?

According to a chart of hominid evolution based on fossil evidence (Lieberman 1975: 175, Fig. 12.1), Homo Erectus lived about half a million years ago and the two hypothesized branches of later evolutionary development, Neanderthal people and modern Homo Sapiens, are placed at about 75,000 years ago and 30,000 years ago, respectively. One approach to explanation of the origin of language is that it evolved from the gestures or sounds of primates (Savage-Rumbaugh et al. 1978; Dingwall 1988: 286; Bickerton 1990). Another major approach has been to equate language with speech and to study how the physical apparatus of speech evolved. Lieberman (1975, 1984) compares reconstructions of the vocal tracts of hominid fossils with those of living non-human and human primates, as well as with human infants, arguing that the two branches of the evolutionary tree led to different types of specialization of the vocal tract. In the case of the Neanderthals, the tract was best suited for chewing, as is true for apes even today. In the case of Homo Sapiens, the vocal tract evolved in a manner which allowed for speech as we know it today.

It is tempting to assume that performativity must have developed as part of evolution of speech itself. There is remarkable evidence that this is probably not the case. Although Neanderthal culture lacked speech, its people apparently invented forms of ritual and were actively involved in artistic expression (both painting and sculpture; Pfeiffer 1982). They were the first to bury their dead, and, moreover, placed various cultural artifacts in the graves, for apparently symbolic reasons (Pfeiffer 1982: chapter 6; Marshack 1976).

Marshack (1976) pushes back the dating of complex symbolic activity to a much earlier time than many researchers are willing to accept. He summarizes evidence for the carving, colouring and decoration of artifacts, all of which strongly suggest that symbol use prospered even before Homo Sapiens. He argues that artifacts probably served as markers in culturally structured intragroup relations and involved age, sex, rank and role differentiation, and that they document a cognitive capacity and competence for abstraction, modelling and manufacture other than that which can be deduced from subsistence tool industries – in other words, they reveal a capacity for culture in the deeper sense of the word – an artificially created reality not directly linked to conditions of the natural world (Marshack 1976: 305). Fragmentary as all this evidence is, it suggests that (1) the capacity for artificially constituted ritual is not dependent on speech itself; (2) that it preceded speech, chronologically; and (3) that it began to develop perhaps 50,000 years ago or even earlier.

A WRITING AND PERFORMATIVITY IN ANCIENT TIMES

Record-keeping versus performativity in writing

How did writing come to serve a constitutive function? This issue is far more amenable to research than that regarding the origin of performativity. There is widespread consensus that full-fledged writing, an arbitrary set of conventionalized graphic symbols, was invented about 5,000 years ago in the Fertile Crescent – the area from Palestine to Mesopotamia (Gelb 1963; Gaur 1984). Both Mesopotamian cuneiform writing and Egyptian hieroglyphics date roughly from this period. Scholars often claim that the prime incentive for the invention of writing was the need for record-keeping (Gaur 1984; Goody 1986, 1987; Harris 1989; Senner 1989). I do not dispute the importance of record-keeping as an incentive for the creation of documents. However, this view places exclusive emphasis on the referential functions of language, ignoring the issue of performativity.

Legal documents in ancient Mesopotamia

The transition from oral to literate culture in ancient and medieval times was by no means smooth or linear (Goody 1986, 1987; Stock 1983). It got off to a good start in ancient Mesopotamia, which had developed a flourishing literary tradition, sophisticated schools for scribes, libraries and so on (Chiera 1938; Kramer 1956; Oppenheim 1964). However, many later societies of the ancient period came and went, and with them their beliefs and practices with respect to writing. Medieval societies had to re-learn some of the lessons about the institutionalization of writing which had been forgotten in the course of time.

Drawing on classical sources (Chiera 1938; Kramer 1956; Oppenheim 1964), Coulmas noted that:

> More than 75% of the … cuneiform inscriptions excavated in Mesopotamia are administrative and economic documents including legal documents, deeds of sale and purchase, contracts concerning loans, adoption, marriage, wills, ledgers and memoranda of merchants, as well as census and tax returns.
>
> (Coulmas 1989: 73)

Were these documents merely after-the-fact records of oral transactions, or was making the document eventually considered an autonomous constitutive act in any of these ancient Near Eastern societies? And if under certain circumstances, documents did eventually become fully performative, how did this happen? Cuneiform scholars have rarely raised these issues, though they often suggest or imply that documents did enjoy some kind of at least quasi-performative status. Chiera (1938) reports that legal transactions were not considered 'complete' unless they were recorded on tablets. The fact that documents were typically imprinted with the seals of scribes or witnesses also attests to their importance in the culture. However, it is not clear whether they authenticated the oral ceremony or the written record itself.

The language of the Code of Hammurapi

A particularly fascinating case in point is the famous Code of Hammurapi from Old Babylonian times, one of the earliest legal codes preserved in writing. This code is inscribed on a 2.25-meter-high basalt column found in modern Iraq at the beginning of the twentieth century and now in the Louvre. The text consists of a prologue, an epilogue and a list of 282 laws, written in an if/then structure, as in 'If a man has accused another man and has brought a charge of murder against him, but has not proved it, his accuser shall be put to death' (Oates 1986: 74). Regarding its function, Oates comments:

> That it is not a 'true' code seems clear. It is far from comprehensive in its coverage and nowhere is there a specific adjuration of judges or other officials to abide by its provisions. Whether the text represents a recording of customary law, a series of legal innovations or even a designation of those areas in need of amendment ... remains uncertain. That the provisions were not Statute Law can be seen from the fact that several abuses explicitly condemned by Hammurapi ... were again 'legislated against' in a later edict ...
>
> (Oates 1986: 74)

Hammurapi's purpose in setting up this stele is set forth in ambiguous language at the beginning of the epilogue:

> These are the laws of justice which Hammurapi the able king has established. ... That the strong may not oppress the weak, to give justice to the orphan and to the widow, I have inscribed my precious words on my stele and established it in Babylon before my statue called 'King of Justice'.
>
> (Oates 1986: 75)

This passage appears to suggest that the document is a record of laws which had previously been constituted in an oral ceremony. However, there is also evidence for incipient performativity in this famous text. The epilogue contains a long list of vivid curses, arguing for at least some attempt to imbue the code *on the column* with performative power. I will return to this issue of the performative significance of curses later in this chapter.

THE TRANSITIONAL LANGUAGE OF ANGLO-SAXON WILLS: A CASE STUDY

I turn now to a summary of our case study of Anglo-Saxon legal documents (Danet and Bogoch 1992a, 1992b). With the end of the Roman Empire, literacy went into decline in the West, for the most part continuing to flourish only within the confines of the Church. In early medieval times, the uses of writing began to spread once more, all over Europe (Stock 1983; McKitterick 1990). It was only in medieval and early modern Europe that writing became sufficiently institutionalized so as to be, in Stock's (1983) preferred phrase, irreversible. He argued that 'Up to the eleventh century, western Europe could have returned to an essentially oral civilization. But by 1100 the die was cast' (Stock 1983: 18).

English society between the fifth and eleventh centuries was largely an oral society. Most people, including kings, were illiterate. Outside the Church, no authority was vested in written texts. The ability to write was not even considered essential for the litterati, the elite clergy who were educated in Latin. Only scribes were allowed to put quill to parchment, though their role in the composition of documents is not known (Clanchy 1979).

While the ability to read and write remained unnecessary for most social functions until the end of the Anglo-Saxon period, access to the written word became increasingly important. Initiated by the clergy to record transfers of property to the Church, the use of documents eventually extended to records of other governmental and commercial transactions as well (Clanchy 1979). The conveyance of land and bequest of property continued to be primarily oral acts, performed according to verbal rituals and witnessed by trustworthy individuals (Whitelock 1979, 1986 [1930]). Records of such acts were regarded with suspicion, and in many instances this distrust was justified; forgeries were common (Clanchy 1979).

The corpus

The corpus of the case study consisted of the complete set of 62 wills in Old English that have survived from the Anglo-Saxon period, and was assembled from collections of documents edited by Whitelock (1986 [1930]), Harmer (1914), Robertson (1956 [1939]), Napier and Stevenson (1894) and Whitelock (1968). The actual period studied is a span of about 250 years, beginning with the date of the earliest surviving will, 805AD, and ending with the last one dated approximately at the time of the Norman conquest in 1066.

Table 2.1 presents a model for the analysis of the language of constitutive ritual in documents. It lists seven linguistic features of documents, in three main categories: meta-comments about writing; linguistic realization of the performative act of bequeathing; and decontextualization. The table summarizes the differences between modern and Old English wills. While no one will has all of the features described below, most have at least several of them. In identifying these features, we have drawn of the literature of differences between speech and writing (Biber 1988; Akinnaso 1982a, 1982b, 1985; Tannen 1982; Chafe and Tannen 1987).

Meta-comments about the new medium

Whereas modern documents take the act of writing for granted, Anglo-Saxon wills reveal self-consciousness about using a new medium. For example, one will opens with a record of instructions to the scribe:

> I Ealdorman Alfred command to be written and made known in this document to King Alfred and all his councillors …
>
> (Whitelock 1979: 97)

The wills also often make explicit references to the oral ceremony which constituted the binding act of bequeathing, as in:

> Then I wish it to be given out for my soul just as I now said to my friends with whom I spoke.
>
> (Harmer 1914: 33)

Linguistic realization of the act of bequeathing

The openings of Anglo-Saxon wills are anything but standard, indicating that creating documents was a novelty. Only a tenth of the

Table 2.1 Linguistic features of Anglo-Saxon vs. modern English will

Feature	Anglo-Saxon wills	Modern wills
Meta-comments about writing	present	absent
Realization of act of bequeathing	linked to oral ceremony	autonomous
Opening strategy	non-standard	standard
Consistency	inconsistent	consistent
Secondary means to strengthen act of bequeathing	carried over from oral practice or transitional	writing-specific
Witnesses	reference only, or touching the document	signature
Curses	present	absent
Binomial expressions	present	present
Evidence of planning	present with lapses	present
Patterns of reference	situated	explicit
Dating	no date	date specified
Involvement of testator	high	low
Direct address	present	absent
Evaluative expressions	present	absent
Hedging	present	absent

Reproduced from Brenda Danet and Bryna Bogoch (1992a) 'From Oral Ceremony to Written Document: The Transitional Language of Anglo-Saxon Wills', *Language and Communication* **12**(2): 99.

wills open with a strategy resembling that of a modern will, as in that of King Alfred the Great:

> I Alfred, King of the West Saxons by the grace of God and with this witness declare how I wish to dispose of my inheritance after my death …
>
> (Whitelock 1979: 534)

This type of opening is cast in the first person present, like those of modern wills. Contrast this with the opening of the will of Æthelstan:

> In the name of Almighty God I Æthelstan the Atheling declare in this document how I have granted my estates and my possessions.
>
> (Whitelock 1986 [1930]: 56–7)

Although this opening also starts off like a modern will, the second half reveals that Æthelstan has already bequeathed his property, in a previous oral ceremony. It also illustrates another characteristic of many Anglo-Saxon wills – the lack of consistency of person or tense in the realization of the act of bequeathing. While this will is consistently in the first person, it mixes the present and past tense – there are two tenses in Old English, a present and a preterit, which in most cases is used as a simple past (Carlton 1970). What we refer to for convenience as the past is actually the preterit used to describe past action. Other openings are inconsistent in person but not in tense. In a modern will, the voice and tense, not only of the opening strategy, but of the text as a whole, must be consistent. In a few cases, the text is consistent in person and tense but cast in the third person. In such cases there is no attempt to transfer performativity to the document; the scribe is simply taking the stance of a reporter – in effect communicating, 'read all about it – Alfred made a will'. If Anglo-Saxon wills were intended only as a record of the oral ceremony, a third-person narrative version, or even a sketchy list of donations, together with some identification of the testator, would have sufficed. Yet, fully three out of five wills are cast in the first person – either in entirely consistent fashion, or nearly so. Moreover, the narrative type of document was not only far less common, but disappeared fairly quickly.

Second-order performatives: witnesses and curses

The wills contain evidence of two types of device to strengthen the act of bequeathing. Witnesses are sometimes explicitly mentioned as having been present and heard the oral declaration. Such references to witnesses do not have implications for performativity of the document because they only report on the act of witnessing the oral ceremony. However, in other cases, a list of witnesses appears with a cross next to each name, much like a list of signatures in present-day legal documents. A phrase such as 'I ... consent and write and confirm it with Christ's cross' is often added.

These are not signatures in the modern sense because all writing on the document, including the ostensible signatures and the cross, was done by the scribe (Earle 1888: xxxvi–xxxvii; Clanchy 1979). Still, there is performative significance to the fact that witnesses often touched the cross with their sword or hand. Touching the cross is a medieval equivalent of the modern signature, a transitional act, since it reveals close links with the physical manipulation of symbolic objects common to oral ceremonies, and yet points toward literacy, in that individuals are relating to graphic marks on the parchment.

A particularly fascinating aspect of the wills, with important implications for performativity is the inclusion of curses in the concluding section. Twenty-five of the 62 wills contained such 'whoever' curses, addressed to anyone who tampers with the will, as in:

> And he who shall detract from my will which I have now declared in the witness of God, may he be deprived of joy on this earth, and may the Almighty Lord who created and made all creatures exclude him the fellowship of all saints on the Day of Judgment, and may he be delivered into the abyss of hell to Satan the devil and all his accursed companions and there suffer with God's adversaries, without end, and never trouble my heirs.
>
> (Whitelock 1986 [1930]: 86–7)

These curses are both an expression of widespread magical beliefs and practices, often pagan in origin, and evidence of the strong influence of Catholicism on public life. This was a period in which religion and magic were inextricably fused, as is evident in related practices of putting documents on altars or copying them into holy books. Curses were commonly used in many aspects of everyday life, as an attempt to exert control over the supernatural and social world (Kieckhefer 1990; Flint 1991). Excommunication from the Church was the ultimate curse (Vodola 1986).

We hypothesized that curses are especially likely to be mobilized in documents which are struggling towards performativity. To test this hypothesis, we compared wills with two other types of Anglo-Saxon documents – land grants and royal writs. We compared the set of 62 wills with 112 royal writs and 73 land grants. Like wills, land grants involve public ceremonial acts which create new, legally binding situations. In speech-act terms, both therefore involve declarations. Writs, in contrast, are private letters, a kind of assertive, whose purpose is to notify some particular individual of an event. Thus, we expected curses to be more common in the wills and land grants than in writs. Also, since writs were private letters to specific individuals, kings might care less about their long-term preservation than in the case of documents of public import, such as wills and grants, and therefore would be less likely to mobilize curses to protect them. In fact, six out of ten land grants and leases, and four out of ten wills include one, compared to only one in five writs. Thus, these results strongly support the thesis that curses are mobilized as part of the latent effort to transfer performativity to the document.

Stylization: binomial expressions

Linguistic stylization also contributes to performativity. It is universally found in oral ritual genres of communication. One of the most common forms is parallelism – the foregrounding of certain aspects of text or discourse by the introduction of extra regularities not called for by the basic rules of language (Leech 1969: 56–8). An extremely common form in our documents is the use of binomial expressions – word pairs such as *mid mete 7mid mannum* ('with cattle and men') or *write 7theafie* ('confirm and consent'). We found over 100 different binomials in the corpus, with an average of four per will, though only about a quarter of them occurred more than once; thus, what is common is not any given expression but the general phenomenon of binomials. The case for preoccupation with language *qua* language is especially strong when the pair is redundant, as in the Old English for 'house and home,' or 'statements and provisions'. While binomials may be partly a form of oral residue, left over from oral ceremonies, I believe that they also perform a new function in documents. Like oral ritual language, written ritual language must also be marked linguistically to be effective. As Rappaport (1971) has stressed, stylization contributes to the unquestioning acceptance of utterances in ritual contexts. It provides a kind of verbal 'cornstarch' in written documents too, fostering psychological closure (Herrnstein-Smith 1968; Danet 1984).

Decontextualization

One of the most striking features of the language of Anglo-Saxon wills is their context-dependence: testators refer to property and persons in ways which assume that others will know who or what is meant. Often, shared knowledge of members of the community would be necessary in order to carry out the wishes of the testator. Such patterns of reference are situated in the flow of interpersonal communication among persons who have ongoing face-to-face relationships (Biber 1988; Tannen 1982; Chafe and Tannen 1987). The will of Bishop Theodred of London is especially rich in context-bound references to property. Among the goods which he bequeaths are:

> ... two hundred marks of red gold, and two silver cups and four horses, the best that I have, and two swords, the best that I have.
>
> (Whitelock 1986 [1930]: 2–3)

To modern eyes, Theodred's bequest is quaint: how is one to know which horses and swords he considered his 'best'?

These texts often refer to people without identifying them in any way. This contrasts sharply with modern practice, which identifies individuals by first and last name, title, address, identification numbers, and so on. Most commonly, testators are presented by name only, as in 'This is Ælfgifu's request to her royal lord' (Whitelock 1986 [1930]: 21). Almost as common is the combination of name and title or role. Kings, archbishops and bishops refer to themselves this way, as in: 'I Alfred, King of the West Saxons' (Whitelock 1979: 535). In two cases, testators were designated as 'the son, of ...', as in 'This is the will of Leofwine, Wulfstan's son' (Napier and Stevenson 1894: 122). Only once is the testator identified by location: 'This is the will of Wulfgeat of Donington' (Whitelock 1986 [1930]: 55).

Beneficiaries are sometimes identified by their name and blood relationship to the testator, as in 'Wynflæd bequeaths to her daughter Æthelflæd her engraved bracelet and brooch' (Whitelock 1986 [1930]: 11), or they are identified by their social role, as in 'my servant Viking' (Whitelock 1986 [1930]: 83).

Another important aspect of decontextualization is the practice of dating documents. Once again, this practice serves to objectify documents and to disassociate them from the immediate context in which they were created. Even well into the twelfth century, documents were rarely dated in England. During the Anglo-Saxon period there was, as yet, no standard way of reckoning time (Earle 1888). Only one of the 62 Old English wills is dated.

In some cases, testators and scribes locate the making of the will in time by mentioning events in their personal or collective lives, a common practice not only in the Anglo-Saxon period but well into the Norman one. For instance, three wills were made as testators embarked on dangerous pilgrimages to the Holy Land. Thus, one will concludes:

> This is the agreement which Ulf and his wife Madselin made with [God] and with St Peter when they went to Jerusalem.
>
> (Whitelock 1986 [1930]: 94–5)

THE FUTURE OF PERFORMATIVITY

Let us now leap forward in time once again, to consider the future of performativity in the twenty-first century and beyond. Four new technologies – electronic mail, fax, video, and virtual reality – raise major new issues about performativity. In this speculative section of the chapter, I will argue that we have paid so much attention to processes of decontextualization of the verbal content of texts that we have ignored the functions of the text-as-object, and that our experience of the materiality of texts is now being undermined, challenged and transformed by these new technologies. Secondly, I will consider the possibility that in the future, video-taped oral ceremonies or, eventually, fully virtual events, may supplement or even replace some kinds of documents and the face-to-face ceremonies in which they are manipulated.

Text-as-object in literate culture

We have seen that in oral cultures, ritual typically involves not only the uttering of verbal formulas but also the manipulation of critical objects, in settings which strongly appeal to the senses. In manuscript and print culture, too, the physical presence of texts-as-objects and our aesthetic experience of them have been necessary components of performativity in many important settings.

In Anglo-Saxon England, the oral ceremony for the transfer of lands was often accompanied by the transfer of a symbolic object such as a clod of earth, or a knife or sword belonging to the donor (Earle 1888; Clanchy 1979). When documents came into use, knives were sometimes attached to them, to make the transfer real (Clanchy 1979: 24). Even seals sometimes had three-dimensional volume, as in the Anglo-Norman document dating from the 1220s which is displayed in the endpapers of Clanchy (1979). The wax seals of about 50 persons, each a separate small, round, fairly flat object with the individual's personal symbol imprinted in a raised relief technique, are attached individually to the document by small parchment strips serving as loops, making a kind of thick fringe all along the bottom of the document. The photograph of this document suggests not only that the fringe could be touched, but that the individual symbols on the seals could be 'read' by touch, much as Braille writing is read by the blind (Clanchy 1979: endpapers).

We moderns might smile patronizingly at such practices, dismissing them as magical hocus pocus left over from oral culture. Ostensibly, we rely on the verbal meanings of texts alone to manage our affairs. However, in many instances the thingness of documents and various sensuous features of them have helped us to preserve the cultural fiction that marks inscribed on clay, parchment, or paper can change the world. *Texts have in fact retained a fetish-like importance which, ironically, has become more visible just as it is being undermined.*

We have seen that there are many instances in which the manipulation or reading aloud of a written document are still part of an oral ceremony today. Just as oral ritual appeals to the senses in a host of ways, documents and ceremonies involving them may do so too. First, the document is something we can hold and touch. In addition, any or all of the following may appear in a document: rich, distinctive texture of the material on which the text has been inscribed, e.g. parchment; special size and shape of the document, larger than ordinary letter-size, or a rolled-up scroll, as in a graduation diploma; fancy lettering, whether hand-inscribed or printed; prominent ceremonial colour, notably, the red of ribbons and seals on notarized documents; more generally, seals of all kinds, often with visual images as well as verbal components; gilt lettering for seals, as on passports, a carry-over from medieval manuscript illumination, which Conquergood (1983: 134) suggests was used to enhance the importance of texts in the eyes of illiterates. When signing international treaties, the parties usually exchange the pens they have used to sign the documents, and documents are passed between the parties in impressive-looking leather or simulated leather folders. All these uses of visual and tactile stimulation instill a sense of awe in constitutive situations.

Loss of the aura of the document in the electronic era

Like all physical objects, documents have an aura (Benjamin 1969a, 1969b). The aura of an object includes its presence in time and space, its sensuous features as perceived by the beholder, the changes it may have undergone over time, and the history of the hands that have touched and held it.

> Experience of the aura ... rests on the transposition of a response common to human relationships to the relationship between the inanimate or natural object and man. The person we look at, or who feels he is being looked at, looks at us in return. To perceive the aura of an object is to invest it with the ability to look at us in return.
>
> (Benjamin 1969b: 188)

The new media of electronic mail and fax transmission are undermining the aura of texts. When texts are transferred from one computer to another by electronic mail, there is no automatically generated object to hold in the hand. Hard copies are optional. We read and delete electronic mail messages, or store them on a mainframe computer or on diskettes. Moreover, in routine printing, at least, texts lack all the flourishes just discussed. Also, electronic texts are easily modified by recipients. Thus, this new medium threatens our notion of the authoritative binding text.

In the case of faxes, there is a paper copy at both the sender's and the recipient's end. However, the paper that the recipient touches is not the paper that the sender handled. Moreover, paper which is distinctive in size or texture cannot be used, though at least the visual image of everything appearing on the document can be transmitted. Thus, the image of a seal can be transmitted, but without gilt or coloured trimmings. Of course coloured faxes are becoming a reality too, but at best an image of the document is transmitted, rather than 'the thing itself'. Also, at least in the current state of fax technology, the paper on which messages are transmitted is generally flimsy, the quality of the printing is often quite poor and tends to fade.

The critical question is, then: can texts transmitted in these modes autonomously fulfil the performative functions at issue in this chapter? Will future diplomats present their credentials solely by electronic mail or by fax, instead of appearing before heads of state? Can treaties between nations be constituted entirely by electronic means, without a formal ceremony in which the parties sign documents? Did Yitshak Rabin and Yasir Arafat have to meet and shake hand on the White House lawn, in order to make peace? Could educational institutions dispatch diplomas to graduates electronically, saving the expense, time and trouble of elaborate commencement ceremonies? Until now, there has been a fundamental need for these ceremonies, and for an object which makes the constitutive act palpably real. At least in the near future, I believe, they are unlikely to be replaced by texts without tangible, visible physical presence. Electronic mail and faxes can be used to negotiate the form and content of documents, and even to send advance copies of the text ahead, but there will be strong pressure to continue to conduct face-to-face ceremonies to conclude performative acts.

Electronic Data Interchange: contracts without physicality

There is one apparent exception to my case: Electronic Data Interchange (EDI) – a system of electronic contracting in the business world. Although EDI-based contracts are not yet legally binding, participants in the system are increasingly treating them as such (Emmelhainz 1990). Why is EDI so immediately acceptable as an autonomous, performative mode but not the electronic transmission of diplomatic credentials or graduation diplomas?

Actually, even in print culture, some kinds of binding legal relationship have routinely been created without fanfare. Signing the documents for a bank loan is routinely done without dressing up, in ordinary rather than set-aside ceremonial time, etc. Moreover, in contrast to diplomas and treaties, such documents lack aesthetic flourishes like those described above.

It appears that the aestheticized dramatization of newly constituted relationships has been important, first of all, in connection with major changes in the life cycle of the individual – marriage, graduation, religious confirmation. Secondly, when the constitution of important collective relationships is at stake, ceremonies and the manipulation of objects, including texts, also tend to be important. Signing treaties and submitting diplomatic credentials are instances of changes in the life cycle or status of collectivities – nations, in these instances.

Video wills

In some cases, video technology may upstage the written document. People are beginning to make video wills, bequeathing their property before the camera, either reading aloud a previously composed written will or speaking directly to their heirs, whether or not they are actually present. Obviously, reading a text aloud is a form of literate residue, an obsolescent choice in an era of change, experiment and transition to new, mediated forms of orality. Video technology makes it possible to constitute binding social relationships in a manner which records the visual and aural components of an oral event, perhaps even making written texts obsolete. At the present time, video wills are merely supplementary to legally recognized, generally written ones. As yet, they have no independent performative status of their own, just as written wills were only supplementary to the oral ceremony in Anglo-Saxon England. There is already a small trend to create video wills, in both the United States and Israel, the two countries with which I am most familiar (Negev 1990; Bechar-Israeli 1992; Danet and Bogoch 1992a).

In a video will a person can once again address beneficiaries directly. Imagine that an elderly woman is making a video will. Having arranged a group of objects on a table beforehand, she addresses each of her children, in turn, before the camera. She points to a sculpture, saying 'This sculpture is for you, Tom'. If the children are present at the filming, we have something very close to the traditional oral ceremony. If, on the other hand, the testator addresses the beneficiaries directly, even though they are not present, we have something of a cross between the oral ceremony and the written document. The film can later be shown to them and others as the way of 'publishing' the will after the person's death, just as a written will is read aloud after the person's death.

Attractive as the thought of returning to something approximating the oral ceremony may be, we no longer live in small face-to-face communities like those of the Anglo-Saxons. The authorities in modern, large-scale societies will still require objective, context-free identification of the parties. Perhaps a compromise is possible: a return to second-person, concrete, contextualized language in the recorded ceremony itself, combined with an accompanying means to identify the parties. But what about the aura of the text? Can a video-tape have the aura of a written document? On the face of it, a strip of video-tape is very unprepossessing! Will we find ways to dramatize its Special status, for instance by storing it in a special box of impressive qualities? How will we protect it from being tampered with? What means might be used to authenticate such a tape? One Israeli man improvised a clever solution: he placed a clock on the table at the start of the film. Since it remained on the table throughout the film, anyone later viewing the film could tell at a glance if a segment had been cut out!

Constitutive ceremonies in virtual reality rooms?

The new technologies of virtual reality open up still other possibilities bordering on science fiction (Benedikt 1991; Heim 1993). They change the inputs in one's sensorium, so that one is 'somewhere else in time and place' instead of being 'here and now'. In some versions of the technology, the individual dons a special helmet and gloves and 'feels', 'hears', 'smells' a host of simulated sensations.

I have argued that texts-as-objects and the appeal to the senses in constitutive ceremonies have been vital components of print culture. One possible prediction as we move into digital culture is that, since we cannot do without documents and ceremonies when changes in the life cycle of individuals and collectivities are at stake, they will persist in digital culture too, not just during a time of transition, but in the long run. But we should also open our minds to the possibility that virtual reality technologies may someday be used to conduct fully autonomous constitutive ceremonies, among persons who only virtually present to one another. Such a possibility is envisaged by the science fiction writer William Gibson, much admired by virtual reality pioneers (Gibson 1984; Benedikt 1991; Heim 1993). Already, video conferencing is being used by corporations for business meetings – apparently for negotiations, thus far, but not for constitutive acts.

All ritual requires a 'leap of faith' for participants to believe in its efficacy and often involves some kind of simulation. In the realm of religious ritual, taking Communion in Catholic ritual is a way of virtually partaking of substances from the Lord's Supper; for Jews, eating matzoth while reading aloud the Haggadah at the Passover Seder is a way to relive, as it were, the experiences of the exodus from ancient Egypt. As we have seen, in the realm of secular ritual, too, there is a leap of faith, and there is an appeal to the senses, albeit greatly reduced. Perhaps more fully virtual rituals can also be experienced as efficacious in the future. Thus, we should separate the necessary leap of faith from quite different matters – establishment of technical and legal means to guarantee the authenticity and binding quality of such virtual ceremonies and to validate the identities of the parties. Progress on these matters is being made all the time. At a January 1996 exhibit of new technologies in Jerusalem, one software developer claimed to have made major advances in both voice recognition and handwritten signature recognition.

Either of these just might be the breakthrough necessary for authentificated, virtual constitutive ceremonies to become possible.

Recall now Marshack's (1976: 305) argument that the Neanderthals of 50,000–70,000 years ago revealed a capacity for culture in the deeper sense of the word – an artificially created reality not directly linked to conditions of the natural world. His words are uncannily appropriate to the present context as well: the artificial reality of the future will be detached from the conditions of the natural world to an extent unprecedented in the history of human culture.

Already, close observation of interaction in cyberspace, especially in popular synchronous chat-modes such as IRC (Internet Relay Chat) and MOOs (Multi-User Domains, Object-Oriented), reveals that participants simulate aesthetic experience all the time. For example, they 'pour each other drinks', type in 'loud noises' in the manner of comics (*bang*, *POW*), 'hug' and 'kiss', send each other 'New Year cards', describe the look of a 'room', and so on (Danet 1995; Danet et al. in press; Turkle 1995).

Even more fascinating is the fact that people are experimenting with the online simulation of constitutive ritual, finding the ethereality of cyberspace remarkably conducive, rather than off-putting, as many might have expected. Of particular relevance are virtual mock weddings. These often hilariously funny events are usually partly planned, and partly improvised. Originally, I had thought of them as merely a form of good fun, one instance of the rampant playfulness in synchronous chat modes. Research is beginning to show that, rather than being merely playful, mock weddings are also a means for virtual couples to give symbolic expression to their *real* feelings (Jacobson and Dana 1995). In a deeper sense than many of us have anticipated or may be willing to accept, then, *the virtual is real*. The lived experience of individuals online belies the perception that what is simulated is merely playful and 'doesn't count'. In short, our understanding of what is 'virtual' vs. what is 'real' is now undergoing radical revision (Heim 1993; Turkle 1995).

At the present time, communication in cyberspace is mainly textual – people chat by typing. As real-time communication becomes more fully multimedia, and people can include sound, graphics, and video in their messages, we will be able to simulate a richer range of aesthetic experience. In the light of these and other developments just reviewed, I believe it would be premature to dismiss fully simulated, legally binding, constitutive ritual as mere wild fantasy.

REFERENCES

Akinnaso, F. N. (1982a) 'On the Differences Between Spoken and Written Language', *Language and Speech* **25**(2), 97–125.

Akinnaso, F. N. (1982b) 'The Literate Writes and the Nonliterate Chants: Written Language and Ritual Communication in Sociolinguistic Perspective', in W. Frawley (ed.), *Linguistics and Literacy*, pp. 7–36. New York: Plenum.

Akinnaso, F. N. (1985) 'On the Similarities Between Spoken and Written Language', *Language and Speech* **28**(4), 32–59.

Austin, J. L. (1970a) *How to Do Things with Words.* Oxford: Oxford University Press.

Austin, J. L. (1970b) *Philosophical Papers.* Oxford: Oxford University Press.

Bechar-Israeli, Haya (1992) 'Video Wills as an Aspect of the Transition from Literacy to the New Orality', unpublished MA thesis, Department of Communication and Journalism, Hebrew University of Jerusalem (Hebrew).

Benedikt, Michael (ed.) (1991) *Cyberspace; First Steps.* Cambridge, M.A.: MIT Press.

Benjamin, Walter (1969a) 'The Work of Art in the Age of Mechanical Reproduction', In Hannah Arendt (ed.), *Illuminations,* trans. H. Zohn, pp. 59–67. New York: Schocken.

Benjamin, Walter (1969b) 'On Some Motifs in Baudelaire', in Hannah Arendt (ed.), *Illuminations,* trans. H. Zohn, pp. 155–201. New York: Schocken.

Biber, Douglas (1988) *Variation Across Speech and Writing.* Cambridge: Cambridge University Press.

Bickerton, Derek (1990) *Language and Species.* Chicago: University of Chicago Press.

Carlen, Pat (1976) *Magistrates' Justice.* London: Martin Robertson.

Carlton, C. (1970) *Descriptive Syntax of the Old English Charters.* The Hague: Mouton.

Chafe, Wallace L. and Tannen, Deborah (1987) 'The Relation Between Written and Spoken Language', *Annual Review of Anthropology* **16**, 383–409.

Chiera, Edward (1938) *They Wrote on Clay.* Chicago: University of Chicago Press.

Clanchy, M. T. (1979) *From Memory to Written Record: England, 1066–1307.* Cambridge, MA: Harvard University Press.

Conquergood, Dwight (1983) 'Literacy and Oral Performance in Anglo-Saxon England: Conflict and Confluence of Traditions', in David W. Lanham Thompson (ed.), *Performance of Literature in Historical Perspectives.* New York and London: University Press of America.

Coulmas, Florian (1989) *The Writing Systems of the World.* Oxford: Basil Blackwell.

Daly, Lloyd WIlliam (1967) 'Contributions to a History of Alphabetization in Antiquity and the Middle Ages', *Collection Latomus* vol. XC. Bruxelles: Latomus, *Revue d'Etudes Latines*.

Danet, Brenda (1984) 'The Magic Flute: a Prosodic Analysis of Binomial Expressions in Legal Hebrew', *Text* **3**(4), 139–69. Special issue, *Studies of Legal Discourse*, Brenda Danet (ed.).

Danet, Brenda (ed.) (1995) *Play and Performance in Computer-mediated Communication*. Special issue, *Journal of Computer-mediated Communication* **1**(2). URL: http://shum.huji.ac.il/jcmc/vol/issue2/vol1no2.htmI or URL: http://www.usc.edu/dept/annenberg/vol1/issue2/

Danet, Brenda. Submitted for publication 'Books, Letters, Documents: The Changing Aesthetics of Texts in Late Print Culture'.

Danet, Brenda and Bogoch, Bryna (1992a) 'From Oral Ceremony to Written Document: The Transitional Language of Anglo-Saxon Wills', *Language and Communication* **12**(2), 95–122.

Danet, Brenda and Bogoch, Bryna (1992b) '"Whosoever Alters This, May God Turn His Face From Him on the Day of Judgment": Curses in Anglo-Saxon Legal Documents', *Journal of American Folklore* **105**, 134–67.

Danet, Brenda, Ruedenberg, Lucia and Rosenbaum-Tamari, Yehudit. In press '"Hmmm Where's All That Smoke Coming From?": Writing, Play and Performance on Internet Relay Chat', in Sheizaf Rafaeli, Fay Sudweeks and Margaret McLaughlin (eds), *Network and Netplay: Virtual Groups on the Internet*. Cambridge, MA: AAAI/MIT Press.

Dingwall, William Orr (1988) 'The Evolution of Human Communicative Behavior', in *Linguistics: The Cambridge Survey*, Vol. III, Frederick J. Newmeyer (ed.), *Language: Psychological and Biological Aspects*, pp. 274–313. Cambridge: Cambridge University Press.

Earle, J. A. (1888) *A Handbook to the Land Charters and Other Saxonic Documents*. Oxford: Clarendon Press.

Emmelhainz, Margaret A. (1990) *Electronic Data Interchange: a Total Management Guide*. New York: Van Nostrand Reinhold.

Flint, Valerie (1991) *The Rise of Magic in Early Medieval Europe*. Oxford: Clarendon.

Gaur, Albertine (1984) *A History of Writing*. London: British Library.

Gelb, I. J. (1963) *A Study of Writing*, 2nd edn. Chicago: University of Chicago Press.

Gibson, William (1984) *Neuromancer*. New York: Ace.

Goody, Jack (1986) *The Logic of Writing and the Organization of Society*. Cambridge: Cambridge University Press.

Goody, Jack (1987) *The Interface Between the Written and the Oral*. Cambridge: Cambridge University Press.

Harmer, F. E. (1914) *Select English Historical Documents of the Ninth and Tenth Centuries*. Cambridge: Cambridge University Press.

Harris, Roy (1989) *The Invention of Writing*. Oxford: Pergamon.

Heim, Michael (1993) *The Metaphysics of Virtual Reality*. New York: Oxford University Press.

Herrnstein-Smith, Barbara (1968) *Poetic Closure: A Study of How Poems End.* Chicago: University of Chicago Press.

Hibbitts, Bernard J. (1992) 'Coming To Our Senses: Communication and Legal Expression in Performance Cultures', *Emory Law Journal* **41**, 873–960.

Hibbitts, Bernard J. (1995) 'Making Motions: The Embodiment of Law in Gesture', *Journal of Contemporary Legal Issues* **6**, 51–81.

Jacobson, David and Dana, Adrianne (1995) 'Play and Not-Play in Cyberspace: Frames and Cues in Text-based Virtual Reality'. Paper presented at the Annual Meeting, American Anthropological Association, Washington DC, November 1995.

Kieckhefer, Richard (1990) *Magic in the Middle Ages.* Cambridge: Cambridge University Press.

Kramer, S. N. (1956) *From the Tablets of Sumer: Twenty-five Firsts in Man's Recorded History.* Indian Springs, Colorado: The Falcon's Wing Press.

Leach, Edmund (1976) *Culture and Communication.* Cambridge: Cambridge University Press.

Leech, Geoffrey (1969) *A Linguistic Guide to English Poetry* London: Longman.

Lieberman, Philip (1975) *On the Origins of Language: An Introduction to the Evolution of Human Speech.* New York: Macmillan.

Lieberman, Philip (1984) *The Biology and Evolution of Language.* Cambridge, MA: Harvard University Press.

Marshack, Alexander (1976) 'Some Implications of the Paleolithic Symbolic Evidence for the Origin of Language', in Stevan R. Hamad, Horst D. Steklis and Jane Lancaster (eds), *Origins and Evolution of Language and Speech.* Annals of the New York Academy of Sciences, vol. 280. New York: New York Academy of Sciences.

McKitterick, Rosamond (ed.) (1990) *The Uses of Literacy in Early Mediaeval Europe.* Cambridge: Cambridge University Press.

Moore, Sally Falk and Myerhoff, Barbara G. (eds) (1977) *Secular Ritual.* Assen: Van Gorcum.

Murray, David W. (1977) 'Ritual Communication: Some Considerations Regarding Meaning in Navajo Ceremonials', in Janet L. Dolgin, David S. Kemnitzer and David M. Schneider (eds), *Symbolic Anthropology: A Reader in the Study of Symbols and Meanings,* pp. 195–220. New York: Columbia University Press.

Myerhoff, Barbara G. (1977) 'We Don't Wrap Herring in a Printed Page: Fusion, Fictions and Continuity in Secular Ritual', in Sally Falk Moore and Barbara Myerhoff (eds), *Secular Ritual,* Assen: Van Gorcum.

Napier, A. S. and Stevenson, W. H. (1894) *The Crawford Collection of Early Charters and Documents. Anecdotia Oxoniensia, Medieval and Modern* No. 7. Oxford: Oxford University Press.

Negev, Eilat (1990) 'Now Video Wills', *Yediot Ahronot,* 12 January 1990, pp. 30–1 (Hebrew).

Oates, Joan (1986) *Babylon*, revised edn. London: Thames & Hudson.

Ong, Walter J. (1982) *Orality and Literacy: The Technologizing of the Word*. London: Methuen.

Oppenheim, A. L. (1964) *Ancient Mesopotamia*. Chicago: University of Chicago Press.

Pfeiffer, John E. (1982) *The Creative Explosion: An Inquiry into the Origins of Art and Religion*. Ithaca, NY: Cornell University Press.

Rappaport, Roy A. (1971) 'Ritual, Sanctity and Cybernetics', *American Anthropologist* **73**, 59–76.

Roberts, Simon (1979) *Order and Dispute: An Introduction to Legal Anthropology*. Harmondsworth: Penguin.

Robertson, A. J. (1956 [1939]) *Anglo-Saxon Charters*. 2nd edn. Cambridge: Cambridge University Press.

Savage-Rumbaugh, Sue, Rumbaugh, Duane and Boyson, S. (1978) 'Linguistically Mediated Tool Use and Exchange by Chimpanzees (Pan Troglodytes),' *The Behavioral and Brain Sciences* **1**, 539–54; 614–16.

Searle, John (1976) 'A Classification of Illocutionary Acts', *Language in Society* **5**(1), 1–23.

Searle, John (1979) *Expression and Meaning*. Cambridge: Cambridge University Press.

Senner, Wayne (ed.) (1989) *The Origins of Writing*, pp. 27–42. Lincoln and London: University of Nebraska Press.

Stock, Brian (1983) *The Implications of Literacy*. Princeton: Princeton University Press.

Tambiah, Stanley J. (1968) 'The Magical Power of Words', *Man* **3**, 175–288.

Tambiah, Stanley J. (1985) *Culture, Thought and Social Action*. Cambridge, MA: Harvard University Press.

Tannen, Deborah (ed.) (1982) *Spoken and Written Language: Exploring Orality and Literacy*. Norwood, NJ: Ablex.

Turkle, Sherry (1995) *Life on the Screen: Identity in the Age of the Internet*. New York: Simon & Schuster.

Turner, Victor W. (1977) 'Symbols in African Ritual', in Janet L. Dolgin, David S. Kemnitzer and David M. Schneider (eds), *Symbolic Anthropology: A Reader in the Study of Symbols and Meanings*, pp. 183–94. New York: Columbia University Press.

Ungerleider-Meyerson, Joy (1986) *Jewish Folk Art*. New York: Summit.

Vodola, Elizabeth (1986) *Excommunication in the Middle Ages*. Berkeley: University of California Press.

Whitelock, Dorothy (ed.) (1968) *The Will of Aethelgifu: A Tenth Century Anglo-Saxon Manuscript*, trans. and ed. Dorothy Whitelock. Oxford: Roxburghe Club.

Whitelock, Dorothy (ed.) (1979) *English Historical Documents 500–1042*. London: Oxford University Press.

Whitelock, Dorothy (ed.) (1986 [1930]) *Anglo-Saxon Wills*, originally published by Cambridge University Press. Holmes Beach, FL: William W. Gaunt and Sons.

THREE

Performatives constituting value: the case of patents

Charles Bazerman

INTRODUCTION

Some symbolic systems take certain symbols very seriously. These symbols are given great weight as the fundamental pieces in the game enacted within the system. Symbolic systems based on sacred texts grant great power to those utterances which are designated the words of god, so that all other utterances are held accountable to these divine utterances, which have a kind of trump value. In financial and other economic discourses, amounts of money are an essential referent; here the notorious bottom line is the discursive trump card. In commerce (and the regulating law of commerce), designation of property and ownership are powerful symbolic representations.

Each of these systems requires valid specific instances of these valued classes of symbols in order to continue as vital scenes of social action. A religion based on divine utterances would be in great difficulty if no words of god could be certified, so as to anchor the faith. Literary criticism without valued literature would have little to talk about. Finance with no dollars or kronor is bankrupt. A system of commerce with no designated property and no designated owners would negotiate precious few deals. Thus the symbolic systems depend on the creation or designation of instances of valued symbols.

Although in a symbolic system, a certain class of utterances may carry great weight, each instance must be accepted as belonging to that class and thus admitted as a powerful symbol in the discourse. Each dollar must be recognizable as legitimate – issued in the proper form by the proper authorities who continue to put full faith and credit behind the paper – and not counterfeit or child's play-money. In the Old Testament burning bushes and other miraculous occurrences are reported by Moses and his colleagues as authorizing certain words as the words of god. Literary scholars have procedures for establishing the true text, which then becomes a referent of great power in critical discourse; similarly, accountants have well-known and regulated procedures for determining and certifying the figures that represent financial assets and liabilities.

PROCEDURES FOR CREATING VALUED SYMBOLS

In some discourses the procedures by which powerful symbols are born into the discourse are left entirely invisible, and we simply trust the ethical probity of the utterer that the symbol indeed represents the valued commodity it purports to, as when emotions are reported within intimate conversations. Sometimes the creation of valued symbols is regulated by an external procedure enforced by some sort of discursive police, such as the Securities Exchange Commission. But sometimes the status of the symbol must be petitioned for within the symbolic system itself, perhaps through elaborated and regulated procedures. That is, the term or utterance must apply for a valued status within the discursive system by engaging in a set of discursive practices of application or value-seeking.

Law, both civil–commercial and criminal, provides many instances of such procedures for application for a status within the law. The nature of the law is such as to encourage precisely the activity of status-seeking. The law is a specialized discursive system that orders and regulates activities in many other spheres of life. However, for any life concern to be brought under the law it must be brought into the legal chambers with its legal talk and texts, first by the passage of legislation that brings that general class of affairs under some legal umbrella, and secondly by suit in individual cases claiming that this case falls under the law. Thus where there is no law concerning cheating at sports, there can be no legal discourse about such cheating, unless it were brought under some other class of activity which was covered by law, such as assault with a deadly weapon. Then, for trial to be brought, a case must be made, such as before a grand jury, that the events are potentially definable as those covered by law; the final determination of the definition of events and assignment of historical roles and responsibilities are then decided in the court proceeding. Moreover, in order to bring a case before the law, a complainant must establish legal standing in the case; that is, that person must be legally definable as having a legitimate interest in the case. Then, ordinary events of life, in order to be converted into legally valid evidence, must be introduced through well-established procedures and must pass discursive tests, as specified in the rules of evidence. Thus representations of medical conditions would not exist within a legal proceeding unless deemed admissible by the court and then presented through records or witness testimony of the sort deemed valid. Further, in so far as the legal system makes a claim to be fair, equitable, and non-arbitrary, each of these translation and status-granting procedures must be held up for legal evaluation and review; for example, the legal standing of the complainant or the admissibility of any testimony may each be litigated.

Law in most countries is ancient (or based on ancient models), rife with precedent, procedures and rituals of authority, presenting an aura of stability and regularity. The methods by which individuals, events or statements obtain status or standing in the form of powerful legal symbols are well-established in formulas encased in rules. The use of any such formula can be considered a specific speech act (Austin 1962; Searle 1969; Danet, this volume). If the speech act meets all the appropriate general and local contextual considerations, abides by all the encasing rules and fulfils all its discursive activities, then the necessary status is obtained and the symbol or utterance enters into legal play.

THE PATENT AS LEGALLY CREATED VALUE

Patents are just such legal statuses granted to ideas through well-known procedures encased in regulations. Through the successful negotiation of the patent procedure, a person having an idea for some useful improvement in a product or process can have his/her idea deemed an ownable property and him/herself the owner for a prescribed period. During these years he/she owns a monopoly on the invention, and all who wish to use the idea must meet his/her terms for a licence. The advantage to be drawn from patents is in the system of commerce and finances, where patents can potentially be converted into money. However, because law regulates the commercial system and designates ownable property, eligible owners and methods for transfer of ownership and licensing, the status of patent must be established within the legal system before any idea has any value as an owned property within the world of commerce.

That patents are of great commercial value is indicated by the frequency with which products or their wrappers are imprinted with patent numbers, a compact identification of the patent status. This numerical symbol, of course, indexes against more complete documentation and description on file with the patent offices of the issuing governments; however, short of any legal procedure that would question the validity or extent of the patent, the patent number counts sufficiently as full sign of the legal status.

In the early years of incandescent lighting, which I have examined in relation to a project in progress on the discursive activity surrounding the emergence of Edison's system of centralized power and light (Bazerman 1993, 1995, forthcoming), the development and control of the industry hung on which patents were granted to whom. In the 1880s, when the technology was being transformed from a laboratory experiment into a widely available commercial product, Edison companies frequently discussed in publications directed at investors and potential investors the security and extensiveness of their patents as well as litigation to maintain the strength of the patents. Ritual lists of the patent numbers were common. The designation of ideas as patented property and the assignment of that property is a weighty, valuable matter.

HISTORY OF THE PATENT SYSTEM AND FORMS OF DOCUMENTS

The system of patents in the Anglo-American world was the remnant of the Renaissance English royal practice of granting monopoly privilege, and the documents surrounding patents took the typical forms of royal petition and decree. In reaction to royal abuses, parliament outlawed all royal monopolies for the single temporary monopoly granted to the inventor of a new good, under the belief that invention would advance the economic well-being of the country. Moreover, since invention created new value, a monopoly was not sequestering a previously open part of the economy, but was only granting temporary privilege for a value that would not have existed without the invention.

Once the idea of privilege dependent on specific value to the state emerged, it became necessary to create a mechanism whereby individuals might request this privilege and present their claim to it for evaluation. In England this led to a registration procedure followed by a litigation in the courts when the patent was contested. This system remained in effect until 1852.

In the Anglo-American colonies patents were granted on an individual basis by courts and local legislatures. The framers of the United States Constitution, to regularize and limit this practice, made patents and copyrights a federal responsibility. The first US patent law placed responsibility for approving patents on three cabinet members, determined that the application was to include a specification and drawing, and if possible a model, but did not prescribe anything further about the form of the application. The earliest extant application reveals that the rhetorical emphasis was on the deserving character of the petitioner and the great economic value to befall the United States, rather than the specific technical improvement. The actual patent grant consisted of a brief formal declaration signed by the president and the attorney general, containing only a one-sentence general description of the invention.

Because the burden of evaluating the applications was too much a drain on the time of the cabinet officers, in 1793 the law was revised to become simply a registration system with no evaluative procedures. The application, from the examples on file, turned to a description of the invented object, cross-referenced to a drawing. Models (not necessarily working) were also to be provided to the patent office. The grant consisted only of official testimony that the papers were filed and the fees were paid. Since no check was made of prior art and the putative inventor had to make no case beyond presenting the object and paying fees, many lawsuits developed. Apparently, within the litigation, two crucial issues emerged: the identity of the actual inventor and what exactly was being claimed as novel in the patent. Thus, in order to provide legal standing for these issues, by 1830 patent applications typically had two new elements: the formulaic opening identifying the putative inventor and a closing statement identifying the claim.

In 1836 a new patent law was passed, reintroducing examination and establishing a patent office with examiners. This law establishes the system we still have in effect, with some modifications from later law, most extensively in 1870 and 1952. The form of the patent in effect at Edison's time, was first specified in the 1836 legislation and was followed in practice. Moreover, the procedures and criteria for examination (aimed at preventing excessive litigation) were established both by the law and the practices of the newly formed patent office. These examination procedures and criteria further focused the task of the application, which rhetorically was aimed at passing through procedures and criteria to gain approval (Bazerman 1995).

THE FORM OF PATENTS AT EDISON'S TIME

Thus, by the time of Edison, the generic form of patent application and grant were stabilized in much like the modern form, spelled out in legal regulation and encased in bureaucratic procedures of evaluation. Now, as then, a patent, usually a printed document, describes an invention, identifies its inventor and declares particular aspects of the invention as original (the claim); it further carries some official designation of the patent-granting body, a patent number and a date from which the patent right begins. In late nineteenth-century United States, the patent typically opened with one or more technical drawings, signed by the inventor and two witnesses. The first page of text was headed by 'United States Patent Office', with subheadings identifying the inventor and the name of invention, followed by the formula 'Specification of Letters Patent [number], dated [date]'. The text then opened in the form of a letter 'to all whom it may concern', followed by the formulaic opening paragraph;

> Be it known that I, [name], of [city and state], have invented a new and Improved [object or process]; and I do hereby declare that the following is a full and exact description thereof, reference being had to the accompanying drawing and to the letters of reference marked thereon.

A general elaboration of the invention and its improvements over prior art is followed by a detailed description of the invention and its operation, typically introduced by a formula such as 'To enable those skilled in the art to fully understand and construct my invention, I will proceed to describe it.' The description is usually cross-indexed to the illustration through reference letters. The patent then ends with precise claims of novelty, prefaced by some such language as 'I claim as new, and desire to secure by Letters Patent ...'. The signature of the inventor and two witnesses again appears at the end.

Then, as now, the reigning patent law identified the specific elements to be put into the patent application, and thus the elements that will appear in the final patent grant which borrows the specification directly from the application. The law suggests the content, organization and even some of the phrasing of the patent.

Because the genre of application within the patent system establishes a single legal force of a coherent legal action (despite secondary multiple uses that may be made of this document), we can by-pass some of the usual complications when we try to consider both extended utterances and written texts as speech acts. If we consider patent applications as speech acts, we can most simply see that if one's application for a patent meets all the conditions for a patent, then one's application for a patent will be a success, and a patent should be granted, as the illocutionary force will be complete, and the patent examiner will be compelled to approve the application. If not, you can take the examiner to the appeals board or court. The courts and surrounding legal bodies then interpret and certify whether all conditions of success or felicity conditions are met, enforcing a relationship between *illocutionary* force and *perlocutionary* effect and thus bringing the interpretive procedures to the surface and making participants accountable for their interpretations. This makes patent and other similar legal procedures different from most speech acts, where illocutionary forces are not even linked to an anticipated perlocutionary effect (asserting that you are happy does not direct how your listener might respond); in any event, perlocutionary effect is usually up to the free choice of the hearer (as a call for help may be ignored).

CONDITIONS FOR A SUCCESSFUL PATENT APPLICATION

Now let us examine some of the conditions that must be met by a successful application and how the various parts or features of the text may be related to that success.

To obtain a patent you must have an idea for an object or process. This object or process must be useful. It must be novel. You must have invented it. Thus all these items must be asserted in the specification. As we have seen, in Edison's time the text of the patent opens with an identification of the inventor and the assertion of invention which is new and useful. A description of the invention follows, supported by an illustration. However, since you do not yet have the patent, the patent requiring approval, you must cast the application in the form of a petitionary letter, closing with some petitionary language like 'I claim as new and wish to secure by letters patent ...'. This petitionary format would be further framed by a cover letter, a standard form of which is given in a Scientific American pamphlet of 1881:

> To the Commissioner of Patents:
> Your Petitioner, a resident of ——, ——, prays that letters-patent be granted to him for the invention set forth in the annexed specification.
> signed

These petitionary features clearly identify that the person intends the document as a request, that the petitioner intends the receiver to understand this as a request, that the petitioner desires the receiver do what is requested, that the text is communicated to the receiver who is capable of interpreting the text, that the petitioner believes that the person receiving the request (the Commissioner of Patents) is able to grant such a request, that the request is for something that the receiver would not already have done in the normal course of affairs, and all the similar social and psychological conditions that must be met for a request to be granted, of the sort that Searle (1969) spells out.

The nature of the request, however, is that the receiver declare that a representation of an object or process be considered a patent. That is, the petitioner must assert that his/her idea meets the criteria of a patent so that the receiver will then declare the representation to be a patent protecting the idea. Therefore we must look into the propositions or representations embodied in the patent application.

PROPOSITIONAL ACTS IN THE PATENT APPLICATION

Searle (1969) points out that every speech act has a propositional content, and that proposition consists of acts of reference and acts of predication. On one level, the act of reference of the application is to the commissioner declaring a patent and the predication is that the commissioner will do it. That would be the standard propositional content of a request. However, the commissioner's declaration is based on an evaluation (to be performed by a patent examiner) of the object or process represented in the specification and the claims predicated of that object or process. Thus, the key propositions are to the item for which patent status is sought. Because there is an examination process done by the receiver that extends beyond the representation created by the petitioner, we must consider the propositional acts in two stages – as represented and as received, and what conditions must be met in each instance for success of the patent application.

The patent refers to the self, the act of invention and the object or process which represents the invention. Thus the patent opens with the identification of the applicant, a representation of the act of invention and details of the object. The largest part of the patent is given over to the representation of the object in the form of illustrations, description of the parts of the object in relation to the illustrations and a description of its operation, use and/or construction. From the point of view of the writer, these representations rely on the writer indeed believing that these represent him/herself, his/her actions in inventing and, most importantly, the object or process he/she has conceived. The inventor need not have brought this idea to working perfection, so the reference is to an imaginative construction that the inventor is in the process of bringing into physical realization. These representations share information about the idea seeking patent status not only with the patent examiner for the purposes of evaluation, but also (after the patent is granted) with others, allowing them to use the idea after the period of protection.

The propositional act, however, also consists of predications as well as of reference. The inventor, in making a patent application, represents him/herself, therefore, as having of a certain date the idea for a particular kind of device or process, that he/she believes this idea is workable and useful, and that it is an improvement of a substantial kind and therefore is an invention; and that, moreover, the novel improvement can be characterized within specific claims. The applicant may always be in bad faith concerning any of these representations, but in forwarding the application the inventor must present him/herself as sincere in these representations. It is up to the patent examiner to evaluate these representations as accurate and inaccurate, and therefore give public, legal approval to the validity of these representations, turning the individual's belief about his/her ideas into publicly certified knowledge.

PATENT EVALUATION PROCEDURES

The procedures for evaluation (whereby the illocutionary force of requesting a patent is converted to a state of belief on the examiner's part that will legally compel the desired perlocutionary effect of granting the patent) are, however, limited, attending only to specific aspects of the representations in the application. The inventor's representation of name and geographical location are accepted on the oath of the inventor. The date of filing is a matter of record of receipt. There is no procedure for determining whether the idea is workable, beyond obvious violations of physical laws (so that perpetual motion machines are not patented); the workability is left to the future of the product development. Similarly, the usefulness of the object is left to the later judgement of the marketplace. Thus, if the idea is unworkable or unuseful, the patent will be of no financial value and will be abandoned, making the patent monopoly moot and insignificant.

Since the patent does not represent actual produced and marketed objects, the representation is only of an idea. The idea itself is embodied in the patent description, so that there is no further examination of whether there is an idea here or whether this is the idea the inventor had. Patent descriptions are rejected usually only for lack of clarity or specificity, i.e. that the document is vague as to what the idea is.

The major forms of examination in patent office practice are primarily intertextual. The patent descriptions and claims are compared to the file of existing patents and to other representations of the current state of the art, such as textbooks and encyclopedia. Thus, only novelty is examined, leaving agnostic even the question of whether this novelty is an improvement (for improvement is equivalent to the usefulness of the novelty). The most sensitive item for novelty is the claim in which the breadth and generality of the intellectual property is defined, establishing the extent of the patent owner's rights.

Having passed through the defined procedures and intertextual examination, the patent is granted and the specification of the application becomes part of the patent grant. This successful speech act has passed tests of its perfection as a well-made symbol with due recognition of the contextual symbols of law, textbook knowledge and prior patents. In this manner, a new legal object of property is declared and assigned. All questions concerning the patent must then refer to the legal entity, for the life of that legal entity. Any attempt to challenge the patent must attempt to undo the speech act creating the legal entity. After the patent expires, the symbolic value is officially dead and all legal suits, contracts, licensing payments, restrictions on use, and the like, expire. Residual effects on secondary communicative systems, such as the history of technology, may remain, as patent documents become historical artifacts, but their primary symbolic force vanishes and the legal object is no more.

THE CREATION OF VALUE WITHIN DISCURSIVE SYSTEMS

To conclude, I return to the larger puzzle for all symbolic systems: how various entities come to have place and significance within discursive systems such that they are attended to, amass privileges, acquire a stability of meaning and value, and serve multiple functions for people differentially located in the system. Discovering the procedures by which terms gain weight and meaning within a system will tell us much about the nature and character of reference. It will also tell us about the way in which different social systems are bound together and held accountable to each other, as well as to the way certain discourses become self-contained and self-perpetuating. Then, understanding how the status once obtained operates as a dynamic element in the discursive system will tell us much about what language does and how it does it. Finally, seeing how that status – granted, maintained and modified – then translates into other social systems will tell us much about the flow of discursive power among social systems. We will learn in greater detail how the world works, through language.

REFERENCES

Austin, John (1962) *How To Do Things With Words*. Oxford: Oxford University Press.

Bazerman, Charles (1993) 'Patent Realities: Legally Stabilized Texts and Market Indeterminacies', *The Narrative Construction of the Anxious Object*. John Hultberg (ed.). Göteborg: University of Göteborg, pp. 5–12.

Bazerman, Charles (1995) 'Systems of Genre and the Enactment of Social Intentions', *Genre and the New Rhetoric*. Aviva Freedman and Peter Medway (eds). London: Taylor & Francis.

Bazerman, Charles (forthcoming) *The Languages of Edison's Light.* Cambridge, Mass.: MIT Press.

Scientific American (1881) *Reference Book.* New York: Munn and Company.

Searle, John (1969) *Speech Acts.* Cambridge: Cambridge University Press.

FOUR

Contracts as social action

Anna Trosborg

1. INTRODUCTION

The field of legal language within the written medium is unique with regard to distinctive lexical features, such as technical terms, archaic expressions, etc., and it is renowned for its syntactic complexity, which has given rise to a number of studies of these aspects (see, for example, Danet 1985: 278–87). Recent years have witnessed a shift of focus to pragmatic aspects (e.g. Gunnarsson 1984, Kurzon 1986, Werther and Helmersen 1989).

In this volume, Bazerman takes up the issue of how performatives constitute value in the case of patents, and Danet is concerned with 'speech, writing and performativity' in a historical perspective. She points out that 'legal documents contain evidence of a latent struggle to transfer performativity from speech to writing'. As for written documents, they pervade our daily lives, in official legislation as well as private transactions.

This chapter deals with the language used to express legal speech acts in simple contracts within the field of English Contract law. The central objects of study are regulative functions (directive, constitutive and commissive speech acts) with a particular view to establishing realization patterns of these rhetorical functions. The language of authentic contracts is analysed for socio-pragmatic occurrence and pragmalinguistic realization of regulative acts, and the choice of individual strategies can be interpreted in terms of the face redress required by the socio-pragmatic situation.[1]

2. REGISTER AND MEDIUM DESCRIBED COMMUNICATIVELY

The framework to be employed in this chapter is founded on the assumption that in order to get his/her message satisfactorily across, a sender will rely on a strategic cost/benefit analysis weighing the need for face redress against the necessity of propositional clarity and directness. Language is seen as a rich variety of options available for the sender to select the linguistic means which may best further his/her aims and achieve the receiver's cooperation to that end. Thus the linguistic output signals may be interpreted as politeness strategies reflecting the sender's intentional and strategic selection from the range of options available to him/her.

For this purpose, a three-dimensional model for formulating the sender's communicative intentions is applied. The parameters of the model are as follows: (i) domain/subdomain to allow for an adequate characterization of the 'register' involved in the discourse; (ii) sender/receiver constellation in order to reflect the socio-spatial relations and relative power of the interlocutors; (iii) communicative function for specifying the criteria according to which the language user can select the linguistic means for formulating a particular message.

This approach is in agreement with Brown and Levinson's (1987) concept of strategic and intentional behaviour on the part of the sender and with the limitations imposed on the operational scope of the parties to the individual contract by the existing legal framework comprising the law of contract.

2.1 Domain/subdomain

The underlying concept of the domain/subdomain dimension is Trosborg 's (1991) distinction between 'legal language' as the superordinate term for all instances of language used within all relevant subdomains (e.g. documents, textbooks or professional literature) embodied in the area of law, and 'the language of the law' as the specific term referring to language as realized specifically in legal documents, i.e. texts covered by the scope of common law and statute law, namely (i) simple contracts and deeds, and (ii) legislation, respectively. I have restricted my analysis to simple contracts (see section 3.1).

2.2 Sender/receiver constellation

The sender/receiver relations are defined as 'symmetrical' vs. 'asymmetrical' according to the relative authoritative status of the interlocutors, taking into account the extent to which the parties may be said to be insiders or outsiders of the domain/subdomain involved.

2.2.1 Sender/receiver relations in a legal perspective

Contractual communication is unique in that the relative intentions of the parties are expressed on to print by the assistance of an intermediary filter someone who is learned in the law – with a particular reference to the legislative limitations – the contractual basis – and with a view to the dispute-settling institution: the courts of justice. In contracts, the parties to the contract are specified in the introduction and by their signature, and each party accepts 'the agreement' as enforceable by the court: 'It is this day mutually agreed between ...'; 'Now it is hereby agreed (and declared) as follows: ...'; 'Now this deed witnesseth as follows ...'.

Basically, the parties to the contract are both senders and receivers. The parties are senders in that before the contract is drawn up by a lawyer, they have agreed on the subject matter of the contract, its contents, i.e. the specific 'promise' and 'consideration', and the particular circumstances and conditions involved. They are receivers in that they verify and witness the agreement by their signature, and thus approve the contents of the contract.

This procedure forms a contrast to the one-way traffic in law-texts, in which the legislative body sets up rules to be obeyed by the citizens. The successful enactment of the law (by means of the so-called promulgation formula) is a necessary condition for 'laying down the law' and marks the act in question as a declaration.

Because of the nature of simple contracts, either party may be said to hold something of great value and interest to the other – 'promise' and 'consideration', respectively. This, combined with the fact that the parties witness the contract by their respective hands, is the prime motivation for claiming that the relative level of authority is symmetrical.

The distribution of roles is fixed in that the parties are designated a 'title' according to the role they play, e.g. principal/agent, seller/buyer or franchisor/franchisee. Where the parties are identified as corporations, persons representing them and invested with the proper authorization will sign the contract on behalf of the corporation.

Apart from the parties to the contract themselves, there may even be another receiver of the contractual message, namely 'the dispute-settling institution' – a court of justice. Thus Werther and Helmersen claim that:

> one could say that to any contract there is one further potential receiver, namely the authority/instance which may be involved in settling disputes about the contract as may arise. Thus the parties are communicating with an impersonal, abstract and institutional receiver, which does not necessarily receive the message.
>
> (Werther and Helmersen 1989: 11)

The potential receiver may be characterized as the 'hidden hand' of the communicative process of the legal discourse as realized in contracts. It forms the basic scope for the individual contract and its inherent authoritative status imposes restrictions on the parties, as the contents of the contract have to be in conformity with the legal framework, and it forces the parties to avail themselves of politeness strategies in order to reduce the face-threatening acts (FTAs) (see Brown and Levinson 1987) of the directive speech acts involved, as well as the incorporated intentions of the law with their subtle allusions to remedies and sanctions if the parties do not comply with their contractual duties and obligations. Compare:

> The special use of *shall* is one of the most characteristic markers of the legal register; it means not only 'Do X', but also 'If you don't, we have sanctions'.
>
> (Albrecht and Bülow-Möller 1984: 26)

There seems to be asymmetrical power relations between the potential receiver and the parties to the contract as their scope and liberty of action is restricted and limited by the mere institutional authority of partly the rules of contract law, and partly the courts constructing and administering such rules.

2.2.2 *Sender/receiver relations in a linguistic perspective*

The contractual proposition is uttered in relation to differentiable receivers: (i) the parties entering into contractual relations, and (ii) lawyers who will construct and interpret the contract in accordance with the legislative framework in case of a dispute. The difference between the various 'audiences' may be illustrated in terms of Fleck's (1981) distinction between exoteric ('outsiders') and esoteric ('insiders') receivers. Myers (1989: 3), who has applied Brown and Levinson's (1987) politeness theories on a set of scientific texts, makes a claim that the distinction is very important in respect of FTAs involved in communicating a message, as politeness involves displaying to the exoteric group the proper respect for the face of members of the esoteric group, and furthermore, the same act may be an imposition on one of these audiences but not on the other.

The function of the intermediary filter of the communicative process – the lawyer – is to ensure that the contents of the contract are in agreement with the scope for dispositional freedom on the part of the parties to the contract as limited by the legal framework. In this respect, legal discourse within the scope of the language of the law can be described as formula-based communication with the form side orientated mainly towards the esoteric audience jurists and lawyers. The content side is mainly orientated towards the exoteric group – the parties to the contract – as their relative particular data, decisions and declarations of legal intent make up the content side of a contract. Obviously, the functional side relates to both groups, as both the intentions of the parties and the intentions of the legal framework will manifest themselves in the contract.

2.3 Communicative function: regulative speech acts

For the specific purpose of constructing contracts, language is used as a means of 'ordering human relations', i.e. language is used with a regulative function. In his taxonomy of illocutionary acts, Searle (1976) outlines two major categories of regulative acts – directives and commissives – with the same 'direction of fit', 'world-to-words', the illocutionary point of which is the speaker's intention to regulate the world, as opposed to, for example, representative speech acts where the words are adjusted to match the world ('words-to-world').

Establishing classificatory kinship between requests and promises would simplify Searle's taxonomy. However, in his taxonomy the two categories are different:

> whereas the point of a promise is to commit the speaker to do something (and not necessarily to try to get himself to do it), the point of a request is to try to get the hearer to do something (and not necessarily to commit or obligate him to do it).
>
> (Searle 1976: 12)

Attempts to assimilate the two categories have been made, suggesting either that promises are really a species of requests to oneself, or that requests place the hearer under an obligation. Searle, however, accepts neither solution but commits himself to 'the inelegant solution of two categories with the same direction of fit' (Searle 1976: 12).

The present framework suggests a classification in which directives and commissives are subclasses of the category of regulative acts. While legislative power is clearly exercitive, the commitment in contracts can be established either as an obligation issued by one party over the other (i.e. directive), or by a party committing him/herself (i.e. commissive).

Within a very general definition, the nature of a contract may be defined as 'a legally binding agreement [...] imposing rights and obligations on the parties which will be enforced by the courts' (Redmond 1979: 19). The language of simple contracts refers to mutual rights and obligations in relation to 'promise' and 'consideration'. I shall now consider the 'nature' of the underlying linguistic functions for distributing such rights md obligations: directive and commissive acts.

2.3.1 *Directive acts*

A directive is an illocutionary act by means of which the addresser tries to influence the behaviour of the addressee. Directives are impositive acts which have been defined as follows:

> Impositive speech acts are described as speech acts performed by the speaker to influence the intentional behaviour of the hearer in order to get the latter to perform, primarily for the benefit of the speaker, the action directly specified or indirectly suggested by the proposition.
>
> (Haverkate 1984: 107)

In outlining the terms of the contract, rules are formulated with the intent of ordering human relations. One party of the contract (e.g. principal, seller, franchiser) imposes a certain behaviour on the other party (e.g. agent, buyer, franchisee) and vice versa.

A directive is a 'face-threatening act' involving a threat to the addressee's negative face, which has been defined as 'the want of every "competent adult member" that his actions be unimpeded by others' (Brown and Levinson 1987: 62). An addresser issuing a directive attempts to exercise power or direct control over the intentional behaviour of the addressee and in this way intrudes on the right to freedom of action. In order to lessen the impact of the imposition on the addressee, the addresser has recourse to politeness strategies. The explicitness with which the act to be performed (or not performed in the case of prohibitions) is formulated is referred to as the directness level of the directive.

2.3.2 *Directness levels of directive acts*

When issuing a directive, various options are available to the addresser. Within the theory of Brown and Levinson (1987: 62), the directive can be expressed 'on record' or 'off record', i.e. with or without explicit directive force, respectively. If the former option is selected, the addresser can voice the directive with or without face redress by using mitigating devices. Table 4.1 provides a list of directives used as an instrument for analysing legal speech acts of English Contract law (Trosborg 1991).[2] In the case of unmodified imperatives and unhedged performative utterances, the directive is phrased explicitly without face redress and serves as an order. Likewise the modals *shall* and *must* are employed to impose a high degree of obligation on the addressee. Face redress, on the other hand, can be obtained by means of conventionally indirect directives, either in the form of (i) 'hearer orientated' questions concerning the ability/willingness of the addressee to perform a certain action, e.g. by the use of the modals *can/could* or *will/would*, or by 'permission statements' through the application of the modals *may/might* or *can/could*, or (ii) 'speaker based' *want*-statements expressing the addresser's desires and needs. Finally, directives can be performed indirectly with no explicit marker of the impositive intent (i.e. 'off record'). These categories are adapted for the purpose of analysing legal contracts (see section 3.2).

2.3.3 *Commissive acts*

According to Austin (1962: 156), 'the whole point of a commissive is to commit the speaker to a certain course of action'. Obvious examples are utterances including the verbs *promise, vow, pledge, covenant, contract, guarantee, embrace* and *swear*. Adopting Austin's categories for further development, Searle takes over Austin's category of commissives in its original form with the only objection that certain verbs included by Austin according to Searle 'do not belong

Table 4.1 Request strategies (presented at levels of increasing directness)

Situation: Speaker requests to borrow Hearer's car.

Cat. I	**Indirect request**		
	Str. 1 Hints	(mild)	I have to be at the airport in half an hour.
		(strong)	My car has broken down. Will you be using your car tonight?
Cat. II	**Conventionally indirect** (hearer-orientated conditions)		
	Str. 2 Ability		Could you lend me your car?
	Willingness		Would you lend me your car?
	Permission		May I borrow your car?
	Str 3 Suggestory formulas		How about lending me your car?
Cat. III	**Conventionally indirect** (speaker-based conditions)		
	Str. 4 Wishes		I would like to borrow your car.
	Str. 5 Desires/needs		I want/need to borrow your car.
Cat. IV	**Direct requests**		
	Str. 6 Obligation		You must/have to lend me your car.
	Str. 7 Performatives		
	(hedged)		I would like to ask you to lend me your car.
	(unhedged)		I ask/require you to lend me your car.
	Str. 8 Imperatives		Lend me your car.
	Elliptical phrases		Your car (please).

in this class at all' (1976: 11). He refers to verbs such as *shall*, *intend* and *favour*.

Searle repeats that:

> Commissives then are those illocutionary acts whose point is to commit the speaker (again in varying degrees) to some future course of action.
>
> (Searle 1976: 11)

The sincerity condition is intention. The propositional content always refers to the carrying out of some future action on the part of the speaker. The speaker's commitment to carry out the act described in the proposition can be expressed through an explicit performative verb or by means of the modal verb *will* functioning as an implicit performative:

The Distributor *promises/covenants/guarantees* ...
Each party hereby *agrees* that it *will* ...

Commissives and directives differ as regulative acts with regard to 'face-threat'. Per definition (as specified by the 'felicity conditions'[3] of promises), promises are in the interest of the hearer (and at the cost of the speaker). The speaker can only promise 'felicitously' if the intended act is in the interest of the hearer. For this reason, an act of promising is not face-threatening to the hearer. An explicit statement of the promise is therefore desirable, and indirectness and/or hedging would only weaken the obligation and make it legally invalid.

In contrast, directives are issued for the benefit of the speaker and at the cost of the hearer; they are face-threatening acts to be adjusted in communication relative to interlocutor and communicative intention.

3. EMPIRICAL DESIGN

3.1 The data

The data of the investigation has been drawn from a corpus of legal language within the specific field of contract law comprising three individual corpora (Danish–English–French). Each corpus consists of one million running words and covers six types of text relevant to the subject: (i) statutes, rules and regulations; (ii) travaux préparatoires; (iii) judgments; (iv) contracts; (v) legal textbooks; and (vi) articles in law journals.

The body of contracts consists of: (i) bilateral simple contracts; (ii) unilateral simple contracts; and (iii) deeds (contracts under seal), altogether 69 individual contracts amounting to a total of around 210,000 running words. The data subjected to analysis are the compiled simple contracts (163,500 words).[4] For a more detailed description of the corpora, see Dyrberg et al. (1988).

3.2 The classificatory instrument

The purpose of the analysis was to isolate all occurrences of regulative acts and analyse the pragmalinguistic realization patterns of the directive, constitutive and commissive acts by means of which the parties to a contract are committed.

A combination of computational analysis and manual tagging was used for examining the contracts for the relevant speech acts. For a detailed presentation of the quantitative methods employed, see Blom and Trosborg (1992).

The classificatory framework outlined in sections 2.3–2.3.3 (see Table 4.1) was adapted and modified to allow for the classification of regulative acts observed in the corpus. Table 4.2 summarizes the categories used as an instrument of classification. The unmarked category in Table 4.1 relates to Cat. I, 'constitutive rules' in Table 4.2. Statements which do not include performative verbs, or modals functioning as implicit performatives, may still serve the purpose of regulating behaviour. Sentences used to explain or define expressions and terms in the contract or to supply information concerning the application of the statute, or part of it, are part of constitutive rules (cf. Kurzon 1986: 23).

Cat. II (Table 4.2) includes 'permission' and the category of 'rights', which comprises 'assignment of benefit' (a) and 'limitation of liability' (b). An utterance listed under 'assignment of benefits' involves a dual function; it distributes a right to whomever is entitled to it and a latent duty on the party not entitled to it – irrespective of

Table 4.2 Domain-specific hierarchy of strategies for issuing regulatives

Regulative strategies for simple contracts (presented at levels of increasing directness)

I.	Constitutives	unmarked
II.	Permission	allow[–] • can • could • grant[–] • may • might • need not • [VP] no obligation • offer[–]
	Rights	(a) shall/will {"benefit"} [± negation] (b) shall/will {"limitation of liability"} [± negation]
III.	Obligation	are to • has to • have to • is to • must • obligate • obliged to • shall • should • will
	Prohibition	can [negation] • may [negation] • shall [negation] • will [negation]
	Performatives	demand[–] • order[–] • request[–]
IV.	Promises	accept[–] • acknowledge[–] • agree[–] • certify[–] • commit[–] • confirm[–] • covenant[–] • declare[–] • guarantee[–] • promise[–] • represent[–] • understand[–] • undertake[–] • warrant[–]

[ ]: symbol for syntactic item
{ }: symbol for semantic item denoting stated value or equivalent
–: symbol for morphological item

which party makes the utterance. 'Limitation of liability' is a pragma-semantically related subcategory, in which the right assigned is some kind of debt reduction, restriction as to commitment, etc. (e.g. *neither party shall be liable for ...*).

As the analysis of contracts revealed an empty slot for Cat. III (speaker-based preparatory conditions) in Table 4.1, this category was exempted from the classification.

Cat. III of Table 4.2 comprises the categories 'obligation' and 'performatives' (transferred from Cat. IV in Table 4.1) and an additional category 'prohibition'.

Finally, the scale was enlarged with Cat. IV, 'promises'. The performative verbs typically employed with commissive intention are *promise, covenant, undertake, commit, offer, acknowledge, agree* and *consent*. In agreement with Searle (1976: 11) verbs like *intend* and *favour* (which are suggested by Austin as performatives) are not treated as performatives, as intentions and favours are 'weak' expressions unable to commit the speaker legally. *Shall* is treated as an implicit performative, though generally with a directive function. The modal *will* functions as an implicit performative expressing the addresser's obligation to carry out the act described in the proposition.

4. THE USE OF REGULATIVES IN ENGLISH CONTRACTS

The corpus of contracts was analysed for the occurrence of regulative acts. Performatives were not used to indicate directive force. Instead, modal auxiliaries were used as 'implicit performatives'. The results (see Table 4.3) show a predominance of direct acts (Cat. III, statements of obligation and prohibition), which amounted to 46.3 per cent of the total number of observed strategies. Unmarked strategies (Cat. I, constitutive rules) were employed frequently (22.7 per cent). In Cat. II, conventionally indirect strategies were only expressed by means of permission statements (5.8 per cent); besides, 'assignment of benefit' (6.6 per cent) and negated limitation of liability' (3.4 per cent) occurred. Strategies querying preparatory conditions (hearer's ability/willingness to carry out the desired act) and speaker-based strategies expressing wishes and desires, which occur frequently in everyday conversations (Trosborg 1991), were noticeably absent.

Commissive acts were realized by means of performatives

explicitly expressing promises (9.5 per cent). Obligation expressed by implicit performatives realized by the modal *will* amounted to 4 per cent.

In the following, the realization types of regulative strategies observed in the corpus are discussed and exemplified.

4.1 Direct directives

4.1.1 Obligation

As is apparent from Table 4.3, the direct strategies of Cat. III are the most frequently used directives in English contracts. Statements of obligation amounted to 39.5 per cent, and the subcategory of prohibitions to 6.8 per cent. Imperatives and performatives were not observed.

Table 4.3 Distribution of categories of regulatives in per cent

Cat. I	**Constitutives**				
	Statements:	lexical main verb	10.7		
		be-constructed	5.5		
		shall	3.2	19.4	
	Predictions:	*shall*	3.2		
		will	0.2	3.3	22.7
Cat. II	**Rights**				
	Permission:	lexical	0.2		
		may	5.4		
		can	0.2	5.8	
	Assignment of benefits:		6.6		
	Negated assignment:		0.6		
	Limitation of liability:		1.1		
	Negated limitation of liability:		3.4	11.8	17.6
Cat. III	**Obligation**				
	Prohibition:	*may/can* + neg	0.3		
		shall + neg	6.0		
		will + neg	0.5	6.8	
	Obligation:	*are to*	0.7		
		must	0.6		
		shall	38.0		
		lexical	0.2	39.5	46.3
		will	4.0		50.3
Cat. IV	**Promises**		9.5		9.5

In order to express obligation in legal contracts, the modal *shall* is used almost exclusively (38 per cent). *Shall* is used to express the illocutionary force of an order. The addresser – one party to the contract – directs the other party to do X. By signing the contract, the addressee undertakes the obligation:

> Commission *shall* be paid on a quarterly basis and *shall* be based on the previous quarter's nett sales.
>
> (4–001)

> Employees *shall* work such overtime as the Company from time to time thinks necessary according to the needs of its business.
>
> (4–014)

As in (4–001), the illocution is frequently constructed by the application of passivization, involving agent suppression, and/or by the use of a non-human subject. Those are prominent features of the legal register and may be explained in terms of face redress in order to reduce the face-threat involved in issuing a directive.

4.1.2 Prohibitions

In addition to statements expressing obligation, the regulation of behaviour can be made by issuing prohibitions. Again, the modal *shall* is used almost exclusively (6 per cent out of 6.8 per cent of the strategies observed):

> Each party hereby agrees that it will use such confidential information solely for the purposes of this Agreement and that it *shall not* disclose, whether directly or indirectly, to any third party such information other than as required to carry out the purposes of this Agreement.
>
> (4–015)

> This agreement *shall not* be assigned by the Owner without the prior written concern of the Distributor.
>
> (4–018)

4.2 Rights

4.2.1 Permission

Permission generally issues from some authority, which is often the speaker (addresser) – the performer of the speech act. In contracts, a symmetrical relation holds between the two parties, either of which is able to grant permission to the other party (discretionary authority):

> The Hirer *may* determine the hiring at any time by giving one month's previous notice in writing expiring on one of the days appointed for payment of rent.
>
> (4–015)

> The Owner hereby *grants* to the Distributor [...] the sole and exclusive right to licence, sub-licence and generally to market, distribute and support the Software.
>
> (4–047)

> The company hereby *gives* the officer *permission* to reside with his wife and children in the dwellinghouse and premises [...] as the company's representative.
>
> (4–006)

Statements of permission, which made frequent use of lexical verbs (e.g. *grant/give permission*), amounted to 5.8 per cent of the total number of strategies.

4.2.2 *Assignment of benefit/liability*

The examples below are linguistic manifestations of the subcategories: (i) assignment of benefits; (ii) negated assignment of benefits; (iii) limitation of liability; and (iv) negated limitation of liability, respectively:

> The Company *shall have power* [...] to carry on its business alone or in association with any one or more persons (whether natural or legal) or by any one or more subsidiary companies.
>
> (4–026)

> The duty to disclose contained in this clause *shall not impose* on either party any obligation to develop any such modification or improvement.
>
> (4–027)

> The Carrier *shall be relieved of its obligation* to perform the Contract to the extent that the performance thereof is prevented by failure of the Trader.
>
> (4–038)

> *No liability* whatsoever *shall be accepted* by the Contractor for any alterations or additions carried out in contravention of this Clause.
>
> (4–059)

4.3 Constitutive rules

Examples of constitutive rules typically involve lexical main verbs such as *mean, apply, include, exclude,* which are not performative verbs, and constructions with *be* + copula:

> 'ACCIDENT' *includes* exposure resulting from a mishap to a conveyance in which the Assured is travelling.
>
> (4–021)

> All accounts *are payable* in accordance with the terms contained in the Supplier's invoice for the Equipment.
>
> (6–004)

Future reference by the use of the modal *shall* may indicate a constitutive spelling out a rule of the contract with a legal effect:

> ANY notice required to be served upon the Owner or Hirer hereunder *shall be deemed* to be duly served 48 hours after posting if sent by first class recorded delivery post.
>
> (4–053)

4.4 Commissives

By making a promise, a party to the contract commits him/herself before the law. Promises were typically expressed by means of performative verbs, such as *agree, undertake, acknowledge, warrant, accept*:

> The Supplier *warrants* to the Customer that the Equipment marketed by the Supplier is believed to be free from defects of workmanship and materials.
>
> (4–057)

> The Licensee *acknowledges* that the copyright in [...] all written, printed and photographed matter supplied by the Grantor under this agreement [...] shall belong to and remain vested in the Grantor.
>
> (4–027)

The verbs *promise* and *covenant* were observed but they were not in frequent use.

5. DISCUSSING THE FINDINGS

When discussing the present findings, I briefly compare the use of regulative acts in contractual communication with the occurrence of regulative acts in legislative texts (Trosborg 1991) and with the use of directives in conversational English.

In both types of legal documents, the category of direct directives dominates (legislation 47.6 per cent, contracts 46.3 per cent) with mandatory *shall* as the single most frequently used subcategory (legislation 21.4 per cent, contracts 38 per cent). A higher number of constitutives in statutes (39.3 per cent), as compared with contracts (22.7 per cent), reflects the very function in the former of establishing rules and regulations.

Commissives occurred only in contracts. A difference was observed in the use of explicit performatives in directives compared with commissives. Strategies of the prototype *I hereby order you to do X* were rarely observed, neither in statutes, nor in contracts, whereas strategies of the type *I hereby promise to do X* amounted to 9.5 per cent in contracts. This difference can be explained with reference to the face-threat (see sections 2.3.2–2.3.3) involved in the two acts. When trying explicitly to enforce the desired behaviour (which is for the benefit of the sender and normally at the cost of the receiver) on to the receiver, the sender openly threatens the receiver's right to remain unimpeded. This explains why explicit performative verbs are avoided.

On the contrary, when issuing a promise, the speaker commits him/herself (and not someone else) to carry out the act specified in the proposition, but does not impose on the other party. The promise is at the cost of the sender and believed to be for the benefit of the receiver. For these reasons, a promise can be emphasized by being made explicit by means of a performative verb.

When comparing the directives observed in English Contract Law with directives observed in everyday conversations, the selection of directness levels differs markedly in the two domains (see Trosborg 1991).[5] The strategies used most frequently in everyday conversational English belong to the category of conventionally indirect directives, a finding which is in agreement with those of previous studies (e.g. Ervin-Tripp 1976 (American English); Blum-Kulka et al. 1989 (British and American English)). Querying the hearer's ability/willingness to perform a given act (*Could you spare me a cigarette?/Would you mind mailing this package for me?*) amounts to 50.6 per cent of the total number of strategies observed in conversational English, while statements of the speaker's wishes and desires (*I would like you to send me a parts list*) amount to 16.9 per cent, altogether comprising 67.5 per cent of the total number of strategies. These strategies occur neither in contract law, nor in contracts.

The most frequent category in the language of the law and in contracts is direct ordering (47.6 per cent and 46.3 per cent, respectively), which is the category employed least frequently in the conversational data (9.6 per cent). As for individual strategies, statements employing the modal verb *shall* are specific to legal English. Imperatives were not observed at all in the language of the law. In everyday conversation, orders are issued downwards in rank by means of imperatives (*Bring me the file*), or the strategy is used as an indicator of solidarity between interactants of equal status (*Hand me the paper, will you?*).

The modal *must* (deontic use) was not observed at all as an illocutionary force indicator of a directive in contract law, and it was employed only infrequently in contracts (0.6 per cent). *Must* is used in conversational English in directives issued by authority figures, and it also occurs in statements in which the speaker wants to express enthusiasm as to the realization of the propositional content (*You really must go and see that film*). The modals *should/ought to* were utilized only in rare cases in contract law, when a directive was intentionally weakened, and not at all as realizations of directives in contracts. These modals are typically used to express suggestions and convey pieces of advice in conversational English.

Statements of permission occur in all three domains. In contract law, permission is supplemented with the categories of 'assignment of rights' and 'limitation of liability'. The category 'assignment of benefits' is particular to contracts.

The observed differences in the use of directives in English Contract Law compared to the use in conversational English cannot be ascribed to a difference between the written and the spoken medium. Samples of directives in written English (a corpus of business letters) also shows a predominance of conventionally indirect strategies and a low proportion of direct strategies (Pilegaard 1990).

It is argued here that the pragmatic characteristics of the law pertains to the dependence on extra-linguistic institutions and must be interpreted within the sociopragmatic constraints of the situation. Furthermore, a consideration of the 'felicity conditions' of directives and commissives (see Searle 1969: 64–6) is helpful in throwing light on the selection of directives in the language of the law.

The declaration realized through the enactment formula is particular to legislation and so is the authority of legal institutions. In legislature, the addressee's willingness to perform is not questioned – the authority of the legislature is unquestionable; in contracts, the parties are obligated by their signatures. These factors explain why we do not find directives of the kind *Can/could/would you do X?* in the corpus. This type of directive is by far the most frequent in conversational usage, due to a balance between being adequately polite (conventional indirectness) and a demand for explicitness (the proposition to be performed by the addressee is explicitly stated).

The total absence in the language of the law of *want*-statements (the speaker's wishes and desires for X to take place), which in conversation is realized as *I want/would like X* can be explained with reference to the 'sincerity condition'. This strategy is a statement to the effect that the speaker sincerely wants X to take place. However, as the legislator's demands become law when enacted, there is no point in stating sincerity.

In legislative discourse, the condition of authority is crucial. The legislator is in a position of authority over the addressee, a factor which is decisive in the selection of directness levels utilized in the language of the law. It explains the high proportion of direct acts and may even influence acts seemingly offering the addressee freedom of action.

As regards the examples above, employing the modals *may/shall*, the modal verb *may* has been pointed out as indicating the illocutionary force of a permission, while acts employing the modal verb *shall* were treated as having the illocutionary force of orders. Legal writers have stressed the need to distinguish between the two modals of legal language – *shall* to be used with 'mandatory' and *may* with 'directory' force (Craies 1971: 229–30), i.e. *shall* implies obligation or duty and *may* implies permission. However, the illocutionary forces of order and of permission have in common an authoritative source – the legislature. As pointed out by Kurzon (1986: 23), once an authorized body, such as a court, has been given power by the occurrence of *may* to effectuate the legal rights of a person or class of persons, it is very difficult for it not to exercise that power.

The distinction between *may* and *shall* may also be neutralized in everyday language, e.g. a manager may tell one of his/her employees to leave his/her office by saying *You may leave now*, in which case the manager's wish is to be understood as a command. In contrast, in contracts one party does not hold power over the other. In this symmetrical power relationship, 'permission means permission', and the sincerity of the offer (made legally valid by the parties' signatures) is crucial, hence the explicit promises employing performative verbs.

The lack of imperatives in legislative texts may be due to the distance between the legislature and the body of addressees, who are never directly addressed. In the case of the citizens, this may be due to the intervention of mediators (as interpreters of the law to laymen). When addressing parties to a contract, a lack of imperatives may be interpreted as adherence to the principle of face-saving.

The occurrence of statements with directive intention without performative marking observed in both conversational English and the language of the law needs to be commented on. In the conversational data, these utterances are indirect directives (hints), in the sense that the intended directive force can be neglected by a non-cooperative hearer. This is not so with the unmarked statements of the language of the law which make up constitutive rules. In spite of the lack of directive markers, these statements belong to the body of rules which come into function as directives by means of the promulgation formula (in statutes)[6] and signatures (in contracts); hence they function as regulative acts on a par with explicit directives.

Concerning the use of politeness markers, the illocutionary force of directives in everyday conversations is often hedged or mitigated by the inclusion of politeness markers (*I wonder if you could possibly …*). In the language of the law, mitigators are almost absent (unlike the language employed in judgments and mediation). However, one device, which has been observed to occur frequently, is defocalization of agent as well as patient.

The sender/receiver perspective of a regulative act presents a particular point of interest. In face-to-face interaction, when the speaker issues a directive, the hearer is generally the addressee. In writing, a high level of explicitness is often necessary. If the sender avoids mention of the addressee as the agent of the desired act, thereby downtoning the impact of the directive on the requestee, the directive is potentially ambiguous with regard to addressee. In legislation, however, the roles are predetermined: the legislative body as regulator has an authoritative position in relation to the citizens who are to obey the laws. Consequently, the regulated party need not be explicitly mentioned in law-texts. This explains why only 19.4 per cent of the observed directives in contract law have a human subject. Depersonalization can be used (without risking ambiguity of agency) as a way of mitigating the impact of a directive on the addressee, as in *such sum shall be recoverable, regard shall be had*.

A contract is drafted with the intention of stating as clearly as possible the rules, rights, obligations, etc., which regulate the parties. Desired action is not hinted at but explicitly stated, and it is the drafter's obligation to be as clear as possible in every aspect of agreement in the interest of the contractors and in order to avoid litigation. As agency is not predetermined, ambiguity and defocalizing reference with the intention of blurring agency must be prevented (at least in principle). This explains the higher number of human agents specified in contracts (57.8 per cent compared with 19.4 per cent in law-texts).

The high number of directives employing a non-human subject in law-texts is due to the fact that the law operates by laying down its own constitutive rules with legal actants as subjects, such as 'this act', 'the provisions of this section', 'a statutory instrument', 'the guarantee'. In contracts, non-human subjects are referred to as 'conditions of the contract', such as price, data, amount, licence fees, etc.

6. CONCLUDING REMARKS

This chapter has analysed the occurrence of legal speech acts in English contracts. An analysis has been presented of directive acts observed in the corpus, revealing the communicative acts of statements of obligation, statements of prohibition, statements of permission (involving 'assignment of rights', 'limitation of liability' and 'assignment of benefits'), as well as constitutive statements as directive acts typical of the language of the law. Explicit commissive acts occur as affirmative statements.

When comparing directives in documents with directives observed in everyday conversations, it has been shown that the selection patterns, drawn from a continuum of directness levels, differ. Legislative texts and simple contracts show a predominance of direct strategies (statements of obligation and prohibition), whereas conversational English favours conventionally indirect strategies.

I have argued that this difference can be ascribed to the external factors of the social situation, rather than to a difference in medium (written vs. spoken). Furthermore, it is not just a matter of the English language of the law being more direct than conversational English (no imperatives were observed); it is a question of selecting strategies to express a specific communicative function in a particular sender/receiver relationship within the considerations of the 'felicity conditions' of the act in question and of the socio-pragmatic requirements of the situation.

NOTES

1. This research has been financed partly by The Danish Research Council for the Humanities and I would like to express my gratitude for their support. The chapter is based on my findings published in a preliminary version as Blom and Trosborg in *HERMES* **8** (1992), The Aarhus School of Business. It has also appeared in revised form as part of my article 'Statutes and Contracts: An Analysis of Legal Speech Acts in the English Language of the Law' (Trosborg 1995).
2. For previous classifications of directives, which build on Austin (1962) and Searle's (1969, 1976) theories, see for example, Brown and Levinson (1987), Blum-Kulka *et al.* (1989).
3. 'Felicity conditions' relate to a given illocutionary act, which can be performed under various social conditions. Socioeconomic requirements relate to specific social situations.
4. For the purpose of well-defined sender/receiver relations, I have chosen to leave out potentially unilateral contracts as they may contain an overall illocutionary force tending towards promise. Those are as follows: (i) certain types of 'deeds'; and (ii) certain types of 'simple contracts' (options, tenders, rewards).
5. The data of comparison derive from dyadic conversations between native speakers of English elicited by means of role simulation material constructed on the basis of anticipated illocutionary acts with a directive function. The role relationships between the two participants varied along two parameters: 'dominance' and 'social distance', and the situations involved a high 'degree of imposition'.
6. Compare Fotion's (1971) notion of a master speech act.

REFERENCES

Albrecht, Lone and Bülow-Möller, Anne Marie (1984) *Practical Text Analysis – How to Read Between the Lines*. Copenhagen: Samfundslitteratur.

Austin, J. L. (1962) *How To Do Things with Words*. New York: Oxford University Press.

Blom, Bjarne and Trosborg, Anna (1992) 'An Analysis of Regulative Speech Acts in English Contracts – Qualitative and Quantitative Methods', *HERMES* **8**, 83–110.

Blum-Kulka, Shoshana, House, Juliane and Kasper, Gabriele (eds) (1989) *Cross-cultural Pragmatics. Requests and Apologies*. Norwood, NJ: Ablex Publishing Corporation.

Brown, Penelope and Levinson, Stephen C. (1987) *Politeness. Some Universals in Language Use*. Cambridge: Cambridge University Press.

Craies, W. F. (1971) *A Treatise on Statute Law*. Ed. S. G. G. Edgar, 7th edn. London: Sweet and Maxwell.

Danet, Brenda (1985) 'Legal Discourse', in *Handbook of Discourse Analysis*, vol. 1, ch. 11. London: Academic Press.

Dyrberg, Gunhild, Faber, Dorit, Hansen, Steffen Leo and Tourney, Joan (1988) 'Etablering af juridisk tekstkorpus', *HERMES* **1**, 209–29.

Ervin-Tripp, Susan (1976) ' "Is Sybil there?" The Structure of Some American English Directives', *Language in Society* **5**(1), 25–66.

Fleck, L. (1981) *The Genesis and Development of a Scientific Fact*. Chicago: University of Chicago Press.

Fotion, N. (1971) 'Master Speech Acts', *Philosophical Quarterly* **21**, 232–43.

Gunnarsson, Britt-Louise (1984) 'Functional Comprehensibility of Legislative Texts', *Text* **4**(1/3), 71–105.

Haverkate, Henk (1984) *Speech Acts, Speakers and Hearers*. (Pragmatics & Beyond, V: 4.) Amsterdam/Philadelphia: John Benjamins Publishing Company.

Kurzon, Dennis (1986) *It is Hereby Performed ... Explorations in Legal Speech Acts*. (Pragmatics and Beyond, VII: 6.) Amsterdam/Philadelphia: John Benjamins Publishing Company.

Myers, Greg (1989) 'The Pragmatics of Politeness in Scientific Articles', *Applied Linguistics* **10**, 1–35.

Pilegaard, Morten (1990) 'Linguistic Politeness in Intercultural Business Correspondence'. Paper presented at International Pragmatics Conference, Barcelona.

Redmond, P. W. D. (1979) *General Principles of English Law*. Plymouth: Macdonald and Evans.

Searle, John R. (1969) *Speech Acts*. Cambridge: Cambridge University Press.

Searle, John R. (1976) 'The Classification of Illocutionary Acts', *Language in Society* **5**, 1–24.

Trosborg, Anna (1991) 'An Analysis of Legal Speech Acts in English Contract Law', *HERMES* **6**, 65–90.

Trosborg, Anna (1995) 'Statutes and Contracts: An Analysis of Legal Speech Acts in the English Language of the Law', *Journal of Pragmatics* **23**, 31–53.

Werther, Charlotte and Helmersen, Ole (1989) 'Konflikt eller konsensus. Del: II. Sproglige analyser af agent- og eneforhandlerkontrakter', *ARK* 49. The Copenhagen Business School.

FIVE

A scientific community and its texts: a historical discourse study

Ellen Valle

INTRODUCTION

The notion of the *scientific community* has been central, implicitly or explicitly, to our understanding of modern science. From the 'invisible college' of the seventeenth century to the citation networks and research groups of modern sociology of science, both scientists themselves and those who study them have assumed the existence of a community, under whatever name and at whatever level of organization, within which the activity we today call science is actually carried out. The scientific community is, to a considerable extent, self-defining and self-policing. It is this community that (i) decides (within constraints set by the society at large) what are the legitimate concerns of science and what kinds of questions can meaningfully and legitimately be asked; (ii) sets the criteria by which the validity of findings is to be evaluated; and (iii) defines the body of concepts, entities and propositions which are accepted – until displaced by other, newer ones – as 'scientific knowledge'. The mechanisms whereby this codification of concepts and information into 'knowledge' takes place may be explicit, in the form, for instance, of statements by scientific commissions; more often, however, it takes place implicitly, above all by means of various (inter)textual practices. The scientific community also sets admission criteria for new members, appoints gatekeepers (editors, referees) to regulate members' access to publication, and deals with cases where the rules of the community are flouted by members, such as scientific fraud. The community is, of course, by no means monolithic. On the contrary, it is divided into innumerable disciplines and networks. *Vis-à-vis* the society at large, however, the community tends to maintain a united front.

The concept of the scientific community has been widely applied in language for special purposes (LSP) and discourse studies. The case for the scientific community as a discourse community has been presented in detail by Swales (1990), who formulates explicit criteria for such communities, such as shared communication goals, specific genres and special lexis. A detailed and 'hands on' approach to the relationship between the scientific community and the texts it generates has been developed by Greg Myers. Myers (1990), for instance, examines the construction of scientific knowledge as a joint activity shared in by the writer(s) and the other members of the community; this is not a metaphor but a literal reality, describing the way in which writers, their colleagues and various gatekeepers – editors, referees and (last but far from least) those who control access to research grant money – all modify the original text until it satisfies the demands of the entire community, balancing the originality of the writer's claim against its acceptability. This process of co-construction cannot normally be approached through the text itself, since the traces have almost, by definition, been obliterated. It is accessible, laboriously, through such techniques as the comparison of various drafts, examination of the comments in the margins of manuscripts, and interviews with writers and other persons involved. In a historical setting these techniques are, in general, impossible, since all that is available is the final version of the text; the drafts have been destroyed and the persons involved are dead. In at least one case, however, the process has been painstakingly recreated (Bazerman 1988). Here the various drafts and versions of Newton's work on optics, combined with surviving lecture notes and correspondence, and with the 'opposing' texts to which Newton was responding, allow some access, almost three centuries later, to the process whereby a new kind of rhetoric was constructed.

The textual representation of the scientific community as such, on the other hand, has been discussed by a number of writers, such as Charles Bazerman, Dwight Atkinson, and the 'Uppsala group' (Britt-Louise Gunnarsson, Björn Melander and Harry Näslund). Some of these studies (in particular Bazerman 1988, 1991, 1993) have been intensive analyses of single texts, making use of traditional rhetorical and literary analytical techniques but often with a discoursal interpretation. While these studies are highly revealing of the rhetorical techniques available at a given time, we do not know to what extent these techniques were actually made use of by 'ordinary', run-of-the-mill writers in routine scientific texts. Other studies have been based on large longitudinal text corpora, showing the relationship between writer, text and community, and its development through time, on the basis of a smaller or larger number of carefully defined textual, rhetorical, discoursal and linguistic features; the features selected are often, though not always, those suitable for computer-based analysis. Corpus studies may focus on one or more individual disciplines, as in the case of the Uppsala project (economics, technology and medicine – Gunnarsson et al. 1994), or on scientific texts published in a particular journal across a long time-span (Atkinson 1992, 1993); this may be either a general scientific publication, such as the *Philosophical Transactions of the Royal Society* (Atkinson 1993), or a specialized journal, such as the *Edinburgh Medical Journal* (Atkinson 1992). All of these approaches have their own advantages and drawbacks.

The study reported in the rest of this chapter represents a compromise between these various factors: it deals with texts in a relatively diffuse disciplinary cluster, the life sciences, published in a general scientific journal over a period of 160 years. During the period represented by these texts, the life sciences gradually evolved from their relative lack of a separate identity in the seventeenth and early eighteenth centuries, into a cluster of autonomous disciplines in the nineteenth and especially the twentieth centuries. We can expect this gradual emergence of a separate disciplinary identity to be reflected in the texts.

THE LIFE SCIENCES IN THE EIGHTEENTH AND NINETEENTH CENTURY IN ENGLAND

Background, corpus and methods

The findings presented here are based on a larger study (Valle 1993), in which I examine certain rhetorical, pragmatic and textual characteristics of a corpus of texts in the life sciences (including biology, medicine and natural history) published in the *Philosophical Transactions of the Royal Society of London* during 1711–1870. The Royal Society, founded in 1660, is one of the oldest European scientific societies still flourishing today, and its *Philosophical Transactions* is the oldest scientific journal with an unbroken history of publication.[1] The society and its journal are thus an important source of information for the history of the scientific community and scientific writing.

In this chapter I look at changes in the way the discourse community is represented in the texts during this 160-year period. The question is approached through three rhetorical features: (i) the subject matter of the texts and their general rhetorical structure; (ii) the implicit or explicit 'recipient' or addressee of the text; and (iii) the presence or absence of an explicit text 'motivation', i.e. statement of purpose. These particular features were chosen (out of the large range of possible ones) because they are relatively easy to identify in a particular text by 'manual' analysis, thus making it possible to observe trends in a large but non-computerized corpus. At the same time, they seem to reveal something genuinely significant about the way the texts serve the needs of the community at a particular time. Before clarifying the precise content of these features, I first briefly describe the corpus.

The study corpus is based on the *Philosophical Transactions of the Royal Society of London*, 1711–1870. Sampling took place at 50-year intervals in 10-year blocks, i.e. 1711–20, 1761–70, 1811–20 and 1861–70. Within this period, the corpus consists of all those texts whose primary subject is within the domain of the life sciences: in modern terms, biology, botany, zoology, human or animal anatomy and physiology, and theoretical and applied medicine. For purposes of more detailed analysis of pragmatic text features, this corpus was further reduced to a more manageable size by a second sampling, taking either every second or every third consecutive text within each block. The numbers of texts in each block and their mean length are shown in the Appendix (p. 95).

The indices of the community studied, as listed above, were subject matter, implicit or explicit addressee, and presence or absence of an overt statement of the purpose of the text. The first of these is what might be called a *paradigmatic* index. It reflects the research interests of the community at a given period; more precisely, it indicates what kinds of natural phenomenon are considered legitimate subjects of scientific inquiry and what kinds of things can legitimately be said about them.[2] To some extent this can be seen as overlapping with the *cognitive layer* of Gunnarsson and her colleagues (see the chapter by Britt-Louise Gunnarsson in this volume). The extent to which these topics are either random and varied or tend to concentrate on a few main topics reflect the degree of integration of the community. The implied or expressed addressee of the text might be called a *pragmatic* index, reflecting the way that the community and his own position in it was perceived by the individual writer; this again overlaps with Gunnarsson's *social layer*. Finally, the presence or absence of an explicit statement of the purpose of the text and/or the research can be seen as a *rhetorical* index. In the final analysis, however, these divisions and labels are more or less arbitrary: all texts (or all writers) have rhetorical and discoursal goals, and use various textual – ultimately at one level or another linguistic – means to achieve them.

The changing paradigmatic focus of the community

There are some interesting tendencies perceptible in the topics with which workers in the life sciences were preoccupied at various periods. Here I first look briefly at the texts in each block separately, and then summarize the main trends.

In Block I (1711–20), there seem to be few individual topics which are of systematic interest. Twenty of the 51 texts (39.2 per cent) consist of random reports on isolated and usually 'freakish' phenomena and events. Sample titles include: *Several Observations in Natural History, made at North Brierley in Yorkshire* (1713: xviii); *An Account of a praeternatural Tumour on the Loins of an Infant, attended with a Cloven Spine* (1720: iii).[3] These cases have come more or less randomly and accidentally to the attention of the writer: it is not uncommon for a text to begin in some such form as 'A butcher did this morning bring me in the Head of a Calf (which he had taken out of a Cows Belly ...' (1712: iv), or 'About two Years ago the Manservant of a Neighbouring Clergyman complained to me of excessive Pains in and about his Stomach' (1716: iv). Rhetorically, these texts consist in most cases entirely of the reporting of observed facts. The text type is descriptive, narrative or expository; at the very end there may be a few sentences of general discussion. The observations are only rarely placed in a broader cognitive, not to mention theoretical, frame of reference. An analysis of the information structure of the texts would probably show an almost total absence of assumed or shared information; definite articles, where they occur, are almost always textually determined, i.e. they are used for purposes of textual cohesion alone rather than to indicate assumed common knowledge.

But there are also texts of another kind, which fit explicitly or implicitly into a particular framework of knowledge. I tentatively call this text category *systematic* texts. These are equally random in subject matter. What they have in common is that their purpose is to fill a gap in an existing system of knowledge. Two of these texts report experiments carried out to answer a particular question: *Experiments and Observations of the Effects of several sorts of Poisons upon Animals, etc.* (1712: ii) and *An Account of some Experiments relating to the Specifick Gravity of Human Blood* (1719: iii). The first of these is predominantly expository in rhetorical strategy and consists of a report of results; the second is rhetorically for all practical purposes a 'modern' scientific text, beginning with a statement of shared knowledge ('It is well known from the Observations of Mr. Leeuwenhoek and others that … '), then describing the writer's own experiments and findings, discussing their significance and how they fit in with what is known, anticipating disagreement from others and ending with a 'opening', suggesting questions for further research.

In other words, some texts are already written within an existing framework of knowledge, to which their purpose is to contribute. This aim is sometimes revealed in the title: *An Account of the external Maxillar, and other salivary Glands: Also of the Insertions of all the Lymphatics (as well above as below the Subclavians) into the Veins; which Glands and Insertions have not hitherto been mentioned, or not truly described by any Authors* (1720: ii).

The total number of such systematic texts, even at this early date, is 26, or 50.1 per cent. In terms of number of pages, the proportion is even higher, since these texts tend to be above average in length.

It would thus seem that the random, fact-collecting nature of early scientific activity, at least in the life sciences, has perhaps been somewhat exaggerated. Already at this period, systematic investigation within an accepted body of knowledge and conceptual apparatus – what we can loosely call a scientific paradigm[4] – represents the largest single type of text. This trend will be further strengthened in subsequent blocks.

The majority of texts in Block II (1761–70) still consist of case reports on fairly random topics, indicating that biological scientists in the Royal Society did not have any particular research agenda. Randomness of subject matter, however, no longer necessarily entails surprisingness or unusualness. Only six of the 35 texts dealing with human biology now include such expressions as 'uncommon' or 'monstrous' in the title (*An extraordinary Case of three Pins swallowed by a Girl and discharged at her Shoulder* (1769: iii)). Three texts, on the other hand, are rhetorically quite complex and include fairly extensive theoretical discussion. The other 26 evidently represent the norm for their period: they describe an individual case and draw some, usually limited, inductive generalizations from it. This normally involves a switch from exposition (description or narration) to argumentation, signalled linguistically again by tense-switching.

There is also a relatively new kind of text, of which there are seven examples. This is the foregroundedly general, theoretical text, often argumentative and even polemical in rhetorical strategy, in which the writer deliberately sets out to answer a particular question, for instance in physiology, and in which reference to particular cases is subordinated to this scientific and rhetorical purpose. Examples are *Essay on the Use of the Ganglions of the Nerves* (1764: xxxiii) or *A Description of the Lymphatics of the Urethra and Neck of the Bladder* (1769: liv). Here the gap which the writer sets out to fill is not so much in knowledge of the facts as such as in their interpretation. The facts are taken as given and known; what is at issue is their interpretation. These texts demonstrate the increasing cumulativeness of biological and medical science in this period, as shown by the numerous references to earlier texts.

Block III (1811–20) is quite different from the earlier ones, and its structure in terms of both topic and rhetoric is considerably simpler. There is now only one text which can be classified as falling into the 'curiosities' category, *An Account of a Family having Hands and Feet with supernumerary Fingers and Toes* (1814: vii), and this too includes some general discussion. In other words, all the texts (with one partial exception) fall into the systematic, 'gap-filling' category. There are seven texts on a new subject, which will be of increasing interest throughout the nineteenth century – that of animal fossils and their correct classification. There is only one text on practical medicine, but 19 on human physiology and 31 on animal physiology. There are two dominant topics of interest: the various properties of the blood and the way in which the nervous system is linked with and affects other physiological processes. Two examples must suffice: *Some additional experiments and observations on the relation which subsists between the nervous and sanguiferous systems* (1815: xxiv), and *Some account of the fossil remains of an Animal more nearly allied to Fishes than any of the other Classes of Animals* (1814: xxviii).

In terms of their rhetorical structure, these texts are not necessarily particularly complex; many if not most of them offer data either with no discussion or only a brief and non-argumentative discussion. Above all, many of these texts lack the most important signal of cumulativeness in scientific texts, i.e. overt intertextuality in the form of references to earlier writing on the same subject.

In some respects, Block IV (1861–70) is the simplest of all. In terms of subject matter, the 57 texts fall fairly neatly into three categories: (i) those dealing with animal anatomy and/or physiology (27 items or 47.4 per cent); (ii) those dealing with human or non-specified anatomy and/or physiology (20 items or 35.1 per cent); and (iii) those dealing with fossil structure and taxonomy (10 items or 17.5 per cent). All the texts are systematic or gap-filling, at least in the narrow, Baconian, non-theoretical sense. There are no random case reports and no strictly medical texts. The latter have presumably been taken over by this time by specialized medical journals.

PRAGMATIC AND RHETORICAL PRACTICES: ADDRESSEE AND MOTIVATION

This part of the analysis attempts to combine two approaches to the description of modern scientific texts.[5] The first of these is Swales's (1990) genre-based approach, known as the 'CARS' model ('creating a research space'). Swales has identified certain more or less standardized rhetorical 'moves' in the introduction sections of scientific articles. These moves accomplish such things as establishing the centrality of the writer's topic in terms of the goals of the community, identifying a specific 'niche' and, finally, occupying it. The CARS model has been found to be more or less standard for article introductions across a wide diversity of disciplines at least in modern Anglo-American scientific writing; it describes the structure of a standardized genre in terms of its rhetorical features. Myers (1989), on the other hand, has looked at scientific articles from the discourse–pragmatic point of view, as turns in an ongoing 'conversation'; he interprets these and other strategies in terms of the politeness and face-saving needs present in scientific communication, as in any other situation where individuals are speaking to and/or about each other. Myers sees the need to 'motivate' the text as a mitigation of the imposition both on the community at large, demanding journal space, and on the individual reader, demanding his/her time. The justification of the text (more specifically the research article) is the *claim* which it presents. For Swales, on the other hand, it is the empty 'niche' which offers the writer the necessary research space. Since science aims at exhaustive coverage, any gap in the community's collective knowledge automatically justifies an attempt to fill it.

For both Swales and Myers, the 'addressee' of the text is the scientific community as a collective body. According to Myers, it is towards this collective community, rather than towards any particular individual, that 'humility' is implicitly expressed on the part of the writer. The latter's paramount goal is community acceptance of his/her claim.[6]

In the corpus texts, there is often an 'ostensible addressee' who is overtly addressed. This is particularly common in the first two blocks of the corpus, due to the standard epistolary form of the texts; findings and observations are personally reported to the Royal Society via letters addressed to the President, the Secretary or some other Fellow. This ostensible addressee, however, often is not the one with whom the writer is actually concerned. The distinction is similar to that of the 'implied reader' of a literary text, who differs from both the narratee (in this case the ostensible addressee) and the actual reader of the text. In a few cases the letters are 'exophoric', i.e. are ostensibly addressed to an outsider (an interesting example is the series of letters in Block II, addressed to Linnaeus at Uppsala).[7]

The term 'motivation' is used actively rather than passively: how the writer 'motivates' the text, i.e. justifies his claim on journal space and on the reader's time and attention. It is thus functionally related to the strategies identified by Swales, but can take quite different forms. If the statement of text motivation is defined strictly, i.e. as the presence at or near the beginning of the text of a sentence (representing the move to occupy the empty niche) such as 'The purpose of this paper is to do X' or 'In this paper I do X', or alternatively, of a sentence such as 'the purpose of the research described here was to determine X', then at least in the earlier blocks not many texts present this feature. If, however, we look at *implicit* motivation of the text, in terms of the goals of the community, the outcome is different.

1711–20

Block I has only a few examples of explicit text motivation. One text, a non-systematic case report, begins:

> Sir, The strangeness of the following Relation will easily excuse me for troubling you so soon with another Letter.
>
> (1712: iv)

Another, at least semi-systematic letter from Leeuwenhoek,[8] begins:

> Gentlemen, In compliance with your desires, I here send you a Copy of the Observations which I communicated to the great Pensionary Monsieur Heinsius, concerning the Membranes ...
>
> (1714: ii)

One, addressed to a Bishop, begins:

> My Lord, The Curiosity which I here send your Lordship is so far beyond anything that I have had the honor to communicate to your Lordship, or that I have ever met with, that I presume your Lordship will think it fit to communicate to the Royal Society.
>
> (1715: v)

These examples show that the motivation of the texts (all in overt epistolary form) is conceived of in personal terms. The mitigation of the claim on the reader's attention is expressed in personal terms, either to some individual or to the Royal Society as a group of individuals, rather than to an anonymous scientific community.

There is only one text out of the 25 which seems explicitly to be stating the writer's intention of filling a gap in knowledge, and even that is somewhat ambiguous, being at least equally concerned with practical prevention:

> Among the Accounts which the Royal Society hath had of the Mischiefs ensuing the swallowing of divers sorts of Stones, I do not remember any Case wherein the lesser Stones of Fruits ... have produced any dangerous Symptoms, especially in the Stomach alone. ... But the following Case will shew the Danger even of these lesser Stones. And I have acquainted the Society with it, on purpose to prevent Dangers, if it should be thought it to publish it in the Transactions, for a warning to others.
>
> (1716: iv)

A long, flowery and interesting opening is the following one:

> It is generally acknowledg'd, that the exact Observation of internal Diseases, and the faithful Accounts of External Tumours, and extraordinary Cases in Chirurgery, have contributed very much to the Advancement of Medicine. Hippocrates and Galen, and other ancient Fathers of Medicine, have set us fair Copies of this; and the Moderns, happily following their Footsteps, have illustrated this Matter by many

> curious Observations and Reflections. The Royal Societies and Colleges of Virtuosi, that are now over all Europe, have taken much pains in this Affair, and have given us many Instances and Examples of Extraordinary Cases in Medicine, which are of great use to all the Practisers of Physick and Chirurgery. According to these laudable Examples I shall, for the Satisfaction of the Curious and Ingenious, give a true and faithful Account of an extraordinary Excrescence cut off from the cheek of a Man, which weighed Nineteen Pounds, and the Patient entirely recover'd in a few Weeks time.
>
> (1717: vi)

This is a very clear expression of the writer's sense both of community and of the cumulativeness of scientific knowledge. The text itself is a purely expository one, with no argumentation or theoretical frame of reference either implicit or explicit. In fact, at the end of the text (rhetorically a key position, second only to the beginning), the writer explicitly repudiates any intention of interpreting his findings:

> I have given a true and plain Account of this extraordinary Case from certain Information; I have contented myself to relate only Matters of Fact, without making any Observations or Reflections on it; for I leave it to the Philosophers and Virtuosi to make their own Reasonings and Refinements as seems best to themselves.
>
> (1717: vi)

This is an early statement of the anti-theoretical, anti-speculative stance already noted, which recurs repeatedly throughout the corpus. The scientific community is seen as engaged on a collective enterprise, the purpose of which is to collect information but not to interpret it; that is deferred to an indefinite future when all the data will (presumably) be available.

The one text in this block which does explicitly refer to the 'design' (i.e. purpose) of the text is a highly contumacious letter. It refers to other writers, but lacks any mitigation of face-threatening acts, and shows considerable resentment against those who have disagreed with him:

> Before I engage in the principal Design of this letter; which will be to prove, that the Venereal Disease, when it came to be confirmed, was … I shall endeavour to refute the Opinion of those Persons, who believe it to have its rise there [in Naples], if any such shall remain, who have read my former letter.
>
> (1720: ii)

Summing up, in the early eighteenth century only one text out of 25 refers explicitly to the purpose of the text; eight have some sort of implicit statement of purpose. The humility *vis-à-vis* the community, and the justification of claiming the readers' time, however, is seen in personal rather than anonymous terms. There is not yet any notion of a 'niche' to be occupied; that implies ecological crowding. Here, on the contrary, the scientific space is so empty that one can wander around at will, observing here and there and reporting what one sees.

1761–70

In Block II a new type of motivation appears, exemplified by a text from 1764 (addressed to another Fellow of the Royal Society (FRS)). Despite its length, I quote it almost in its entirety:

> [Dear Sir,] The honor I received, by being elected a fellow of the Royal Society, excites me through gratitude to offer that learned body whatever occurs to me new, or worthy attention in the animal world; and the respect I bear you, dear sir, for your learning and goodness ... and the encouragement you have constantly shewn towards promoting natural history, emboldens me to transmit to you this paper containing the descriptions of a very singular species of Wasp and Locust ... which I met with in the Island of Jamaica. I made what search I could find in the natural historians, but cannot find that they have ever been taken notice of, therefore are as yet unknown to the learned, or non-descripts. I therefore offer them by your means to the inspection of the Royal Society, to be inserted in the Transactions, if deemed worthy their attention.
>
> (1764: vi)

This text is interesting on several accounts. First of all, it turns out to serve the function of the covering letter to the editor of the journal; it is followed by the straightforward description of the specimens, with no textual modulation at all. There have been a few cases before this in which the accompanying personal letter has been to some extent distinct from other parts of the text, especially when the letter has been sent by some foreign correspondent personally to some English FRS, who has then communicated it to the Royal Society. This letter, however, is meant directly for publication. Secondly, it expresses humility before the scientific community, i.e. the Royal Society, but here again this is formulated primarily on a personal basis, as in the preceding block. Above all, this seems to be the first time that we find an explicit statement of a gap in knowledge. The writer has searched the literature, but finds no mention of the species in question. The concept of the 'non-descript' is one that will recur in this and the next block. Nature is no longer an unmapped wilderness; the paths have been drawn, and must be followed. In short, the existence of at least a general knowledge frame within which new observations must be located in order to be meaningful, is now explicitly recognized. In hind-sight, this can be seen as a forward-looking text motivation: the writer is occupying his niche. From the point of view of contemporary natural history, on the other hand, it might be viewed in terms of the 'great chain of being', which along with the paradigm of natural theology (the attempt to explain all nature as the benevolent design of God) dominated much of English natural history in the eighteenth century. The implicit or explicit addressee, towards whom humility is expressed, is in any case the Royal Society, ambiguously or simultaneously as a concrete group of individuals and as representing the scientific community.

Another example of a motivation which today would be represented by a genre of its own is the following, presented at least partly on social rather than on scientific grounds:

> The respect, with which the late Dr Bradley, Astronomer Royal, and Savilian professor of astronomy in this University, was treated by the learned of all countries, and the esteem, in which he was held by your Lordship, and the Society over which you preside, must naturally make the world desirous to be acquainted with the circumstances of that illness, which occasioned his death, especially as his disorder was in itself rather uncommon.
>
> Under these circumstances I flatter myself, that I shall do what will be very agreeable to your lordship, and the Society, if I lay before you, and that learned body, a detail of the several particulars attending the case of so very worthy, and excellent a member, collected as well from the best inquiries I could make, as from the observations made by myself, who attended him in his last hours, and assisted at the opening of the body.
>
> (1762: cii)

This should presumably be seen as fulfilling the function of an obituary, combined with a normal scientific case report, followed by some brief general discussion concerning Bradley's illness.

I give the motivations of two other texts from this block of the corpus to show the enormous range present at this time. The first is from a rural clergyman from Cornwall (and an FRS):

> Perhaps you may not have forgot that, in the year 1765, I sent a specimen of native tin, to be deposited in the Royal Society's Museum; and though the account of it, published in the Transactions of the year following, was not such as I wish, yet I am steadily intent on paying my duty to the Society, and obviating (as far as lies in my power) all doubts relating to natural knowledge.
>
> (1769: vii)

This motivation reveals to how great an extent the Royal Society was still a club for like-minded gentleman amateurs. Yet this text is contemporary with the following one, from 1764. This is an 'advanced' and polemical text, motivated implicitly, though not explicitly, by a gap in the theoretical literature concerning the interpretation of phenomena. It is again necessary to quote at length:

> The ganglions of the intercostal nerves, first discovered by Fallopius, are oblong and very hard bodies; the uses of which have not been satisfactorily ascertained by anyone. Few anatomists have indeed entered deep into the subject, except the learned J. M. Lancisi, who imagined them muscles sui generis. ... And in order to give an idea of the structure of all other Ganglions, he particularly describes and delineates that of the first cervical Ganglion.
>
> This theory has the misfortune to be erroneous in its foundation. For Haller and other succeeding anatomists have not been able to discover ...
>
> (1764: xxxiii)

The same writer has another text later in the block, motivated on similar grounds but again with something new. He first refers to his own previous publications on the subject of the ganglia, and the debate which arose from them, and continues:

> I was not, till lately, capable of proving this by experiments, with which I beg leave once more to trouble the Royal Society, as they much support the new uses assigned to ganglions, in the Essay published in the LIVth volume of Philosophical Transactions, and open a new field of anatomical research and philosophical speculation, not without some prospect of advancing the practice of medicine in nervous diseases, with the knowledge of the nervous system.
>
> (1770: iv)

This seems to be the first time in the corpus that the motivation of the text includes both filling a theoretical gap and offering an opening for future research, again both in the acquisition of data and in their theoretical interpretation ('philosophical speculation'). The text also offers an extensive survey of the European literature on the issue at debate, both for and against the writer's own view. Ostensibly, he is addressing the Royal Society; implicitly, he is speaking to a geographically broader but scientifically more specialized community. But texts like this are rare and a majority of the texts in this block still contain no motivation at all.

Summing up, we can say that in the second half of the eighteenth century, the notion of an established domain of knowledge, and of the need to define and 'reserve' a niche to be occupied by a text, begins to occur, especially in natural history, where it is associated with description and species classification. The statements of motivation and the accompanying expressions of humility, however, are still largely addressed on a more or less personal basis to the Royal Society as a known group of individuals, rather than to the scientific community at large.

1811–20

In Block III we find an interesting form of text motivation. Where earlier texts were either reports of random observations or designed to fill a gap in systematic knowledge, we now frequently find the two combined. The writer is interested in a particular question and happens to have come across a specimen or exemplar helping him to answer it. What this presumably means is that entirely random observations are no longer acceptable to the scientific community as represented by the Royal Society. An example of such a combined motivation is the following:

> This is a consequence of an unusual, and hitherto, I believe, entirely unnoticed structure. ... My attention was called to this structure, by having received from my friend Mr. Herbert Ryder, the assay master to the mint at Madras, the bones of the skull of a cobra de capello.
>
> (1818: xxiv)

There seems to be only one text with an entirely accidental motivation, entitled *An Account of a Family having Hands and Feet with supernumerary Fingers and Toes* (1814: vii). Here too, however, at least some systematic motivation is revealed, though only halfway through the seven-page text. Interestingly, this is immediately followed by both an optimistic view of the future of science and by a restatement of the Baconian ideal of science:

> Numerous examples of the hereditary propagation of peculiarities have been recorded: all family resemblances, indeed, however trifling they

> may appear to a common observer, are interesting to the physiologist, and equally curious. ... In every department of animal nature, accumulation of facts must always be desirable, that more reasonable inductions may be established concerning the laws which direct this interesting part of creation ... nor is it altogether vain to expect, that more profound views, and more applicable facts await the researches of men, who have as yet only begun to explore this branch of natural history, by subjecting it to physical rules.
>
> (1984: vii)

It is probably not accidental that the only text in this block of the corpus which does not, at the beginning at least, imply a gap in systematic knowledge, is also the one to contain such a view of the nature of scientific inquiry.

Four of the 25 texts now contain an overt statement of the purpose of either the research or the text. I give two examples:

> The following experiments were begun with a view to ascertain the manner in which certain poisons act in destroying life.
>
> (1815: vi)

> I here attempt a description of it, and also submit a few remarks on the genus.
>
> (1819: vii)

Other kinds of motivations are also explicitly stated. One such is an explicit claim of priority (the only one, as far as I know, in the entire corpus):

> Having performed the high observation for the Stone in a manner less severe and less dangerous for the patient than that now in use ... I am desirous of having it put upon record in the Philosophical Transactions, that at the same time it is made public, my claim to the first adoption of this mode may be established, which could not be so well done, were I to postpone the present communication.
>
> (1820: xvi)

Summing up, the main difference between this and the earlier two blocks is that totally unmotivated texts have now disappeared, and the motivation is less personal. The random, accidental aspect, however, has not totally disappeared. The writer is aware of the gap to be filled, but is able to do so because of information or evidence which has come more or less accidentally to his knowledge.

The most important change, however, is probably that the implicit addresses of the texts – the group towards whom the imposition is felt to occur and towards whom humility is expressed – is increasingly no longer the Royal Society, but the scientific comn nity at large.

1861–70

In Block IV the situation has again changed. Many of the texts n begin in a way which anticipates modern generic practice, with creation of a niche by means of references to the literature and pointing out of a gap. This gap may be: (i) a lack of knowledge the facts; (ii) contradictory explanations of the data; or (iii) what writer considers to be an incorrect explanation.

The motivation is now often stated at least semi-explicitly. C text, for example, after a brief survey of the literature, continues: is not my intention to enter upon any description of the many str tures ... I confine myself strictly to the structure and elaboration the teeth themselves' (1861: xx). Another embeds the text purp in a relative clause: 'The investigations of which I now commu cate the results were made ...' (1862: xxxvi). One text makes purpose very explicit; this is pragmatically understandable in t the writer is bringing new evidence to refute criticism of an earl paper of his own:

> In a communication ... that was read before the Royal Society, Januar 1863, I brought forward experimental evidence which had conducted to view the immunity. ... The opposition that this view received on th evening of its announcement induced me to extend my experiments, ... I have deemed it desirable to present this further communication, i which the whole subject is concisely reviewed with the aid of the new matter that has been brought to light.
>
> (1863: v

Some texts now have an highly 'stripped' and simple statement purpose: 'The chief purpose of the present paper is to describe convolutions ...' (1863: xv), or 'I propose in the following notes relate some observations respecting the formation and growth the bones of the human face' (1868: iv). On the other hand, there still some texts which do not present any explicit motivation at aside from the fact that the information has recently come to writer's attention or that he has recently made some interesti observations. While sometimes this seems a mere oversight, oc sionally these texts strike a rather anachronistic note in this block the corpus. They tend also to be characterized by a lack of refere to other writers, and in that sense do not seem to be embedded the community. These texts, however, are no longer the random observations of the earlier periods; on the contrary, they are often highly systematic. These texts I have elsewhere called *authoritative texts* (Valle 1993). The impression of *ex cathedra* authoritativeness is due in part to the absence of humility before the community, suggested by the omission both of text motivation and of any overt intertextuality.

In conclusion, almost all texts in Block IV contain an implicit statement of motivation, and many of them an explicit one. The implicit addressee and target of humility is now, with a few exceptions, not the Society, as in earlier blocks, but the scientific community at large.

GENERAL DISCUSSION AND CONCLUSIONS

What we find in the corpus with respect to paradigmatic text practice, i.e. subject matter and text rhetoric, is a gradual narrowing down of the acceptable range of topics and an increasing systematicity, i.e. an embedding of the texts in a known and codified frame of knowledge. This can be seen, on the one hand, as an increasing 'control' by the scientific community over what is acceptable as a scientific text, or, on the other hand, as the increasing engagement of the writers in the European scientific community, although to some extent in a dialectic and polemical relationship due to basic differences in biological paradigm. With regard to addressee and text motivation, we find, on the one hand, an outward trend from the face-to-face, 'personal' Royal Society, to the Society perceived as a scientific organization, to the even more abstract disciplinary community. On the other hand, this is accompanied by an increasing frequency of explicit statement of motivation. The two are presumably related: a text addressed to the Royal Society, or to a particular individual within it, did not need to be justified, since the Society existed for just that purpose, and the Fellows knew each other personally.[9] The imposition was thus perhaps less onerous.

The main general conclusion which I find suggested by the data is that, while certain trends are apparent over the long term, they are less linear than might have been expected. In particular with regard to the paradigmatic embedding of the texts and their topical systematicity, there are texts in the very first block which are highly systematic, locating both their research problem and their conclusions within an existing frame of knowledge. However, in the very last block there are texts which start and end with no epistemological framing at all. This is presumably to be understood in terms of the powerful Baconian ethos which seems to have dominated English biology, more perhaps than other disciplines, throughout the period covered by the corpus. In pragmatic terms, the general trend is more consistent, from a discourse community identified with the Royal Society as a concrete group of individuals, to the Society more abstractly, to a yet more abstract discipline-based research community.[10] These two trends – the increasingly strong pragmatic anchoring in the extended community and the persistent lack of paradigmatic embedding, at least as a acceptable rhetorical alternative – seem to some extent to be contradictory; the relationship between rhetoric and pragmatics in the texts needs to be further clarified.[11]

The history of the Royal Society has been documented in considerable detail, above all for the early period, from 1660 to the end of the seventeenth century (most recently by Hunter 1989; Hall 1991). Almost all work dealing with this period emphasizes the empirical and experimental orientation of the Royal Society, and its 'Baconian' project, i.e. the focus on the large-scale and cooperative collection of data without any preconceived theoretical frame of reference. Theory was perceived as dangerous, since it might bias the perception of reality. It should follow, if at all, only after all the relevant data are known. The Baconian programme was also strongly associated with natural history, based primarily on collection, description and classification, and only secondarily on analysis or explanation. While later periods have received considerably less attention, and the existing histories tend to focus on institutional issues rather than ones of scientific paradigm, it seems evident on extratextual grounds as well that a somewhat ambivalent attitude towards theoretical 'speculation' never quite disappeared from the English life sciences. The term 'empirical' is widely used in this context. In the corpus studied here, an antitheoretical stance is found both in texts reporting 'direct' observations of natural phenomena and in those which report experiments; in the latter case the writer reports methods and results sometimes in very great detail, but does not attempt to interpret these results or draw theoretical conclusions from them.

The Royal Society enjoyed almost from the beginning a very high reputation among European scientists. By the eighteenth century it was viewed unofficially as the representative body of English science, and in the nineteenth century it became officially so. Nevertheless, it is important to keep in mind that it was founded as a face-to-face discourse community, in a quite literal sense. Its purpose was to advance 'natural knowledge' through weekly meetings, at which experiments could be demonstrated and papers presented for debate. The early papers are thus quite naturally addressed either to a personal recipient or to the Royal Society as a concrete body. Likewise, the lack of differentiation of topics at this time is consistent with the Baconian project which was the explicit goal of the Royal Society. Gradually, with the growing differentiation of disciplines, it is the specific disciplinary community rather than the scientifically heterogeneous Royal Society as such which is addressed. The range of topics, however, is still dictated by the interests of the English biological sciences. These are in general, throughout the corpus, empirical rather than theoretical, in keeping with the strong empirical emphasis on English science. In the nineteenth century, as we have seen, there is a growing emphasis on the description and classification of fossil and living species. This interest arose in part from cross-section with another discipline, geology, and led ultimately to the Darwinian revolution. But that, as they say, is another story.

APPENDIX

Original and restricted corpus. The analysis of subject matter is based on the original corpus, the analysis of motivation and addressee on the restricted one.

Block		**Items**	**Pages**	**Mean**
I	1711–20	51	355	7.0
II	1761–70	89	592	6.7
III	1811–20	76	731	9.6
IV	1861–70	57	2018	35.4

	Texts	**Pages**	**Mean**
I	25	216	8.6
II	29	162	5.6
III	25	226	9.0
IV	19	559	29.4

The means for number of pages are somewhat misleading since in all blocks the range is very great. In the last block in particular, there are monographs of well over 100 pages as well as brief reports of 10–15 pages. The general trend over the period as a whole, however, is fairly well reflected by the means. Consistency between the blocks is in terms of number of texts rather than number of pages. Since part of the study deals with text macrostructure, the unit of analysis has to be the text as a whole – the 'bulk' size in terms of number of pages is at this stage less relevant.

NOTES

I owe thanks, for valuable comments on earlier drafts of this chapter, to several members of my own community: in particular, Dwight Atkinson, Britt-Louise Gunnarsson, Risto Hiltunen and Jacqueline Välimäki.

1. With the exception of brief interruptions during the early years of the Royal Society.
2. The fact that a topic is not represented in the corpus does not necessarily mean that it was an 'illicit' topic at that time; this absence may be due simply to chance or to a greater interest within the community in other topics. Since, however, each block covers a 10-year period in a journal of general rather than specialized science, the total absence of some topic is at least indicative of a strong lack of interest in that topic. In any case, fairly safe conclusions can be drawn as to the degree of diffuseness versus focus of the community interests at a given time.
3. Text references are to year of publication rather than volume, since the former is more informative for the reader not familiar with the *Philosophical Transactions*. Spelling and capitalization are as in the original; I have not considered it necessary to add the usual 'sic' after odd or inconsistent spellings.
4. The ostensible lack of a paradigm is, of course, itself paradigmatic: it reflects a conception of science which rejects hypotheses, theory-formation and speculation, in its most extreme form any generalization at all, even inductively from the data. This radical view has been called 'vulgar Baconianism' (Hunter 1989: 222). It defines the role of science as confined to the cooperative collection of empirical data.
5. There is, of course, a risk involved in any attempt to apply to historical data models developed to describe rhetorical strategies used by modern writers; the needs and goals of earlier writers may have been, and in fact probably were, different. If such strategies are not observed in earlier data, two quite different interpretations are possible: on the one hand, it can be assumed that at any given time the text genres used will

have served the needs of the contemporary community, in which case we can in fact 'read off' information about the community from the texts; or, on the other hand, that earlier writers did not have available the strategies which would have served their needs, that these strategies evolved gradually into their present form, and that this evolutionary process can be traced in the texts. The problems of false teleology are the same as those inherent in any attempt to trace a process of change backwards from the present; Mayr (1982: 47–51) has written on the problem from the point of view of the biologist.

6. For Myers it is the wider, exoteric community which is the direct addressee and the smaller, esoteric community which 'overhears' the text. It might more plausibly be the other way around; texts are presumably addressed most directly to the relatively small group who are actively involved in the particular research problem or theoretical controversy and who have the necessary knowledge to interpret the nuances of the text.
7. An interesting analysis of the implied reader of modern biological texts has been presented by Gragson and Selzer (1993).
8. The letters from Leeuwenhoek addressed to the Royal Society were all translated from the Dutch, presumably by the Secretary of the RS. This should make us approach their linguistic interpretation with caution. At the level of text rhetoric and pragmatics, however, the use of translated texts is probably less dangerous than at the microlinguistic level.
9. Until the twentieth century, only Fellows were allowed to present or publish papers. A non-Fellow might submit a paper through a Fellow.
10. Nothing has been said here about citation practices. They were, however, increasingly directed (a) outside the Society, (b) outside English science, to the broader European community. (Throughout the corpus there are only a few sporadic references to American scientists.)
11. Previous work, to which these findings can most directly be compared, is that of Atkinson (1992, 1993). The first of these deals with a community narrower than the present one, represented by the *Edinburgh Medical Journal*; the second with a broader community, represented by all texts in the *Philosophical Transactions*, regardless of discipline. Atkinson's findings are too complex to be briefly summarized here, but the general trends are in the main similar to mine. There are, however, some differences, probably due to real differences between the discourse of the life sciences and the physical sciences in England, especially in the nineteenth century.

REFERENCES

Atkinson, Dwight (1992) 'The Evolution of Medical Research Writing from 1735 to 1985: The Case of the *Edinburgh Medical Journal*', *Applied Linguistics* **11**, 337–74.

Atkinson, Dwight (1993) 'A Historical Discourse Analysis of Scientific Research Writing from 1675 to 1975: The Case of the *Philosophical Transactions of the Royal Society of London*'. PhD Dissertation, University of Southern California.

Bazerman, Charles (1988) 'Between Books and Articles: Newton Faces Controversy', in *Shaping Written Knowledge: The Genre and Activity of the Experimental Article in Science*. Madison, WI: University of Wisconsin Press, pp. 80–127.

Bazerman, Charles (1991) 'How Natural Philosophers Can Cooperate: The Literary Technology of Coordinated Investigation in Joseph Priestley's *History and Present State of Electricity* (1767)', in Bazerman and Paradis (eds), pp. 13–44.

Bazerman, Charles (1993) 'Intertextual Self-Fashioning: Gould and Lewontin's Representations of the Literature', in Selzer, J. (ed.), pp. 20–41.

Bazerman, Charles and Paradis, James (eds) (1991) *Textual Dynamics of the Professions: Historical and Contemporary Studies of Writing in Professional Communities*. Madison, WI: University of Wisconsin Press.

Gragson, Gay and Selzer, Jack (1993) 'The Reader in the Text of "The Spandrels of San Marco"', in Selzer, J. (ed.), pp. 18–202.

Gunnarsson, Britt-Louise, Melander, Björn and Näslund, Harry (1994) 'LSP in a Historical Perspective', in Brekke, M., Andersen, Ø., Dahl, T. and Myking, J. (eds) *Applications and Implications of Current LSP Research*. Vol. II. Fagforlaget, Bergen, pp. 878–918.

Hall, Marie Boas (1991) *Promoting Experimental Learning: Experiment and the Royal Society*. Cambridge: Cambridge University Press.

Hunter, Michael (1989) *Establishing the New Science: The Experience of the Early Royal Society*. Woodridge: The Boydell Press.

Mayr, Ernst (1982) *The Growth of Biological Thought: Diversity, Evolution and Inheritance*. Cambridge, Mass.: Belknap Press.

Myers, Greg (1989) 'The Pragmatics of Politeness in Scientific Articles', *Applied Linguistics* **10**, 1–35.

Myers, Greg (1990) *Writing Biology: Texts in the Social Construction of Scientific Knowledge*. Madison, WI: University of Wisconsin Press.

Selzer, Jack (ed.) (1993) *Understanding Scientific Prose*. Madison, WI: University of Wisconsin Press.

Swales, John (1990) *Genre Analysis: English in Academic and Research Settings*. Cambridge: Cambridge University Press.

Valle, Ellen (1993) 'Talkative Community: Rhetorical, Textual and Pragmatic Features in Royal Society Texts, 1711–1870'. Unpublished Licentiate Thesis, University of Turku.

SIX

On the sociohistorical construction of scientific discourse

Britt-Louise Gunnarsson

Scientific language and discourse emerge in a cooperative and competitive struggle among scientists to create the knowledge base of their field, to establish themselves in relation to other scientists and to other professional groups, and to gain influence and control over political and socioeconomic means. In every strand of human communication, language and discourse play a role in the formation of a social and societal reality and identity. This is also true both of the formation of the different professional and vocational cultures within working and public life and of the formation of different academic cultures.

Historically, language has played a central role in the creation of different professions and academic disciplines, and it continues to play an important role in the development and maintenance of professional and institutional cultures and identities. Societal, social and cognitive factors all play important roles in the construction of professional cultures. Professionals try to create a space for their field within society. They try to establish themselves in contact and competition with others within their group as well as with other groups. Their knowledge base and its linguistic forms are created in a societal and social framework.

THE CONSTRUCTION OF PROFESSIONAL DISCOURSE

To understand fully the historical development of professional language and professional communication, we must study it in its rich and varied totality. We must study the dynamic processes behind the construction of professional language. The question is, therefore: What constitutes these processes? That is, what dimensions or layers are involved in the construction of professional texts and discourse?

In this dynamic process. I distinguish three layers: one relating to *cognitive* types of activity, one to *societal* and one to *social*. Professional culture is built up via these dimensions, which means that all three must be considered in order to get a full picture. Written texts as well as spoken discourse are constructed as cognitive, societal and social activities within the different professions and branches of working life. The term professional language and discourse is used here in a wide sense, which includes scientific discourse.

If we begin by considering the *cognitive layer*, we find that each profession has a certain way of viewing reality, a certain way of highlighting different aspects of the world around it. Socialization into a profession means learning how to discern the relevant facts, how to view the relations between different factors. We are taught how to construct and use a grid or a lens to view reality in a professionally relevant way. Language, texts and spoken discourse help us in this construction process. We use language in the construction of professional knowledge. At the same time, language is developed and consolidated through this construction process.

With regard to the professional group as a whole, we find that its professional language has developed as a means of expressing this professional view of reality. Economic terminology, economic text patterns, and economic text and discourse content have developed as a means of dealing with reality in a way that is appropriate for economic purposes. Built into the cognitive structure, there are also attitudes and norms. The economic perspective thus involves attitudes and norms regarding what is economically relevant and right.

The knowledge base of a field has a network of relations with other fields. The cognitive structure of a professional language thus reveals its dependence on and relationship towards other knowledge domains, and this knowledge-based network can vary over time. In metaphors, in terminology, in modes of reasoning, in diagrams, the contribution of adjacent fields to the construction of professional knowledge is revealed. For example, many fields owe a debt to statistics, psychology, mathematics, sociology, physics, economics, politics and religion, and this debt can be seen in the language that is used.

The cognitive layer is, of course, related to psychological processes within the individuals concerned, but it is also related to how these actors as a group perceive and understand reality in professional communication.

Secondly, as regards the *societal layer*, each professional group also stands in a particular relationship to the society in which it operates; it performs certain functions and is given a certain place within that society. The members of a profession play a role in relation to other actors in society, and the professional group acts in relation to other groups. They play – or do not play – a role on the political scene, within the business world, in the education system, in relation to the media, etc. And this cluster of societal functions is essential for language. It is through language that professional groups exert their societal function. If they are going to play a role on the political scene, they have to construct their communicative behaviour in a way that is adequate for that purpose. Their relationship to written texts and spoken discourse and to different genres is also important. Professionals adapt to established genres, but are also involved in forming new ones.

The societal layer is, of course, related to economic and political factors. It is related to power and status patterns in society.

Thirdly, regarding the *societal layer*, every professional group, like other social groups, is also formed by the establishment of an internal role structure, group identity, group attitudes and group norms. The need for a professional identity, for a professional we-feeling, for separation from the out-group, has of course played an important role in the construction of professional group language and constantly motivates people to adapt and be socialized into professional group behaviour. Socialization into a group also means establishing distance from people outside the group.

The three layers are strongly related to the emergence and continuous re-creation of professional language, and they are a part of the construction of professional language and discourse. Historically, language is constructed in relation to all these layers. The cognitive establishment of the field takes place at the same time as the professions fight for their place in society and for the strengthening of their group in relation to other groups.

SCIENTIFICALITY IN ECONOMICS ARTICLES, 1730–1980

As an example of this interplay between the cognitive, societal and social layers, I will discuss some of the results of a study on scientificality in economics articles from 1730 to 1980. All the texts covered by this study belong to the same genre, that of the scientific article in economics, and they are all written by Swedes for a Swedish expert audience. They are, however, constructed within quite different context frames. Swedish society has, quite obviously, undergone radical change since the eighteenth century.

Changes have also taken place within the economic scientific community: (i) Economic knowledge has grown immensely over the 250-year period studied; (ii) Science in general and the philosophy of science have undergone changes. Statistics and empirical methods have developed. Positivism has become a widely accepted paradigm; (iii) Economics as a profession has gradually become increasingly established and recognized. In 1980, economists are highly valued professionals, and economic scientists and economic research are considered highly important to society; (iv) The economic scientific community has grown immensely between 1730 and 1980. The number of practising economists, economic scientists and students of economics has increased, as has the number of economics journals and conferences.

Important changes have thus taken place relating to economic science, science in general, the economic profession and the economic scientific community. The claim that I will make in this chapter, however, is that language and discourse are essential elements in the construction of science, in profession-building and in the shaping of the scientific community, and that academic genres play important roles in this process of construction: of scientific knowledge, of the role of scientists in society, and in the growth and strengthening of the social network among scientists. The correspondence between, on the one hand, the societal role played by scientists and their discourse community and, on the other, the scientificality of the texts they produce, that is the cognitive layer, will be discussed with reference to Swedish economics and articles written in Swedish in that field.

THREE PERIODS OF SWEDISH HISTORY

This study concerns texts from three periods of Swedish history, namely the eighteenth century (period 1), the early twentieth century (period 2), and the latter part of the twentieth century (period 3). In my analysis of the sociohistorical construction of scientific discourse I have focused on the relationship between the scientificality of the texts and society and the scientific community, and I will therefore start off by characterizing these three periods.

Period 1: 1730–99

The first period which is called the *Era of Liberty* in Swedish history, is contemporary with the *Age of Enlightenment*.[1] Economically and politically, Sweden, which in the seventeenth century was a European power, lost its dominion in Poland and the Baltic countries in the early eighteenth century. The economy of the country was ruined after a long period of war. The beginning of the eighteenth century saw major changes taking place in Sweden. There was a new political situation: the monarchy lost its political power, and parliamentary parties became the effective rulers.

The economic growth of the country was the main political aim, and the mercantilist doctrine was declared as the great saviour of Sweden. There was considerable interest in science and technology, but no discipline was as highly esteemed as the economic sciences. Economic ideas provided the background to the programme to make Sweden important again (Lindroth 1978; Frängsmyr 1989).

Academically, the Era of Liberty saw all the useful sciences flourish, and scientists like Carl von Linné and Anders Celsius brought fame to Uppsala University. This university, the oldest in Scandinavia, was founded in 1477, and around 1740 it was attracting around 1,000 students (Lindroth 1978: 31). There was also a high level of scientific activity outside the universities, and in 1739 the Swedish Academy of Sciences was founded, which from the very beginning became the gathering place for the learned in Sweden at the time (Lindroth 1967). The Academy made the very important decision that its Transactions should be presented in the Swedish language. Previously Latin had been the language of the academic world, but by about 1740 Swedish was gaining ground as an academic language (Lindberg 1984).

The eighteenth century saw a remarkable increase in written publications of all kinds. According to bibliographies of publications in Sweden, 450 publications appeared in the sixteenth century, 4,600 in the seventeenth century, ten times as many, and 150,000 in the eighteenth century, that is 30 times as many as the century before (Svensson 1985: 61). It was also during the eighteenth century that the first journals appeared in Sweden.[2]

If we turn to economics, we find a similar phenomenon. The first economic periodicals appear in the 1730s (Gunnarsson and Skolander 1991: 60–4). During the eighteenth century 34 economics journals appeared: 13 on political economy, three dealing with trade and 18 with the economy and agriculture (ibid.: 38; cf. Lönnroth 1991: 17).

In 1741 the government decided that Uppsala University should have a professorial chair of economic sciences.[3] The Swedish chair was attached to the Faculty of Law, but covered natural sciences, agriculture and trade, as well as law and the economy. The role of Swedish as an academic language became especially strong within the new economic discipline. In the letter from the Government to the Chancellor concerning the 1741 professorship in economic sciences, the use of Swedish was enjoined not only for lecturing but also for disputations (Annerstedt 1912: 286). The first holder of the Uppsala chair was Anders Berch. Besides Berch's professorship, three more chairs were created in economic sciences during that era in Sweden and Finland, which at that time was a part of Sweden (E. Gunnarsson 1988).

This interest in economics did not last, however. The mercantilist doctrine was found to be no saviour of the Swedish economy. New ideas – liberal and physiocratic ones – became fashionable towards the end of the century. From a peak in 1760, the number of economics journals rapidly declined (Lindroth 1978; see also Johannisson 1980).

Figure 6.1 shows how the rise in the number of periodicals or journals came to a sudden halt.[4] On the vertical axis there is one line for each journal appearing. The length of the line along the

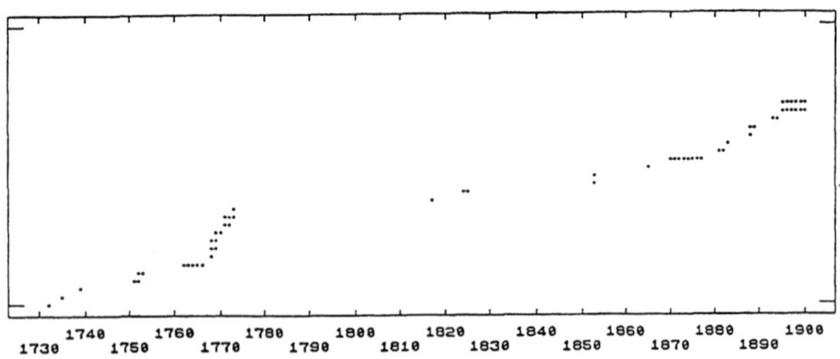

Figure 6.1 Swedish periodicals in political economy, 1700–1900

horizontal axis shows how long the journal appeared. As we can see, there is a period of more than 100 years when hardly any Swedish economics journals were published.[5] On an academic level, too, interest in economic sciences ceased. Of the four chairs created in the eighteenth century, three became chairs of botany and one – that held by Berch – was devoted more and more exclusively to law (E. Gunnarsson 1988: 122).

Sweden was rather backward economically until the late nineteenth century. Banks were established in the eighteenth century, but many of them were closed down in the early nineteenth century, and not until around 1860 was there a more stable banking system. Swedish engineers rapidly became highly skilled, but not until the second half of the nineteenth century did industry start to specialize and use large-scale production. Thinking within political economy also lagged behind.

> Because of language and differences in political and economic conditions, the most advanced international thinking in political economy could not be fully understood in Sweden at the time it was written. Published economic texts were often translations or home-cooked versions of texts in other languages in order to make them fit less advanced economic and social conditions.
>
> (Lönnroth 1991: 40)

If we now turn back to the eighteenth century, the economists of that time were the reformers of society. They most certainly played a role in society, and a very highly valued one at that. Quite a few people considered themselves experts and wrote about economic matters. Only to a very small extent, however, was their aim to debate theoretical or methodological matters among themselves. They were much more concerned with the reform of society. Interest in the economy and economic sciences did not lead to the formation of a scientific community, which perhaps explains why the academic discipline of political economy and the journals disappeared so suddenly when public interest evaporated.

Period 2: 1895–1905

The second period is the period around 1900, more precisely 1895–1905. The economy had developed, and Sweden was an industrialized country, with a diversified network of industries involved in large-scale production. It had an elaborate banking system, and laws regulating joint-stock companies.

On the academic scene, there were now a few professorial chairs devoted to the study of economics. One of the professors, David Davidson, started *Ekonomisk Tidskrift* (a Swedish journal of economics) in 1899. A few other economics journals were also launched around the turn of the century. Economists were organized in *Nationalekonomiska föreningen* (Swedish Association of Economics), established in 1877, and the professionalization of economists began.[6]

There were still relatively few students at the universities, and, as just mentioned, only a few chairs of economics. Some of the holders of these chairs did, however, become famous, like Knut Wiksell (full professor in 1901) and Gustaf Cassel (full professor in 1904). Eli Heckscher was not yet a full professor but became one in 1909. The Golden Age of Swedish economics had dawned. There is no doubt that the economists active in that period were in the process of establishing a scientific community of their own; the birth of the famous Stockholm school is often dated to the end of the 1920s, marked by Gunnar Myrdal's dissertation *Prisbildningsproblemet och föränderligheten* from 1927 and Erik Lindahl's book *Penningpolitikens mål* from 1929.[7]

What characterizes the economists of around 1900, however, is their twin role, as scientists writing for colleagues and as social reformers and educators writing for lay people in popular science journals and in newspapers. All the economists mentioned were frequent popularizers of their economic theories, possibly because they needed a larger audience than the rather small community of economists of the time. This dual aspect of their role when compared to the later period is striking.

Period 3: 1975–85

The last period is around 1980, more precisely 1975–85. Swedish society is now a modern society in every respect. Sweden has six universities, two schools of economics, several regional colleges, and an agricultural university at which economics is also taught. The number of chairs has increased from two in 1900 to 25 around 1980, and the number of students studying economics at different levels has increased dramatically. The number of economics journals has increased, even though it must be noted that some, for example the former *Ekonomisk Tidskrift*, is now written in English instead of Swedish and bears the name *Scandinavian Journal of*

Economics. Economists. like all other scientists today, have become more specialized. They keep to their professional type of publication: they write in newspapers, popular science journals and booklets much less than the economists of the second period.

SCIENTIFICALITY IN TEXTS

I will now discuss the economics articles produced during the three periods referred to (eighteenth century, around 1900 and around 1980), focusing in particular on their ways of expressing scientificality.

Categories and criteria

A comparison of texts and their content over as long a period as three centuries will necessitate abstractions and generalizations. What is considered to be science and scientificality varies over time, as does what is considered to be economics. If we look at scientific periodicals from the eighteenth century and compare these with periodicals from the 1980s, there are, of course, major differences, for example in terms of authors, readers, size, layout, content, types of article included and language. A comparison like the one undertaken here must therefore retain both form-bound and abstract criteria. To be able to study changes in scientificality in economics articles, the analysis must proceed from general categories and criteria that are applicable to texts from three centuries.

First, the concept of *scientificality* has been given many definitions, partly due to its varying character. The definitions vary with time, type of science, discipline and school. Quite obviously, scientific ideals have varied from time to time, and, not infrequently, the concepts of scientificality of a certain period can be related to a general scientific spirit. So-called paradigm shifts can be of a more general as well as of a more discipline-specific nature (Kuhn 1970). What is regarded as science also varies between the two main types of science, the natural sciences and the social sciences (cf. Bazerman 1988). It can also vary from school to school.

The term 'scientificality', as it is used here, refers to the way in which content is structured and expressed, and is based on three criteria: classification, theory and experiment/observation (see p. 110 below). These criteria are considered to be constitutive of science in a general perspective. The aim is not to discuss the deeper development of science, but to look at it from the vantage point of the structure of its content.

Secondly, focusing specifically on *economics* means that we must also take into account the substantial changes that have arisen in perspective over the three hundred years that are considered here. The Swedish political economists of the eighteenth century[8] were very much concerned with population growth and mobility, and with the need for wealth. Agricultural questions were a part of their discipline, as were different types of industry. The first professor of economic science in Sweden established various collections as part of his teaching at the university, e.g. models of ploughs and samples of cloth (Liedman 1986). The range of topics dealt with in economics is less wide nowadays, largely as a result of increased specialization in both society in general and the academic world in particular. The same trend towards greater specialization also holds true of the last hundred years. Economic history, for example, was established as a separate subject in Sweden in 1929 (Henriksson 1991: 154–5). To ensure a certain stability of content, the texts discussed here all belong to a corpus consisting of economics articles dealing with 'banking and the monetary system' (see p. 109 below).

Thirdly, *scientific periodicals* and *journals* also vary over time. The first scientific periodicals appeared, according to Kronick (1976: 77–8), towards the end of the seventeenth century, and the first in Sweden appeared in the early eighteenth century. Of course, these early examples did not take the form of the modern scientific journal as we know it today, with its editorial board, its fixed set of subsections and its layout. They resembled their predecessors: the erudite letter, the book-in-parts, the *Messrelationen* (periodical publication associated with commercial fairs), calendars, almanacs and the like (Kronick 1976: 59–67).

It is not always easy to distinguish the early periodicals from newspapers of the same period. Kirchner gives the following definition of the early periodical:

> The periodical of the seventeenth and eighteenth century is a publication founded with a view toward indefinite duration, which appeared in more or less regular issues, and for a generally circumscribed group of readers with similar interests, which was produced by means of mechanical duplication, and whose individual issues are recognizable as the (periodically) reappearing parts of a unified whole, and which with

> its own particular speciality or field of knowledge strives for a diversity of contents.
>
> (Kirchner 1942: 32–3, English translation quoted from Kronick 1976: 18)

The term 'journal' was popularly applied from very early on to the publication of learned news and information (Kronick 1976: 19). 'Journal' is also used by Kronick as a category name for some of the early types of periodical. In his discussion of the genre of the journal, he differentiates between (i) Periodicals (Journals), (ii) Transactions (Proceedings), (iii) Abstract (Extract) Journal, (iv) Review (Bibliographic) Journal, (v) Serial Collection, (vi) Dissertation (Academic Writings) and (vii) Almanacs and Ephemerides (ibid.: 29). The articles from the eighteenth century discussed in this chapter are taken from categories (i) Journals and (ii) Transactions.

The journal has not remained unchanged over the last hundred years. The first scientific journal in economics in the more modern sense appeared at the end of the nineteenth century. Even in such a short perspective, the concept of what is appropriate in a journal article shows considerable variation. Tribe's study of 'The Economic Journal and British Economics, 1891–1940', for example, draws attention to changes as to where different content categories are placed within the journal (Tribe 1991).

The criteria of a journal in this study follow the classification used in bibliographies and library catalogues for economics periodicals and journals. The term 'scientific periodical and journal' is used with reference to journals whose authors are full members of their discourse community, as is the intended audience.[9]

Material

The economics articles chosen for closer analysis belong to a corpus of 360 articles which are being studied from text-linguistic and semantic perspectives within a research programme at Uppsala University.[10] The articles within this larger corpus are from three fields: economics, medicine and technology. Within each field, articles dealing with two subjects have been chosen. The corpus comprises articles from six periods: 1730–99, 1800–49, 1850–80, 1895–1905, 1935–45, 1975–85. Within each period, 60 articles have been studied, 30 scientific articles and 30 classed as 'popular science'.

The scientific articles dealt with in this study are taken from the subcorpus of economics articles. They all deal with the banking and credit system. Five articles from the eighteenth century have been analysed, five from the period 1895–1905, and five from the period 1975–85. The articles from the two periods of the twentieth century are taken from leading scientific journals, those around 1900 from *Ekonomisk Tidskrift* and those around 1980 from *Ekonomisk Debatt*.[11] The eighteenth century articles are collected from more varied sources: scientific periodicals, journals and the like.[12]

Method

One purpose of the Uppsala studies of texts for specific purposes is to trace the development of the scientificality of the texts. For these studies I have elaborated a model and a method of text analysis based on the concept of 'cognitive world'.[13] The aim of this method is to find a means of comparing the content of specialist texts from different fields, subjects, genres and periods. The categories used for the analysis are therefore rather abstract.

At an abstract level, the content of such texts can be said to vary with regard to a number of *cognitive worlds*: the *scientific world*, the *practical world*, the *object world*, the *private world* and the *external world*. My 'world' concept has similarities with the 'schema' concept which we find in theories within cognitive psychology. The five worlds are possible knowledge structures, which means that they form a background for idealized authors when they construct texts and for idealized readers when they try to build up a mental representation of the text they read.

Within each world, certain abstract categories are discerned that are common to different texts. On one level these categories relate to different *aspects*. Within the scientific world: *theory*, *classification* and *experiment*. Within the practical world: *work* and *interaction*. Within the object world: *phenomenon*, *part-focused* and *whole-focused*. Within the private world: *experience* and *conditions* of a personal kind. Within the external world: *conditions* and *measures* of a social, economic and political kind.

On another level these categories relate to different (time) *dimensions*: *cause*, *phenomenon*, *process* and *change*.[14] Figure 6.2 shows the five cognitive worlds and their related aspect and dimension categories.

The categories of Figure 6.2 relate to the invariant text universe. The worlds and categories, however, also appear in variant forms. For our analyses of language for special purposes (LSP) articles at

		Cause C		Phenomenon F		Process P		Change R
Scientific world (Sc)	Theory (TE)	TE rel. C	–	TE rel. F	–	TE rel. P	–	TE rel. R
	Classification (CL)	CL rel. C	–	CL rel. F	–	CL rel. P	–	CL rel. R
	Experiment (EP)	EP rel. C	–	EP rel. F	–	EP rel. P	–	EP rel. R
Practical world (Pr)	Work (WK)	WK rel. C	–	WK rel. F	–	WK rel. P	–	WK rel. R
	Interaction (IT)	IT rel. C	–	IT rel. F	–	IT rel. P	–	IT rel. R
Object world (Ob)	Phenomenon (FN)	FN rel. C	–	FN rel. F	–	FN rel. P	–	FN rel. R
	Part focused (PF)	PF rel. C	–	PF rel. F	–	PF rel. P	–	PF rel. R
	Whole focused (WF)	WF rel. C	–	WF rel. F	–	WF rel. P	–	WF rel. R
Private world (Pi)	Experience (EC)	EC rel. C	–	EC rel. F	–	EC rel. P	–	EC rel. R
	Personal situation (PS)	PS rel. C	–	PS rel. F	–	PS rel. P	–	PS rel. R
External world (Ex)	Soc. econ. conditions (CO)	CO rel. C	–	CO rel. F	–	CO rel. P	–	CO rel. R
	Soc. ekon. measures (ME)	ME rel. C	–	ME rel. F	–	ME rel. P	–	ME rel. R

Figure 6.2 Invariant text universe

Uppsala, we have described one text universe for the medical field, another for the technical field, and a third for the economic field (Gunnarsson 1989a: 20–2). The abstract categories are given a more specific description: the dimension *phenomenon* becomes *disease* in the medical universe, *technique* in the technical universe, and *economic situation* in the economic universe.

The text content of the articles from this century in our corpus has been classified proposition by proposition (content unit by content unit) with regard to world, aspect and dimension.[15] If a content unit is classified as belonging to the scientific world, it is also classified as either theory, classification or experiment/observation. If it belongs to the external world, as either measure or conditions. The same content unit has also been classified with regard to the dimension focused on.

Below are a few examples of our categorizations of the economics articles. Note that these categorizations were based on the proposition (the content unit). The examples below give longer extracts, covering several propositions categorized in the same way.

(1) World: *Scientific*; Aspect: *Theory*; Dimension: *Process*[16]
The fundamental argument for floating exchange rates is based on the law of supply and demand. The rate should, quite simply, be adjusted so as to bring the market into equilibrium. If there is a temporary rise in the rate, the supply will increase while the demand falls, and the rate will be forced down to its equilibrium level.

(2) World: *Scientific*; Aspect: *Classification*; Dimension: *Process*[17]
The same factors as give rise to balance-of-payments surpluses and deficits when exchange rates are fixed will, when rates are allowed to float, result in appreciation or depreciation of the currency.

(3) World: *Practical*; Aspect: *Work*; Dimension: *Phenomenon*[18]
For the country's exporters and importers, it is now also possible to raise 'composite' international loans, i.e. loans issued in a basket currency.

(4) World: *Object*; Aspect: *Phenomenon*; Dimension: *Phenomenon*[19]
This large quantity of older silver coins also necessitates a certain caution in the issue of the new coins.

(5) World: *Object*; Aspect: *Phenomenon*; Dimension: *Result*[20]
In recent years, however, this restrictive policy has proved a major hindrance as regards fully meeting the needs of commerce.

(6) World: *Private*; Aspect: *Experience*; Dimension: *Phenomenon*[21]
For my own part I must admit that the 5-mark piece seems to me a highly inconvenient coin, which one can hardly accommodate in a civilized purse.

(7) World: *External*; Aspect: *Measures*; Dimension: *Cause*[22]
This rule was of an entirely provisional character, because at that time nothing whatsoever was known about the quantity of coins which commerce in the country would require following the introduction of gold coin as legal tender.

(8) World: *External*; Aspect: *Conditions*; Dimension: *Phenomenon*[23]
The design of general economic policy and inflation sensitivity in the

dominant country may, for example, differ from those found in the smaller country.

Results of the cognitive analysis

Table 6.1 presents some of the results of our analysis of articles dealing with the banking and credit system, written during the eighteenth century (period 1), around 1900 (period 2) and around 1980 (period 3). The table shows the average proportion of the text material devoted to each world – Scientific world (Sc), Practical world (Pr), Object world (Ob), Private world (Pi), and External world (Ex).[24] As we can see from the table, the texts from the first period move within the scientific world to a very limited extent; only 3 per cent of this text material has been classified as belonging to the scientific world, which in this case means that the texts contain classifications. All the other four worlds are fairly well represented in the texts from the first period. In particular, we can note the high proportion devoted to the private world, 28 per cent. Compared with the texts from the later periods, we can also note the high proportion of the practical world, 14 per cent.

As regards the texts from this century, Table 6.1 shows an increase in the proportion of the 'scientific world' from 18 per cent in the texts written around 1900 to 62 per cent in those from around 1980. What decreases most is the 'external world', from 48 per cent of the texts around 1900 to only 18 per cent eighty years later.

Tables 6.2 and 6.3 show the types of scientific content found in the texts from periods 2 and 3. Table 6.2 presents results relating to the average proportions of the three aspects within the scientific world – Theory (Th), Classification (Cl) and Experiment/Observation (Ep) – and to the proportions of the two aspects within

Table 6.1 Cognitive worlds in economics articles 1700, 1900 and 1980

Period	World				
	Sc %	Pr %	Ob %	Pi %	Ex %
1700	3	14	32	28	25
1900	18	5	25	4	48
1980	62	1	19	0	18

Table 6.2 Aspects in economics articles 1900 and 1980

Period	Aspects				
	Scientific world			External world	
	Th %	Cl %	Ep %	Co %	Me %
1900	78	4	18	41	59
1980	68	19	13	31	69

Table 6.3 Dimensions in economics articles 1900 and 1980.

Period	Dimensions			
	Cau %	Phe %	Pro %	Res %
1900	4	34	34	28
1980	19	23	36	22

the external world – Conditions (Co) and Measures (Me). The numbers recorded in the table headed 'aspects' relate to the proportion of each aspect, i.e. theory, classification, experiment, *within* the specific world.

As Table 6.2 shows, 'theory' is the most prominent single aspect within the scientific world. Note, however, that 'classification' became relatively more important than 'theory' in the period between 1900 and 1980. All scientific aspects have, of course, increased in the texts, but 'classification' more than the others. Within the cognitive category 'external world', 'conditions' have decreased relatively more than 'measures'.

Table 6.3 shows the proportions of the four dimensions Cause (Cau), Phenomenon (Phe), Process (Pro), and Result (Res) in the texts from periods 2 and 3, and here we should note that the numbers in Table 6.3 refer to average proportions of the entire texts. As the table shows, the economics article of 1980 is devoted more to 'explanations of causes' than the article of 1900 (19 per cent compared with 4 per cent), and less to mere descriptions of phenomena (23 per cent compared with 34 per cent).

As these figures show, the modern article is more directly concerned with science. External matters are kept out of the texts to a large extent, and the focus is on subject-specific topics. The same trend has been found as for the medical articles in our corpus, and it is almost certainly a general trend within science (see Melander 1989, 1991). Our findings indicate that the development of Swedish economics articles during this century seems to parallel the development of British articles. The study of British journals of economics from 1891 to 1940 reported in Tribe (1991) points to a similar trend towards a gradually higher proportion of scientific content in the articles, from 1915 onwards.

Finally, I have counted the number of references in the articles from the three periods. In the five economics articles from the eighteenth century there is no reference to other economists, which of course is in accordance with the general scientific level found in these articles. However, in the articles from the second period (around 1900), too, the lack of references to other scientists' work is striking. Of the articles from 1900, only one makes any reference to the work of other researchers. In contrast to this, all five articles from 1980 have references to their authors' own work and that of others. These results can be compared with those presented by Bazerman (1988). He found not only a qualitative difference as to the use of references in *Physical Review* articles, but also a striking quantitative difference between articles from 1980 and earlier articles, published before 1930 (ibid.: 165).

SOME EXEMPLARY TEXTS

Texts from period 1

The texts of period 1 are characterized by hardly any scientificality in the sense in which I have used that word here, that is, with regard to discussion of theories, classifications and reporting of observations or experiments. What also characterizes these texts from the end of the eighteenth century, as compared with those from this century, is their much higher proportions of 'private' and 'practical world'. A further striking feature is that these articles, taking their examples from private, practical and public life, seem to be preaching a message. Their resemblance to religious texts is striking, as the following two extracts show.

(1) Yea, I dare say that a *Banque* that does nothing more than take large *Capitals* and let them lie barren is in the long run a certain means of

> bringing ruin upon a *Republique*. For just as our Limbs must wither when the circulation of blood ceases, so must the People perish in poverty when the money arteries in the body of the *Republique* are clogged or severed.
>
> (Carleson 1734)[25]

> (2) If I imagine a society of people who are satisfied with the simplest needs, like those of animals, in my mind I can ultimately abstract Credit from their way of life. When a flock of wild humans join together for no other purpose than to pursue hunting and trapping, they need no other civil laws than those that secure their lives from assault and their simple rights of ownership from robbers. Their chief or superior is no different as regards his clothing, consumption, or having a royal court, from the person who executes criminals: thus the State in effect has no needs. The right of judgment and punishment can be carried out without cost: no other martial arms are necessary than those that can be mustered at the slightest signal to defend the community with the same weapons that are in daily use for hunting animals. Their trade takes the form of exchange of commodities: no other needs can arise and no services be required than those that can be paid for with parts of animals or with some tool for killing the same. Should there be such confidence between another with a loan, then it would probably either be backed up by a sound security or the creditor would claim his right directly, by right of might or by other means allowed by their society, if the debtor should refuse to repay the loan. If such a transaction is ultimately to be called Credit, it is nevertheless of such negligible importance as hardly to deserve the name, especially since such a society can very well exist without it.
>
> (Kryger 1767)[26]

This preaching, however, is not a general feature of the writing of the time. In another study focusing on medical articles from the eighteenth century, I did not find this trait in the twelve articles analysed dealing with pox and cataract. Those scientific articles have the characteristics of modern science, that is they contain classifications, theoretical discussion and presentations of experiments. They do not adopt a religious tone. In the medical articles there were also, even in the eighteenth century, some references to other researchers' work, that is, the ongoing debate between scientists was reflected in the articles (Gunnarsson 1988).

Texts from period 2

Compared with the texts from the eighteenth century, the texts of period 2 are more dominated by the 'scientific world'. What is characteristic of these texts as compared with those from period 3, however, is the central role played by the 'external world'. The following two extracts, taken from texts published in 1900, show this focus on the external world. Below each extract is shown our categorization of the world, aspect and dimensions of the passage quoted.

(3) The silver dollar, like the gold coin, is legal tender. Virtually all minting of this coin has taken place in the period since 1878. In 1873 it was legislated that the Union, which then still had inconvertible paper currency (greenbacks), which had driven the metal currency out of circulation, was going to abandon the double currency standard and adopt the gold standard. But even before the stipulated time for the readoption of metal coinage – January 1, 1879 – this law had been overturned, and the double currency standard had been reintroduced. This was accomplished by the so-called Bland Act of February 28, 1878, which once again elevated the silver dollar to the status of the principal coin.

(Davidson 1900)[27]

Categorization: World: Ex; Aspect: Me; Dimension: Pro, Res

(4) To return to the policy of the 70s, forcefully to bring to completion the currency reform was the basic premise in the bill the government put before parliament in the autumn of 1899. To a certain extent, this bill can be regarded as a continuation of the reform of the banking legislation that had been accomplished immediately prior to this, and which essentially consisted in strengthening the institution that maintains the country's gold standard. This policy marks the definitive abandonment of the bimetal sympathies of the 80s, the recognition in principle of the ascendency of gold. Even after the cancelling of the Indian silver coins and the abolition of the Sherman Act, a German silver commission could be appointed. But after the well-known American delegation's stalemate as a result of India's unwillingness to re-open her mints to silver or rather owing to that nation's determination to convert to the gold standard, bimetallism was virtually dead politically. The German government was merely facing the consequences of the true state of affairs.

(Cassel 1900)[28]

Categorization: World: Ex: Aspect: Me; Dimension: Pro, Res, Pro, Res

Texts from period 3

The results relating to the texts from this century pointed to an increase in scientificality in texts between period 2 (around 1900) and period 3 (around 1980). The texts of period 3 are characterized by a higher proportion of 'scientific world'. In these articles, theories are presented to a much larger extent, and we also find more classifications. Causes are explained to a larger extent in 1980 than in 1900. Extracts 5 and 6 illustrate this modern type of economics article.

(5) There are, of course, a number of objections of a theoretical nature to be levelled against the theory of purchasing power parity. If a country has made technological progress in its import-competitive sector, it might very well see an appreciation of its currency, even though it might have a higher rate of inflation than its trading partners. Shifts in demand can produce such results, as can shifts in preferences regarding assets or shifting expectations. Nevertheless, purchasing power parity theory possesses a rather strong intuitive credibility, not least from the perspective of monetary theory.
(Södersten 1980)[29]

Categorization: World: Sc; Aspect: Th; Dimension: Pro, Res, Phe

(6) The influence on inflation exerted by the bottom line of the budget is normally assumed to take place via the amount of money in circulation. It is called 'inflation-driving financing via the currency presses'. But it should also be possible to imagine that the budget deficit as such could create inflation. Even if the budget is financed, for example, by the public buying premium bonds, the wealth of the general public increases, which might be seen as leading to greater demand and heightened inflation. But a comparison of the rate of inflation in Figure 1 and the two measures of budget balances in Figure 2 seems to indicate that no such connection exists.
(Lybeck 1981)[30]

Categorization: World: Sc; Aspect: Th; Dimension: Cau, Pro, Cau, Pro, Cau

DISCUSSION

The interest of the differences observed between the economics articles from the three periods lies mainly in their relationship to changes in the external context. Changes in the scientificality of economics texts are signs of the development of economics science and of science in general. It is by means of discourse practices that science is created, and changes in these practices are an essential part of the development of science.

Scientific language and discourse are also essential elements in profession-building and in the shaping of the scientific community. Changes in the discourse practice thus reflect changes in the societal role played by scientists and the scientific community in society.

In the case of Swedish economics, the results of this investigation show how the creation of a modern scientific community has proceeded in steps. The scientificality of texts, has increased and also changed character. As an explanation for this stepwise process, I have found it appropriate to distinguish three different stages: a *pre-establishment stage*, an *establishing stage* and a *specialized stage*. These stages are characterized by the varying roles played by the scientists as individuals and as a group in society:

Stage 1. The pre-establishment stage.
The scientist – or perhaps we should just say expert – acts mainly within society.

Stage 2. The establishing stage.
The scientist acts within the scientific community as well as within society.

Stage 3. The specialized stage.
The scientist acts mainly within the scientific community.

The three stages characterized by the different roles played by economists with regard to society may be assumed to be reflected in the scientificality of their respective texts, leading to different degrees of and means of expressing scientificality. Texts from stage 3 can be expected to be more scientific than texts from stage 1, and more purely scientific than texts from stage 2.

If we now turn back to the results of this study, I would argue that the three periods studied can be said to form three different stages. The texts from period 1 (the eighteenth century) lacked scientificality in the sense in which I have used that word here, that is, with regard to discussion of theories, classifications and reporting of observations or experiments. There were no references to other scientists in the eighteenth century economics articles studied. The writers acted as preachers or educators, spreading their economic message. As was mentioned in the discussion of Swedish history, interest in economy and economics saw a boom in the middle of the eighteenth century. This interest, however, did not lead to the formation of a scientific community. The chairs in political economy were dissolved and the economic academic discipline more or less disappeared. Economics journals ceased to appear. Though interest in the discipline was considerable for a short period, no scientific stable community was formed. This period can therefore be characterized as a *pre-establishment stage*.

The texts of period 2 are characterized by a high proportion devoted to the 'external world', as well as the 'scientific world'. There are very few references to other economists at this stage. Economic scientists were becoming more and more established. The scientific community, however, was still quite small, and its members were still also actors within society. They played a dual role in this period, which can be called the *establishing* stage.

The texts of period 3 on the other hand, are characterized by a high proportion of 'scientific world'. Theories are presented to a much larger extent in the articles from 1980 than in those from 1900. We also find more classifications and explanations of causes. There are also regular references to other scientists' work. In the 1980s, we have a well-established academic community with a large group of specialized scientists writing for the in-group and mainly dealing with internal scientific matters. We also find a much lower proportion of 'external world' in these modern economics articles than in the older ones. Economists are mainly actors within the academic community; their role in society outside this world is no longer of any great importance. They are specialists at this stage, which I have accordingly called the *specialized* stage.

CONCLUSION

Language and science are mutually constructed and constituted on three planes, the cognitive layer (the scientific content), the societal layer (the scientists' role in society) and the social layer (relations within the group). This construction process has been in progress since the first economists tried to establish themselves as scientists, and it is still continuing. In Sweden the process began in the seventeenth century. However, it was not until the middle of the eighteenth century that Sweden became a national writing community. Swedish was gradually accepted as a scientific language, and the construction of economic science and the economic scientific community was related over a long period to the development of Swedish as a language of economics and also to the Swedish economics article as a genre. During the three periods covered by this study, economics articles were parts of this process, and they still are. These articles serve as one tool for economic scientists in their construction of their scientific reality and identity.

NOTES

1. In Gunnarsson and Skolander (1991) I present an overview of Swedish history and of the history of the Swedish economy and economic sciences. The summary here is based on that overview.
2. *Daedalus Hyperboreus*, which appeared in 1716–17, is considered the first Swedish scientific journal. It was edited by Christopher Polhem and Emanuel Swedenborg.
3. It was the fourth chair in Europe, preceded only by three chairs in Prussia. The first chair was set up in Halle in Prussia in 1727, the second in Frankfurt an der Oder, also in 1727, and the third in Rinteln in 1730 (Liedman 1986: 27). In both Sweden and Prussia the state had power over the universities, which could explain why those countries had chairs in political economy before England and France (Sandelin 1991: 3).
4. Figure 6.1 is based on Lundstedt (1969).
5. A few scientists did write about political economy (Lönnroth 1991: 27–33). Most famous was the botanist C. A. Agardh, who also published in the field of political economy (Wadensjö 1987). Agardh chose the pamphlet and small-book form for his publications, however, as did other economists of the time.
6. The same development seems to have taken place among British economists around the turn of the century (Tribe 1991).
7. Eskil Wadensjö, personal communication.
8. I have relied on the classification of economists found in bibliographies and overviews in the field of history of science and ideas.
9. For each periodical we have determined the intended audience on the basis of prefaces, subtitles, programme presentations in first volumes, etc. (see Gunnarsson, Melander and Näslund 1987 and Gunnarsson and Skolander 1991).
10. The studies have been carried out by the Research Group on Discourse in the Professions at the Department of Scandinavian Languages at Uppsala University.
11. *Ekonomisk Debatt* is a national economics journal started in 1973. It can

be said to be the present-day scientific debate forum for economists in the Swedish language.

12. The twentieth-century corpus is described in Gunnarsson, Melander and Näslund (1987), and the eighteenth- and nineteenth-century corpus in Gunnarsson and Skolander (1991).
13. The model and method are described in English in Gunnarsson (1989b, 1990, 1992).
14. The analysis also covers the categories *text type* and *role*.
15. Also with regard to *text type* and *role*.
16. Det grundläggande argumentet för rörliga växelkurser bygger på lagen om tillgång och efterfrågan. Kursen bör helt enkelt anpassas så att marknaden kommer i jämvikt. Om kursen tillfälligtvis stiger så ökar utbudet under det att efterfrågan minskar och kursen drivs ned till sin jämviktsnivå.
17. Samma faktorer som vid fasta växelkurser ger upphov till över- och underskott i betalningsbalanser kommer vid flytande kurser att få växelkursen att apprecieras eller depricieras.
18. För landets exportörer och importörer finns det numera också möjlighet att ta upp 'sammansatta' internationella lån, dvs lån utgivna i korgvaluta.
19. Denna stora mängd af äldre silfvermynt fordrade också en viss försiktig begränsning i utgifvandet af de nya skiljemynten.
20. Denna begränsning har emellertid under senare år visat sig synnerligen hindersam för ett riktigt tillgodoseende av rörelsens behof.
21. För min egen del måste jag tillstå, att 5-markstycken förefalla mig vara ett högst obekvämt mynt, som man knappast kan få in i en civiliserad portmonnä.
22. Denna föreskrift hade en allt igenom provisorisk karakter, ty man hade på den tiden ingen som helst erfarenhet af hur mycket skiljemynt landets rörelse skulle kräfva efter införandet af guld som kurantmynt.
23. Uppläggningen av den allmänna ekonomiska politiken och inflationskänsligheten i det dominerande landet kan t.ex. avvika från den som förekommer i det mindre landet.
24. My discussion of the scientificality of the economics articles from the second and third periods is based on results presented in Melander (1989, 1991).
25. Ja, jag tör säja, at en *Banque* som intet annat giör än tager stora *Capitaler* emot och låter dem ligga ofruktbara, är et säkert medel at i längden fördärfwa en *Republique*. Ty lika som Lemmarne måste förtwina när blodens gång afstadnar så måste Folket af fattigdom förgås när penninge-ådrorne i *Republiquens* kropp tillstoppas eller afskiäras. (Carleson, C., 'Om penninge-loppets befrämjande'. In *Hushåldsråd*, 1734.)
26. Så länge jag föreställer mig människor, uti et Samhälle, som äro nögda med de enklaste behof, sådana, som djuren tarfwa; så kan jag

ändteligen, i mina tankar, söndra Crediten ifrån deras sammanlefnad. När en flock willa människor förenar sig, til ingen annan afsigt, än att lefwa af jagt och djurfång; så behöfwa de inga andra borgerliga lagar, än dem, som försäkra deras lif ifrån öfverwåld, och deras enfaldiga egande rättigheter, ifrån röfwerier. Deras Förman eller Öfwerhet, är ej skild, uti kläder, förtäring eller Hofhållning, ifrån den, som förrättar skarprättaresyslan. Således har Staten egenteligen inga behof. Domare- och straffrättigheten kan utöfwas utan kostnad: inga andra krigsrustningar äro af nöden, än at på minsta wink löpa tilsamman, och förswara sig med samma wapn, som dageligen brukas, til djurens fällande. Deras handel sker genom waru-utbyte: inga behof kunna ibland upkomma, och inga tjenster begäras, hwilka ej med några qwarlefwor af djur, eller med något werktyg til deras dödande, kunna betalas. Skulle ock förtroendet imellan några sträcka sig så långt, at den ene, wid besynnerliga tilfällen, lånte åt den andra; så sker det dock antingen emot säker pant, eller långifwaren skaffar sig genast rätt, genom näfwerätten, eller andra hos dem tillåtna medel, då lån-tagaren nekar, at återställa lånet. Om ändteligen en sådan afhandling skal kalla Credit; så är dock densamma af så ringa betydelse, at han knapt förtjenar namnet: i synnerhet som et dylikt Samhälle wäl kan bestå, honom förutan. (Kryger, J. F., 'Om Crediten'. In *Stats- och Hushåls-Journal*, 1767.)

27. Silfverdollarn är liksom guldmynten lagligt betalningsmedel. Så godt som all prägling af detta mynt har skett under tiden efter 1878. År 1873 bestämdes det genom lag att unionen, som då ännu hade oinlösligt pappersmynt (greenbacks), hvilket drifvit metallmynten ur rörelsen, skulle öfvergifva den dubbla myntfoten och öfvergå till guldmyntfot. Men redan före den för återinförande av klingande valuta bestämda tidpunkten – den 1 jan. 1879 – hade denna lag upphäfts och den dubbla myntfoten återinförts. Detta skedde genom den s.k. Blandlagen af den 28 febr. 1878, hvilken åter upphöjde sifverdollarn till hufvudmynt. (Davidson, D., 'Den senaste reformen af Förenta staternas penninge – och bankväsende'. In *Ekonomisk Tidskrift*. 1990.)
28. Att återgå till politiken från 70-talet, at med kraft bringa myntreformen till afslutning var grundtanken i det lagförslag som regeringen på hösten 1899 framlade för riksdagen. I viss mån kan detta förslag betraktas som en fortsättning på den reform af banklagstiftningen, som nyss förut genomförts, och som väsentligen gick ut på att stärka den institution, som uppehåller landets guldmyntfot. Denna politik betecknar det definitiva uppgifandet af de bimetallistiska sympatierna från 80-talet, det principiella erkännandet af guldets seger. Ännu efter inställandet af de indiska silfverpräglingarne och Shermanlagens upphäfvande kunde en tysk silfverkommission tillsättas. Men sedan den bekanta amerikanska delegationens ansträngningar strandat på Indiens ovilja att åter öppna sina myntverkstäder för silfret eller fastmer på detta lands bestämda afsikt att övergå till guldmyntfot, var

bimetallismen såsom praktisk politik död. Tyska regeringen drog endast konsekvenserna af sakernas verkliga läge. (Cassel, G., 'Till afslutningen af den tyska myntreformen'. In *Ekonomisk Tidskrift*. 1900.)

29. Det finns i och för sig flera invändningar av teoretiska slag som kan riktas mot köpkraftsparitetsteorien. Om ett land har tekniska framsteg i sin importkonkurrerande sektor kan det mycket väl få en appreciering av sin växelkurs även om det skulle ha en högre inflationstakt än sin handelspartners. Efterfrågeförändringar kan ge liknande resultat, liksom förändrade preferenser beträffande tillgångar eller förändrade förväntningar. Köpkraftsparitetsteorien har dock en tämligen stark, intuitiv trovärdighet, inte minst ur ett penningsteoretiskt perspektiv. (Södersten, B., 'Växelkurser och växelkurspolitik'. In *Ekonomisk Debatt*. 1980.)
30. Det inflytande som budgetsaldot utövar på inflationen brukar i allmänhet antas ske via penningmängden. Man talar om 'inflationsdrivande finansiering via sedelpressarna'. Men man skulle även kunna tänka sig att budgetunderskottet i sig skulle kunna skapa inflation. Även om budgetunderskottet fnansieras t ex genom att allmänheten köper premieobligationer, stiger förmögenheten hos allmänheten vilket skulle kunna tänkas leda till ökad efterfrågan och snabbare inflation. Men vid en jämförelse mellan inflationstakten i figur 1 och de två måtten på budgetsaldo i figur 2 verkar inte något sådant samband finnas. (Lybeck, J. A. 'Den svenska inflationen sedd genom Solow's glasögon'. In *Ekonomisk Debatt*. 1981.)

REFERENCES

Annerstedt, C. (1912) *Uppsala universitets historia, Bihang III. Handlingar 1695–1749*, Uppsala.

Bazerman, Charles (1988) *Shaping Written Knowledge. The Genre and Activity of the Experimental Article in Science*, Madison, WI: University of Wisconsin Press.

Frängsmyr, Tore (1973) 'Den gudomliga ekonomin. Religion och hushållning i 1700-talets Sverige', in *Lychnos, Lärdomshistoriska samfundets årsbok 1971–1972*, Stockholm, pp. 217–44.

—— (1989) *Gubben som gräver. Människor och miljöer i vetenskapens värld*. Stockholm: Författarförlaget Fischer & Rye.

Gunnarsson, Britt-Louise (1988) 'Medicinsk facktext i 1700-talets Sverige', in *Ingemar Olsson 25 augusti 1988*, MINS 28, Inst. för nordiska språk, Stockholm, pp. 125–39.

—— (1989a) *Facktexter under 1900-talet 2. Metoder för textanalys på makro- och mikronivå*. FUMS Report 145, Uppsala University.

—— (1989b) 'LSP Texts in a Diachronic Perspective', in C. Laurén and M.

Nordman (eds), *Special Language: From Humans Thinking to Thinking Machines,* Clevedon, PA: Multilingual Matters, pp. 243–52.

—— (1990) 'The LSP Text and its Social Context. A model for Text Analysis', in M. A. K. Halliday, J. Gibbons, and H. Nicholas (eds), *Learning, Keeping and Using Language, Vol. II,* Amsterdam, PA: John Benjamins Publishing Company, pp. 395–414.

—— (1992) 'Linguistic Change within Cognitive Worlds', in G. Kellermann and M. D. Morrissey (eds), *Diachrony within Synchrony: Language History and Cognition,* Frankfurt am Main: Verlag Peter Lang, pp. 205–28.

Gunnarsson, B.-L. and Skolander, B. (1991) *Fackspråkens framväxt: terminologi och ordförråd i facktexter från tre sekler 1. Projektpresentation och materialbeskrivning.* FUMS Report 154, Uppsala University.

Gunnarsson, B.-L., Melander, B. and Näslund, H. (1987) *Facktexter under 1900-talet 1. Projektpresentation och materialbeskrivning.* FUMS Report 135, Uppsala University.

Gunnarsson, Elving (1988) *Från Hansa till Handelshögskola. Svensk ekonomundervisning fram till 1909,* Acta Universitatis Upsaliensis, Studia Oeconomiae Negotiorum 29. Uppsala.

Henriksson, Rolf G. H. (1991) 'Eli F. Heckscher: The Economic Historian as Economist', in B. Sandelin (ed.), *The History of Swedish Economic Thought,* London and New York: Routledge, pp. 141–67.

Johannisson, Karin (1980) 'Naturvetenskap på reträtt. En diskussion om naturvetenskapens status under svenskt 1700-tal', in *Lychnos. Lärdomshistoriska samfundets årsbok 1979–1980,* Stockholm, pp. 109–54.

Kirchner, Joachim (1942) *Das deutsche Zeitschriftenwesen, seine Geschichte und seine Probleme 1. Von den Anfangen des Zeitschriftenwesens bis zum Ausbruch der Französischen Revolution,* Leipzig: Harrasowitz.

Kronick, David A. (1976) *A History of Scientific and Technical Periodicals. The Origins and Development of the Scientific and Technical Press 1665–1790,* 2nd edn. Metuchen, NJ: The Scarecrow Press.

Kuhn, Thomas S. (1970) *The Structure of Scientific Revolutions,* 2nd edn, enlarged, Chicago: University of Chicago Press.

Liedman, Sven-Eric (1986) *Den synliga handen. Anders Berch och ekonomiämnena vid 1700-talets svenska universitet.* Stockholm: Arbetarkultur.

Lindberg, Bo (1984) *De lärdes modersmål. Latin, humanism och vetenskap i 1700-talets Sverige,* Gothenburg studies in the history of science and ideas 5, Göteborg.

Lindroth, Sten (1967) *Kungl. Svenska Vetenskapsakademiens Historia 1739–1818. Band I: 1–2. Tiden intill Wargentins död (1783),* Uppsala.

—— (1978) *Svensk lärdomshistoria. Frihetstiden,* Stockholm.

Lönnroth, Johan (1991) 'Before Economics', in B. Sandelin (ed.), *The History of Swedish Economic Thought,* London and New York: Routledge, pp. 11–43.

Lundstedt, Bernhard (1969) *Sveriges periodiska litteratur 1645–1899. Bibliografi, Del I-IN,* Stockholm.

Melander, Björn (1989) *Facktexter under 1900-talet 3. Resultat från kognitiv analys*. FUMS Report 148. Uppsala University.

—— (1991) *Innehållsmönster i svenska facktexter*, Skrifter utgivna av institutionen för nordiska språk vid Uppsala universitet 28, Uppsala University.

Sandelin, Bo (1991) 'Introduction', in B. Sandelin (ed.), *The History of Swedish Economic Thought*, London and New York: Routledge, pp. 1–10.

Spilich, G. J., Vesonder, G. T., Chiesi, H. L. and Voss, J. F. (1979) 'Text Processing of Domain-Related Information for Individuals with High and Low Domain Knowledge', *Journal of Verbal Learning and Verbal Behavior* **18**, 275–90.

Svensson, Lars (1985) 'Om 1700-talets bokproduktion', in U. Teleman (ed.), *Det offentliga språkbruket och dess villkor i Sverige under 1700-talet*, Nordlund 7, Institutionen för nordiska språk, Lund University.

Thorndyke, P. W. (1977) 'Cognitive Structures in Comprehension and Memory of Narrative Discourse', *Cognitive Psychology* **9**, 77–110.

Tribe, Keith (1991) The Economic Journal and British Economics, 1891–1940, Unpublished dissertation, Keele University.

Wadensjö, Eskil (1987) 'Ekonomporträttet: Carl Adolph Agardh', *Ekonomisk Debatt* **2**, 139–46.

SEVEN

Parameters of institutional discourse

Jan Anward

This chapter has as its point of departure the following problem: every utterance entails a context.[1] Sounds or gestures or lines emerge as utterances only as figures against a contextual ground. However, structural resources for utterance construction are very rarely designed relative to particular contexts, but are provided by design features internal to linguistic systems. Nevertheless, utterances constructed from such structural resources are typically well-designed in particular contexts, often in fine detail. How is this possible? How does structure make contact with function?

In my view, the best answer to this question is an answer along Darwinian lines: language systems are both products of independent laws and selected by various arenas of use (Hurford 1987: 15–35). Humans, unlike all other species, have the capacity to acquire systems of syntactically structured symbols, but the potential lexical and structural resources of such systems are crucially adapted to expressive spaces made available by significant arenas of use.

1. DIVISIONS OF SAYING

Starting with Anward (1983), a study of how classroom interaction might influence students' language development, I have been exploring a line of inquiry where expressive spaces, the 'environments' to which language systems adapt, are shaped by the 'divisions of saying' operating within significant social activities. Consider, for example, the following sequence from a lesson in fifth grade:

(1) **Classroom interaction, fifth grade**[2]

T1:	Är det nån som vet vilken planet som åker runt närmast solen Arne	Is there anyone who knows which planet goes around closest to the sun Arne
A1:	Saturnus	Saturn
T2:	Nä	No
	Benny	Benny
B1:	Markillus eller nåt sånt heter den	Marcilly or something like that is it called
T3:	Merkurius ja	Mercury yes

What is said in this sequence can also be said as (2), by a single speaker.

(2) Den planet som åker runt närmast solen heter Merkurius	The planet that goes around closest to the sun is called Mercury

That what is said is (1) and not (2) reflects the division of saying in this variety of teaching, where things are normally said through the classical three-part sequence of teacher question, student response and teacher evaluation. A similar pattern prevails in writing as well, where textbook exercise and textbook solution to exercise substitute for teacher question and teacher evaluation, respectively:

(3) **Grammatical drill**

Exemplen nedan består vart och ett av flera meningar. Gör om varje meningsserie till en enda mening genom att byta ut det kursiverade ledet mot *ett* relativpronomen. Ibland måste du då också göra andra ändringar av texten. Skriv på ett löst blad.

a) Hon gillade bara violinisten. Hon bad *honom* spela en känslosam melodi.

The examples below each consist of several sentences. Make a single sentence out of each sentence series by substituting *one* relative pronoun for the italicized expression. Sometimes you must change other things in the text. Write on a separate sheet.

a) She only liked the violin player. She asked *him* to play a sentimental tune.

(Bratt et al. 1974: 157)

(4) **Solution to grammatical drill in (3)**

a) ... *vilken/som* hon bad spela en känslosam melodi.

a) ... *who/that* she asked to play a sentimental tune.

(Bratt et al. 1974: 167)

This division of saying has definite consequences for student contributions to teaching. Of the students' turns in the cited lesson, 54 per cent consist of, at most, one syntactic phrase, and 87 per cent consist of, at most, one simplex clause (Anward 1983: 120). Simplifying drastically, we can say that the student role in this variety of teaching selects language systems, versions of linguistic competence, which do not include subordinate clauses. This, in turn, creates a curious tension between the competence projected by language drills such as (3) and the arena in which students are meant to acquire this competence. Put bluntly, we could say that in the context of language drills students are often taught language resources that cannot be used in that very context.

In this chapter, I develop the environmental side of this line of inquiry. I isolate three functionally distinct strata of talk in social activities – activity talk, topic talk, and text talk – and describe which divisions of saying are operating in these strata in three types of social activity, which all give rise to institutional discourse (Agar 1985): teaching, interrogation/interview and therapy. In this way, I arrive at a 'parameterized' notion of institutional discourse, where the patterns of division of linguistic labour in activity talk, topic talk and text talk can be used to classify concrete discourses into subtypes of institutional discourse. I argue that these patterns of division of linguistic labour express the points of the social activities involved, and can thus establish a link between social activity types, expressive spaces available to participants in particular activities, and language resources selected by these expressive spaces.

2. THE FUNCTIONAL STRATIFICATION OF TALK

To take something as an utterance means placing it in a context. This context normally involves two situations: a situation in which the utterance occurs, C, and another situation, a described situation, D, which is linked to C through the meaning of the utterance. In C, the utterance is furthermore embedded in a speech event: it is being uttered by a Speaker to an Addressee about a Topic in a Language within a social Activity.[3]

Following a respectable tradition in functional linguistics (Bühler 1934; Jakobson 1960; Hymes 1974; Silverstein 1985; and others), we can derive a functional stratification of talk from the relation of an utterance to the components of its context. To begin with, we can make a distinction between *indexical* function and *topic* function of talk. In its indexical function, talk serves to record the dynamics of the speech event, by indexing continuity and change in the identity of its components, their properties and their relations to each other. Identity of Speaker and Activity, property of Speaker, relation between Speaker and Addressee, and relation between Addressee and Topic are just a few examples of indexical information signalled by talk (for a comprehensive overview, see Saville-Troike 1985). A crucial property of indexical information is that it cannot be denied, except by a metacomment (Levinson 1979; Anward 1986). For example, if someone asks you (5a) in Swedish, you cannot use a simple *nej* (no), as in (5b), to deny that the social relation indexed by the second person singular pronoun *du* (thou) holds between you and that person, but have to use a metacomment such as (5c). In other words, (5b), as an answer to (5a), can never mean the same as (5c).

(5)	a.	Har du en tändsticka?	Have thou got a match?
	b.	Nej	No
	c.	Vi är inte du med varandra	We are not thou with each other

To use Wittgenstein's (1921) distinction between what is said and what is shown, indexical information is always shown, never said.

The topic function of talk can then conveniently be linked to what is said by talk. While in its indexical function, talk serves to show non-deniable aspects of the speech event, in its topic function, talk serves to say deniable things about a situation, which need not be the situation in which the speech event occurs. The situation which a stretch of talk says something about, the *topic* of that stretch of talk, may be the speech event in which that stretch of talk occurs, the situation in which that speech event is embedded (C), or another situation (D).

In ordinary conversation, as Bergmann (1990) shows, talk about C can always interrupt talk about D, and neither the transition from D to C nor the transition from C to D requires an overt display of topic shift. Ordinary conversation is *locally sensitive*, in Bergmann's terms. This suggests that the idea that talk has just one topic at a time might be wrong. Instead, we might think of ordinary conversation as always operating with three active and linked topics: the speech event, the situation C, and the situation D. Shoshana Blum-Kulka has even suggested (personal communication) that there may be several D situations active in a single conversation. For example, in the family dinners analysed by her, talk about the food, talk about table manners, talk about 'my day' and talk about political affairs may alternate. If there are no marked transitions between these topics, then we may well draw the conclusion that they are simultaneously active.

Let us adopt this multi-topic notion of talk. Talk occurs as part of a speech event (e) in a situation (C), which is linked to one or more situations distinct from it (D, D′, D″ ...). Talk provides information about all these components of the context, by indexing aspects of the speech event (e), and by treating the speech event (e), the situation in which it is embedded (C), and the other situations (D, D′, D″, ...), as simultaneously active topics. This means that aspects of the speech event can be both indexed and talked about, which opens up the possibility for an indexed aspect of the speech event to be denied through talk which takes the speech event as topic, as in (5c).

3. ACTIVITY TALK

A consequence of this multi-topic nature of talk is that a stretch of talk, without ceremony, may be heard as talk which indexes and describes the very social activity in which it occurs. Consider the following example, the opening of the lesson from which (2) was extracted:

(6) **Classroom interaction, fifth grade**

T1:	Vi ska börja i OÄ idag	We'll start in OÄ today
	me lite historia	with some history
	Å de ska vi hålla på till jul	And we'll keep on with that until Christmas
	Dom här två veckorna som e kvar	These two weeks that are left
	Å då ska vi tänka oss lite grann ut ifrån jorden	And then we'll move a little bit away from Earth
C1:	Ska vi ut i rymden	Are we going out into space
T2:	Lite grann kanske	A little maybe

This part of the lesson serves to identify and phase the current activity. In the first utterance of T1, the current activity is glossed as *OÄ* (*orienteringsämne*, i.e. 'orientation subject', a cover term for natural and social science subjects) and *historia* (history). Since history is only one of the various subjects covered in OÄ, the glossing of the current activity as history can be taken as a partitioning of OÄ, an interpretation which is further strengthened by the second and the third utterance of T1, where this partitioning is provided with a temporal frame, establishing the current activity as a distinct phase of OÄ. In the fourth utterance of T1, and further in Cl and T2, the topic of that phase is then identified.

The teacher's utterances in (6) are all performative (Austin 1962) in that they change the activity they are embedded in, not merely describe it. Thus, the next phase of her OÄ teaching, which the teacher introduces in T1, is created and defined through the very sequence T1–C1–T2. Talk like this, which serves to change, through showing or through saying, the very activity in which it is embedded, I will call *activity talk*. In more detail, activity talk serves to identify the current activity, its current and next phases, its current and next topics, and the current and next alignments[4] of its participants. In (6), we saw examples of how activity talk establishes current activity, next phase and next topic. In (7), the continuation of (6), there is an example (indicated by →) of how activity talk changes alignment, by identifying a next speaker.

(7) **Classroom interaction, fifth grade**

	C1:	Ska vi ut i rymden	Are we going out into space
	T2:	Lite grann kanske	A little maybe
	D1:	Åâh de e skoj	Wow that's fun
	T3:	Vad vet ni om rymden	What do you know about space
		Hur tror ni världen ser ut	How do you think the world looks like
	E1:	*brings a chair*	
	F1 and other students: *raise their hands*		
	T4:	Tack	Thanks
→		Fredrik	Fredrik
	F2:	De e svart	It is black
	T5:	De e svart	It is black

The unit which is instrumental in establishing such *activity facts* is typically not a single utterance, but a sequence of verbal and nonverbal turns, which combine to bring about an activity fact. Such a sequence is fundamentally an interactive unit, since activity facts must attain intersubjectivity. This means that cases such as the first utterance of (6) and the indicated utterance in (7), where an activity fact is established by a single utterance and without overt contributions from other participants, are not typical, but require special contexts of use, which automatically supply what is normally achieved through sequence and interaction in ordinary conversation.

The variety of teaching exemplified in (2), (6) and (7) is such a special context. What reduces sequence and interaction in this kind of social activity is a division of saying, which confines the establishing of activity facts to one participant only, the teacher. Whatever the teacher says or shows about the activity of teaching becomes a fact, while whatever a student says or shows about that same activity attains only the status of a proposal, which must be ratified by the teacher to become a fact. This means that an activity fact can be established by a teacher utterance alone, as exemplified by the first utterance of T1 in (6), by a sequence of teacher utterances, as exemplified by the second and third utterances of T1, or by any sequence of teacher utterances and student proposals which ends with a teacher utterance, as exemplified by the fourth utterance of T1, C1 and T2.

This division of saying also accounts for turn-taking in this variety of teaching. Consider Sachs, Schegloff and Jefferson's (1974) ordered options for next speaker selection: (i) current speaker selects other; (ii) other self-selects; and (iii) current speaker self-selects. Since identity of next speaker is an activity fact, it can only be established by the teacher. This means that the teacher freely can select next speaker, both as current speaker and as other. A student selection, though, attains, at most, the force of a proposal, which must be ratified by the teacher to become a fact. A successful student selection consequently has two components to it: a student proposal and a teacher ratification. Other-selection by students is rare, as are attempts by students to keep the floor. Self-selection by students, according to the second option, is in contrast a recurring pattern, where the two components of a student selection are conventionalised as bidding and nomination (Sinclair and Coulthard 1975). This is exemplified in (7), where the bidding is in Fl and the nomination is the indicated utterance in T4.

The variety of teaching exemplified in (2), (6) and (7) is fundamentally different from conversations among peers, where activity facts are interactively established, with possible participation of all ratified participants. As a consequence, activity talk is much less frequent in conversation, where topic selection and turn-taking are seldom regulated through talk, but just done. Furthermore, there are conventionalized forms of activity talk in teaching, such as bidding and nomination, which are completely absent from conversation.

4. TOPIC TALK

A stretch of talk within a social activity may also be heard as *topic talk*, talk about a topic that is the current object of that activity. Such talk may alternate with talk about a topic that is somehow 'outside' the social activity in question. The latter kind of talk must of course also be understood as topic talk, but within another activity. Note that it is completely in accord with the model developed so far that an activity may involve several simultaneous topics. It is also to be expected that one and the same stretch of talk may be heard both as activity talk and topic talk, since a stretch of talk can perfectly well both say things about a topic and show things about the activity in which the topic is embedded.

Just as activity talk is used to establish facts, topic talk is used to establish *truths* about the current topic of an activity. By 'truth', I do not mean truth in any absolute sense, but only 'truth for all practical purposes', something which is held to be true by participants during further talk about that topic.

The lesson, whose opening has been shown in (6) and (7), switches into topic talk at T3:

(8) **Classroom interaction, fifth grade**

T3:	Vad vet ni om rymden	What do you know about space
	Hur tror ni världen ser ut	How do you think the world looks like
E1:	*brings a chair*	
F1 and other students: *raise their hands*		
T4:	Tack	Thanks
	Fredrik	Fredrik
F2:	De e svart	It is black
T5:	De e svart	It is black
F3:	Fullt me prickar	Full of dots
T6:	Me prickar	Of dots
	E de stjärnorna ja	Is that the stars yes
	David	David

In (8), two truths are established. The first truth is 'It is dark in space', which is established by the sequence T3–F2–T5, a classical three-part sequence of teacher question (T3), student response (F2) and teacher evaluation (T5). In this case, the teacher evaluation accepts the student response, by repeating it. The second truth is 'Space is full of stars', which is established by the sequence T3–F3–T6, a classical three-part sequence augmented with an other-initiated other-repair (the second utterance in T6).

Truth-establishing sequences in teaching are not always classical three-part sequences. The simplest formats of such sequences are:

a. Teacher assertion
b. Teacher question – Student response – Teacher evaluation
c. Student question – Teacher response
d. Student assertion – Teacher evaluation

A teacher turn can also include a repair or formulation of a preceding student turn, as in the second utterance in T6. And, finally, we get more complex sequences, combinations of the simple sequences above. (1), where the truth expressed in (2): 'The planet which goes around closest to the sun is called Mercury' is established through a combination of teacher question, student response, negative teacher evaluation, another student response, teacher repair of that response, and a positive teacher evaluation, is a good example.

As is evident from the simple formats a–d, truth-establishing sequences in teaching always end with a teacher turn. Just as the teacher is the only participant to establish activity facts, the teacher is the only participant to establish truths about the topics dealt with in teaching.

Again, this is in marked contrast to conversation among peers. Consider the following excerpt from a conversation among four physicians. One of them, A, has just discovered a funny-looking map on the wall:

(9) **Conversation: four physicians**

A1:	De där e minsann till å me sionistisk propaganda	That is even sionistic propaganda
B1:	Den där	That
C1:	Va	What
B2:	Jaså De e inte turistartat	Is it[5] It is not 'touristic'
A2:	Näej absolut inte	No certainly not
B3:	De e de inte Nähä	It is not ≈OK≈
A3:	Undrar var i all sin dar han fått tag i den	Wonder where on earth he got hold of that

(Talsyntax 1974)

The truth established in this sequence is the proposition expressed by A1: 'That [i.e. the map on the wall] is sionistic propaganda'. Unlike the truths in (1) and (8), this truth is interactively established. B2 reacts to A1 with a non-committing *jaså* and presents a tentative alternative interpretation, in the form of a negative declarative with the force of a question. This alternative interpretation is then rejected by A2, and B3 accepts this rejection. With this, both A and B have subscribed to the truth of the proposition expressed by A1, and the truth is established. A3 can then proceed to talk further about the map. In contrast to teaching, conversation among peers involves a division of saying where truths are established by all ratified participants together.

This does not mean, of course, that all participants necessarily take part in the establishing of each truth. Although all participants should have their say in each truth-establishing sequence, factors such as competence, motivation and responsibility effectively limit participation, producing sometimes fairly asymmetric dialogues in what is, in principle, egalitarian activities (see Linell 1990b). In (9), for example, two of the physicians involved in the conversation are inactive. Nevertheless, they accept the truth, as is shown by the further development of the topic. The way their silence (or near-silence) is interpreted is suggested by the Swedish proverb *Den som tiger samtycker* (The one who is silent assents).

5. TEXT TALK

Not all truths established about a topic within an activity are worth saving as results of that activity. This makes it desirable for participants to mark certain truths established within a round of an activity as results of that round. Together, these truths constitute what I will call the *text* produced in that round of the activity. A single truth belonging to the text will be called a *text segment*, and talk used to establish the text of the current round of an activity will be called *text talk*.

The lesson, which has been unfolding in (6), (7) and (8), continues in this way:

(10) **Classroom interaction, fifth grade**

T6:	Me prickar E de stjärnorna ja David	Of dots Is that the stars yes David
D2:	Dom som åker ut i rymden å tittar ner på jorden ser de ut som en boll med massa gropar å sånt	Those who go out into space and look down at the Earth it looks like a ball with a lot of holes and things

T7:	Så jorden e en boll	So the Earth is a ball
D3:	Ja	Yes
T8:	Ha	≈OK≈
	Så du tror alltså att jorden e rund	So you think the Earth is round
D4:	Ja	Yes
T9:	Eller vet du säkert	Or do you know for certain
D5:	Ja	Yes
T10:	Ja de vet du säkert Fredrik	Yes you know for certain Fredrik
F4:	Förr i tiden trodde dom den va platt å när dom åkte till jordens ände ramla dom ner	In the past they thought it was flat and when they went to the end of the Earth they fell down
T11:	Ha	≈OK≈
	Vi ska titta på de lite	We'll look at that a little
	Men först ska vi se va vi vet om jorden nu	But first we'll see what we know about the Earth now
	Vi vet att jorden e rund	We know that the Earth is round
G1:	Ja	Yes
T12:	Då ritar vi en liten jord här då	Then we draw a little Earth here then
	draws a circle on the blackboard	
	Va vet vi mer	What do we know more

In (10), there is an elaborate sequence, starting with D2 and ending with T12, in which 'The Earth is round' is established both as truth and as text segment. The teacher formulates D2 in T7, and then leads D through two successive versions of 'The Earth is round', as belief and as certain knowledge. Then there is an attempt by F to introduce a new proposition. However, this proposition is deferred until later, and the teacher returns to 'The Earth is round', re-establishes it as truth, in T11, and, so to speak, puts it on the blackboard, in T12. This is the start of a phase of the lesson, where the teacher and the students successively identify the Moon, the Sun and the planets. These are drawn on the blackboard, to form, eventually, a complete picture of the Sun and the planets. Then, the teacher moves on to other topics (the medieval picture of the world, Copernicus, Galilei and Bruno). Finally, the students are told to work individually on an exercise in their workbooks. In this exercise, there is another picture of the Sun and the planets, and the students' task is to fill in the names of the Sun, the Moon and the planets (including the Earth).

There is thus a recurrent pattern in this lesson. Certain truths are established through talk and put on the blackboard in an early phase of the lesson. These truths are then the very truths that the students are required to reproduce in the final phase of the lesson. In my analysis, these truths are part of the text of that lesson, what is to be learnt from that lesson.

Unlike the other text segments, which are established once in talk and once on the blackboard, the first text segment established in the lesson, 'The Earth is round', is established three times: twice in talk and once on the blackboard. By separating the establishing of 'The Earth is round', in T11, from the drawing of a round Earth on the blackboard, the teacher can show to the students that the current phase of the lesson is one where text segments end up on the blackboard. This 'rule' can then serve as an interpretive frame for the remainder of the phase.

Text segments, like truths, are established by one participant only in the variety of teaching we are looking at, the teacher. In this respect, too, teaching contrasts with conversation among peers, where text segments are established interactively by all ratified participants. Consider, for example, the complete sequence spent on the map on the wall in the conversation sampled in (9).

(11) **Conversation: four physicians**

A1:	De där e minsann till å me sionistisk propaganda	That is even sionistic propaganda
B1:	Den där	That
C1:	Va	What
B2:	Jaså	Is it
	De e inte turistartat	It is not 'touristic'
A2:	Näej absolut inte	No certainly not
B3:	De e de inte	It is not
	Nähä	≈OK≈
A3:	Undrar var i all sin dar han fått tag i den	Wonder where on earth he got hold of that
D1:	Titta där	Look
	De e liksom slag	It's like battles
A4:	Hela faderullan	The whole thing
D2:	Israel air-strikes	Israel air-strikes
C2:	Jaha	≈OK≈
D3:	De e luftslage va	It's the air-battle isn't it
A5:	De va katten	I say
	De e tydligen från israeliska propagandaministeriet	It's apparently from the Israeli ministry of propaganda
	Å sen e där en lampa bak som	And then there's a lamp behind it which

	lyser precis överallt <u>där</u>	lights up in every place <u>where</u>
C3:	<u>Ja</u>	<u>Yes</u>
A5:	israelerna slogs	the Israeli fought
B4:	De va ju som sjutton	That's really something
D4:	Va var har vi hamnat riktit	Where are we really
C4:	Ja	Yes
A6:	Ja just de	Yes right
	Ja e oskyldig	I'm innocent
D5:	Okej vi tror dej	OK we believe you

(Talsyntax 1974)

There are two truths established in this sequence: 'The map is Israeli propaganda' and 'The map shows the air battle [between Israel and the Arab nations in 1967]'. These truths are established by A and B (Al through B3), and by D and A (D1 through the first utterance of A5), respectively. Then, in A5, A proceeds to formulate these truths and proposes to establish them once more, which all other participants agree to do (B4 through C4). In the sequence A5–C4, then, two truths are established, for the second time, by all participants. This sets this sequence off from the two sequences preceding it, in each of which one truth is established, for the first time, by only two of the four participants. This contrast is, in my view, best interpreted as a contrast between topic talk (A1 through the first utterance of A5) and text talk (the second utterance of A5 through C4).

It might be thought that text talk is primarily a phenomenon of formal, institutional contexts. In such contexts, the text of a round of an activity is quite often actually codified as a written text, and measures may be taken to ensure that the written text adequately reflects what was arrived at through talk. At a formal meeting, for example, what is going into the minutes and what is not is often explicitly stated, and there are routines for selecting who will take the minutes and who will verify them. However, the example of text talk in conversation in (11) suggests a rather different picture, namely that text talk is primarily a conversational phenomenon. Surely, the functional motivation for text talk, to mark what has been achieved through talk, is not lacking in conversation. Formalization of text talk as controlled representations in more permanent media would then be a secondary development, shaped and selected by various institutional contexts.

6. FURTHER DIVISIONS OF SAYING

So far, I have only contrasted the polar opposites of conversation and teaching. In conversation, all participants together establish activity facts, truths and text segments; in teaching, there is only one participant, cast in the professional role of teacher, who establishes activity facts, truths and text segments. The 'lay' persons in teaching, the students, do none of these things.

I will now turn to activities where the establishing of truths and text segments follow a different pattern from those found in teaching and conversation. My first example comes from a study of police interrogations by Linda Jönsson (Jönsson 1988; Jönsson and Linell 1991). Consider the following extract from an interrogation:

(12) **Police interrogation**

A1:	Vem monterade bort bandspelaren	Who disconnected the tape recorder
B1:	Ja vi höll väl på båda två Han va ju lös om ja säjer De va ju bara de att vi tog bort kablarna å sen	Well, we were at it both of us It was loose if I say It was just that we disconnected the cables and then
A2:	Den va inte fastmonterad alltså	It wasn't mounted then
B2:	Nä De va bara kablarna	No It was just the cables
A3:	Kommer du ihåg vem som gjorde de då	Do you remember who did it then
B3:	Ja tror vi drog i'n båda två	I think we pulled at it both of us
A4:	Jaha	≈OK≈
B4:	Vi satt i var sitt säte	We sat in separate seats
A5:	Mm	Mhm
B5:	där fram	in the front seat
A6:	Man kan säja att ni hjälptes åt att ta bort den där	One could say that you helped each other to disconnect that one
B6:	Ja i stort sett	Yes more or less

(Jönsson 1988: 113)

There are two truths established in this sequence: 'The tape recorder was not mounted' and 'B and his accomplice, C, removed the tape recorder together'. These truths also appear in the policeman's written report, in the following formulation:

(13) **Interrogation report**

Stereon låg lös i bilen och kamraterna hjälptes åt att ta bort sladdarna
The stereo lay loose in the car and the mates removed the cables together

(Jönsson 1988: 115)

The history of 'The tape recorder was not mounted' is this: assertion by B1 – formulation proposed by A2 – formulation accepted by B2 – formulation in A's written report. The history of 'B and C removed the tape recorder together' is this: question by A1 – answer by B1 – question by A3 – answer by B3 – formulation proposed by A6 – formulation accepted by B6 – formulation in A's written report. In both cases, the proposition involved is first established as a truth by the layperson, and then established as a text segment through a formulation by the professional which is accepted by the layperson.

But this is not the only pattern found in police interrogations. Consider another extract from the interrogation sampled in (12):

(14) **Police interrogation**

B1:	Ja vet inte riktit om vi *clears throat* fick me oss för vi (p) fick den dumma idén att när vi väl kom in så va de en bandspelare i bilen	I don't really know if we *clears throat* took it with us because we (p) got the stupid idea that when we came inside then there was a tape recorder in the car
A1:	De va samma bil de	That was the same car that
B2:	Ja	Yes
A2:	Mm	Mhm
B3:	(p) Å ja vet inte om (p) Vi tog dän den i alla fall men ja vet inte om vi (p) för vi har ju den inte me oss hem i alla fall	(p) And I don't know if (p) We took it away in any case but I don't know if we (p) because we don't have it with us home in any case
A3:	*writes* (p) Nä den hittades utanför	(p) No it was found outside
B4:	Den hittades Mm	It was found Mhm

(Jönsson 1988: 113)

Note that A3 is established as a truth by the policeman alone. The reaction in B4 marks that truth as already settled. Thus, beside truths clearly established by the layperson, there are also some truths established by the professional.

My second example comes from a medical interview:

(15) **Physician–patient interaction**

A1:	Ja hmm å tarmen sköter sej	Well ah and the bowels are doing all right
	helt å hållet	completely

B1:	Ja de gör den	Yes they do
A2:	Inga besvär me den	No troubles with them
B2:	Nää	No

(Ullabeth Sätterlund-Larsson, personal communication)

I have no access to the medical record based on this interaction, but otherwise, we find the same pattern as in (12). The proposition involved in this sequence goes through the history of question by A1 – answer by B1 – formulation by A2 – acceptance of formulation by B2. In my interpretation, this proposition is, again, first established as a truth by the layperson, and then established as a text segment through a formulation by the professional which is accepted by the layperson.

As in police interrogations, though, not all truths are established by the layperson. When a physician reports a test result, for example, that report is immediately established as a truth.

Interrogations, interviews and similar activities, such as news interviews (Heritage 1985) and job interviews (Adelswärd 1988), thus have a division of saying where truths are established either by the layperson or by the professional, and text segments are formulated by the professional, accepted by the layperson and recorded by the professional. Whether or not records are routinely signed by the layperson differs from activity to activity, as does the accessibility of records to laypersons and others.

My final example is a therapist's account of a psychotherapy session:

(16) **Psychotherapy session, therapist's account**
Två månader in på terapin önskade X ett längre uppehåll och angav barnpassningsproblem som orsak. Hon löste situationen när hon förstod att terapin i så fall skulle upphöra. När jag tolkade detta som uttryck för rädsla och en önskan om distans till mig, svarade hon att hon i terapin ser frånstötande sidor hos sig själv och att hon också blir rädd att ingen ska tycka om henne, om hon inte är lika glad som förut.

After two months of therapy, X wanted a longer pause, claiming problems with child care as cause. She solved the problem when she understood that the therapy would come to an end in that case. When I interpreted that as an expression of anxiety and a wish to keep the distance to me, she said that she sees ugly sides of herself in the therapy and that she becomes afraid that no one will like her, if she is not as merry as before.

Besides describing the establishing of an activity fact by the therapist ('Therapies do not admit of longer pauses'), (16) describes the following process (simplifying somewhat): X establishes 'X wants a longer pause' as a truth. This truth is then formulated by the therapist as 'X wants a longer pause, because she is afraid of therapy', and then further formulated by X as 'X wants a longer pause, because she is afraid of the consequences of therapy'. In this case, then, we have a proposition which is first established as a truth by the layperson, and then interactively established as a text segment through successive formulations by the professional and the layperson. This text segment is then recorded by the professional and forms the basis of the account in (16).

In psychotherapy sessions, at least of the psychodynamic type, we thus find a division of saying where truths are established by the layperson, and text segments are interactively established by the professional and the layperson together, and then recorded by the professional.

7. HOW DIVISIONS OF SAYING RELATE TO ACTIVITIES

I will now argue that the relation between a social activity and the division of saying operating there is an inner one, that a particular division of saying is a direct expression of the social activity in which it operates.

Consider first, teaching. Teaching is the activity of bringing about learning with respect to something (Hirst 1973). More specifically, teaching involves one or more teachers, one or more students, some kind of subject matter (M), and something to be learnt about that subject matter (L(M)). If M is a theoretical subject matter, then L(M) is a text about M, and learning is manifested in reproduction of this text. Thus, the point of teaching is to bring about reproduction of texts about some subject matter by students.

What does it mean to say that teachers bring about text reproduction by students? I will use an extension of Goffman's notion of *principal* (Goffman 1981: 144–5, 226) to explicate this aspect of teaching. For Goffman, the principal of an utterance is the one whose position is expressed by the utterance. This means, among other things, that the principal of an utterance is answerable to the adequacy of that utterance, its truth, ethical value, correctness, appropriateness, beauty, etc. I now propose to extend this revised notion of principal of X, as the one answerable to the adequacy of X, to activities, topics and texts. The principal of an activity is thus the one answerable to the adequacy of that activity; the principal of a topic is the one answerable to the adequacy of what is said about that topic; and the principal of a text is the one answerable to the adequacy of that text.

In teaching, the teacher is principal of activity, topic and text. Teachers, unlike students, know which texts are to be taught and learnt. Thus, teachers naturally assume responsibility for what is happening, working to make it characterizable as teaching and learning, and for what the students are saying, working to make it characterizable as reproduction of the current text. Moreover, whoever knows the text about a topic, knows that topic, and whoever is ignorant of the text about a topic, is ignorant of that topic. This is summarized in the format below, which I will refer to as the *activity format* of teaching. To achieve maximum generality, I have substituted Professional and Layperson for Teacher and Student, respectively.

Teaching

Point:	Layperson(s) reproduce a text about some subject matter
Principal of activity:	Professional
Principal of topic:	Professional
Principal of text:	Professional

The point of interrogations and interviews is the production of a text by Professional about some topic that Layperson has privileged access to, often a segment of Layperson's life world or life story (see Mishler, this volume). It thus follows that Layperson is normally the principal of the topic of such activities. However, in many cases, Professional has other means of getting information about Layperson: witnesses, police investigations, medical tests, documents, etc. This information about Layperson has Professional as its principal (see Hydén, this volume). Thus, I suggest that interviews and interrogations typically operate with two topics: one describing Layperson from 'within', topic (i), the other describing Layperson from 'without', topic (o). The activity format of interrogations and interviews is then:

Interrogation, interview

Point:	Professional produces a text about Layperson
Principal of activity:	Professional
Principal of topic (i):	Layperson

Principal of topic (o):	Professional
Principal of text:	Professional

The point of (psychodynamic) therapy, finally,[6] might be described as a guided rewriting of Layperson's life story by Layperson (White 1991). The activity format of psychotherapy is thus:

Psychotherapy

Point:	Layperson produces a text about Layperson
Principal of activy:	Professional
Principal of topic:	Layperson
Principal of text:	Professional and Layperson

Activity formats are not mechanical causes of behaviour, but abductively established 'norms', which participants work to match, in so far as they share an understanding of what they are doing (for this notion of norm, see Heritage 1984, especially ch. 4). In other words, participants take the behaviours they find in an activity as indexical of that activity (Anward 1994), and may go to some length to secure such behaviours in an activity, thereby maintaining the identification of that activity as a particular kind of activity.

Consider the following extract from the lesson we have been looking at:

(17) **Classroom interaction, fifth grade**

T1:	Var tror ni jag är lättast då	Where do you think I'm lightest then
H1:	På månen	On the Moon
T2:	Upp med handen upp med handen	Hands up hands up
	På jorden eller månen	On Earth or on the Moon
	var är jag lättast	Where am I lightest
	Inge	Inge
I1:	På månen	On the Moon
T3:	Ja förstås	Yes of course

The answer in H1 is correct, as shown by the reaction to I1, and clearly audible. Yet the teacher does not accept it, but uses it instead as an occasion for rule quoting. Then she nominates another student, who produces exactly the same answer. This time it is accepted and established as a truth. I suggest that this interactive work is meant to maintain the activity format of teaching, where it is the teacher that is principal of the activity. H1 is taken as an occasion for rule quoting and not as the correct answer that I1 shows it to be, precisely because H1 violates the activity format of teaching, by speaking without having been nominated.

It is then a small step to propose that divisions of saying are the outcomes of methods designed to establish and maintain certain activity formats. In particular, seeing to it that you are the one who establishes the relevant parts of X, i.e. that you get an independent final say about each successive part of X, is a basic method of claiming and maintaining the role of principal with respect to X. Thus, the principal of an activity will seek to establish the facts of that activity; the principal of a topic will seek to establish the truths about that topic; and the principal of a text will seek to establish the segments of that text.

If two or more participants are principals of X, they will both seek to establish each successive part of X, which means that they must interactively negotiate a shared final say about each successive part of X, in accordance with the logic of closings, as described by Schegloff and Sachs (1973). Thus, in therapies, therapist and patient will negotiate a final say about each text segment, which, however, for the record, will count as the patient's say, since it is the patient that produces the text. In interrogations/interviews, professionals do not have to negotiate the formulations of text segments, since they are the sole principals of texts. However, if a text segment is also a truth about a topic (i), then Professional has to submit that text segment for acceptance to Layperson, since it is Layperson that has the final say on that kind of topic. In this way, we derive the contrast noted above between text-establishing sequences in interrogation/interview and therapy.

If divisions of saying are ways of maintaining activity formats, mainly through strategical use of final sayings, then it follows that a particular activity format is compatible with a considerable variation in other features of divisions of saying. Consider again the varieties of saying in teaching:

a. Teacher assertion
b. Teacher question – Student response – Teacher evaluation
c. Student question – Teacher response
d. Student assertion – Teacher evaluation

Attested teaching methods (Rasborg 1975) span the whole range from methods dominated by (a), lecturing, through methods dominated by (b), recitation, and methods dominated by (c), expert systems, to methods dominated by (d), project work. The persistence of methods dominated by (b) across all kinds of subject (Bellack et al. 1966; Lundgren 1972) must therefore be due to some factor beyond the teacher's role as principal of activity, topic and text. In Anward (1983: ch. 7), I argued that teacher control, implemented through the teacher's role as principal of activity, topic and text, can be seen as a means to restrict classroom discourse to text reproduction by the students, the very point of teaching. But it is essential that teachers exert the right amount of control. Too much teacher control eliminates student contributions altogether, while too little control is insufficient to restrict classroom discourse to text reproduction. Briefly, then, methods based on (b) are persistent because they allow teachers to reduce classroom discourse to text reproduction without excluding student contributions.

A similar argument can be constructed for interrogations/interviews (and for therapies, but that would require a rather lengthy exposition, which I will have to refrain from here). If the essential component of professional control in interrogations/interviews is getting the final say about each text segment, then there is room for variation in other features of divisions of saying. As Linell (1990a) has shown, this kind of variation is also attested. Interrogations/interviews range from form-filling activities, where professionals ask laypersons very specific questions, to activities where laypersons present unsolicited accounts of their cases, leading up to advice-seeking questions. Since professional control is there to ensure the production of a professional text, we might expect professionals to tend towards the form-filling end of the range. This is counter-balanced, though, by great variation in relative competence and motivation among professionals and laypersons across the full range of interrogation/interview activities, topics and participants, which means that there is no single optimal division of saying for interrogations/interviews. Interrogations/interviews are thus similar to conversations among peers, where asymmetric constellations of competence, responsibility and motivation among participants may override the egalitarian nature of the activity and sustain quite asymmetric divisions of saying (Linell 1990b).

This kind of variation, compatible with a single activity format, might give us a clue to the origin of the activity formats I have been looking at. Asymmetric discourse in an egalitarian activity may be taken as evidence for a non-egalitarian activity format. If a certain participant is the only one to establish activity facts in an instance of an activity, for example, the activity may be perceived by new participants as an activity where the role of principal of that activity is limited to one participant only, which is, effectively, the beginning of a new activity format. When role differentiation is further reinforced by recruitment to the new role of professionals, whose selection and training often lie outside of the activity itself and are carried out by other professionals, then the distance between an egalitarian activity and the modern activities of teaching, interviewing, and therapy is more or less covered.

NOTES

1. For invaluable input to this chapter, I am grateful to Viveka Adelswärd, Shoshana Blum-Kulka, Charles Goodwin, Marjorie Harness Goodwin, Eva Lindberg, Per Linell, Ulrika Nettelbladt, Bengt Nordberg, and Ullabeth Sätterlund-Larsson.
2. I am using a transcription notation without much detail. Utterances, i.e. stretches of talk bounded by a single contour, are introduced by capital letters. Non-verbal turns are in italics. (p) marks pauses. Simultaneous utterances and/or events are underlined.
3. Although a context of this general form is necessarily invoked when something is taken as an utterance, we need not assume that all its components are active in all cases. There are well-known genres, where one or more of these components are not focused, not identified or even suppressed. In public signs ('No right turn', for example), in recipes and in instruction manuals, the sender is neither focused nor identified. In poetry, the addressee is not identified. And in formal language instruction, a described situation is neither focused nor identified (Anward 1990). These components are not missing, though, since it is always possible to refocus them. We might for example, link the example sentences of a thesis to a described situation and so derive an illuminating *roman-à-clef*.
4. In the sense of Goffman (1981), who decomposes the notions of Speaker and Hearer into the more primitive notions of Animator, Author, Principal, Addressee and Recipient, which can combine to yield a number of distinct *participant statuses*.
5. The Swedish response items *jaså* (in B2), *näej* (in A2), and *nähä* (in B3) are hard to translate. Roughly, *jaså* is a news receipt token, in the sense of Heritage (1984), i.e. *jaså* weakens *ja* (yes) from an indication of acceptance to an indication of uptake, without further commitment. The partial reduplication in *näej* makes *nä* (no) more emphatic, while the stylized partial reduplication in *nähä* (and *jaha*) marks the matter reacted to as already settled. The approximate character of the translation is indicated by ≈.
6. Other types of activity format exist too, as Bengt Nordberg (personal communication) reminds me. The study groups investigated in Anward

(1990) combine a lay principal of activity and a professional principal of topic and text. Advisory activities would seem to combine a lay principal of topic (i), a professional principal of topic (o) and a lay principal of text. So does the teaching activity analysed in Linde (this volume), where the point of the activity is the reproduction of a skill, rather than the reproduction of a text In such a case, text segments will be variations on the theme 'Layperson knows this now and is happy that (s)he does'. In other words, we have a topic which is a combination of topic (i) with a lay principal and a topic (o) with a professional principal. As a consequence, each text segment needs to be negotiated, and Linde shows that they are indeed negotiated. And further formats are certainly conceivable.

REFERENCES

Adelswärd, V. (1988) *Styles of Success*, Linköping Studies in Arts and Science 23, Linköping.

Agar, M. (1985) Institutional Discourse, *Text* **5**, 147–68.

Anward, J. (1983) *Språkbruk och språkutveckling i skolan*, Liber, Lund.

—— (1986) Emotive expressions, in Ö. Dahl (ed.), *Papers From the Ninth Scandinavian Conference of Linguistics*, Stockholm, 39–52.

—— (1990) Språkspel i språkcirklar, in U. Nettelbladt och G. Håkansson (eds), *Samtal och språkundervisning*, Linköping Studies in Arts and Science 60, Linköping, 147–68.

—— (1994) Semiotics in Educational Research, in *International Encyclopedia of Educational Research*, vol. 6, Pergamon Press, Oxford, 5411–17.

Austin, J. L. (1962) *How To Do Things with Words*, Clarendon Press, Oxford.

Bellack, A. A., Kliebard, H. M., Hyman, R. L. and Smith, F. L. (1966) *The Language of the Classroom*, Teachers College Press, New York.

Bergmann, J. (1990) On the Local Sensitivity of Conversation, in I. Marková and K. Foppa (eds), *The Dynamics of Dialogue*, Harvester Press, Hemel Hempstead, 201–26.

Bratt, B., Ehnmark, K., Heidenfors, K., Ormaeus, N. G. and Pettersson, Å. (1974) *Kombisvenska: Grundbok 3*, Utbildningsförlaget, Lund.

Bühler, K. (1934) *Sprachtheorie*, Fischer, Jena.

Goffman, E. (1981) *Forms of Talk*, University of Pennsylvania Press, Philadelphia.

Heritage, J. (1984) *Garfinkel and Ethnomethodology*, Polity Press, Cambridge.

—— (1985) Analyzing News Interviews: Aspects of the Production of Talk for an Overhearing Audience, in T. A. van Dijk (ed.) *Handbook of Discourse Analysis 3: Discourse and Dialogue*, Academic Press, London, 95–117.

Hirst, P.H. (1973) What Is Teaching?, in R.S. Peters (ed.) *The Philosophy of Education*, Oxford University Press, London, 163–77.

Hurford, J. (1987) *Language and Number*, Blackwell, Oxford.

Hymes, D. (1974) *Foundations in Sociolinguistics*, University of Pennsylvania Press, Philadelphia.

Jakobson, R. (1960) Concluding Statement: Linguistics and Poetics, in Th. Sebeok (ed.) *Style in Language*, MIT Press, Cambridge, Mass, 357–70.

Jönsson, L. (1988) Polisförhöret som kommunikationssituation, *Studies in Communication* 23, Department of Communication Studies, University of Linköping, Linköping.

Jönsson, L. and Linell, P. (1991) Story Generations: From Dialogical Interviews to Written Reports in Police Interrogations, *Text* **11**, 419–40.

Levinson, S. C. (1979) Pragmatics and Social Deixis: Reclaiming the Notion of Conventional Implicature, *Berkeley Linguistic Society* **5**, 206–23.

Linell, P. (1990a) De institutionaliserade samtalens elementära former: om möten mellan professionella och lekmän, *Forskning om utbildning* **4**, 18–35.

—— (1990b) The Power of Dialogue Dynamics, in I. Marková and K. Foppa (eds) *The Dynamics of Dialogue*, Harvester Press, Hemel Hempstead, 147–77.

Lundgren, U. P. (1972) *Frame Factors and the Teaching Process*, Almqvist & Wiksell, Stockholm.

Rasborg, F. (1975) *Undervisningsmetoder och arbetsmönster*, Aldus, Stockholm.

Sacks, H., Schegloff, E. A. and Jefferson, G. (1974) A Simplest Systematics for the Organization of Turn-taking in Conversation, *Language* **50**, 696–735.

Saville-Troike, M. (1985) *The Ethnography of Communication*, Cambridge University Press, Cambridge.

Schegloff, E. A. and Sacks, H. (1973) Opening Up Closings, *Semiotica* **8**, 289–327.

Silverstein, M. (1985) The Functional Stratification of Language and Ontogenesis, in J. V. Wertsch (ed.) *Culture, Communication and Cognition: Vygotskian Perspectives*, Cambridge University Press, Cambridge, 205–35.

Sinclair, J. M. and Coulthard, M. (1975) *Towards an Analysis of Discourse*, Oxford University Press, Oxford.

Talsyntax (1974) *Läkare diskuterar eutanasi*, Text E6:1, Department of Scandinavian Languages, Lund.

White, M. (1991) *Postmodernism, Deconstruction and Therapy*, Dulwich Centre Newsletter 3/1991.

Wittgenstein, L. (1921) *Tractatus Logico-philosophicus*, Routledge, London.

EIGHT

Evaluation as linguistic structure and social practice[1]

Charlotte Linde

1. INTRODUCTION

The study of discourse and the professions is necessarily concerned with the question of how linguistic structure and social practice, specifically professional practice, relate. While there have been many excellent studies describing examples of professional discourse, we do not yet have principled answers to the question of how this intersection is best described. In particular, what is lacking is an analysis of the appropriate and effective units and levels of analysis for both the linguistic and social components.

This formulation of the issue assumes that an effective description must have a structural component, that is, that it will assume a hierarchical organization of linguistic structures such as word, sentence, discourse unit, etc. At the same time, it assumes that professional discourse has a form of organization of its activity which is not purely specified by a description of the linguistic structure alone, but which is also responsive to a separate organization of work tasks and interaction. The first of these concerns is a central one within linguistics; much of the work of discourse analysis has been to extend the identification and analysis of structural units above the level of the sentence to the level of discourse.[2] The description of the micro-organization of the social practice of work, specifically professional practice, is considerably less advanced; it is not yet clear whether there are general organizing structures which are more particular than the general principles of interaction proposed by conversation analysis, and yet more general than the idiosyncratic structure of each professional task, dictated by differing material, technical, organizational and interactional components. That is, the structure of turn-taking is too general a description, the structure of discourses about how to do brain surgery or land an aircraft are too specific. Thus, one serious issue facing any attempt to describe professional discourse is to find a way to unite these two levels of organization together in a single, unified analysis.

Using as data novice users' evaluation of a new computer-based communications tool, this chapter demonstrates that evaluation as a linguistic and social phenomenon can be an important site for unifying these two levels of analysis. Evaluation is a major component of the linguistic structure of discourse. It is also an important part of social interaction, and has serious consequences for real-world decisions. Thus, an analysis of evaluation necessarily gives an account of the relation of linguistic structure and social practice.

2. WHAT IS EVALUATION?

Evaluation is an extremely pervasive phenomenon in language. We may include as evaluation any instance of a speaker indicating the social meaning or value of a person, thing, event or relationship. – 'I like it', 'I don't like it', 'She's smart', 'She's awful', 'It's terrible the way they treat you in hospitals', 'All used car salesmen can't be trusted', 'Blast this machine, anyway', 'I'm so stupid at computers', 'I wish I had a more powerful computer'. Evaluation may thus be viewed as an important part of the moral dimension of language, providing indications of the social order which the speaker reproduces by assuming. For example, Goodwin and Goodwin (this volume) explicate an extremely complex example of the construction of a contested evaluation: the construction of the meaning of police and victim behaviour in the Rodney King case.

Evaluation has been most fully analysed within the linguistic study of narrative structure. Let us begin with the definition of evaluation, taken from Labov's classic work on narrative:

> Evaluation [is] the means used by the narrator to indicate the point of the narrative, its *raison d'être*: why it was told, and what the narrator is getting at. There are many ways to tell the same story, to make very different points, or to make no point at all. Pointless stories are met (in English) with the withering rejoinder, 'So what?' Every good narrator is continually warding off this question: when his narrative is over, it should be unthinkable for a bystander to say, 'So what?' Instead, the appropriate remark would be, 'He did?' or similar means of registering the reportable character of the events of the narrative.
>
> (Labov 1972: 366–7)

To expand this definition, when we examine evaluation, we find that there are two dimensions of evaluation: *reference to reportability* and *reference to social norms*.

The notion of reportability makes use of norms of predictability of events, contrasting events that can be expected and events that are out of the ordinary. Completely expectable events cannot form the basis of a narrative, since they would be likely to elicit some version of the formulaic challenge 'So what?' which calls into question the speaker's right to take up the floor with unimportant or irrelevant material. An apparently ordinary event must be known to be or constructed as being out of the ordinary before its narration can be justified. Thus, a sequence like 'I saw John today and he said hello to me' is not normally, in itself, reportable. It might be reportable under unusual circumstances, for example, that John is known to scorn social convention and to avoid all greetings, or if John and the narrator have not been on speaking terms. For such a narrative to be told, these circumstances either must be known to the addressees or must be made known to them. In comparison, a sequence like 'I got hit on the head with a beer bottle and they took me to the hospital and I had to have fourteen stitches' is universally reportable, and its telling requires no further justification (Linde 1993).

The other dimension of evaluation used to structure narratives is reference to social norms: moral comments or demonstrations of the way the world is, the way the world ought to be, what proper behaviour is, and the kind of people that the speaker and addressees are. This is one particular form of normative judgement: what kind of behaviour can be expected of a good person. Evaluation of this sort forms the heart of narrative; oral narrative is much more about coming to agreement on the moral meaning of a series of actions than it is about the simple reporting of those actions (Polanyi 1989; Linde 1991, 1993).

3. LINGUISTIC STRUCTURE OF EVALUATION

In order to understand evaluation as social practice, it is first necessary to understand how it functions within the many varieties of discourse structures, rather than concentrating only on its function within narrative. To do this, it is helpful to distinguish three kinds or levels of evaluation: *incidental evaluation*, *constituent level evaluation*, and *topic level evaluation*. These differ in their relation to the structure of the discourse, in the scope of the material evaluated and in their preferred response from interlocutors.

Incidental level evaluations are produced in passing:

(1) That's excellent, that just worked dandily.[3]

(2) Page 39 shows you how to add them. But it's not working for me.

(3) Well, this is the second time I, I'm adding New Entry now. Hopefully.

These are small evaluations, made in passing (here excerpted from their contexts). They work at the sentence level or lower. Their scope is relatively small (in our data), evaluating parts of the technology or immediate experiences in learning or using it, rather than the technology as a whole, or the entire experience of learning or using it. They frequently do not receive a response from their recipient.

Constituent level evaluations occur as structural components of a discourse unit, for example, the point of a story or the outcome of a diagnosis of who or what is at fault These are evaluations which are required of components at a given point in the discourse structure. Their scope can include the entire discourse unit. A response to constituent level evaluations must be negotiated and agreed on by the parties before the discourse unit can be completed.

Topic level evaluations are found in cases in which the purpose of the discourse is to arrive at an evaluation, for example, an evaluation of the quality of a new piece of technology. These represent actual negotiations focused on value and the appropriate actions to take. Such topic level evaluations have the discourse form of argument. (See Goguen et al. (1983) and Schiffrin (1984) for analyses of argument discourses which have this character.)

Within discourse analysis, incidental level evaluation and constituent level evaluation have previously been conflated in discussions of narrative, resulting in a structurally anomalous description of evaluation (Labov 1972; Linde 1981, 1993). The structural anomaly is that, unlike all other components of narrative structure, evaluation has neither a specified form nor a specified placement relative to other components. It may appear anywhere in the narrative and may be realized at any level of linguistic structure: sentential, phrasal, lexical, phonological, paralinguistic, etc. Separating the two levels of evaluation moves towards eliminating this anomaly, since it is incidental level evaluation which is pervasive, while constituent level evaluation can be located as a discourse constituent within a discourse unit. Goodwin and Goodwin (1992) define a distinction between assessment signals and assessment segments; these appear to correspond to incidental level evaluation and constituent level evaluation, although they are defined in terms of interaction structure rather than discourse structure.

Topic level evaluation has not been previously been defined as such, although there have been a number of studies on argument structures and planning structures (Grimshaw 1990; Linde and Goguen 1978; Schiffrin 1984). Such a definition would require studies of the varieties of discourse units which function to produce a mutually agreed-upon evaluation.

4. EVALUATION AS A NEGOTIATION

In addition to its structural role in discourse, evaluation also plays an important role in the immediate and long-term social interaction. Evaluation is not produced by a single speaker, but must be negotiated among the participants. That is, it is not sufficient for one person to offer an opinion about the new technology. The speaker must obtain agreement from the other participants, or if that is not possible, at least discover the participants' opinions and how they relate to the speaker's opinion. Hence, negotiation is necessary. Negotiation of evaluation is particularly necessary when it is a communications technology which is being evaluated, since such a technology requires all, or almost all, of the group to use it for it to be valuable (Grudin 1988; Markus and Connolly 1990).

There are several possible forms of negotiation. One is a formally defined discourse genre, found in such activities as political, business or labour negotiations. The other is not a formal negotiating session around the bargaining table. Rather, it is the moment-by-moment process of social and linguistic actions which leads to an implicit agreement. (See Linell and Fredin (1995) for a discussion.) In the data of this study, negotiations are of this second kind – tacit and embedded within other activities. The task at hand is understood to be learning to use the technology. In the course of this activity, one speaker may offer an evaluation and other participants agree or disagree. This may lead to a change on the part of one or more participants in the way in which they evaluate the technology.

But arriving at a decision about the technology is never formally stated as the topic of the interaction.

Perhaps the most striking difference between formal negotiation genres and the informal or embedded negotiations which characterize these data is that in formal negotiations participants often begin with apparently fixed positions which they then slowly modify. In contrast, in these informal negotiations, participants appear to avoid strongly fixed initial positions which might provoke conflict.[4] (It may be relevant that both sites studied consist primarily of female workers. It would be very valuable to do a comparative study of this kind of negotiation to see if there are marked gender differences. It is undoubtedly also relevant that the participants all knew that tapes of their learning sessions would be studied by the designers of the technology they were attempting to learn.)

We must also distinguish between the immediate and long-term consequences of a negotiation of evaluation. The negotiation of an evaluation has the immediate linguistic consequence that the participants can continue their interaction. It may or may not mean that they actually agree or will act in accordance with that evaluation. The long-term consequences have to do with what people will actually do about adopting and using the technology. These are more complex and take effect over a much longer time period; they thus require more extensive and focused data collection to study.

4.1 Prior studies of negotiation in narrative

Linguistic studies of the negotiation of evaluation have focused on narrative. These studies show that the moral meaning of evaluation is produced not only by the speaker, but by a process of negotiation between speaker and addressees. An addressee may show understanding and agreement of the speaker's evaluative construction by providing an evaluation in the course of the story, after it, or by following it with a second story with the same evaluative point (Sacks 1992).

Although agreement is the preferred response, the addressee may not always agree with the evaluation of a narrative, but may rather disagree with the speaker's meaning, and supply an alternative evaluation for the same events. In such a case, the speaker and addressee must then negotiate what the point of the story will be on that particular occasion of telling, since it is difficult, if not impossible, for storytelling to proceed if the interlocutors do not share a basic agreement on moral meaning. The following, from Polanyi (1989), is an example of such negotiation of possible evaluations of a narrative about fainting during rush hour on the New York City subway. The speaker compares conditions on the subway to the Nazi treatment of the Jews:

(4) Yeah, the closest thing I can compare it to, and I never experienced *that* ... and it's probably a *frac*tion of what *that* experience was ... but I think ... of the way the Jews ... were herded into the cattle cars ... [material omitted] And it's just as dehumanizing.

This is an extremely strong claim about the meaning of the narrative, which the addressees refuse to accept. One of the addressees comments on the speaker's earlier account of how she was treated by people in the subway car when she fainted:

(5) But people were pretty nice, hm?

This question rejects the characterization given by the narrator of the subway as being like concentration camp transportation, a very strong characterization. The rejection is implicit. She does not say 'You can't say that', or 'Nothing is comparable to the Nazi cattle cars'. But she does propose a characterization of the people as 'pretty nice' which is completely incompatible with concentration camp transportation. The speaker then reforms the meaning she claims for her narrative into one which can be mutually acceptable. In fact, the participants all end by agreeing that fainting is a weird experience, a much weaker claim than the one proposed by the original evaluation.

Charles Goodwin (1986) gives a complex example of disagreement on the evaluation of a narrative told to a varying group of two to four addressees about what may have been a fight between racers at a local auto race. Two alternate evaluations are proposed, one by the speaker and one by two of the other participants. The first is that there really was a big fight at the race track. The alternative evaluation is that it was all a show, not really a fight at all. The participants never do arrive at an evaluation they can all agree on. Rather, the participants who disagree with the main speaker drift away, leaving him with an audience of one, who is willing to agree with his assessment of the events as a big fight, thus allowing the speaker to conclude the narrative.

The general finding of both these studies is that in white middle-class conversational settings, interlocutors must come to some kind of agreement on the evaluation of a narrative. These conversational settings contrast with other forms of discourse in which unresolved conflict or confrontation is expected, for example formal debates or political demonstrations. They also contrast with the discourse norms of other groups, which can be quite different. For example, Marjorie Goodwin (1990) has shown the prevalence of dispute and disagreement in the discourse of African-American pre-adolescent speakers. However, for those communities who hold agreement in narrative as the preferred stance, agreement is usually achieved so seamlessly that the process is hardly noticeable. This is why examples like the two above are so rare, and so important. If there is an initial disagreement, speakers must work to find a level of evaluation that they can agree on. And if they cannot do this, then the interaction cannot continue, as Charles Goodwin's example shows. Either there is a complete breakdown, or the participants reconstitute themselves so that those who agree can continue. We will see this as a more general principle in the use of evaluation in all settings, not only in narratives. In all speech situations which do not admit extended unresolved contestations of meaning, when speakers come to a disagreement on evaluation, they must reach some form of agreement, even if it is an agreement on the value of agreeing to disagree, before the interaction can continue.

5. THE DATA

As we shall see, the situation of people learning to use a new technology is rich in opportunities for evaluation. For this reason, the data for this study are taken primarily from the Picasso Project, a joint project of the Institute for Research on Learning and Philips Electronics NV. This project attempted to develop new methods for the design of learnable and usable consumer electronics products, through the use of observational studies of users and the inclusion of social scientists as well as designers in the design process. The project team designed a unified computer communications tool which included fax, file transfer, remote screen sharing and control, and chat facilities (Allen et al. 1991). The team picked a work site and studied its work practices before the introduction of the new technology, using ethnographic field observations, video-taping and interviews. We then introduced the new technology and studied how it was learned and used. Based on these studies, we then jointly redesigned the tool to make it easier to learn and more suitable for uses which fit the users' work practices. We then studied the response to the new design in the same way.

The two workplaces we studied were a graphics design firm, whose two partners lived and worked 50 miles apart, and a small private welfare agency with several sites which provides housing and training for the mentally handicapped. These two workplaces were similar in that both had co-workers who worked at a distance and frequently had to make special arrangements to deliver urgent documents to one another – including driving long distances, going to local copy shops to fax documents, or hiring taxis to deliver documents immediately. They differed in the degree of sophistication about computers that the participants possessed. In the case of the graphics designers, they were quite familiar with the Macintosh platform, regularly used graphics and desktop publishing programs, and most crucially, expected that part of maintaining professional competence in their field required continuing to learn new computer programs. In contrast, the workers in the welfare agency were relatively unfamiliar with computer technology. Some of them had used a Macintosh before, some had used the older Apple II (a very different design), and none of them expected that they would continue to learn new technologies as part of their ongoing career path.

The data collected in this project proved to be an ideal site for studying the social construction of evaluation; because the situations it set up are exactly those which require a great deal of evaluation. A new technology was introduced into people's work worlds. It is conventionally expected that anything new in the environment requires evaluation. For example, it is part of American workplace etiquette to notice and comment on a co-worker's new hairdo, new beard or new car. It is also very frequent for speakers to comment on a new feature of the workplace: a new coffee pot, a strange noise in the ventilator system, a rearrangement of the cafeteria. In the data of this study, it is a new technology to be learned which is the basis of evaluative notice. In this situation, speakers make reference to norms of what a useful or learnable device is, and what a competent learner can be expected to accomplish. During the course of learning, when problems arise, the need arises for a diagnosis about where the problem is located – in the technology or in the person. This again elicits a great deal of evaluation.

Furthermore, the act of learning itself requires evaluation. Learning of any sort, whether based in the school or in the workplace, is never a decontextualized activity which consists of the reception of factual information. Learning is relational. In order to learn anything, the learner must have some sense of what it means to learn it, what kind of identity would be assumed by knowing it, what community of practice one might be joining in learning it. (See Eckert and Wenger (1994) for a discussion of the relation of learning and identity; Lave and Wenger (1991) for an argument for the essentially social nature of learning.) In the case of learning a new technology, the learner must make some judgement about what the technology is good for, whether it should be learned, whether the potential learner is the kind of person who is able to master it. As I have discussed elsewhere (Linde 1996), learning within small work groups of the kind studied here includes major negotiations about who will be capable of learning, who will be designated as the resource person or expert in the group, what will the consequence be if someone is not willing or able to learn. For these reasons, a situation of learning is an extremely rich site for the elicitation of evaluations.

Also, evaluation contributes to the larger and very important issue of whether the technology will be enthusiastically adopted, grudgingly adopted or not adopted. These are decisions which are arrived at by a group, and which therefore require group negotiation. However, it must be stressed that this process of group negotiation is by no means the only factor affecting the adoption of a new technology. There are a variety of complex factors determining the introduction of a new technology, including pressures on management to introduce new technologies, pressures on workers to accept management decisions about new technologies, economic influences, etc. Indeed, very frequently the users of a new technology have no influence on the decision to introduce it into the workplace. Nonetheless, this process of users establishing their joint view of the value of the technology being introduced does have an important effect on whether a new technology will be used cheerfully or grudgingly, fully or minimally, with ownership or with sabotage.

5.1 Negotiation of evaluation of technology

Now let us turn to the evaluation of technology. Just as the evaluation of a narrative of a past event must be negotiated, so also must an evaluation of a new and salient feature of the immediate environment.

Example (6) is an interaction focused on a new computer communications technology that the speakers are in the process of learning. The two speakers are attempting to send an electronic fax. They are trying this functionality for the first time, and are not certain how to do it, or whether they have succeeded. They are waiting for an unambiguous indication that the fax has been transmitted.

(6) A: Well, my telephone's hanging up.
B: My little telephone disappeared. My telephone went away. It came back, it's got its little thing, little, little receiver hung up.
A: Um-hm.
B: OK, you should *have* it now. So there's gotta be some way that you can figure out how to print it out. Or, I guess
[
A: Or just to look at it.
B: you want to make a document out of it on your machine, and then print it out. You know, this is gonna be fantastic if this works. This is just going to be ... out of this world. Just like Christina said it was. If we can get it to work.

This is a very clear, if provisional, evaluation of the technology.

5.1.1 *Negotiation of the usefulness of the technology*

In the following example, the two partners in the graphics design firm have been trying to figure out how to send a fax using the new technology. They both agree that the process is time consuming; the discussion turns on whether the wait is better than their previous practice of driving 50 miles between their separate work sites to deliver documents. There is also a diagnostic negotiation about whether the delay is intrinsic to the technology, or a temporary delay caused by the participants' inexperience.

(7) A: Um-hm, I think it's coming. My little machine is buzzing.
((The fax document starts to open on A's screen, and with a short delay on B's screen also.))
A: There ya go! (pause) Okay, can you s—, uh, you can read it I gather.
B: I haven't, no, I haven't got it yet.
(Pause)

B: Yeah, this is just a. this is just kind of a time consuming uh ... I mean it's obviously a lot better than a trip up to Berkeley, right?
A: Uh, yeah, and once you know you have hafta be patient you don't hafta
B: You know, on the other hand (unclear) you could ... and you could take off your fax, call me up, and we could've had this done 10 minutes ago.
A: Yeah, yeah, but it's, you know, the first time is always ... is always
[
B: No, no. I mean in terms of the length of time it takes

The speakers both attend to the length of the delay in transmission. B begins by claiming that although the operation is time consuming, it is still shorter than the time it would take her to bring the document to Berkeley where A lives. A agrees. B then changes position, arguing that she could have sent the document more quickly by conventional fax technology. A argues that the delay is due to the fact that this is the first time they are attempting to use this functionality.

This negotiation ends without a final resolution. The participants make the immediate decision to continue their learning session, but have not yet determined whether the new technology will be worth using once they have learned it. This lack of resolution is possible because this is their first session with the new re-design of the technology and they are not yet certain that they understand it. Thus the negotiation can conclude with a partial but not final agreement.

5.2 Evaluation of self and manual

In example (8), D, the main speaker, is attempting to learn how to send a fax for the first time, and has been having difficulties with it. C, her colleague, who is no more experienced than she is with the technology, has been searching the instruction manual for instructions. D negatively evaluates both herself for being stupid and the manual for being badly organized.

(8) C: '3.3.1 creating a text uh, text file.' ((Reads out loud, then shows manual to D.))
D: Well uh what I'm asking is, how do *I* know being stupid me that I am, just average Joe, that creating a text file is the next step in scanning? It doesn't say anything about scanning. I mean how
[

H: Yeah but it

D: do I know that that go—, that's the next step? It seems like it should say 'Steps for Scanning: A B C D E' instead of like throwing in a new thing saying 'Creating a Graphics File' or whatever.

C: Yeah but I think that's what you have to do. You scan documents and in order=

D: OK but tell me what I'm supposed to do.

This excerpt shows a very strong sequence of evaluations by D. The example forms part of a situation in which she has just requested help from a colleague, and was handed the same piece of documentation that she herself had just been looking at. This can be taken as an implied criticism of her competence. In accordance with this interpretation, she offers an evaluation of herself as stupid, which may be at least partially ironic. But she also offers a criticism of the documentation as not accommodating the average Joe. This is a complex evaluation, a co-construction of the person and her relation to the technology and its supporting documentation.

The extent, or strengths of this evaluation also requires comment, since it is considerably stronger than most of the evaluations in this corpus. It comes at a point when C has given D a repeat of the same information that he had given her before, information which she has already rejected as inadequate. It is possible that her extremely strong evaluation represents a kind of volume increase on her prior response. Such an increase in intensity would presuppose that she, whether stupid or not, average Joe or not, has the right to expect comprehensibility from the manual, and that if she does not find it, she has the right to request assistance from a colleague.

5.3 Evaluation of a functionality

Example (9) is an evaluation that comes after a session of experimenting with the CHAT functionality. CHAT is a real-time text exchange function, also called Conference in some systems. The user types a message, which immediately appears on the addressees' screens. In this example, it is D herself who has initiated the experimentation by saying, 'I want to do the Chat thing'. After learning to use it, and succeeding in a communication session involving much joking, D ends the session with an evaluation.

(9) When would we ever need to use this? If we had laryngitis or something and couldn't talk on the phone?

This is a direct evaluation of the functionality, framed as a joke. (I might note that it seems that all the participants who interact with this functionality seem to find it a rich source of jokes.) In this case, D's joking rejection of the functionality is based on the difference between her computer use and that of the designers of CHAT programs. D turns on her computer occasionally, and must use a modem to use CHAT or other transfer functionalities. Most computer designers have their computers turned on most or all of the time, and work on computers which are hardwired into a network, which does not require them to connect by modem. They are therefore always available for a CHAT session, unlike the participants at both of these test sites, who must either schedule a regular time to be on-line at the same time, or must telephone to ask their colleagues to turn on their computers and modems.

6. RELATION OF LINGUISTIC STRUCTURE AND ACTIVITY STRUCTURE

Having seen the range of types of evaluation of a new technology, let us now consider the relation between the linguistic structure and placement of evaluation, and the structure of the ongoing activity of the interlocutors.

6.1 Evaluation as end marker

One major function of evaluation is to serve as an end marker for a discourse unit, a section of activity, etc. This finding is familiar from studies of narrative and planning (see also Goodwin and Goodwin, 1992). As we have already seen, a speaker cannot end a narrative until there has been agreement on the point of the narrative. One very specific example of evaluation as an end marker is the use of evaluation in agenda management.

In prior work on the management of the agendas of informal meetings (Linde 1991), I have shown that evaluation can serve as a preclosing bid. This work showed that one very common way of ending an agenda item at a meeting is by an evaluation of some feature of the discussion: whether it is the work that has just been done, the plans that have been made or one of the topics discussed. One form of preclosing is an evaluation of the prior discussion.

Rather than continuing the topic, the speaker steps back from it to give an indication of what it means, what its value is, etc. Such evaluations may be simple statements like

(10) Well that's OK.
(11) Good for you. I'm glad that that worked well.

Such evaluative preclosing bids often involve the use of proverbs, aphorisms, etc. Or they may be elaborate and detailed evaluations of the entire topic. In example (12), in discussing a client's desire to repeat his name on every page, the two designers have agreed that three repetitions is enough. Then the participant who is not the designer of this project provides the following evaluation, a summary of the preceding discussion which serves as a preclosing:

(12) In fact, I think you sort of shoot yourself in the foot if you are too obvious.

Evaluation of the technology is a particularly common form of the use of evaluation as a marker of the end of a section of discourse, in this situation in which the novelty of the technology makes it particularly salient. In the following example, the participants have explicitly agreed to close their working session. They end this negotiation with an overall evaluation of the new technology.

(13) A: All right now, are there other things we wanna try here?
B: Uh, lemme tell you something.
A: OK
B: I dunno about you, but I'm getting tired.
A: Yeah.
B: It's been sort of a longish time.
A: OK
B: This is not a bad learning session.
A: No: (unclear)
B: <u>It's a lot of fun</u>, and maybe we're going to uh, experiment some more later or something.
A: <u>OK. It seems like everything's really working very neatly so far</u>.

The discussion of agenda management looked at a particularly high level of structure – design projects that formed the topics of discussion of a work meeting. We also find evaluation as an end marker of smaller units of activity, such as the activity of diagnosing the nature of, and responsibility for, trouble with the technology. Further pursuit of this observation will require a more precise definition of activity units. Whether such a definition is possible will depend on the specific kinds of activity that speakers are engaged in.

6.2 Evaluation as gap filler

Because of the nature of this technology, the data include cases of people working together on the telephone, with large gaps in the interaction introduced by the technology. That is, if one person decides to send another a fax, it can take between one and two minutes for the fax to be received. If the work group needs the document to continue with their work, the technological delay has introduced an unavoidable interactional gap. This is particularly problematic for telephone work, since the co-workers cannot see one another, do not know what the other is doing in the gap, may not be sure that the channel is still open, and cannot put down the phone since they do not know when to pick it up again. One solution to these problems is to fill the gap with talk. One very appropriate kind of talk to put into this gap is evaluation of the technology, since, as we have already seen, evaluation is nearly always relevant. Incidental level evaluation may be placed at most or all points in the discourse. In particular, in these sessions, the technology is relatively new to these users, and hence particularly available for comment.

Example (7) above shows a clear instance of evaluation as gap filler. As we have already seen, the speakers in that situation are waiting for the fax to be transmitted, and for the technology to give them some indication of its state. They begin by discussing the immediate state of their screens and their understanding of what should be done. They then use the evaluation as a further gap filler while waiting for a signal of how to proceed.

7. THE SOCIAL PRACTICE OF EVALUATION

Let us now consider evaluation as a part of the social practice of jointly learning a new technology. It might appear that evaluation is always relevant – a speaker may evaluate any feature of the situation at any time. While this claim is too broad, it points at an important fact about evaluation: evaluation constitutes the social determination of the meanings of one's self, one's actions, and one's environment. This is almost the definition of relevance.[5]

In order to understand the practice of evaluation, an analysis must specify what is evaluated, and how. It also must specify when, if ever, evaluation is not appropriate. For example, the welfare agency members use little or no evaluation in the early stages of the first learning session, even when faced with difficulties and frustrations. They appear to take the position that they will not evaluate the technology until they have learned it. And indeed, the first round of evaluation that they do in this situation is diagnostic – 'Is it our fault, or is it the machine?'

In contrast, the workers at the graphics design firm, who have a great deal more experience with computers, begin a provisional form of evaluation immediately, evaluating how wonderful the technology will be if it does work, as we saw in example (7). In both cases, actual evaluation of the technology does not begin immediately.

In a situation like the evaluation of a new technology, it is also important to understand the effect of evaluation on action. There are at least three levels at which evaluation has an effect.

First, as we have already seen in the case of narrative, speakers must agree on the evaluation of a discourse before they can proceed with that discourse. Disagreement leads either to a focus on the disagreement itself or to a dissolution of the speech situation. Some form of agreement, even if it is only an agreement to disagree, must be reached before the discourse can continue on its initial topic.

Secondly, speakers must also agree on an action to allow the activity to proceed. That is, if an action which requires more than one actor is proposed as being valuable, worth trying, etc., the interlocutors must agree to do it before it can actually get done. This is, of course, a very common case in the learning of a communications technology, since this is a technology which is intended to support group work, and therefore requires group action. That is, it is of no value for one person to try to learn to send a fax by computer if the intended recipients do not agree to learn to retrieve and read it.

Finally, speakers must agree about the value of an artifact to proceed with appropriate group action about adopting, rejecting or modifying that artifact. This is a long-term decision. It is not so much determined by any one interaction, but by the sum of them over a fairly long period. This is a relatively unexplored area and which would merit considerable study.

It would be an unnecessary limitation to consider only the

evaluation of the technology in isolation. In fact, there is a wide range of topics related to the technology for which there is intensive evaluation. These include the technology itself, the nature of the problem, the possible uses of the technology, the relation of the technology to personal and job identity, and social relations and job definitions.

7.1 The technology

This kind of evaluation, which we have already discussed extensively, is a determination of the value of the technology itself.

7.2 The nature of the problem

If a problem arises, it requires a diagnosis that there is a problem where it is most likely to be located, and then, what it is. Frequently, especially for inexperienced users, occurrence of a problem requires them first to determine whether the problem is in the technology or in their own understanding. This can lead to complex and serious discussions of who or what is to blame. Novice users will frequently blame their own lack of understanding rather than the technology. (See Norman (1988) for a discussion of how bad design can lead users to the construction of themselves as incompetent or stupid.) Indeed, some of the novice users in this study appeared to be unaware that bugs in new technologies can be frequent and serious. This led them down long wrong trails of diagnosis, attempting to find what they had done wrong in situations in which the technology itself was at fault.

7.3 Possible uses of the technology

Part of the task of learning a new technology is to understand it well enough to determine its possible uses for current tasks, or its ability to support activities that are not part of current work practices because they are not currently easy enough to do, or are not possible at all. This determination of the possible uses of a new technology is one area where we see a great deal of creativity at work.

7.4 Personal and work identity

The act of evaluating a new technology involves a characterization not only of the technology but also of the person doing the evaluation. It is a serious matter to take an evaluative stance towards a new technology: to claim to like it, dislike it, be able or unable to learn it, to become an expert on it, to outpace or lag behind one's co-workers in learning it. Issues of taste always raise issues of identity. In short, by saying what one likes or dislikes, one says who one is. We see speakers managing these issues as part of their practice of negotiating evaluation.

7.5 Social relations and job definitions

When a new technology is introduced into a workplace, it has the potential to change relations between co-workers, and indeed even the definition of a job itself. For example, if co-workers who previously had the same expertise and job title develop expertise with the new technology at different levels, this produces a change in their relative positions. If someone is unwilling or unable to learn a new technology when use of that technology has become part of that person's job responsibilities, then that person has become deskilled relative to the new definition of the job. All of these possibilities become issues for speakers as they negotiate evaluations: the display of what might be considered merely individual taste in fact has serious consequences for group relations.

8. EFFECTS OF EVALUATION: SOME QUESTIONS

We have discussed evaluation in relation to the microstructure of linguistic and interactional units. This study now allows us to pose a number of important questions for further study at the macro-level.

Do many incidental evaluations add up? That is, what is the cumulative effect of many small evaluations which have not necessarily received a response at the time? Do they contribute to the overall direction of the interaction, or to the long-term fate of a new technology? Answering these questions requires a study of how a new technology is or is not adopted. While adoption studies are relatively common within the study of technology, they are usually aimed at the macro-level of economic and labour forces. These questions can be answered only by a multi-level study of evaluations in interaction, and the ways in which they reinforce or contradict the larger-scale forces which affect adoption or rejection of a technology.

What is the relation of evaluation to action, specifically adoption of the technology? There is a bias in this corpus towards praise of the technology since the subjects know that the designers will see the tapes. In different circumstances, the group learning the new technology may contain an advocate for it, may have all members enthusiastic about the technology before it is introduced, or may have had it forced on them. What effect does each of these configurations have on the nature of evaluation, and ultimately on the nature of adoption?

When does silence mean consent, and when does it mean resistance? (See Scott (1990) for a discussion of the forms of discourses of resistance, including silence, foot dragging, covert criticism and outright rejection.) This question requires an understanding of when response is expected, and hence when absence of response is hearably absent. My hypothesis is that incidental evaluation does not presuppose a response and hence silence means consent. In contrast, constituent level evaluation does presuppose response. This also requires further study.

9. CONCLUSION

This chapter shows that evaluation is a complex phenomenon which stands at the crossroads of linguistic and social structures. Understanding it requires descriptions of the interaction of constraints at multiple levels of structure, including discourse structure, interactional structure and the operational demands of the situation in which the interaction takes place. Doing this shows the possibility of studying the relation of linguistic structure and social practice, and demonstrates one extremely rich site for developing such a model.

NOTES

1. This chapter would not have been possible without the work of my colleagues on the Picasso Project: Christina Allen, John de Vet, Rob de Vogel and Roy Pea. I owe a great debt to the people who consented to be test subjects, and who thus agreed to the triple nuisances of beta testing, videotaping and social scientists. I am also grateful to my colleagues for helpful comments and advice at various stages of this work:

Penny Eckert, Rogers Hall, Brigitte Jordan, Per Linell, Kären Wiekert, Helga Wild and the members of the Institute for Research on Learning's Interaction Analysis Laboratory.

2. See Linde (1981, 1995) for an analysis of discourse studies from the point of view of structural and non-structural descriptions.
3. The specifically evaluative material is underlined.
4. I am grateful to Karin Aronsson for this observation.
5. This discussion refers to the practice of evaluation in American English. There is no reason to believe that such practice is universal. Undoubtedly, languages differ widely in their social practice of evaluation. The comparative study of evaluation as a social practice would be of great value both for linguistics and for the understanding of the range of variation of a social practice.

REFERENCES

Allen, Christina, de Vet, John, de Vogel, Rob, Linde, Charlotte and Pea, Roy (1991) *Picasso Project Final Report*. Institute for Research on Learning Technical Report Series.

Eckert, Penelope and Wenger, Etienne (1994) From School to Work: An Apprenticeship in Institutional Identity. *Working Papers on Learning and Identity* **1**. Institute for Research on Learning.

Goguen, Joseph, Linde, Charlotte and Weiner, James (1983) Reasoning and Natural Explanation, *International Journal of Man-Machine Studies* **18**, 521–59.

Goodwin, Charles (1986) Audience diversity, participation and interpretation, *Text* **6**(3), 283–316.

Goodwin, Charles and Goodwin, Marjorie Harness (1992) Assessments and the Construction of Context, in Alessandro Duranti and Charles Goodwin (eds) *Rethinking Context: Language as an Interactive Phenomenon*. Cambridge University Press, Cambridge, pp. 147–89.

Goodwin, Marjorie Harness (1990) *He-Said-She-Said: Talk as Social Organization among Black Children*. Indiana University Press, Bloomington, IN.

Grimshaw, Allen (1990) *Conflict Talk: Sociolinguistic Investigations of Arguments in Conversations*. Cambridge University Press, Cambridge.

Grudin, Jonathan (1988) Why CSCW Applications Fail: Problems in the Design and Evaluation of Organizational Interfaces. *CSCW 88: Proceedings of the Conference on Computer-Supported Cooperative Work*. ACM SIGCHI and SIGOIS, pp. 85–93.

Labov, William (1972) The Transformation of Experience in Narrative Syntax in William Labov *Language in the Inner City*. University of Pennsylvania Press, Philadelphia.

Lave, Jean and Wenger, Etienne (1991) *Situated Learning: Legitimate Peripheral Participation*. Cambridge University Press, Cambridge.

Linde, Charlotte (1981) The Organization of Discourse, in Timothy Shopen and Joseph Williams (eds) *Style and Variables in English*. Winthrop Publishers, Cambridge, MA.

Linde, Charlotte (1991) What's Next?: The Social and Technological Management of Meetings, *Pragmatics* **1**, 297–351.

Linde, Charlotte (1993) *Life Stories: The Creation of Coherence*. Oxford University Press, Oxford.

Linde, Charlotte (1995) Discourse Analysis, Structuralism and the Analysis of Social Practice, in John Baugh, Crawford Feagin, Gregory Guy and Deborah Schiffrin (eds) *Towards a Social Science of Language: A Festschrift for William Labov*. Longmans, London.

Linde, Charlotte (1996) 'I Don't Wanna Be Computer Literate': Group Construction of Workplace Learning, Institute for Research on Learning Technical Report, Menlo Park, CA.

Linde, Charlotte and Goguen, Joseph (1978) The Structure of Planning Discourse, *Journal of Social and Biological Structures* **1**, 219–51.

Linell, Per and Fredin, Erik (1995) Negotiating Terms in Social Welfare Office Talk, in Alan Firth (ed.) *The Discourse of Negotiation: Studies of Language in the Workplace*. Pergamon Press, Oxford, pp. 299–318.

Markus, Lynne M. and Connolly, Terry (1990) Why CSCW Applications Fail: Problems in the Adoption of Interdependent Work Tools. *CSCW 90: Proceedings of the Conference on Computer-Supported Cooperative Work*. ACM SIGCHI and SIGOIS, pp. 371–80.

Norman, Don (1988) *The Psychology of Everyday Things*. Basic Books, New York.

Polanyi, Livia (1989) *Telling the American Story*. Ablex, Norwood, NJ.

Sacks, Harvey (1992) Lecture 1: Second stories, 'Mm hm'; Story Prefaces; 'Local news'; Tellability, in Harvey Sacks *Lectures on Conversation*, Vol. II, edited by Gail Jefferson. Blackwell, Oxford.

Schiffrin, Deborah (1984) Jewish Argument as Sociability, *Language in Society* **13**, 311–35.

Scott, James C. (1990) *Domination and the Arts of Resistance: Hidden Transcripts*. Yale University Press, New Haven, CT.

NINE

Critical discourse analysis and the study of doctor–patient interaction

Ruth Wodak

1. COMMUNICATION IN INSTITUTIONAL CONTEXTS

1.1 Aims and goals of critical discourse analysis (CDA)

Like other approaches to discourse analysis, critical discourse analysis (see Fairclough and Wodak 1996) studies real, and often extended, instances of social interaction which take a (partially) linguistic form. The critical approach is distinctive in its view of (a) the relationship between language and society, and (b) the relationship between analysis and the practices analysed. Let us take each of these in turn.

CDA sees discourse – language use in speech and writing – as a form of 'social practice'. Describing discourse as a social practice implies a dialectical relationship between a particular discursive event and the situation(s), institution(s) and social structure(s) which frame it: the discursive event both shapes and is shaped by them. That is, discourse is socially constitutive as well as socially conditioned – it constitutes situations, objects of knowledge and the social identities of and relationships between people and groups of people. Discourse is constitutive both in the sense that it helps to sustain and reproduce the social *status quo* and that it contributes to transforming it. Since discourse is so socially consequential, it gives rise to important issues of power. Discursive practices may have major ideological effects; they can help produce and reproduce unequal power relations (between, for instance, social classes, women and men, and ethnic/cultural majorities and minorities) through the ways in which they represent things and position people. As a result, discourse may be racist or sexist and attempt to pass off assumptions (often falsifying ones) about any aspect of social life as common sense. Both the ideological import of particular ways of using language and the relations of power which underlie them are often unclear to people. Critical discourse analysis aims to make more visible these opaque aspects of discourse.

Critical discourse analysis sees itself not as a dispassionate and objective social science, but instead as an engaged and committed one. It is a form of intervention in social practice and social relationships – many analysts are politically active against racism, or as feminists, or within the peace movement, and so forth. But CDA is not an exception to the normal objectivity of social science – social science is inherently tied into politics and formulations of policy. What is distinctive about CDA is that it intervenes both on the side of dominated and oppressed groups and against dominating groups. In addition, it openly declares the emancipatory interests that motivate it. The political interests and uses of social scientific research are usually more covert.

1.2 CDA and the study of institutional discourse

An approach to the study of language and discourse in context (DISCOURSE SOCIOLINGUISTICS)[1] aims to reveal both explicit and implicit rules and power structures in socially important domains. In modern societies these domains are embodied in institutions which are structured in terms of social power relationships and characterized by specific divisions of labour (see Weick 1985; Mumby 1988; Menz 1991). Within institutions, elites (typically consisting of white males) occupy the dominant positions and therefore possess power. They determine what Bourdieu (1979) calls the 'symbolic market' [*symbolischer Markt*], i.e. the value and prestige of symbolic capital (or certain communicative behaviour). This can be seen most readily in the technical registers used by all professional groups (for example, what in lay terms is often referred to as 'legal language' or 'legalese': see Dressler and Wodak 1989), but it also manifests itself less obviously in the form of preferred styles and certain communicative strategies.

Before I try to grasp the relationship between discourse and institutions in a more detailed way, I would like to begin with a definition of institution which I consider to be important. Mumby stresses the notion of 'organizational cultures':

> This approach conceptualizes organizations as cultures in order to examine the ways in which organization members engage in the creation of organizational reality. Such research generally takes organizational

> symbolism – myths, stories, legends, jokes, rites, logos – as the most clearly visible articulation of organizational reality.
>
> (Mumby 1988: 3)

Mumby argues further that most cultural approaches to organization start out with the concept of 'shared meaning' and 'sense-making'. He criticizes rightly that the concept of power is neglected, that – as we can also illustrate in our case studies – meanings are not shared inside the institution. It is quite the contrary: the everyday life of institutions is characterized by conflicts, by disorders in discourse and by contradictions which are mystified through myths and other symbols of the institution (see Wodak 1996).

Power is therefore regarded as a structural phenomenon, a product of and process by which organization members engage in organizing activity. Organizational power is constituted and reproduced through the structure of organizational symbolism. Power manifests itself in hierarchies, in the access to certain discourses and information, and most certainly in the establishment of the symbols: which myths are considered to be relevant, which ideologies, norms and values are posited relates directly to the groups in power and their interests.

The concept of institutions viewed as cultures with an emphasis on discourse and power lends itself very well for our analyses in the following sections. The specific methodology used in our empirical investigations (the inside-perspective) suggests clearly that institutions have their own 'life', their own rules, insider jokes and stories which are narrated over and over again and serve to strengthen the *status quo* (for example, the typical story of how people 'make' it) . By observing the institutions from the inside, by participating in meetings and other rituals or by following the insiders through their everyday life at work, the mixture and intricacy of all these many discourses became apparent.

Institutions thus have their own value systems which are crystallized in the form of specific ideologies. However, it is important to distinguish between the explicit demands and expectations of the official institutional ideology and the implicit rules underlying everyday behaviour. These two sets of norms often lead to contradictions: for example, van Dijk (1993) discusses a study of managers in large companies who claimed in interviews that foreigners had equal chances of employment and that their companies explicitly supported 'affirmative action', whereas in reality foreigners are actively discriminated against and not employed in this company. Yet, these contradictions are disguised by what Barthes (1974) calls 'myths' [*Mythos*], and in this way they are legitimized. Myths, in this sense of the word, are secondary semiotic systems, which both insiders and outsiders are supposed to believe and which mystify reality. A second reality is constructed and naturalized.[2] A particularly striking example of this in medical institutions is the great knowledge that doctors are supposed to possess and their infallibility: the 'gods in white' [*Götter in weiß*] is a common expression in Austrian German. (See section 4.)

One further aspect of the critical analysis of institutions should also be mentioned here. Investigations of the *status quo* should make it possible to devise and propose different communicative practices for those working in the institution (contributing to training programmes, for example), as well as different approaches from the clients' point of view (see Lalouschek et al. 1987; Lalouschek and Nowak 1989). In this respect, sociolinguistic analysis is particularly important, as a purely sociological analysis tends not to make the individual dynamic processes clear enough. Using the discourse analysis approach, we can see the effect of both explicit and implicit institutional rules and norms in virtually every specific discourse, and we can demonstrate how structures are constantly being reproduced in each specific interaction (see Strong 1979; Ehlich and Rehbein 1986).

2. DOCTOR–PATIENT COMMUNICATION

Research into doctor–patient communication has generally been based on one of two approaches: the medical-sociological approach, which focuses on the institution, and the linguistic approach, which deals with the micro-structural aspects of communication. However, the two approaches have rarely been combined in a single study. Aaron Cicourel, one of the founding figures of doctor–patient research, has shown, on the basis of selected interviews, the advantages of a conversation analytical approach, over quantitative psychological investigations (Cicourel 1981, 1985, 1987). He repeatedly insists that any analysis must take account of the structural framework as well as the different interests of the two main protagonists – the doctor and the patient.

Current American research is increasingly limited to the analysis of individual conversational phenomena, for example question–answer sequences and 'accounts'. Since these phenomena are studied in isolation from the context of the complete discourse, they can only be interpreted up to a certain point (see, for example, Frankel 1983; Todd 1983; West 1984, 1990; Bennet 1985; Freeman 1987; Heller and Freeman 1987; Fisher and Groce 1990). Two findings from recent American work are relevant to the present context and are worth drawing attention to here. Alexandra Todd (1983) describes the clash between the institutional world and the lay world as a 'frame conflict': value systems, the structuring of knowledge and traditions all diverge and cause misunderstanding and conflict. One common concrete manifestation of this is the fact that doctors typically want to arrive as quickly as possible at a diagnosis, while patients often want to explain aspects of their biography and would also like to know the implications of their symptoms or illness. Elliot Mishler (1984) shows that even research on communication remains in 'the voice of medicine', so that scientific interpretations are made from the point of view of medical knowledge and the signals coming from the patients are ignored. I shall return to these approaches later in the discussion of our own findings.

The medical-sociological approach which dominated early work in German-speaking countries lacked the necessary linguistic apparatus. At the centre of this research were case histories and conversations during doctors' rounds (see Köhle and Raspe 1982; Strotzka et al. 1984). Current research based on discourse analysis oscillates between two extremes: from a mainly application-oriented approach to an approach which is concerned with the smallest units of discourse without an exact analysis of context (see Spranz-Fogasy 1987; Ehlich et al. 1989). Thomas Bliesener's (1982) study of doctor–patient conversations represents the first relevant attempt at defining a certain subsystem of everyday life in a hospital using discourse analysis. The doctors' rounds are broken down into their various features and phases, and individual problems in the patients' communication are pinpointed. Here again, however, some important sociolinguistic aspects are not brought in: he does not investigate, for example, whether women and men or old and young patients are treated differently. Yet, he does make the important point that communicative problems will not be solved simply by devoting more time to the patients, as the quality of the doctors' approach and of their conversations with patients also needs to be improved.

Within the department of Applied Linguistics in Vienna, we have incorporated many ideas from both the medical-sociological and the linguistic approach and have recently begun research into case interviews (see Hein et al. 1985; Hein and Wodak 1987; Menz 1991; we have also done extensive research on therapeutic discourse, see Wodak 1986). In a study on general practitioners, Norbert Hein (1985) has shown clearly that there are language barriers between doctors and patients that are attributable to social class differences. Patients from a working-class background were treated condescendingly, and even the suggested treatment for the same symptom (insomnia) was different for working-class and middle-class patients: the former were offered drug prescriptions, the latter were referred to psychotherapists. However, in these studies the definition of the discourse unit was again limited to the exploratory interview itself: everyday life at the institution was only touched upon (for further detail on this area, see Wodak 1987, 1996).

In the next part of this chapter, I shall look in some detail at a study that precisely attempts to analyse discourse in the context of the institution as a whole and which should illustrate my critical, discourse-sociolinguistic approach.

3. DISCOURSE AND CONTEXT: A STUDY OF EVERYDAY LIFE IN AN OUTPATIENTS WARD

3.1 Setting and methodology – the context of the institution

All the studies mentioned so far were carried out from the 'outsider's perspective', that is on the basis of certain preconceived assumptions, specific discourses were extracted from the larger institutional setting and analysed in isolation. The sense of context in relation to the institution and to the daily life of the institution is therefore lost. Given this limited knowledge of the context, the interpretations that are made are only partially valid.

Therefore, one of the key objectives of our study of an outpatients ward at a Viennese hospital was to work from the 'insider's perspective' (this concept has been well defined by Habermas (1981), and has had a great impact on field work research design in the social sciences). This entailed observing and recording complete morning sessions as a single discourse unit, and having discussions with doctors and patients both before and after these sessions. On this basis, it was possible to define new, dynamic categories of analysis, which can be taken together with the familiar categories in interpreting the data (see below).

For an understanding of the context, it is important to realize that the outpatients ward has very low status and prestige in relation to the rest of the hospital. It is a type of outpost and, among other things, serves as a training ground for young doctors, which results in inexperienced insiders working where experienced ones are arguably most necessary. Hierarchy, knowledge, experience and gender are interlinked in a strange and unique way in the outpatients ward. Inefficiency, bad organization and bad training are disguised by the propagation of myths (see sections 1 and 4), and stereotypes emerge: doctors never have enough time, they are never wrong, and there is simply no better way of doing things.

Seven morning sessions were covered in detail and 83 individual conversations were recorded. The age of the patients ranged from 17 to 87 and there were roughly the same number of men and women. Five doctors were observed, three women and two men. The institution itself was very cooperative and supportive. However, some problems did arise, especially when doctors became nervous and felt overburdened by the many contradictory demands imposed on them (see Lalouschek et al. 1990 for details).[3]

The following questions provided the basic framework for the study:

- Which elements of the context are relevant in the interactive process? Is the setting, for example, more important than the experience and personality of the doctors, or is the influence of each element different? What typical discourse patterns can be identified?
- According to Pierre Bourdieu (1979: 355ff), the elite define 'right' language behaviour and possess power, thus the language of the elite is 'symbolic capital'. How is this capital 'invested'? How are differences in knowledge expressed in our specific case? Does a frame conflict (see section 2 above) exist in the outpatients ward? How do doctors convey their power? Which 'power registers' can be identified?
- How are the values and myths of the institution expressed? How are the contradictions between expectations and reality dealt

with? Or to put it more bluntly, how do the doctors cope with their everyday professional life?

3.2 Categories for analysis

In dealing with these questions and assumptions, three dynamic categories were found to be important. First, the emergence of 'patient initiatives' (such as asking for information, relating stories, making complaints or judgements) and the ways in which doctors deal with these initiatives (for instance, by answering, interrupting or ignoring them) bring two conflicting elements into play at the same time: the doctors' exercise of power and the patients' voices.

Secondly, we focused on doctors' problem-solving procedures: the specific discursive way in which doctors deal with each problem manifests the assumed contradiction between explicit rules, myths and actual events.

Thirdly, the verbal negotiation and formation of relationships was analysed: each time a relationship is established, fundamental factors of the management of relationships are applied. For example, if a personal relationship is established, then important rituals of politeness are observed, certain forms of address are used, and so on.

3.3 A typical morning session

3.3.1 *The institutional context*

A male and a female doctor are working together during this specific morning session. Both have just been on night shift and are exhausted. The initial phase is quiet. Then at 11 am there is an announcement over the intercom system to the effect that all cars have to be removed from the hospital car park by 1 pm. This announcement causes an outbreak of chaos because it means that the doctors will have to leave the ward at some time during their work.

3.3.2 *Case study 1: The experienced patient*

The first patient is 60 years old and has a stomach complaint. He is to be prepared for an operation which also takes place in the outpatients ward. The problem that the doctor has to solve is one of non-compliance with official procedures: the patient has apparently taken medication on his own initiative. On the basis of Text 1, it is possible to analyse strategies of problem-solving, as well as specific power registers used with an experienced patient. Through an analysis of the macro-strategies, we can identify specific patterns used to cover up a fault in the procedures on the ward which the patient discovers and exploits. At the same time, this discourse is representative of the quiet initial period in which the patients have much more space than at the end of the morning session. It is important for an understanding of the closer context to know that an experienced patient is the subject of this case.

Text 1[4]

11	DM8:	as pills from today
	P:	[Yes – and yesterday you
12	DM8:	[Well, I hope it works – hmm well
	P:	didn't give me any at all.

* * *

31	DM8:	well – but that's always – that's only the Lasix 80 32
	DM8:	you can get that from us – yes AS WELL
33	DM8:	– you know. Or have you also taken
	P:	[I haven't taken any – – no
34	DM8:	an 80 today as well?
	P:	[I haven't had any – till now
35	DM8:	It says here Lasix 80 milligrammes – – as a daily
36	DM8:	dose – – on the chart. Lasix 80 – – yes there was
37	DM8:	a short break. Oh well
	P:	[I didn't get it – I didn't get it till
38	DM8:	mhm
	P:	Dr X (doctor's name) was er down here
39	DM8:	yes
	P:	with me you know. Gave me that er – Novarin. Apart
40	DM8:	[Yes I see – you didn't
	P:	from that I haven't had any powders – (......)
41	DM8:	get them again till today? – – Yesterday was
	P:	Got them
42	DM8:	[very good
	P:	today and YESTERDAY I took one of my own because
43	P:	if you remember – I asked you
44	DM8:	yes that's fine – GOOD –
	P:	(......) that I stopped taking
45	DM8:	fine – you can start taking them again from today –
	P:	those – the powders you know.
46	DM8:	because you don't need any more infusions.

The doctor begins with an indirect accusation: he accuses the patient of having taken a 'Lasix 80' tablet on his own initiative, even though he receives this drug from the ward anyway (lines 31–4). Obviously, the nurses forgot to give the patient the drug, and he fetched it himself. The accusing voice can be detected in the intonation, especially from the emphasis on the words AS WELL. In line 33, the patient tries to justify himself, but the doctor does not allow him to take his turn. It is not until line 34 that the doctor actually pauses, reformulates his question, and then enables the patient in line 37 to take his turn and begin his story. In his account, the patient reminds the doctor that the doctor had personally given him the instruction to take his own tablets (lines 42–3). The doctor tries as early as in line 42 to interrupt by offering praise and positive comment, but the patient continues. In line 44, the doctor finally manages to interrupt the patient, again with praise, and then closes down the discussion ('fine, good'). The doctor's discursive strategy has therefore served two purposes: to cover up the institution's error and to terminate a potentially embarrassing discussion on an apparently positive note. In the final part of the episode, the doctor re-defines reality, prescribes the same medicine again and legitimizes this with new information (lines 45–6). In this way, he resumes his active role in keeping with his position of power.

This episode leads to the doctor being relatively open towards this (experienced) patient in the continued conversation (not quoted here). This encourages the patient to take another initiative by asking: 'What's the next step? Well, at least here in hospital, I mean', to which the doctor replies: 'Well, when we can let you out depends on the condition of your ulcer, and from the surgery wing, which will obviously be soon ...'. The doctor responds in more detail to questions concerning the patient's stay in hospital – a strategy that serves to block any further non-medical questions. So openness and personal relationships are possible, but only up to a certain point: that is, as long as they remain within the frame determined by the doctor.

However, when the patient takes his third initiative and complains again about the ward: 'I was prescribed the Malox, but I never got any. And that's only one example: first of all that ... but now I know already, if you don't ask ...', he is praised ('that's right') but then the doctor abruptly changes the topic and asks: 'So when did you have breathing problems – would you tell me about it?'. The same pattern as in Text 1 is repeated, but here it is much stronger as the experience of the patient becomes a little too threatening. However, the doctor maintains his formal manner and takes his leave politely. A relatively close relationship has been established. There has been no clash between different 'worlds of knowledge', and so the doctor has to work hard to maintain his authority by using several strategies (interruption, rationalization and topic shift). One particularly subtle aspect was the discursive strategy of combining praise and/or a change of topic – a clever 'packaging' of power.

3.3.3 *Case study 2: The inexperienced patient*

The second patient enters the ward at 9.45 am. She is considered a difficult patient because of her age (87). She is not prepared to take off her hospital gown as there are men present. Here there is a real clash between values and generations, coupled with a total lack of experience on the part of the patient. Through the micro-analysis of this case study, it is possible to make explicit the systematic interaction of different aspects of discourse (speech acts, particles, forms of address, socio-phonological realizations) in the process of making the patient adapt to the institution.

Text 2 contains extracts from the beginning, middle and end of the examination.

Text 2

1	DF2:	Right we'll have to take off the gown too
	P:	(......) don't
2	DF2:	Why not? – We are in the hospital you know. Right –
3	DF2:	now then let's sit down here shall we?
	P:	/quietly/ (...)
4	DF2:	RIGHT take off the gown please.
	P:	[Gown – but I've
5	DF2:	[Take if off please – the gown. We've
	P:	got nothing under the gown.
6	DF2:	got to do an ECG. Right No one's
	P:	(......) Gown
7	DF2:	looking – – well – it's only the doctor
8	DF2:	– isn't it. He's allowed
	P:	[The doctor can look – but
9	DF2:	to look isn't he – right let's sit down here
10	DF2:	shall we. exactly
	P:	[Sometimes he even has to look (......)
11	DF2:	Right – tell me, which was the broken arm?

* * *

64 DF2: She keeps wobbling around – NOW JUST LIE STILL
65 DF2: DON'T KEEP WOBBLING AROUND – OR THE ECG WON'T WORK
66 DF2: QUITE STILL – JUST RELAX OK. Good – – right:
P: [All right – yes.
67 DF2: that's fi:ne.

* * *

221 DF2: But she's sore EVERYWHERE – – she's sore
222 DF2: everywhere. DOES IT HURT THERE TOO?
P: Ah: yes /sighs/ (……) no no
223 DF2: Ah, not there – only the back and there it hurts,
P: [it's OK
224 DF2: right? Yes – and there?
P: It hurts there. [Well – I can feel it but
225 DF2: [not too bad.
P: it's bearable.

The doctor makes four attempts to get the patient to take off her gown. The first is in the form of an indirect speech act using a child-like form of address ('we'll have to … ') [*müß ma*] which I refer to as *pluralis hospitalis.* Then the doctor tries to persuade the patient to comply with her wishes by rationalizing the situation ('we *are* in hospital …') [*wir san ja im Spital*], but again without success. After a structuring signal ('right'), the doctor makes a fresh attempt, this time in the form of a polite but firm request ('take off the gown please') [*tun Sie das Hemd bitte ausziehen*], using a more direct but still distant or polite form of address and a socio-phonological switch into standard German articulation (the first forms are typical Viennese dialect). Finally, when the patient still refuses to oblige, the doctor repeats her request ('take it off please, your gown') [*Ziehn's das aus bitte – das Hemd*] – the imperative form indicating the more peremptory nature of this attempt. She reinforces this with a technical explanation, which the patient does not understand. As the patient still fails to remove her gown, the doctor tries to reassure her that no one else is looking other than her (male) colleague (lines 6–7); the particle 'right' [*gell*] is intended both as a concluding signal and a reassurance. The patient begins to give in, although she still does not seem to be totally convinced (line 8). The doctor picks up this more positive sign, echoing the patient's remark that 'the doctor is allowed to look' and switching to dialect, which helps to bring the two closer together. She follows this up with a further request, softened by the reassuring ('OK'/'*gell*'). The patient again repeats 'sometimes he even has to look', as if to convince herself, and the doctor confirms this before changing the topic with the structuring signal 'right'/*so*. Then the actual examination begins.

Later in the examination, the doctor is unable to control her irritation with the patient and begins to shout at her (lines 64–6). This is followed by a direct request, which is realized in standard German [*Jetzt bleibens aber ruhig liegen*]. Four more demands follow before she resumes a calmer, reassuring tone (line 67). The final section of the discourse (from line 221) is polite and gentle, and the patient is more subdued. The patient is the subject of the discourse but is referred to in the third person singular (line 221). This is a common pattern, but it causes a lot of uncertainty among patients since it is not clear who is actually meant. Only the use of a direct question (line 222) makes it clear that, at that point, it is the patient herself who is being referred to and that a response is required. Finally, the patient concedes that 'it's bearable': a sign that she has, at last, adapted to the institutional frame.

The doctor's manner with the patient ranges from a gentle approach through stiff formality and impatience to harsh authority. These changes are indicated by the character of the various requests (direct and indirect), the different forms of address, and the switches in socio-phonological style. The patient is provided with very little in the way of discursive orientation other than the particles 'OK', 'right', etc., which are used to express reassurance and as structuring signals (beginning or concluding topics). There appears to be a clear correlation between these indicators and certain patterns seem to emerge: for example, indirectness of request is associated with *pluralis hospitalis*, the use of dialect and certain particles.

The doctor's behaviour is a form of exercising power, but it also reflects a conflict that is caused by a number of factors. It is her first professional conversation with a patient that is being recorded. The patient is considered 'difficult', as her 'uncooperative' behaviour slows the examination down, and the doctor has great difficulty in dispelling the patient's fears. Because the case is therefore seen as a disruption of the normal routine, it conflicts with institutional expectations. As a result, no close personal relationship is established between doctor and patient. Helpful explanations and information are not forthcoming precisely when they are most needed, and even when the doctor does attempt a more personal approach, it is characterized by child-like language and *pluralis hospitalis.* This only serves to reinforce the difference in power and the patient's assumed mental inferiority. The frame conflict and the language barriers separating the two participants render cooperative face-to-face communication virtually impossible and, in the end, the patient falls silent.

3.3.4 The disruptive case history

The following patient is treated for the first time by the hospital, i.e. she was not sent by an inpatients ward, but went direct to the hospital and was sent to the outpatients ward by the doctor on duty. The patient is 30 years old, female, from former Yugoslavia, speaks very good German, and has experience of hospitals (since she has already been in hospital and has had colostomy operations). The reason for her hospital visit is a feverish infection which has persisted for some time and bronchitis. In the course of this examination, several disruptions occur which turn the quiet morning into chaos and render the doctors helpless.

1st Disruption

The senior doctor enters the outpatients ward. The male doctor DM8 has been waiting for him in order to discuss the many 'interesting cases'. The senior doctor, however, is 'taken over' (lines 12 and 13) immediately by the outpatient nurse (S1) who needs him for the ergometry, his actual job. Initially, she wants him at first to finish the examination which has just begun (line 12). DM8 is visibly disappointed about this course of events ('allright then' (line 14)).

	DM8:	/phones/ senior doctor – – you
10	S1:	[right – I need]
		/SD enters/
	DM8:	[We've got a few discussions]
11	S1:	the senior doctor.
	DM8:	now
	DF2:	[o.k. let's talk about it – let's talk about it
12	S1:	(Let's
	DM8:	Do the ergometry then
13	S1:	do the ergometry first of all.
	DM8:	[Allright then (……)
14	S1:	We've still got four ergometries to do.

Two other disruptions occur afterwards: bad emergency cases

and unexpected tasks may occur and the number of patients can never be calculated beforehand. The doctor, who had not been expecting such cases, has to alter her expectations of a peaceful morning session. Then, the senior doctor comes in again and takes away the good blood pressure gauge without the doctor, who is doing the examination, noticing. He thereby disrupts the course of the examination and underlines at the same time his position of power.

Following this third disruption there is a problematic conversation between the two doctors (fourth disruption): since the beginning of the examination DM8 has been on the phone to a senior doctor of another ward about the diabetes check-up of the previous patient and has noted down the results as well as the therapeutic instructions without informing DF2. He has therefore taken over the medically relevant, and therefore the interesting tasks – i.e. takes notes of the difficult results, makes detailed phone calls to the senior doctor – without including the other doctor in his actions.

5th Disruption

For the first time DM8 comes in on the examination which is being done by DF2. A misunderstanding occurs between him and the patient since the patient has come as a result of her lung condition and not, as DM8 assumes, because of intestinal complaint.

190 DM8: Yeah, but why is she coming to us – now
[Yes, for an
191 DF2: assessment
P: [because I've still got a temperature – and
192 DM8: [Yes, but, I mean, you know – you were –
P: I can't
193 DM8: you're sure, aren't you – in which department
194 DM8: were you?
P: [What's that got to do with the colostomy bag
195 DM8: No no – that's what I'm saying – look, that's –
196 DM8: difficult of course. Ah – diarrhoea – antibiotics of
197 DM8: course – it all plays a role somewhere
P: [I'm not here because of
198 DM8: [Yes, because of your temperature
P: diarrhoea – I've had diarrhoea since yesterday
199 DF2: [temperature and your
P: but my temperature – temperature I've had anyway
200 DF2: lung condition
P: That's got nothing to do with (......).

DM8 is impatient and wants to postpone this examination which, in his opinion, does not belong in the outpatients ward and just holds up the work, i.e. causes an additional disruption. He signalizes distance by not talking WITH the patient but instead talking ABOUT her ('Yeah, but why is she coming to us – now' (line 190)) and standing next to her without having acknowledged her. (Concerning the problem of talking ABOUT the patient, see case study 2.). A sequence of accusations based on the previous misunderstanding then takes place:

206	DM8:	Mainly because of the lung condition at first
207	DM8:	I thought – the diarrhoea is not so predominant –
208	DF2:	[yeah, well – probably both
	DM8:	that's what you told me; drug resistant diarrhoea
209	DF2:	No, I didn't actually say that – you
210	DF2:	read it. So far I haven't said anything to you about
	DM8:	[well:? – I heard it – as I was on the
211	DF2:	diarrhoea
	DM8:	telephone – it was about diarrhoea
212	DF2:	[I didn't ask her then at all

6th Disruption

The intercom announcement, already mentioned, interrupts the emotionally loaded situation. The reaction to this disruption which burdens the whole outpatients ward, becomes increasingly dramatic. While DM8 removes blood from a patient, he has time to consider the consequences of the intercom request:

309	DM8:	/to P/ can you move the watch away a bit – – – Oh no
310	DM8:	and I've got my course at one o'clock – I don't
311	DM8:	think I've been at the course for three weeks
312	DM8	[And now the car again – where
	DF2:	Hey perhaps we could go there earlier
313	DM8:	should I put it
	DF2:	[Okay, we'll just leave it there
314	DM8:	mmh – there's one. – Is there a thinner one than
315	DM8:	the black one – is the green no the yellow one thinner?

The threatening character of the situation is transferred to the waiting patients and to the whole outpatients ward. Every event, which so far was quite normal, is now seen only in the light of its potential as a burden or a disruption. The event becomes emotional. The illness reports of the patients still waiting to be examined, which so far have remained untouched regardless of the order in which they were collected, suddenly become 'still to be looked at yet'. The number of these patients, which – considering the length of the previous examinations – has never played an important role so far, now becomes a threat: 'How many are there still to come?' The daily routine of the outpatients ward, i.e. that a large number of patients have to be seen within a particular period of time, is perceived as a complete surprise for the doctors and as a considerable affront. This behaviour leads to the whole situation becoming uncontrollable: the burden becomes even heavier than it already is, and any action which might bring about a solution to the situation is prevented.

The final stage of this morning session thus becomes hectic and full of tension, the examinations are significantly shorter, and follow-up discussions are abandoned altogether. Approaches from patients are ignored and a general sense of distance between patients and staff prevails. In the penultimate examination an ECG is refused, even though the patient really ought to have one, as the machine does not work straight away. In the end, the doctor only appears to be concerned with his hunger, and says: 'I'm going to die if I don't get something to eat soon ... '.

3.4 Summary

The texts with their descriptions and analyses were able to show clearly how the external situation influences the (verbal) behaviour of the doctors with their patients as well as with each other. It could also be seen how interruptions, disruptions and burdens are directly transported into the conversation and are simply left there, unprocessed, since the disharmony, emotionally or cognitively – the so-called 'routine chaos' – is not accepted either. The incompatibility of contingency plans is apparent, leaving internal and external factors alone to define the conversation. A more meaningful approach to the disruption, such as perceiving it as routine and part of everyday life, as well as rejecting the 'myth of harmony', would reduce the internal pressure on the personnel and would enable a more flexible approach to the whole situation.

During quiet relaxed periods such as the beginning of the morning session, the doctors are also relaxed and friendly with the patients: the conversations last on average 16 minutes, as do the post-examination discussions and those among the doctors themselves.

The doctors respond to questions and requests for an explanation from the patients – even if the answers are not always 'patient-orientated' – and sometimes the doctor goes beyond simply answering the questions.

As soon as a disrupting and interrupting incident occurs, which in this particular morning session happens to be during a somewhat complicated examination, there is a sudden change in the verbal behaviour of the doctors: the patient discussions become much shorter (on average nine minutes). There are no more complex explanations of the results, nor are there any post-examination discussions. Patients' initiatives are either not requested or are interrupted. It is noticeable that the number of patients' initiatives is minimal. The tense situation is clearly felt and has a direct effect on the verbal behaviour of the patient, just as the relaxed atmosphere of the early morning session virtually prompted patients' initiatives. The uncooperative and problematic patients more than the others are treated differently by the doctors and are accused implicitly of causing additional disruption and burden in the outpatients ward.

The results of this morning session, when taken as an example, are typical and can be applied generally to events in the outpatients ward. Many of the burdening factors, such as the unpredictability of many events or parallels between the examination and the training situation, can be easily recognized through their disfunctionality and can be corrected by implementing suitable organizational methods. However, there is not even a hint of chance there; indeed, the institutional insiders often contribute themselves to an increase in the already overloaded burden. It would therefore be appropriate to ask which behavioural strategies, which expectations and which patterns of interpretation of the institutional members contribute to the contradictions being seen as meaningful and desirable, i.e. that the disfunctionality becomes 'functionalized'.

4. THE MYTHS OF THE OUTPATIENTS WARD

4.1 The functionalizing of contradictions

The previous descriptions and analyses have indicated that these outpatients discussions are highly complex processes, a continual juxtaposition of several actions of equal and subordinate importance.

Examination, treatment, advice, teaching, learning, organization, reorganization and telephone calls all take place at the same time. Shift doctors, senior doctors, professors, head doctors, senior nurses, outpatient nurses, ward nurses, trainee nurses, orderlies, porters, ambulance personnel, service personnel and, finally, patients keep coming and going. Treatments and examinations take place one after the other almost without a break.

These overlapping and contradictory processes and functions lead inevitably to contradictions, a burdening of roles, and to role conflicts between those involved. The creation of myths is one strategy to cover up and hide these internal contradictions. These myths serve to give the contradictions a function which stabilizes the system and maintains the outpatients ward as an institution. In addition, they enable the members of the institution to give meaning to the contradictory role expectations and role conflicts, apparently overcoming them. The following passages show some of the strategies, behavioural patterns and expectations of the institutional insiders which support these myths.

4.2 The myth of the undisturbed, predictable process

The outpatients ward is a highly contingent domain. The course of events is unpredictable due to the many interruptions and disturbances, such as acute emergencies, priority patients, the squeezing-in of patients, and the occurrence of single, unexpected events (intercom announcements, the absence of personnel, machines breaking down). There is a high degree of uncertainty.

One strategy of coming to terms with the instability of the system is expecting the processes to be predictable and uniform, e.g. the examination event. Those involved in the examination perceive the ideal, NORMAL process of, e.g. a patient being prepared for an operation, as the following:

- the patient is called in (by the doctor or nurse)
- the patient takes off his/her vest and lies down on the bed
- one of the two doctors does the examination
- the patient puts his/her clothes back on and returns to the ward
- the examining doctor dictates the results to the other doctor and discusses them with him/her, or the examining doctor writes the results him/herself.
- the next patient is called in

This kind of examination process is, however, a rare exception. The REAL process of an examination as it happened in the ward in question is very different:

- the nurse calls in the patient
- the patient removes his vest and lies down on the bed
- DM8 enters and discusses the results of a previous patient with DF2
- DM8 calls for the patient's medical history
- the patient is greeted
- DF2 begins the examination
- there are no results about P
- DM8 looks for nose drops
- third doctor enters and asks DF2 about another patient, DF2 answers and continues with the examination
- the nurse brings an X-ray of an earlier patient to be checked over
- the ECG has to be repeated since it was not correctly in position
- the results are not in order
- the telephone rings, the nurse answers the call
- the orderly enters in order to take a patient for an operation
- DM8 leaves to fetch the senior doctor
- DF2, P and the orderly wait
- DM8 returns, the senior doctor is busy
- the nurse calls DM8 to the telephone: another patient should be slipped in
- DF2 listens to P with the stethoscope
- a taxi driver knocks on the door and looks for a patient
- two porters announce the patient who was slipped in by telephone
- DM8 dictates the results to DF2
- DM8 leaves again to fetch the senior doctor
- DF2 tells P about the waiting time
- the nurse is on the telephone
- DM8 and the senior doctor enter
- technical discussion between DM8, DF2 and the SD
- the telephone rings, the nurse answers the call
- a patient enters and looks for registration
- the professor enters, talks with the SD and takes the patient with him
- DF2 and DM8 finish writing the results.

The 'normal' process is therefore not quiet, uniform and undisturbed, but rather is characterized by disruptions, is uncertain and constantly in the flux of change. The everyday life in the out-patients ward is a continuous juxtaposition and confusion of different actions and discussions. The disrupted process could trenchantly be described as the normal process. As long as the out-patients doctors and nurses do not accept that most of the disruptions and interruptions are part of the normal routine and that an undisturbed, quiet examination represents an exception to the rule, then they will have to interpret every disruption as an affront and will feel potentially overburdened. Due to their idealized expectations, they are completely at the mercy of the situation and can only come to terms with it through dismissive comments and grumbling.

44	DM8:	ok – they're making me rush around like crazy

* * *

65	DM8:	oh: well: I thought it was …
	DF2:	[yeah, yeah – you have to
66	DM8:	[yeah, yeah, everything – you
	DF2:	get it all wrong, don't you
67	DM8:	have to do everything all at the same time
	DF2:	[three things
68	DM8:	[that's the great thing with us
	DF2:	all at the same time

In moments of overburden, the collective grumbling about the situation, the wards or about people in higher positions seem to have the function of relief and solidarity.

4.3 The myth of efficiency

The interruption, that is the disruption of the examination taking place, is therefore an overriding characteristic of all discussions. These interruptions are caused, on the one hand, by outside events such as telephone calls, intercom announcements or through people entering (doctors, nurses, orderlies, patients, etc.) and, on the other hand, by the doctors themselves: during the examination of a patient, test results of previous patients are discussed, telephone calls are made, there are people leaving the room and people gossiping with doctors who enter the room. Many of the interruptions are necessary and form part of the outpatients routine (outside telephone calls, giving priority to emergency cases, waiting for the senior doctor regarding difficult decisions), yet other interruptions could be avoided. One thing is quite clear: efficient work is impossible under these conditions; anger, disappointment and dissatisfaction are automatic reactions.

One of the ways in which the doctors themselves contribute to the lack of effectiveness due to apparently efficient actions is by discussing the results of previous patients in the presence of the patient being currently examined. This so-called time-saving concurrent event regularly causes further disruptions. This gives rise to confused conversations, misinterpretation and misunderstanding for those patients present since they normally do not have the technical medical knowledge, nor do they know about this habit, which might help them to understand the utterances which only apply to them.

4.4 The myth of time

All disruptions, interruptions and unpredictable events add to the pressure on the staff and their overburdened activity which is already obvious due to the doctors' implicitly contradictory double role of the examiner, i.e. of the expert, and of the pupil. At the same time, this overburden and the constant pressure of time for the members of the outpatients ward have the function of proving the meaning and necessity of the action. After all, the role cliché exists of the doctor who is constantly on call and thus permanently under pressure of time, and who corresponds to the 'prophylactic emergency behaviour'.

One paradox of the tense, pressurized outpatients situation is the time spent waiting for the senior doctor: if, during the examination, the results point to the official clearance for operation or a discharge being questioned, then the senior doctor must be called upon to make a decision; and this means – as in the following case – that everyone must wait for the senior doctor.

110 DF2: Mhmm – so if you think that there's only
/to DM8/
111 DF2: ONE result here – – then you're wrong
DM8: [yes well – – well please
112 DF2: [yes right –
DM8: send him to X (name of senior doctor)

Doctors and nurses, in accordance with the myths of time, efficiency, and predictability of the process, begin to bridge the waiting time with various tasks (sorting card index, heading results sheets), or they start looking for the senior doctor. Only the patient, who was not informed, is unclear about why he must continue to lie half-naked and why, suddenly, the focus of general interest has turned away from him. After a few minutes of waiting he begins to explain the situation for himself:

337 P: Can I put my clothes on again?
DF2: [No, you've still got to wait
338 DF2: a little for the senior doctor – you know – because
339 DF2: we said your ECG was negative – – and you're anaemic
340 DF2: ok.

Although it is late, the long-awaited explanation follows from the doctor. This leads us to the question of how and to what degree the patients and doctors experience the situation differently and to what extent the institutional insiders consider it necessary to inform institutional outsiders about the processes and events.

4.5 The myth of the collective knowledge – the reality of the insiders and outsiders

The complex process of the outpatients ward is daily routine for the insiders of the institution, i.e. the doctors and the orderly staff. They are familiar with the procedures and know their way around the complicated network of the various tasks, people, hierarchies, and the areas of responsibility of the institution. Those who are least familiar with the procedures are, in fact, the patients without whom there would be no outpatients ward. It is normally impossible for the patients to penetrate the complex process, to find their place within these processes, to interpret the procedures correctly and to understand their meaning and purpose. Previous studies of doctor–patient communication show quite clearly that a lack of information for the patient is a part of this type of communication, a lack of information about current procedures and future action, about the illness, technical expressions, results, or about therapy. The fundamental lack of information for the patients often reaches the point where they are not aware of why they are in an outpatients ward at all, what will happen to them or when, why and what the operation is, etc.

1 P: This is an examination, isn't it,
DM8: [An examination, yes:

2 P: for an operation – yes
DM8: [well, well not quite – here it says
3 P: [yes –
DM8: that you've already HAD an operation another
4 P: [I don't know
DM8: operation [you see – I don't know
5 DM8: either – nothing here about it.

Apart from the lack of technical medical knowledge, the patients, if they do not have much experience of hospitals, i.e. a certain measure of 'insider-knowledge', do not have the complex knowledge of the doctors and nurses about the routine procedure of the examination, nor do they know that interruptions and the overlapping of actions and discussions are part of the normal process and that in most cases during their presence in the room only part of the actual event refers to them.

It is noticeable in the discussions examined by us that the doctors never explicitly told the patients when the focus of the conversation was changing, i.e. when the examination was interrupted. This very frequently leads to misunderstandings: the patients react to statements not directed at them; they associate the results of previous patients with themselves and become unsettled; they attach the wrong importance to a question which, due to the interruptions and confusion of various actions, is inadvertently asked more than once; and they thus become unsettled. The verbal routines of the doctors and nurses, with whose help the patients come to terms with the interruptions and changes of issue, are so minimal owing to their daily familiarity with the situation, that they can scarcely offer help to outsiders to cope with the situation. The inability of the institutional insiders to see trouble spots ('organizational blindness') in their own organization often reaches the extent that they forget that, in many cases, when patients enter the room they are probably encountering a completely new situation, or at least one which they do not encounter every day and where they have no complex routines to help them assimilate and find their way in the organization (see, for example, case study 2).

The provision of necessary information during the examination would help the patients to become more cooperative and to understand the examination. Thus, the prevention of unnecessary misunderstandings and disruptions would be a first step on the way to really producing effective action and easing the shortage of time.

5. PERSPECTIVES

Life on the outpatients ward is stressful, the more so when institutional routines are disrupted. As this study shows, it is the 'difficult' patients who are typically held responsible for these disruptions, even when the disruptions are not caused by them, as in the morning we described above: the scapegoat is sought and found outside the ward and not within the structure of the hospital. The clients become the external enemy, the institution protects itself and functionalizes its contradictions. Only an exact analysis of the context, an understanding of everyday life in the institution, and the sequential analysis of the discourses permit a full interpretation of events and the discovery of contradictions and of the ways in which power is exercised. Since what should not be, is not permitted to be, myths and rationalizations are kept alive, this means that any form of reflexion and the possibility of change are excluded. However, the particular study discussed here has shown how applied sociolinguistic research can be beneficial in precisely these circumstances, as it provided the basis for a successful seminar programme on improving communication. The results were quite impressive. The most important consequence of such training was a qualitative change in attitude, in viewing the patient as a partner and person, and not merely as an object.

NOTES

1. Discourse sociolinguistics is one school in CDA (see Fairclough and Wodak 1996; Wodak 1996).
2. 'Man sieht, daß im Mythos zwei semiologische Systeme enthalten sind, von denen eines im Verhältnis zum anderen verschoben ist: ein linguistisches System, die Sprache [...], die ich *Objektsprache* nenne – weil sie die Sprache ist, deren sich der Mythos bedient, um sein eigenes System zu errichten – und der Mythos selbst, den ich *Metasprache* nenne, weil er eine zweite Sprache darstellt, *in der* man von der ersten spricht'. (Barthes 1974: 93).
3. Every morning, there were two doctors present. The doctors stay in the outpatients ward for two months. Every month, one new doctor is integrated, so that a doctor with one months experience always works with a new doctor. They are all young, having just finished their studies. The room itself is very small, 9 square metres, and often about 12 people were inside this small room, which made the chaos even larger.

4. *Transcription symbols*

DM	male doctor
DF	female doctor
P	patient
(......)	inaudible passage
–	break in intonation
– –	short pause
/sighs/ (e.g.)	non-verbal feature
a: (e.g.)	long vowel
YOU (e.g.)	word spoken with emphasis
.	falling intonation
?	question intonation
[	simultaneous speech

REFERENCES

Ammon, Ulrich, Dittmar, Norbert, Mattheier, Klaus (eds) (1987) *Sociolinguistics – Soziolinguistik.* De Gruyter, Amsterdam.

Barthes, Roland (1974) *Mythen des Alltags.* Suhrkamp, Frankfurt/Main.

Bennet, Alexander E. (ed.) (1985) *Communication Between Doctors and Patients.* Oxford University Press, Oxford.

Bliesener, Thomas (1982) *Die Visite – ein verhinderter Dialog.* Narr, Tübingen.

Bourdieu, Pierre (1979) *Entwurf einer Theorie der Praxis.* Suhrkamp, Frankfurt/Main.

Cicourel, Aaron V. (1981) Language and Medicine. In Ferguson, C. and Heath, S. B. (eds) 403–30.

Cicourel, Aaron V. (1985) Doctor–Patient Discourse. In van Dijk, T. A. Vol. **4**, 193–202.

Cicourel, Aaron V. (1987) Cognitive and Organizational Aspects of Medical Diagnostic Reasoning, *Discourse Processes* **10**, 347–67.

Dressler, Wolfgang U. and Wodak, Ruth (eds) (1989) *Fachsprache und Kommunikation.* Österreichischer Bundesverlag, Vienna.

Ehlich, Konrad and Rehbein, Jochen (1986) *Muster und Institution.* Narr, Tübingen.

Ehlich, Konrad, Koerfer, Armin, Redder, Angelika and Weingarten, Rolf (eds) (1989) *Medizinische und therapeutische Kommunikation.* Westdeutscher Verlag, Opladen.

Fairclough, Norman and Wodak, Ruth (1996) Critical Discourse Analysis. In van Dijk, T. A. (ed.) *Discourse Studies. A Multidisciplinary Introduction* vol. 2 Discourse as *Social Interaction.* Sage Publications, London/ Newbury Park, CA.

Ferguson, Charles and Heath, Shirley Brice (eds) (1981) *Language in the*

USA. Cambridge University Press, Cambridge.

Fisher, Susan and Groce, S. B. (1990) Accounting Practices in Medical Interviews, *Language in Society* **19**, 225–50.

Fisher, Susan and Todd, Alexandra D. (eds) (1983) *The Social Organization of Doctor-Patient Communication.* Center for Applied Linguistics, Washington, DC.

Frankel, Richard (1983) The Laying on of Hands: Aspects of the Organization of Gaze, Touch, and Talk in a Medical Encounter. In Fisher, S. and Todd, A. D. (eds) 19–54.

Freeman, Susan H. (1987) Organizational Constraints as Communicative Variables in Bureaucratic Medical Settings: A Case Study of Patient-initiated Referral Talk in Independent Practice Association-affiliated Practices, *Discourse Processes* **10**, 385–400.

Freeman, Susan H. and Heller, Martha S. (eds) (1987) Medical Discourse, *Text* **7**, 1. Special issue.

Habermas, Jürgen (1981) *Theorie des kommunikativen Handelns.* Suhrkamp, Frankfurt/Main.

Hein, Norbert (1985) *Gespräche beim praktischen Arzt.* MA thesis, University of Vienna.

Hein, Norbert and Wodak, Ruth (1987) Medical Interviews in Internal Medicine, *Text* **7**, 37–66.

Hein, Norbert, Hoffmann-Richter, Ulricke, Lalouschek, Johanna, Nowak, Peter and Wodak, Ruth (1985) Kommunikation zwischen Arzt und Patient, *Wiener Linguistische Gazette* Beiheft 4.

Heller, Martha and Freeman, Susan (1987) First Encounters – The Role of Communication in the Medical Intake Process, *Discourse Processes* **10**, 369–84.

Köhle, Karl and Raspe, Hans (eds) (1982) *Das Gespräch während der ärztlichen Visite.* Urban und Schwarzenberg, Munich.

Lalouschek, Johanna and Nowak, Peter (1989) Insider–Outsider: Die Kommunikationsbarrieren der medizinischen Fachsprache. In Dressler, W. U. and Wodak, R. (eds) 6–18.

Lalouschek, Johanna, Menz, Florian, Nowak, Peter and Wodak, Ruth (1987) *Konzept einer Gesprächsausbildung für Ärzte.* Unpublished manuscript, Vienna.

Lalouschek, Johanna, Menz, Florian and Wodak, Ruth (1990) *Alltag in der Ambulanz.* Narr, Tübingen.

Menz, Florian (1991) *Der geheime Dialog.* P. Lang, Bern.

Mishler, Elliot G. (1984) *The Discourse of Medicine. Dialectics in Medical Interviews.* Norwood, NJ, Ablex.

Mumby, Denis K. (1988) Communication and Power in Organizations: Discourse, Ideology and Domination. Norwood, NJ, Ablex.

Spranz-Fogasy, Thomas (1987) Alternativen der Gesprächseröffnung im ärztlichen Gespräch, *Zeitschrift für Dialektologie und Linguistik* **15**(3), 293–302.

Strong, Peter M. (1979) *The Ceremonial Order of the Clinic: Parents, Doctors, and Medical Bureaucracies.* Routledge and Kegan Paul, London.

Strotzka, Hans, Pelikan, Jürgen and Krajic, Karl (eds) (1984) *Welche Ärzte brauchen wir? Medizinstudium und Ärzteausbildung in Österreich.* Facultasverlag, Vienna.

Todd, Alexandra (1983) A Diagnosis of Doctor–Patient Discourse in the Prescription of Contraception. In Fisher, S. and Todd, A. (eds) 159–88.

van Dijk, Teun (ed.) (1985) *Handbook of Discourse Analysis.* Academic Press, New York.

van Dijk, Teun (1993) *Discourse and Elite Racism.* Sage, London.

Weick, Karl (1985) *Der Prozeß des Organisierens.* Suhrkamp, Frankfurt/Main.

West, Candace (1984) *Routine Complications. Troubles with Talk Between Doctors and Patients.* Indiana University Press, Bloomington, IN.

West, Candace (1990) Not Just 'Doctors' Orders': Directive-response Sequences in Patients' Visits to Women and Men Physicians, *Discourse and Society* **1**(1), 85–112.

Wodak, Ruth (1986) *Language Behavior in Therapy Groups.* University of California Press, Berkeley, CA.

Wodak, Ruth (1987) Kommunikation in Institutionen. In Ammon, U., Dittmar, N. and Mattheier, K. (eds) 800–20.

Wodak, Ruth (1996) *Disorders of Discourse.* Longman, London.

TEN

Intertextuality and interdiscursivity in the discourse of alternative dispute resolution

Christopher N. Candlin and Yon Maley

Our concern in this chapter is with a relatively new and still developing professional discourse that is associated with the social practice of mediation, in common law countries like the United Kingdom, the United States of America, Canada and Australia. As a form of dispute resolution in which a third party functions as a go-between to help disputing parties reach a settlement, mediation is proving a very adaptable social practice. It would appear that anything that can be disputed and litigated can now be mediated in either a public, i.e. court annexed, or in a private context. In the light of this popularity and adaptability, we believe it of interest to pursue here the extent to which it is possible to speak of the discourse of mediation as a discrete social and linguistic phenomenon, and, further, to explore and reveal the extent to which the emerging discourse of mediation can be said to draw creatively upon other related and more established professions with their associated discourses. We shall, then, in what follows, set out what we take to be the essential or core forms of mediator discourse. We shall argue that despite these core features, which are defining of mediation, a good deal of internal variation and complexity is apparent in mediator practice and discourse. We shall then explore the nature and extent of this internal heterogeneity, and in doing so we shall draw upon insights which derive from current discourse analysts in intertextuality and interdiscursivity (Foucault 1984; Fairclough 1992). The evidence and illustration for our discussion and analysis are derived from a corpus of real-language data, i.e. transcriptions from tape-recorded and video-taped mediation sessions in divorce and custody matters, in three Australian cities – Sydney, Brisbane and Melbourne.[1]

DISCOURSES AND INTERTEXTUALITY

'Discourse' is often used to refer to connected language in general, a generalization or abstraction which is realized in specific pieces of connected and coherent language, or texts. Discourse in this sense is no more than stretches of connected spoken or written language, 'a view that takes into account the fact that language patterns exist across stretches of text' (McCarthy and Carter 1994: 1). But since stretches of language can hardly be analysed without consideration of the context or social situation in which they occur and on which any interpretation of their meaning depends, then more commonly discourse refers to language *in use*. Thus Brown and Yule comment:

> While some linguists may concentrate on determining the formal properties of a language, the discourse analyst is committed to an investigation of what the language is used for.
>
> (1983: 1)

The distinction between discourse and text, then, becomes a variety of process/product distinction, bearing in mind that the process is always viewed as a socially situated process. Here there are overlaps with other linguistic theories or frameworks, in particular those which are concerned with 'genres' (Swales 1990; Bhatia 1993) or 'registers' (Halliday and Hasan 1985) as functionally and situationally differentiated varieties or styles of language. Sometimes these terms can be used interchangeably, for example, in referring to courtroom language as a register, a genre or a discourse type (Fairclough 1992: 5).

In this chapter, we refer to discourse in a sense which is in no way in conflict with these socially oriented approaches to language use. However, following social theorists like Foucault (1984) and Fairclough (1992), we stress the dynamic and constructive role of either spoken or written discourse in structuring areas of knowledge and the social and institutional practices which are associated with them. A discourse is a way of talking about and acting upon the world which both constructs and is constructed by a set of social practices. Because it is individuals who use discourse, the discourse analyst looks for ways in which the lexico-grammatical, semantic and textual-discursive (in the sense of creating and packaging coherent discourse) options available to and chosen by individuals serve to construct, reinforce, perhaps question, social roles and social behaviour. In addition, describing and explaining a discourse in this way involves hypothesizing the semantic and linguistic exclusions, the meanings that are unwelcome and non-functional in such a context. The exclusions are part of a system of constraints, extra-linguistic, social motives for selecting or rejecting linguistic elements or discursive patterns in the construction of a discourse.

Since discourses are inherently part of social behaviour, they are also inherently cultural. Merry, in her study of legal consciousness displayed in mediation and lower court programmes in the United States of America, further explains:

> Discourses are aspects of culture, interconnected vocabularies and systems of meaning located in the social world. A discourse is not individual and idiosyncratic but part of a shared cultural world. Discourses are rooted in particular institutions and embody their culture. Actors operate within a structure of available discourses. However, within that structure there is space for creativity and actors define and frame their problems within one or another discourse.
>
> (Merry 1990: 110)

We believe that in the exercise of this creativity and problem-framing, discourses draw upon the resources of other discourses associated with other social practices. This process is most likely to occur when, as Foucault suggests (1984: 134), functional correlations across discourses suggest the value of incorporating linguistic elements of various kinds from one text type to another or from one socially situated discourse type to another. Discourses are made internally variable by the incorporation of such *intertextual* and *interdiscursive* elements. Such evolving discourses are thus intertextual in that they manifest a plurality of text sources. However, in so far as any characteristic text evokes a particular discoursal value, in that it is associated with some institutional and social meaning, such evolving discourses are at the same time interdiscursive.

In employing in this context the term 'intertextuality' we refer especially to Fairclough (1992), where Kristeva's (1986) use of the term in reference to the work of Bakhtin is appropriated and extended in the service of an explanation of the connections to be made between discoursal and social change. By intertextuality is meant an inherent property of text where, following Bakhtin (1986), each utterance is a link in a chain of speech communication, or following Kristeva (1986), how texts contain within themselves evidences of the histories of other texts. In short, the argument is that all texts are in some sense intertextual, requiring a Foucaultian archaeology to uncover and explicate how it is that they comprise parts of other texts 'marked off ... and in which the text may assimilate, contradict an echo'. More central to this chapter, however, is Fairclough's convincing illustration of how intertextuality is more than a stylistic phenomenon. On his argument, the study of intertextuality is important for the understanding of social change, in particular revelatory of how, in institutions where orders of discourse are unstable, consisting of internally heterogeneous discursive practices whose boundaries are in flux, this intertextuality becomes integrated into the complex discourse of such institutions as productive interdiscursivity. In such a way, not only are novel (inter)texts constructed, but novel (inter)discourses arise, representing new and as yet not fully stable orders of discourse. Exploring such innovative discourse permits, as here in the context of mediation, the parallel exploration of the innovative social.

MEDIATION AS SOCIAL PRACTICE

Mediation is not, of course, a new phenomenon; it is well known in antiquity and in other cultures (Maine 1875; Hoebel 1964; Gulliver 1979). Evolutionary studies of courts often follow a developmental paradigm and place mediation before courts on time and sociolegal dimensions. On this perspective, 'Mediation precedes courts in time; courts come later and are more formal than mediation bodies' (Friedmann 1953: 13). Weber, for example, considering the evolution of legal systems, drew a picture of 'khadi' justice or dispute settlement, that is informal (charismatic) justice applied by a third party, as a forerunner of the development of what he called 'rational' justice (Rheinstein 1954). However, as writers such as Yngvesson and Mather (1983) point out, the forms of mediation in other, less 'developed' cultures are, and have always been, quite varied, and the borderline between mediation and adjudication, with or without a formal court system, is often quite difficult to draw (Philips 1990; Maley, in press). One point which does emerge clearly from the anthropological studies is that the form of mediation (or third-party intervention in disputes) available in a society or culture is always integral with that society in the sense that it must be seen in relation to other kinds of social structure and roles in the particular society, especially those which support it and give it shape. So Hoebel, in his study of the Ashanti, remarks:

'Whenever mediation is an effective institutional device it has its informal cultural machinery to make it effective' (1964: 16).

Yngvesson and Mather, after discarding the developmental paradigm as inaccurate and simplistic, also argue for an approach to the description and analysis of dispute resolution procedures in both modern and tribal societies that depends on key features of the social and cultural context, i.e. the kind of setting or arena, the use of specialized or unspecialized language, and the degree and kind of organizational complexity (Yngvesson and Mather 1983: 66). In short, dispute resolution procedures available within a society are created from and depend upon a complex of culturally specific, contextual features.

The mediation that is currently available in the USA, Canada, the UK and Australia does not precede court systems in time, in the sense of being left over or vestigial from earlier times. It is a mid and late twentieth-century development. However, like the forms of dispute resolution in so-called 'tribal' societies, it is grounded in and supported by existing social conditions, structures and informal machineries (to borrow Hoebel's term). In these societies, mediation is one of a group of systems of dispute resolution which function quite purposefully and explicitly as an alternative or an addition (Street 1992) to the formal court systems. Mediation, arbitration, conciliation and negotiation are the best known and most widely used of these alternative forms; they have developed as a response to the need for a diversity of systems of dispute resolution within and between complex, industrialized and pluralistic societies.

The driving forces behind the development of mediation as a form of alternative dispute resolution and thus a distinct form of social and institutional practice have been both practical and ideological. The commonly advanced practical rationale for mediation is based upon its claim to be cheaper, faster and simpler than formal court processes that have tended to become prohibitively expensive and increasingly arcane and inaccessible to the layperson. This ideology of mediation builds upon a revulsion to and rejection of the asymmetries of power that such processes realize; instead the literature of mediation stresses notions of accessibility and empowerment. Despite a diversity of frequently competing models of mediation, which we shall be considering later in this chapter, the underlying philosophy and ideology of mediation displays 'singular unanimity' (Silbey and Merry 1986: 8; Adler et al. 1988):

> To settle disputes by providing mutually agreeable solutions provided by the parties themselves; to arrive at settlements through discussion moderated by a third party who has no legitimate power to render a decision or enforce an agreement; to create agreement based upon shared obligations and behavioural change rather than to articulate competing interests and rights.
>
> (Adler et al. 1988: 334)

MEDIATION AS DISCOURSE

The interactions which constitute the mediation process are themselves discursive interactions. Language constructs the process and offers evidence of the strongly articulated ideology which underlies the process. As an example, Text 1 below shows how a mediator explains the way in which this ideology is worked out in the actual process of mediation.

Text 1

MEDIATOR: We do ask that you come and respect each other ... um ... we will have great respect for you, we wont sit in judgment on you and we will be neutral ... so, we don't know you, there's no bias on our part to start with ... um ... we certainly wont be judging either of you. We ask you to have that kind of respect for each other. We also ask you to come here in good faith. ... So that's what mediation is. Are there any questions?

2 MINUTES LATER

When the mediators ask you what your position is, or what you want, they'll want to know what those underlying needs and interests are of yours. You might say that one thing would work for you ... or you might say what you want from others. ... In case of conflict, we would ask you, What would be an option for you?

(F8: Exc)

We note here the informality of tenor (Halliday and Hasan 1985: 26) adopted by the mediator, an important aspect of the 'alternativeness' of mediation as a form of dispute resolution. Tenor, or the relationship between the participants in an exchange (Halliday and Hasan 1985: 26), is realized by interpersonal meanings in the discourse: here, first person pronominal choice and everyday conversational lexis reduce social distance and also, pragmatically, mitigate the imposition of a request. The ground rules of the mediation are expressed as one person asking, not even requesting, cooperation ('we ask you to come in good faith') from another. We may, however, also note, with Bogoch (1994) in the context of lawyer–client interaction, and generally following Habermas's (1984) explanation of how the private sphere increasingly colonizes the public, that this informality does not infringe the claimed authority of the mediator to set out the ground rules of the interaction. What it does do is express quite explicitly what is by far the strongest theme or motif in our Australian data, that of the desirability of consensual agreement and an eschewal of overt conflict. Mediation constructs and is constructed by a discourse of wants, needs, interests and options, and not, as law, by a discourse of rights and obligations. It should be noted here, however, that several recent studies have expressed reservations about mediators' claimed impartiality and the possibility or impossibility of reaching truly consensual agreement (Dingwall 1988; Greatbatch and Dingwall 1989); nonetheless, on this point the expressed ideology of mediators, referred to by Silbey and Merry (1986), and Adler et al. (1988), is unshakeable.

Text 2 provides an example of mediators establishing an environment of choice for the disputant:

Text 2

MEDIATOR 1: Coming back to the property itself, Louise, would you like to tell Alfred what you think would be a fair thing as far as you concerned. You remember that last time you told us that you needed security, and financial security for the future.

WIFE: (cries) … I'm paying the rent, the mortgage, the rates and the school fees …

MEDIATOR 1: So you feel the whole financial burden at the moment is on your shoulders?

WIFE: (Continues itemizing her expenses)

MEDIATOR 2: Alfred, you've heard what Louise has to say. Have you any comments at all on that? How do you feel about her having the house? On what conditions will you give her the house?

HUSBAND: I give her the house.

MEDIATOR 2: Just so I understand what you're saying, Alfred, you'd be content to sign the house over to Louise?

HUSBAND: Yes …

(The discussion continues indecisively for a few minutes)

MEDIATOR 1: Alfred, Alfred, we wont actually say if its a good or a bad option, OK?

HUSBAND: No, no, I don't know …

MEDIATOR 1: You'll decide what's the best option for both of you.

(Discussion about the repair of the roof of the property follows)
MEDIATOR 1: We're talking about the future now. Let's not get bogged down in details.
MEDIATOR 2: Is that what you both think is fair? Louise? Alfred, I get the feeling that you're not very happy ...

(MG3: Exc)

In Text 2, a number of core features of mediator talk – what might be termed the characteristic mediator voice – are present. The mediators summarize and check information received from the disputants. They probe the feelings of the disputants and seek to establish viable options. They deny responsibility themselves for decision-making, yet control turn-taking and decisively steer the exchanges away from unprofitable lines of discussion ('Let's not get bogged down in details'). They seek to establish a forward, not backward perspective for the disputants. They employ one of the most common mediator strategies – a reformulation of the disputant's previous contribution which aims to reframe it, in the sense of influencing the disputant's perceptions of the subject matter. 'So you feel the whole financial burden is on your shoulders?' is a reformulation, a more general and abstract rendering, of the wife's contribution which seeks confirmation, not information. In seeking confirmation of a different version of what the wife has said, the mediator attempts both to empathize with the wife and at the same time identify and isolate an 'issue' or 'concern' which can be later discussed and, it is hoped, resolved. Again the tenor of Text 2 is personal, other-directed and frequently tentative. Personal names, pronouns and modalizations are part of the common currency of mediator talk.

As Foucault (1984) has suggested, discourses are as noteworthy for what they exclude, as for what they include. The exclusions of mediator discourse are few, but in a very real sense criterial. A mediator who employs the voice of blame, or of obligation, cannot truly be said to be mediating. Blame is, or should be, irrelevant to the mediator's role. Perhaps the most important exclusion, however, is that which, as many studies have suggested, distinguishes mediation from adjudication. Decision-making and rule-making are the powers that define the judge's role; their absence defines the mediator's role and hence mediator discourse (Gulliver 1979: 209).

Within such constraints, mediators have available to them a wide range of linguistic forms and discursive strategies as a potential – a set of members' resources on which individual mediators draw and which they use to build up a repertoire that reflects and reinforces the institutional, and within that the contextual/situational requirements of the mediation process. Mediators operate within a particular pragmatic space. In this sense, we recall Bourdieu's approach to discourse as capital (1982, 1991) and Foucault's reference to 'the internal economy of a discourse' (1984: 134).

We turn now to the question of the constitution of the members' resources, i.e. the internal resources of the mediator economy. In determining how they have been built up, we are, in terms of our earlier discussion, exploring the nature and scope of intertextuality and interdiscursivity in mediator discourse.

INTERTEXTUALITY AND INTERDISCURSIVITY

In the above section we have argued that there is an identifiable core of linguistic practices which comprise mediator discourse. Moreover, we have argued that the discourse of mediation is both pragmatically and ideologically driven. The task of the mediator is to move disputants to a certain kind of settlement – consensual, compromising, centred on needs – in a certain kind of way – non-confrontational, non-adversarial – using a structured analytical process. But the impetus to mediation and indeed, the professional workforce from which mediators tend to be drawn, has been dominated by two contrasting and often competing sets of professional practices and ideologies. In the sense of this chapter, they constitute associated, yet competing discourses, those of the law and of the social sciences, particularly counselling and therapy (Fineman 1988; Adler et al. 1988). This complex and critical positioning of mediation in relation to the social practices of adjudication and counselling provides a classic example of interdiscursivity (Fairclough 1992) and also enables a clearer discourse-mediated perspective on a profession whose professional and institutional identity is in the process of being shaped.

MODELLING THE DISCOURSAL COMPLEX OF MEDIATION

The professional literature on mediation recognizes the variation that exists in mediation process and techniques (although it is significant that this variation is always seen as a difference in process and technique, not a difference in discourse). A number of oppositions or different 'styles' of mediation have been proposed. In the literature of mediation, these styles are said to differ on two dimensions: the degree of intervention and the type of intervention. Thus some writers place mediators on a scale or line between 'passive ' and 'interventionist' (Marlow 1987; Gulliver 1979), in which the polar distinction is drawn between a mediator who says very little, but throws the discussion open to the disputants and leaves them to create their own options and solutions and the interventionist who, in contrast, enters actively into both the option-creating and the negotiating process and actively tries to keep the peace between the disputants. More often, however, degree of intervention is seen to correspond, at least broadly, with types of intervention, or styles of intervention in the sense of a *way* of intervening. In this sense, the most common characterization of styles of intervention is that of an opposition between the 'bargaining' and the 'therapeutic'. So Silbey and Merry, working on data from US court-based and community mediation programmes, propose 'two ideal types of mediation style: the bargaining and the therapeutic' (1986: 20). They explain that

> ... the bargaining style tends more towards structured process and towards more overt control of proceedings. In the bargaining style, mediators use more private caucuses with disputants, direct discussion more and encourage less direct disputant communication than in the therapeutic style.
>
> (Silbey and Merry 1986: 20)

They compare this with the therapeutic style in which

> the parties are encouraged to engage in a full expression of their feelings and attitudes. Here mediators claim authority based on expertise in managing personal relationships and describe the purpose of mediation as an effort to help people reach mutual understanding through collective agreements ... a single mediator usually uses both styles to some extent, and a single mediation session has some elements of each style.
>
> (Ibid.: 19ff)

Broadly, the conclusions from our Australian data support those of Silbey and Merry. As anthropologists and social scientists, however, their interest is naturally primarily on the social practices of mediation. Our interest, however, is translating these generalizations about the social practices of mediation into a broader picture of the discourse, or better, discourses of mediation, where the social and discursive practices are taken to be mutually defining. In particular, we are interested in showing how what is called either *bargaining* or *therapeutic* in terms of social practice can be seen as the incorporation and transformation of intertextual and interdiscursive elements into the bank or capital of the mediator economy, to use the analogy suggested above. From this perspective, a complex picture emerges of the building of a set of professional discursive practices to be drawn upon according to the particular institutional environment in which it is used. What matters most is not the individual style of the mediator (although that factor also carries weight), but institutional, structural and ideological factors. If we think of these factors as constituting sectors within the bank or economy of the profession, then members will draw upon these resources of the discourse according to the preferences and imperatives of their sector.

In exploring this further, we may account for this intertextuality and interdiscursivity in terms of what is, for Goffman, a shift of 'footing' (1974, 1981) as the mediator moves for a segment of the mediation from, say, acting as a leader/negotiator to a facilitator/therapist or vice versa. At each shift of footing, discursive practices which predominate in this particular institutional arena are replaced by ones more typical of other arenas. However, it is important, in our view, *not* to see these as borrowings or insertions (as the classic literature on intertextuality might characterize them), but as a utilization of what, in this particular organization, is a relatively rarely deployed resource taken from the common capital of the professional discourse. The new voices revalue the old, creating a *new* construct. This is entirely in harmony with Fairclough's concept of interdiscursivity where conventional elements from particular orders of discourse are drawn upon, creatively evidencing the emergence of new orders of discourse which may then themselves be taken as evidence for social and institutional change.

INTERTEXTUALITY AND INTERDISCURSIVITY IN MEDIATOR DISCOURSE

The concept of intertextuality and interdiscursivity outlined above is one that is indicated and supported by our data. Our chief focus will be on interdiscursivity, which, as we have indicated earlier, we take to be the use of elements in one discourse and social practice which carry institutional and social meanings from other discourses and social practices. These data also indicate that we need to identify three separate aspects of, and questions about, intertextuality and interdiscursivity for the purpose of textual analysis.

1. The nature and source of the intertextual and interdiscursive elements in the professional discourse as a whole.
   'What are these elements? Where do they come from?'
2. The particular internal mix of interdiscursive elements within particular institutional arenas.
   'How do mediators use these elements in that particular professional, institutional context?'
3. The absorption and transformation of interdiscursive elements and their significance within a novel discourse type.
   'What is their value in mediator discourse?'

In the texts that follow, we shall attempt to show how these three intertwined aspects of intertextuality and interdiscursivity are realized in mediation practice.

Text 3

MEDIATOR: I heard you say too earlier Ted ... I don't quite know if this is how you put it ... but you wanted to take the kids out of the middle of the argument.

FATHER: Yeah ... I just looked through this book ... 75% of things they say you should avoid is probably happening at the moment to our kids.

MEDIATOR: It ... just to normalise things ... It probably also happens in 75% of cases as well, you know, we parents, we have the best intentions but ... you do get caught up in the middle and the important thing is that you both be very aware that it's happening and you want to stop it ...].

FATHER: [Yeah ...

MEDIATOR: ... and that's the first big thing ...

(MGI: Exc)

In this excerpt from a mediation with a divorced couple on the matter of custody and access for their two children, the mediator's interventions take on the character of therapeutic discourse. The mediator opens the topic (her prerogative as mediator) by paraphrasing something the father had said earlier (... 'I don't know if this is how you put it ... '). This opening is a preface to the advice on parenting which she then offers ('It probably also happens in

75% of cases as well, you know, we parents, ... '), advice which would not be out of place in a counselling interview. Strictly speaking, mediators are not in the business of offering advice; to do so goes very much against the strong principle that the mediation process should empower the parties and leave them to make their own judgements and decisions. However, in our data on counselling matters in particular, the distinction between mediation and counselling can be difficult to retain. It is easy to see why this would be so. If the mediator pays attention to the feelings and needs of the parties that are creating problems and preventing a settlement, then it becomes difficult to avoid suggesting a course of action that will alleviate those problems. A similar difficulty surrounds the discourse of family planning counsellors as the study by Candlin and Lucas (1985) makes clear.

Given this dilemma, the mediator's strategy in this particular exchange is to generalize, to make her comments seem like a reflection on the world in general rather than on the parties before her. So she begins by commenting on what happens in about '75% of cases', a factual statement of what is normal in good or bad parenting. Lest this generalization seem too impersonal, she then includes herself within the class of parents who have problems with parenting, by using the inclusive pronoun in 'we parents', followed by the general and inclusive 'you do get caught up' (i.e. people in general as well as herself and the parties before her). Having made these general and inclusive statements about parenting, which are only indirectly advisory, she then slides into direct advice by employing a more selective meaning of 'you', i.e. 'the important thing is that you both be very aware'. The mediator goes on to reinforce the frame of good parenting that she has established by a nominalized generalization, 'the first big thing'. The point here, it seems to us, is that the mediator's careful expression of advice reveals an attempt to incorporate a strategy from another, related professional arena and discourse, adapting it to the requirements of a different ideological orientation. It is interdiscursive.

In Texts 1, 2 and 3, the prevailing ideology of mediation is expressed and applied in a hybrid discourse which, as we have shown, owes much to the discourse of counselling and therapy. Its orientation is personal, concerned with feelings and needs. The strategies used to bring the disputants to settlement include advice-giving (Text 3) and the reformulations which attempt to reframe the disputants' perceptions of the issue and the other parties in the dispute (Text 2). Since many mediators, particularly in divorce and family mediation, are also trained social workers, such interdiscursivity is perhaps not surprising.

In the texts that follow, we display mediations in which the discourse has legal intertextuality and interdiscursivity. Text 4 performs the same function in the mediation process as did Text 1. It is the opening preamble or framing of the mediator and expresses very much the same ideology and constructs very much the same process as did Text 1. But here the mediator is also a lawyer, a lawyer with training in mediation skills.

Text 4

There are a few ground rules for the purpose of this conference, I'll briefly outline those ... ground rules. Firstly, there are no interruptions ... there's no verbal abuse or intimidating behaviour on either side during the course of the ... conference ... is that understood by everyone? If one person is speaking ... it's not necessary for one or the other of you to interrupt or interject ... everyone will get ample opportunity to say what they want to say, O.K. Now the conference is 'without prejudice', that means that ... anything said in this conference by either of you, or your respective legal adviser can't be used in any subsequent court proceedings, can't be used in any correspondence, or in any other matter. You understand ... what 'without prejudice' means? Are you happy for the conference to proceed on that basis?

(BLA3: Exc)

Text 4 provides an example of mediatory discourse at the boundary of legal discourse, that is to say it is as close to legal discourse as our earlier texts are to therapeutic. Consequently, just as Texts 1, 2 and 3 exhibited therapeutic intertextuality, Text 4 incorporates and manifests legal intertextuality. In Text 1, the mediator's introduction, stresses the need for mutual respect and consensual problem-solving. Text 4 begins in a similar way by stressing the desirability of consensual agreement, but as the mediator proceeds, the tenor becomes more formal and impersonal than that of Text 1. The statement 'There's no verbal abuse or intimidating behaviour' makes a rule of what was presented by the mediator in Text 1 as a request: 'We ask that you have the same kind of respect for each other.' The functional correlation between legal rule-giving and mediator rule-giving, as here, provides an example of interdiscursivity. Lexical items and phrases like 'verbal abuse', 'intimidating behaviour', 'interject', 'ample opportunity' introduce a formal tenor with legal resonances; and there is manifest intertextuality in the use of the lawyer's phrase 'without prejudice' and as such it also resonates interdiscursively in relation to legal practice.

In Text 5, reproduced below, a young female lawyer is mediating in a property settlement, again in a legal aid office. In this particular model of mediation (which is sometimes called a pre-litigation conference) each party is represented by his or her lawyer, a system which has the intended advantage of giving each party a professional bargainer in the negotiation process, who will safeguard the client's legal rights and ensure that the power balance between the parties is in equilibrium. It is hard to say whether the addition of lawyers as professional negotiators makes the mediator's task easier or more difficult, as the text below shows.

Text 5

LAWYER 2: The other point is on the question of settlement and this is strictly on a without prejudice basis, my client *won't* agree that the house be taken to a valuer. What she'd like to do is, that the house be listed for sale at a price of $160,000, but ... if a reasonable offer is obtained and she consents to it, then ... she'll allow the property to be sold. In effect, she wants, she wants to have some control over either the price or the property.

MEDIATOR: But Tom, yeah, what time period are we talking about?

LAWYER 2: She doesn't want a time period, she just wants it listed for sale like it is now ...

MEDIATOR: Tom, that's not adequate, hasn't it been listed for sale for two years?

WIFE: No, it hasn't.

MEDIATOR: Well, how long has it been listed for sale?

WIFE: Karen, can I just interrupt?

MEDIATOR: Yeah, go ahead.

WIFE: (Explains reason for not listing the house.)

MEDIATOR: OK, but what I'm saying that I'm concerned about is that ... let's just say six months go by and it hasn't been sold, how long do you want it to drag on for? Now I think it's really important that you have some kind of process in place without everyone, you know, the agreement breaking down and everybody having to come back together again, everybody is clear about the mechanism that's going to be used, so that it can get solved. Now one idea, is the one that ... I suggested about getting a valuer after a period of time to value it, and then relist it. You don't have to use the same one, you can use a different one, but I think it's important that everybody go away with some certainty about what's going to happen after today.

WIFE: (Argues about the role of the valuer.)

LAWYER 2: I reckon then we'll leave it the way it is.

MEDIATOR: Tom, there's got to be some mechanism.
LAWYER 2: ... the mechanism's there.
MEDIATOR: It's not good enough.

(BLA1: Exc)

Here the mediator appears at times to be almost a partner in the negotiations, rather than simply a facilitator of other people's negotiations, as 'received' mediator theory prescribes. Her contributions are evaluative, argumentative and controlling. She comments unfavourably on the lawyer's suggestion ('that's not adequate', 'It's not good enough'); she steers them towards decisions ('I think it's really important ... ') and she pushes her own suggestions ('Now one idea, is the one that ... I suggested ...). In all this she acts more as a negotiating lawyer herself (albeit an impartial one), than as a helpful but non-interventionist facilitator. No doubt because she is interacting as much with other lawyers as with the parties, her contributions are *of the same kind* as legal bargaining and negotiating as it occurs in lawyer–lawyer interactions or in judicial interventions in some courts of law, for example in arbitration or conciliation matters. They are again examples of the interdiscursivity we have been referring to throughout. The point we would first want to make here on the role of such interdiscursivity in building discourse, is not that the mediator is acting like a lawyer, but that her lawyer-like contributions are a valid component of mediator discourse in this setting. Suggesting, arguing, negotiating are discourse strategies aimed to bring parties to settlement. In this setting, with these interactants, they resonate interdiscursively with the discourse of the law.

Secondly, lawyer-like though these strategies may appear in this segment of the mediation, their value (in the Saussurean sense) to the total discourse has to be seen within the particular institutional arena and in relation to the discourse elements or components of the mediation. The value of a linguistic or discoursal element is the meaning it carries within a system of paradigmatically related elements. Within the context of mediation, evaluations and suggestions do not necessarily have the same value in the sense of the same meaning or rhetorical function as they do in the context of the law. Their value is conditioned by the pragmatic space they occupy within the particular context. Here in the pragmatic space of mediation, the parties participate voluntarily (although in this case there is strong financial incentive for them to do so) and the mediator's role, though influential and in some instances quite powerful, can be no more than persuasive. Certainly, it is less persuasive than a similar contribution from a judge in a court of law would be, or even advice from counsel in the conduct of a law suit. Another way of saying this is that in law, evaluating, suggesting, negotiating may combine or contrast (de Saussure 1959) with deciding or rule-making as a paradigmatic set of legal functions. In the context of mediation, the option of deciding or rule-making is not available as a mediatory function; we would say it is an 'exclusion' of the Foucaultian kind (1984). Evaluating, suggesting, negotiating are paradigmatically related to other functions and related strategies which have interdiscursive relationships with counselling and therapy.

Texts 6 and 7 exemplify clearly how intertextual elements from different social practices and different discourses combine interdiscursively in the new or host hybrid social practice and discourse. The texts are taken from the same mediation session as Text 5, above, with the same mediator and participants. In Text 6 discussion is continuing about the disposition and sale of the marital home:

Text 6

HUSBAND (Darren): Well, why do you want to lock it in for 12 months, why are you suggesting that ...]

LAWYER 1: [She's *not* trying to lock it in for 12, months, you are, you're trying to leave it open]

MEDIATOR: [OK, just let's, just let Darren and Julie talk because I think they might actually get somewhere. Keep going.

HUSBAND: (turning to mediator) I think ... we'd be better off]

MEDIATOR: [Yeah, well, talk to *her*, talk to *her*.

(BLAl: Exc)

The mediator intervenes in this text to control turn-taking, preventing the lawyers from taking a turn and selecting the husband and wife disputants as speakers. Exercising control of process through turn-taking is a powerful strategy for mediators: in this case it allows the mediator, Karen, to facilitate communication between the disputing parties and perhaps set up an improved personal relationship. The aim of improving personal relationships derives not from law – which usually exacerbates them – but builds upon the interpersonal focus of social practices like counselling and therapy, and to that extent is once more functioning interdiscursively.

And, in this case, the mediator's strategy works. The husband and wife talk, the lawyers keep quiet, the mediator intervenes only to check and clarify, and a settlement is reached. Text 7 is a segment of talk at the very end of the session, as it begins to wind up.

Text 7

HUSBAND (Darren): Can I just get one thing?
MEDIATOR: Yeah!
HUSBAND: Julie, can I have your sister's phone number please?
WIFE (Julie): Yes, it's a new one, so I'll give it to you ... I mean Darren, I would be willing to talk to you if I felt as though you would be courteous to me on the phone
HUSBAND: Julie, I don't know why, you could have saved yourself thousands of dollars.
MEDIATOR: Well, Darren, maybe that's not very helpful, may be ...
WIFE: See, that's not the attitude.
MEDIATOR: OK, hold on, maybe what Julie's saying to you is that she'd like to make an effort to deal with you directly, but she wants to know that you try and be patient.
HUSBAND: I would, yeah
MEDIATOR: How about you say that to her?
HUSBAND: Yes! What am I going to say to you, what are you scared about?
WIFE: Because you threatened me before, Darren ...
HUSBAND: Threatened you, how, Julie?
MEDIATOR: Now, look, stop. I don't think this is the time or place to go into the history, or asking questions. What I'm asking you is if you're prepared to say to Julie, that you would like to deal with her directly and you're prepared to be patient.
HUSBAND: Yes, I would, because it would save a lot of time and money.

(BLAI: Exc)

In this text, the previously lawyer-like mediator becomes very counsellor-like. Her explicit aim in this segment is to set up a basis for a cordial relationship between the disputing husband and wife. To this end, she gently chides Darren for not being helpful ('Darren, maybe that's not very helpful ... '), she reformulates Julie's offer in slightly more favourable terms. Julie's rather grudging 'willing to talk' is reformulated as 'she'd like to make an effort to deal with you directly', and again she urges direct communication ('how about you say that to her ...?'). These reformulations are manifestly intertextual. As we mentioned earlier, Fairclough's point is that all dialogue is in various ways intertextual since each turn in some way builds upon the turn before. In reformulations (what

Fairclough calls 'discourse representation' (1992: 118)), the intertextual links are made explicit. However, no two utterances can ever be identical; we have argued elsewhere (Candlin and Maley 1994) that all reformulation involves semantic change on three dimensions which, following Halliday and Hasan (1985), we have identified as the ideational, the interpersonal and the textual. The mediator's reformulation attempts to effect an interpersonal reframing of the disputants' perception of their relationship by an ideational alteration (from 'willing' to 'like to make an effort') and which carries favourable interpersonal meanings of cooperation and good will. The substitution of 'patient' for 'courteous' in her reformulation appears to make less of an imposition upon Darren's face; it is both an ideational and an interpersonal alteration. So, as Foucault and Bahktin have suggested, intertextuality involves the absorption and transformation of elements in new textual contexts.

CONCLUSION

We have argued throughout this chapter for an approach to the description and explanation of mediator discourse which conceptualizes it as a reservoir of members' resources, functioning rather as an economy to be drawn upon. Many of these resources are intertextual and interdiscursive in character. Overwhelmingly, these intertextual elements work interdiscursively as they exhibit links with professional discoursal practices in law, counselling and therapy; at the same time, they are indisputably mediatory in character in their new professional and institutional arena. The advantage of regarding mediator discourse as a resource or as an economy is that it enables us to explain the undoubted variety and heterogeneity that exist *within* mediator discourse. There is a considerable tension still within the profession as to the correct role and weight of both legal and therapeutic intertextuality and interdiscursivity within their professional practice. All would probably agree that it is undesirable for mediator practice to incorporate either legal or therapeutic practice overwhelmingly, or without modification and transformation. Getting the right mix is the concern. It will always be the case that non-institutional mediation concerned with sorting out personal problems rather than legal rights and issues will lean more to the therapeutic. In such cases it is to be expected that the dominant meanings will be interpersonal. On the other hand, mediation in commercial or industrial matters will lean more to the negotiation of rights and duties. Ideational meanings will be dominant. We need to be able to account for the dynamics of regularity and exclusion that define the discourse type and also to be able to account for the variation that occurs depending on the institutional site and particular model of mediation that is being applied. Our argument is that this can best be done by identifying the particular mix of intertextual elements and explaining their interdiscursivity in relation to the particular site and model of practice in question.

NOTE

1. The research on which this chapter is based has been funded by Australian Commonwealth Government grants: an Australian Research Council grant on *Varieties of Arbitral Discourse,* and a National Centre for English Language Teaching and Research grant on *Interethnic Communication and Dispute Resolution.*

REFERENCES

Adler, P., Lovaas, K. and Milner, N. (1988) The Ideologies of Mediation: The Movement's Own Story. *Law and Policy* **10**(4): 317–19.

Bakhtin, M. (1986) *Speech Genres and Other Late Essays.* C. Emerson and M. Holquist (eds), trans. V. W. McGee. Austin, University of Texas Press.

Bhatia, V. J. (1993) *Analysing Genre. Language Use in Professional Settings.* London, Longman.

Bogoch, B. (1994) Power, Distance and Solidarity: Models of Professional–Client Interaction in an Israeli Legal Aid Setting. *Discourse and Society* **5**, 65–88.

Bourdieu, P. (1982) *Ceque parler veut dire: l'économie des échanges linguistiques.* Paris, Fayard.

—— (1991) *Language and Symbolic Power.* Cambridge, Polity Press.

Brown, G. and Yule, G. (1983) *Discourse Analysis.* Cambridge, Cambridge University Press.

Candlin, C. N. and Lucas, J. (1985) Interpretations and Explanations in Discourse: Modes of 'Advising' in Family Planning, in T. Ensink, A. van Essen and T. van der Geest (eds) *Discourse Analysis and Public Life.* Dordrecht, Foris, 13–38.

Candlin, C. N. and Maley, Y. (1994) Framing the Dispute. *International Journal for the Semiotics of Law* **VII**(19), 75–99.

Dingwall, R. (1988) Empowerment or Enforcement? Some Questions about Power and Control in Divorce Mediation, in Robert Dingwall and John Eekelaar (eds) *Divorce, Mediation and the Legal Process.* Oxford, Oxford University Press, 150–66.

Fairclough, N. L. (1992) *Discourse and Social Change.* Cambridge, Polity Press.

Fineman, M. (1988) Dominant Discourse, Professional Language and Legal Change in Child Custody Decision-making. *Harvard Law Review* **101**(4), 727–74.

Foucault, M. (1972) *The Archaeology of Knowledge.* London, Tavistock Publications.

— (1984) *The Order of Discourse,* in M. Shapiro (ed.) *Language and Politics.* Oxford, Blackwell, 108–38.

Friedmann, L. M. (1983) Courts Over Time: A Survey of Theories and Research, in K. O. Boyum and L. Mather (eds) *Empirical Theories about Courts.* New York, Longman, 9–50.

Goffman, E. (1974) *Frame Analysis: An Essay on the Organization of Experience.* New York, Harper and Row.

— (1981) *Forms of Talk.* Oxford, Blackwell.

Greatbatch, D. and Dingwall, R. (1989) Selective Facilitation: Some Preliminary Observations on a Strategy Used by Divorce Mediators. *Law and Society Review* **23**(4), 613–41.

Gulliver, P. H. (1979) Disputes and Negotiations. A Cross-cultural perspective. New York, Academic Press.

Habermas, J. (1984) *Theory of Communicative Action.* Vol. 1 trans. T. McCarthy. London, Heinemann.

— (1992) *Autonomy and Solidarity: Interviews with Jürgen Habermas.* London, Verso.

Halliday, M. A. K. and Hasan, R. (1985) *Language, Context and Text: Aspects of Language in a Social-semiotic Perspective.* Victoria, Deakin University Press.

Hoebel, E. A. (1964) *The Law of Primitive Man.* Cambridge, Mass., Harvard University Press.

Kristeva, J. (1986) Word, Dialogue and Novel, in T. Moi (ed.) *The Kristeva Reader.* Oxford, Blackwell, 36–61.

Maine, H. (1875) *Lectures on the Early History of Institutions.* London, John Murray.

Maley, Y. (in press) From Adjudication to Mediation. To appear in *Journal of Pragmatics.*

Marlow, L. (1987) Styles of Conducting Mediation. *Mediation Quarterly* **18**, 144–9.

McCarthy, M. and Carter, R. (1994) *Language as Discourse.* London, Longman.

Merry, S. E. (1990) *Getting Justice and Getting Even.* Chicago and London, Longman.

Philips, S. U. (1990) The Judge as Third Party in American Trial Court Conflict Talk, in A. D. Grimshaw (ed.) *Conflict Talk*. Cambridge, Cambridge University Press, 197–210.

Rheinstein, M. (1954) *Max Weber on Law in Economy and Society*. Cambridge, Mass., Harvard University Press.

de Saussure, F. (1959) *Course in General Linguistics*. Charles Bally and Albert Sechehaye (eds) Trans. Wade Baskin. New York, Fontana.

Silbey, S. S. and Merry, S. (1986) Mediator Settlement Strategies. *Law and Policy* **8**(1), 7–31.

Street, L. (1992) The Language of Alternative Dispute Resolution. *Australian Law Journal* **66**, 194–8.

Swales, J. (1990) *Genre Analysis*. Cambridge, Cambridge University Press.

Yngvesson, B. and Mather, L. (1983) Courts, Moots and the Disputing Process, in K. O. Boyum and L. Mather (eds) *Empirical Theories about Courts*. New York, Longman, 51–83.

ELEVEN

The interactional construction of narratives in medical and life-history interviews

Elliot G. Mishler

THE INTERACTIONAL PRODUCTION OF NARRATIVE ACCOUNTS

Narrative accounts, or stories, appear with regularity in many types of structured and unstructured interviews.[1] The perspective guiding this study is that the specific structures, functions and meanings of such accounts are produced through the interaction of the two speakers. My analyses focus on the work of story production in clinical and research interviews – on how physicians and researchers question, listen and respond to their patients and respondents, and how the latter clarify, develop and change their stories over their tellings. An analytical description of these features and the interactive process is provided through a sociolinguistic model.

Studies of narratives in informal and formal social contexts – naturally occurring conversations, research interviews, institutional settings and professional encounters – comprise a relatively new area of inquiry in the human sciences. Beginning with a few pioneers in the late 1960s and early 1970s (e.g. Labov 1972; Labov and Waletzky 1967; H. White 1973), research on narrativization in non-literary discourses and texts expanded rapidly, and at an accelerating rate in the past decade. Diversity among investigators in disciplinary backgrounds, conceptual and methodological approaches, and empirical interests is a distinctive feature of current work. Narrative is both a framework for and a source of research topics in a wide range of disciplines.[2]

Specific studies retain distinctive markings of the theoretical and methodological traditions and concerns of researchers' home disciplines. Nonetheless, narrative researchers with different perspectives tend to focus on a common set of general problems: defining the features of different narrative types and genres; specifying contextual influences; analysing their cultural, psychological and social functions. For this reason, diverse studies bear a family resemblance to each other, constituting not a new discipline but an interdisciplinary problem-centred area of research.

Difficulties of cross-disciplinary communication and understanding that might attend diversity are attenuated to some degree by the reliance of many narrative researchers on text-based analytical models of language developed in linguistics, literary criticism and the philosophy of language. This allows connections to be made among different studies, but these models have serious limitations. The features of narratives represented in them are characteristic of sole-authored written texts and formal oral presentations. They do not provide an adequate description of narratives that emerge on-line in interactional contexts, which is a prominent focus of recent work. In contrast, this process is the central topic of this chapter.[3]

One pervasive assumption, reflecting the focus on authorship in text-based models, is that the story which is told – even in ongoing interactional contexts – is the singular possession of one individual, the designated storyteller. Investigators seem to assume that the story has been there all along, located inside the person, waiting to be expressed in response to the eliciting stimulus of a question. The question itself is abstracted from the interactive process and omitted from the analysis.

With this approach, the dynamic process through which a story takes on its specific shape and meaning is lost. The dialectic of speaking and listening, the essential reciprocity between conversational partners, is removed from analysis and absent from the interpretation of the story. Further, there is a tendency to treat the particular story expressed in a specific situation as 'the' story, rather than as one of a number of possible 'retellings'.

In contrast, the alternative approach, adopted here, makes interactional processes the central focus for studies of narratives in social contexts. Applying this perspective to analyses of clinical and research interviews, I show how stories are produced and developed through the interactional work of co-participants in such encounters.

PATIENTS' STORIES: FACILITATIVE AND NON-FACILITATIVE CLINICAL ENCOUNTERS

Diagnostic interviews typically begin with a physician's initial question to a patient about the nature of her/his problem. Patients often respond in the form of a story, offering an account of current distress and its history. I will examine opening sections of two interviews that are markedly different from each other in their respective forms of discourse (Clark and Mishler 1992; Mishler et al. 1989).

Briefly, in previous analyses, we found the first physician attentive to and facilitative of the patient's efforts to give a coherent account of his problem. Further, he invited him into a collaborative treatment relationship. In contrast, the second physician was relatively inattentive and interrupted the patient's account, relying on his medical authority for treatment recommendations. The patients' accounts differed from each other in ways that mirrored these two clinical approaches: one was relatively well developed and contextually grounded; the second was fragmented and repetitive.

In the following analyses, I focus on the patients' initial presentations of their problems and on how their account is shaped and developed through the interaction between them and their respective physicians. The aim is to show how each patient's story is co-produced, over the course of its telling. The interaction at the beginning is emblematic; it foreshadows the rest of the encounter, producing and reproducing the differences between the two interviews summarized above.

To provide an analytical description of patients' and research respondents' accounts as stories, I use a model of oral narratives proposed by Jim Gee, a sociolinguist (Gee 1985, 1991). It emphasizes the social and communicative functions of prosodic and paralinguistic features of speech, such as changes in pitch and intonation contours. The model defines a hierarchically ordered set of structural components of spoken language – from the smallest Idea Unit with a single intonation contour, a next larger unit of Lines that include one or more topically related Idea Units, then successively larger components of the story – Stanzas, Strophes and Parts – each thematically unified at progressively higher levels of generality.

The associated transcription procedure used in the following transcripts represents respondents' stories in terms of these units.[4]

Physicians' and researchers' questions and brief question–answer exchanges are included in the transcripts but not represented as parts of the stories themselves. However, they are essential to the interpretation of how the stories develop.

In Transcript I, a 'Facilitated Story', it appears from the physician's initial reference to the patient's having said he had a 'seizure' that there was some prior conversation – presumably on their walk from waiting room to office. The lengths of uninterrupted silences within both the patient's and physician's initial utterances are unusual. We interpreted these silences as occasions offered by each of them for the other to speak. The patient continues to offer such opportunities as he tells his story. What is noticeable is that the physician does not take up these opportunities. He does not seize upon each pause in the patient's speech as an opening for a question, nor does he interrupt when the patient is talking.

TRANSCRIPT I – CLINICAL INTERVIEW: FACILITATED STORY

D: Okay/ so you said you ha:d a seizure. . . {yesterday?}
P: Uh {Yesterday}
Yesterday about- * . . . . about eleven o'clock/ yes/
D: Hmm *... At work? [P: hmhm] Okay/
STANZA 1
P: Well I'm not really worried/
Itz same thing you told me 'bout not gettin yaknow upset and aggravated/
STANZA 2
and- *. I couldn't have ta- uhm . . . . my boss get me a car Tuesday/ right?
* . . . . An' . . . . I workin on- it was an Audi/
I never did brakes on an Audi before/ yaknow front wheel drive? [D: Yeah]
An' * it was a problem yaknow/
STANZA 3
and I'm down all day long/*yaknow w- back like this here/ like the car's on a lift/ [D: Yeah]
But it's two bolts ya-know/ ya just can't get to em unless you get right up on the caliper/
*And ah twis- jus can twist a little bit with a screwdriver/
*An' I was going like (gang ...)- when ya can see I got a black e:ye/ (laughs)

D: Wha- oh from the seizure/
P: No/ from the caliper/ one of em fell . to the eye/
D: Oh {I see}
P: {An'} an' it hit me there/
STANZA 4
So . . . . Tuesday night/ an' I had this terrible headache and all
*So I slept with a- yaknow with a ice pack . . . . over it all night/ to keep- tryin to keep it from swelling and all/
STANZA 5
*... An' then I went back in * yesterday/ to try to finish it up/
It never took me that long before to finish up a brake job/
[D: .hh hh.]
And * . . . . my boss hadn't got all the parts for it/ so I start working on another car yaknow/
*That's when I ended up having the seizure/
D: Okay/ uhm so:o did your boss or someone else see the seizure happen?
P: Well the other guy that work with me/ he saw it/
D: Did he tell you what it looked like?
P: * . . . . No/ ah (. .) he said I was just shaking like mad/
[D: Yeah] that's what he told me/
D: He said you were shakin/
P: Umhum
D: Okay/

The patient begins his story after the topic for their discussion has been established – a shared understanding that he had a seizure yesterday at work. This allows and prompts him to begin without having to wait for a direct question – and the physician does not ask a question but simply acknowledges their shared understanding with an 'Okay'.

The first part of the patient's story is divided into three stanzas – a two-line couplet followed by two four-line stanzas. In Gee's model, an Idea Unit is defined by a change in stress or pitch referred to as a 'pitch glide'; these are marked by single diagonal slash marks. Lines are specified by their focus on a single topic and may include one or more meaning-related Idea Units. Stanzas are composed of groups of lines with a common theme.

Unitizing a stretch of speech into this set of interdependent categories is not a mechanical process but an interpretive one, based primarily on 'hearing' the talk rather than 'reading' its representation as a text. It requires a speaker's competence in the language on the part of the analyst, who must take into account both content and prosodic features through which speakers mark, relate and distinguish among units of meaning at different levels. Thus, different analysts might parse a stretch of speech, e.g. into Lines and Stanzas, somewhat differently. Further, Gee's rules about intonation contours and pitch glides are based on American English, and quite different rules for specifying basic units of meaning may be required in other languages.

Through the first three Stanzas, the physician does not interrupt the flow of the story either with questions or comments. He speaks only at two points, in response to a direct and an implied question, showing his understanding with 'Yeahs'.

In the opening couplet, the patient presents the evaluative frame (Labov and Waletzky 1967; Labov 1972; Polanyi 1985a) within which he wants his story to be understood: he is 'not really worried' about the seizure since he understands what the physician had told him, presumably in earlier conversations, about not getting 'upset and aggravated'. In the next two stanzas, he describes, as will only become clear later, the background for his seizure: a difficult job given him by his boss of doing brakes on a car with 'front wheel drive'. He does not mention the seizure, nor does the physician interrupt to ask what all of this might have to do with it – although they have both already agreed that the seizure is the primary topic of their conversation.

At the end of Stanza 3, the patient reports getting a 'black eye'. Apparently thinking they have now arrived at their agreed-upon topic, the physician proposes a connection between the seizure and the black eye. His hypothesis is disconfirmed: it was the 'caliper' that hit the patient in his eye.

After this clarifying side-exchange, the patient returns to his story, beginning with a couplet that completes his presentation of the background: a 'headache' and 'swelling' from his black eye and his effort to relieve the problem with an 'ice pack'. He concludes his story, in Stanza 5, noting his continued frustration with not being able to complete the brake job and his starting work on another car. His last line is the point of the story and brings them both back to their topic: 'That's when I ended up having the seizure'. The physician asks for further information – witnesses and what the seizure looked like to them – and ends this episode with an affirmation of having understood: 'Okay'.

I am proposing that the shape of this patient's story – its thematic coherence, with orientation and background sections and a clear stanza structure, and an ending grounded in the account that is the point of the story – reflects the interactive roles that the physician and patient negotiate for this encounter. The physician adopts the role of an attentive listener. Through his silences and by explicitly marking his understanding, he shows he is prepared to listen to the patient's account in his own words and in his own way of telling – even when the patient appears to digress from their agreed topic. The patient takes up the complementary role as narrator. To restate my central argument, the story is interactionally produced. That a different type of interaction might produce a different type of account will be evident in the second clinical interview.

It appears from the way Transcript II, an 'Interrupted Story', begins that there was also some prior conversation before the tape recorder was turned on, perhaps the physician's opening question. The patient states a complaint and then breaks off before launching into the first part of her story. This consists of four stanzas: three of four lines and the couplet of Stanza 2. She begins by recalling for the physician when 'it must have been startin' with 'pains in [her] head'. Another doctor's examination was inconclusive: 'he said somethin about [her] glands'. But over the past four or five weeks, she continues in the third Stanza, it has been 'gettin worse' and now 'it's just terrible'. She has diabetes, we learn from other information in the interview, and in the fourth Stanza reports her concern about her sugar levels that are 'everywhere' and 'still high' as measured by her use of the standard 'finger stickin' procedure.

TRANSCRIPT II – CLINICAL INTERVIEW: INTERRUPTED STORY

P: I can hardly drink water/ [D: hm hm]
Sometimes it bothers me in- in-
STANZA 1
First- remember when it started?
Remember I told you I was in pa- the pains {in my head?}
{D: hm hm}
It must have been startin then/ [D: hm hm]
I don't know what it is/
STANZA 2
The doctor looked at it/ when I came 'n see Sally/
He said somethin about my glands/ [D: hm hm]

STANZA 3
And it's gettin worse now/ it's like painin yaknow?
And it's- uh first it was like- um . well I had some fish/ and
I put lemon on it/ that's when I {noticed-} that's been
{D: hm hm}
about five- [D: hm hm] four weeks ago/ [D: hm hm]
And now it's- it's just terrible/ even coffee hurts it/
So I don't know what it is/ [D: hm hm]
STANZA 4
(. .) and my sugar's . everywhere doc/
.hh I don't know/
I'm doing that finger stickin/. still high/
(. .) .hh [D: ah:m] I don' know/

D: What kinda- Where abouts approximately on the finger stick have you . been findin it/ when you do it?

P: Oh over the- near there- um 270? [D: hm hm] Yeah/ in be- in between there/ [D: hm hhm] uh huh

D: Okay/ .hh uh . and is that pretty constant? Where it is?

P: That's where it always is/ [D: It is?] yeah/ [D: Okay] {uh huh}

D: {ah:h} The last- I was looking in the computer- the last one that I saw in there was about three weeks ago/ have you had blood drawn in the lab since then? [P: uh:m] Or just {(...)}

STANZA 5

P: {I don't} remember/
I was comin so regular {ya-know?/ Cause I was comin-}
{D: Yeah/ Yeah/ Yeah}
I know I was seein Sally like once twice a week/ [D: Yeah]
so- I done forgotten that/

D: Okay/ Okay/ .hh uhm aside from this/ how have you been feeling? I know the blood sugar's been up/ but what- [P: Terrible] Yeah/

STANZA 6

P: Tired all the time/ that tired feelin again/ [D: Yeah.]
An- I don't know/
I eat and I'm still sick/
So .hh I don' know/

D: ah:m .. .hh With respect to this business up here/ is that sore if you're not eating? [P: Yeah] {or is it only if you take-} {P: Yeah/ there's pains in it] yes/ uh huh

STANZA 7

P: Yeah an' it's- it's one- one spot right here/ [D: uh huh]
It's real sore/ [D: uh huh]

But then there's like pains in it/
Yaknow how- I don't know what it is/
D: uh huh Okay/ .hh Fevers or chills?
P: No/
D: Okay/ ah:h Have you been sick to your stomach/ or anything like that?
P: (Sniffles, crying, 9 second pause) I don' know what's goin on.

Although there is a rough chronology in this account, from when the 'pains' started in the first Stanza to the currently worsening situation in the third and fourth, its primary thrust is an expression of considerable distress. Not only is the pain getting worse when she eats, but this is compounded by her not knowing what is going on. 'I don't know' is her repeated and poignant final line in each of the four-line Stanzas; and apparently, as we see in the couplet, another doctor doesn't know either. The physician's responses are restricted to minimal acknowledgements, 'hm hms', which in two instances overlap the patient's speech.

The physician enters the conversation directly only after she reports her own measurement of blood sugar levels in Stanza 4. Since he does not ask about the main topic she has been talking about, namely, her marked distress about her pains and not knowing what is going on, we may assume from his question that he views blood sugar levels as of special significance. He presses her to clarify its exact level and variability, saying he can check the adequacy of her report with laboratory tests listed in the computer – a more scientific basis than her self-report. In Stanza 5, responding to his question about when she last had 'blood drawn in the lab', she says she can't remember since she had been coming in so often to see a nurse, Sally.

He then asks how she has been feeling, 'aside' from her blood sugar's being up. Without the previous context of her report of pain and distress, we might make the mistake of viewing this question as a mark of attentiveness. But in that context, it is clearly inattentive; it suggests he has not been listening to what she has been saying. She responds quickly that she feels 'terrible', is 'tired all the time', eats and is 'still sick', and twice repeats her now-familiar complaint: 'I don't know'.

After Stanza 6, the physician asks about 'this business up here' and whether it's 'sore' if she's not eating. These terms transform her report of pains and distress into euphemisms, but she returns to her own words in her response. Note that his question, as his earlier ones, focuses on a specific physical symptom and that he has not yet referred directly to any of her many characterizations of her distress: that she is feeling terrible, it's getting worse, she's tired all the time, she's still sick, and throughout that she doesn't know what's going on.

He persists with his own medical agenda, asking about whether she's had fevers or chills, or been sick to her stomach. At this point, the patient's control breaks and she begins to cry, coming back again to her deep and pervasive concern: 'I don't know what's goin on'.

In contrast to the first patient's story, this patient's story is relatively less well formed and less developed. Although she tries to provide a context for her problem – its worsening course over time and the situations that elicit pain – and repeatedly states the point of her story, namely, her distress at not knowing what is going on, the physician does not help her develop or elaborate her account. Instead, he interrupts her story with his questions, sidetracking her from stating her problem in her own terms by focusing on a series of physical symptoms – blood sugar levels, fevers, chills, being sick to her stomach. In earlier work (Mishler 1984), I describe the conflict within medical interviews between the 'voice of the lifeworld' and the 'voice of medicine'. This is clearly an instance of such a contrast. By dominating the encounter through the 'voice of medicine', the physician drowns out and undermines the patient's effort to tell a meaningful and coherent story.

I am, of course, proposing that this patient might have told as coherent and well-formed a story as the first patient. The difference between them cannot simply be attributed to presumably different storytelling abilities. Rather, I would argue, each story was interactionally produced, but through different discursive practices – story-facilitative practices in the first case and non-facilitative ones in the second.

RESEARCH INTERVIEWS: THE CO-PRODUCTION OF LIFE HISTORIES

This same process is at work in research interviews. Transcript III shows the beginning section of a life history interview with a woman potter, one of a series from my ongoing study of the lives and work of contemporary craftspersons.

TRANSCRIPT III – POTTER'S INTERVIEW: STORY BEGINNING

E: Right=well perhaps if we MIGHT- a:ah for ME/ it's useful to ask you to begin at the BEGINNING/ [R: hm hm] since I'm interested in ah the history of your work in the CRAFTS/ what brought you INTO IT/ and= [R: OKAY]=how the work has gone SINCE THEN [R: OKAY] E: How did you ah START/ doing the work that you're DOING? What- ah what led you into . THE WORK?

PART I. Fine Arts Degree

STROPHE 1. Art as option

STANZA 1. Art class

R: 1. Um:m . . . . probably just from attending SCHOOL
2. and ah . . I- . at the very end of my undergraduate . um . STUDIES/ I took an ART CLASS
3. and I had al- always done . um ART/when I was in HIGH SCHOOL/ and .hh .hh was DOING IT
4. but never really thought of it as an OPTION/of something to do in my LIFE

STANZA 2. Art major/degree

5. and I took it- I took an ART CLASS
6. and on the ENCOURAGEMENT/ of .hh the TEACHER/ I uh . transferred . SCHOOLS/ and en- and ended up transferring MAJORS/ um and started all OVER AGAIN (laugh)
7. .hh so I actually can- you know . [have] one bachelor of FINE ARTS
8. and if I wanted TO/ I could go back and get an- another BACHELOR'S DEGREE/ I ended up with that many CREDITS

Prior to the interview, by letter and telephone, I explained the aims of the study and why I wanted to interview her. On my arrival at her house, we briefly reviewed what the study was about and went through the informed consent procedure before I turned on the tape recorder. The formal interview begins, at the top of Transcript III, with my specifying my interest as the 'history' of her 'work in the crafts'. I offer this as the reason for asking her to 'begin at the beginning' and then restate this request in several different ways: 'what brought [her] into it', 'how did [she] start', 'what led [her] into it'. She indicates her understanding by 'Okays'.

It is apparent from her first statement that she is trying to respond to my question about the beginning of her work. Her initial response is shown in the transcript as two four-line Stanzas that together represent both Strophe 1 and Part I of her extended story.

As it turns out, she speaks continuously for the next 12–13 minutes, without any further comment or question from me and without my interrupting her or interjecting verbally with even a brief acknowledgement. Thus, her full response to my opening question is a lengthy monologue through which I am completely silent, although clearly attentive, for if I were not we must assume she would have stopped before she finished what she wished to say. I will refer to this as her core story.

I first parsed her speech into Idea Units and Lines – there are 100 Lines in the core story. They fall into 27 Stanzas, of which all but four couplets have four lines. In turn, the Stanzas group into 11 thematically unified Strophes, and the Strophes into seven general Parts, or episodes. Together – the Idea Units, Lines, Stanzas, Strophes and Parts – constitute the structure of her story within the framework of this analytical model.

Her core story takes her from her self-defined beginning – her transfer to Art School at the end of her undergraduate studies reported in these first two Stanzas – through her graduation and early work as a potter, her decision to go to graduate school in the crafts, her experiences in making and marketing her work, and her present situation. She makes it clear when she has reached the end of her story by bringing us up to the present, saying that her work has slowed down because she is pregnant but she hopes to get started again after her baby is born and 'goes on schedule'. She ends her story, as we shall see in a moment, by stating that she misses doing the work.

Her story is not only long and well-formed, thematically and structurally, but held together by a strong temporal ordering of events – each successive Part is a next point in time. However, as complete and coherent as it is, this story is not the end of the interview. We continue to talk for two more hours. This offers an excellent opportunity to explore the interactional production of narrative accounts in some detail. The question guiding further analysis is: if she has already told me her story, what did we do together for the next two hours of the interview?

What we did is exemplified in my first question after she finishes her core story, Stanza 27 at the top of Transcript IV, and in her response to it. I ask her where she had been going to school before she transferred, returning us to the beginning of her story.

TRANSCRIPT IV – POTTER'S STORY: FOLLOWING UP THE STORY

STANZA 27. Missing the work

97. and- the last show I had was la- last MARCH
98. um . . I had a show at the uh Riverside Arts CENTER/at the women's studio WORKSHOP/ Oldtown MICHIGAN
99. and uh that was- uh that was very NICE/ to be able to dig- get- get TOGETHER/ and get a show AGAIN/ and stuff like THAT
100. so . I've MISSED IT (laugh)

END OF CORE STORY

E: (Can I) come back uh a little bit to what you were mentioning early on? Where- where were you going to school in the beginning? The place you went before you left?

R: I got my uh Bachelor of Fine Arts at Western University in Kirkland.

E: But you had been somewhere else before?

STANZA A1. Transfer schools

R: A1. Oh I was STUDYING/ um I'd say in several different PLACES

A2. but I was basically getting my sociology psychology degree from DownstateU CITYSIDE

A3. and I transferred for one SEMESTER/. to KIRKLAND

A4. and I just- . I got THERE/ and I took a lot of uh sociology COURSES

STANZA A2. Encouragement/ Drawing ability

A5. but I also took . two . basic non MAJOR-/a design and a drawing COURSE

A6. and at that POINT/ my drawing TEACHER/. encouraged me very very STRONGLY/ 'cause he felt that um I had an ability to- I just had drawing ABILITY/ that he didn't see very OFTEN

A7. and he- he really- you know- it was- it was his ENCOURAGEMENT/ get your PORTFOLIO TOGETHER/ you know you're really GOOD/ you- you just try APPLYING

A8. and you know I got IN/ and everything like THAT

STANZA A3. School wanted students who could draw

A9. but- um the school was- uh WesternU KIRKLAND-/ I don't- I don't know if its still the SAME/ had a pretty . intense FOUNDATION/ for its beginning STUDENTS

A10. and it was difficult to get IN

A11. if you didn't know how to DRAW/ they really- they really didn't want you in THERE
A12. they wanted people that had some good ABILITY/ before they went IN
A13. SO:O

My questions, here and in the remainder of the interview, indicate my uncertainty of understanding or puzzlement about what she has told me. On the whole, I ask about topics and themes she has introduced – here, her transfer of schools and majors – but my questions also reflect my interests and aims. In this unstructured interview, and the general project of which it is a part, my interests were not fully articulated in advance. Rather, I came to clarify them over the course of the interviews. In other words, what I was trying to find out emerged and became clearer as I heard what she and other respondents were saying. In this sense, it is not only her story that is interactionally produced but the study itself.

Thus, asking her where she was going to school before she transferred does not express an *a priori* interest – I did not have this question in mind before I heard her story. Nor, as is evident from its placement at the end of her story, where she is referring to her present situation, does my question follow directly either from the overall narrative line she has followed or what she has just said. I mark this disjunction explicitly to her by my metacomment about coming back to what she was 'mentioning early on'. Finally, I did not have any special interest in the name of the school she attended although this is specifically what I ask for. Rather, my question both marks and signals some puzzlement about what she chose to define as the 'beginning' of her work in the crafts in response to my opening question. In her own comments, she recognized that her shift in majors and schools was late in her college career and abrupt. I am searching for further understanding of this transition by asking about what was happening prior to what she proposed as the 'beginning'.[5]

In a more comprehensive analysis of this interview than can be presented here, I summarize the primary themes expressed in Stanzas and Strophes in the form of propositions, that is, general statements of her aims, actions and evaluations. Of the nineteen propositions that could be distinguished in her core story, the two representing the thematic content of the first two stanzas in Transcript III are: (i) I had always done art but never thought of it as an option of something to do in my life; (ii) I took an art class at the very end of my undergraduate studies, and on the teacher's encouragement transferred schools and majors and started all over again.

Her response to my question after her story, Stanzas Al through A3 in Transcript IV, may also be summarized in three new propositions that connect to these earlier ones but add important information. They bear on my uncertainty, that prompted my question, about this transition and what she means by the 'beginning' of her work: (i) I was taking my degree in sociology and psychology at one college, transferred to another for one semester and continued to take courses in my major; (ii) my teacher in a non-major art course strongly encouraged me to apply to art school because I had unusually good drawing ability; (iii) the school had an intense programme and only selected students who knew how to draw, and I got in.

Her core story is not contradicted by this new information. Nonetheless, her elaboration begins to transform it. She is clarifying what made art a feasible and reasonable choice for her at that time. Fundamentally, this comes down to her teachers' encouragement in recognition of her talent, that is, her drawing ability. It turns out there was not one but two teachers – the first at the earlier college campus, and the second at the one to which she transferred. And finally, there was the ultimate encouragement of admission to a highly selective art school with an intensive programme. This dual theme of her talent and its recognition reoccurs at other points in her life, which we hear about in other sections of the interview.

After Stanza A3, I ask her what year she transferred from one campus to another. Her response goes well beyond the limited focus of the question. She reports quick acceptance by the Art School because she was a very good student with high marks. Her discovery that there was excellent equipment and facilities 'really opened [her] eyes', and she 'started really becoming serious', deciding she was going to 'see it through to the end', that she was going to 'get [her] degree'. These remarks provide a fuller context for our understanding her decision to pursue art as a serious option.

Despite this new information, I am apparently still puzzled by the ease and rapidity of her transition to art at this late stage in her undergraduate studies. In particular, I am unclear about why she took an elective art course when she transferred to the second school, and I ask if she has 'any sense of why' she took a drawing course. She repeats what she said in the first Stanza of her core story – that she had 'been doing art' and 'drawing ... all the way in high school ... but never really thought that it was an option'. Instead, she had been 'into studying sociology and psychology ... doing very well and very excited'. But – a significant 'but' – 'a few events happened'. Specifically, she was becoming 'very unsatisfied' with her 'work with teenagers in a behavior mod program', 'getting disillusioned with the field', but 'not really enough to leave it'.

She then refers to a critical but previously unmentioned event in her 'personal life', namely, she had 'recently left [her] husband', ending a 'brief and not- not very happy (laughter) marriage'. Unfortunately, he was still attending the school she was at. Recognizing she 'was getting disillusioned' and that she 'really kind of wanted to leave the area', her college art teacher 'strongly suggested' that she go to the other school 'just for one semester and take a look'. This teacher felt she had 'motivation' and 'some talent', wanted her to continue with art and thought there were many more options for her in the Art Department at the other school. When she got there, 'it didn't take much to persuade me to stay because . it was so beautiful', much like the place where she had grown up and remarks, further, that she had been finding it increasingly 'bothersome' to face the hazards of living in the city.

Her response helps resolve my puzzlement about the ease and rapidity of her transfer to the second school, as well as about her taking an elective drawing course while continuing with courses in psychology and sociology. The strong encouragement of her first college art teacher re-affirms the theme of recognition of her talent we found earlier. She adds significant new information, primarily reasons for wanting to leave where she was: growing disillusionment with her chosen field; the lack of art options; the presence of her ex-husband from an unhappy marriage; her dislike of the city as a place to live. Finally, the beauty of the area helped persuade her to stay.

Immediately after she says how 'bothersome' it was to live in the city, I ask if she had any support from her family when she shifted direction to the arts. Although she has just mentioned the beauty of the area where she grew up, she has not referred to her family either here or at any earlier point in the interview. Not directly connected to her core story or other topics or themes she has introduced, my question interrupts the flow of her account and reflects my own interests in family influences on the pursuit of careers in the arts and crafts. Nonetheless, she seems to accept the question as appropriate and responds that her family 'basically wasn't involved' in her life since she was seventeen when she left home, escaping from a not 'very good childhood' where she was 'abused . physically'. Her family did not give her 'much emotional or financial support' and essentially 'they weren't there'. For example, they have not come to her major shows.

However, she continues, she has had other supportive 'friends and people', among whom there is Roger. She met him 'immediately' after she arrived at the school and, 'that was another reason why I (laugh) didn't want to go back'. That was nine years ago. They married and are still together. Roger has been 'supportive', 'very encouraging', 'one of the most positive influences' and a 'positive force in my life as far as my art work goes'. This is another significant item of information, not mentioned in the core story, that adds to the complexity of reasons for her staying at the new school. More than that, it bears on her switch to art. And beyond that, as we learn later in the interview, Roger's support sustains her development and work as a one-of-a-kind potter – from her initial efforts to produce and market her work, through graduate school, to the present where she is moderately successful competing in shows and selling through crafts galleries.

All this new information – the multiple reasons that emerge about why she left where she had been, why she stayed where she went, why she chose art as an option and continued to work in the crafts – are not simply additions to her core story. Without contradicting it, they transform it. And this transformation takes place through the dialectic of questions and responses in the interview, the ways in Paget's terms that 'questioning practices' and 'the answers given continually inform the evolving conversation' (Paget 1983: 78).

There is much more to the interview. The sections I have discussed occupy only about the first half hour of a two and a quarter-hour interview. My aim, within the limits of space, has been to show in some detail how the dynamics of the interview, the dialectic of questions and responses, produces the account we traditionally assign to the respondent. We have, of course, been listening to her story and not mine – it is important to be clear about this point. However, it is equally important to be clear that 'her story' is only one retelling, one of many stories she might have told about her life and work in different contexts and with a different interviewer. The shape, structure, content of the story she told me reflects what we were doing together – it was interactionally produced.

DISCUSSION

The idea that accounts are interactionally produced is hardly new. It is central to ethnomethodology, conversation analysis and various interpretive research traditions. But it has had little influence on the diverse field of narrative studies. I suggested two possible reasons for this neglect: the dominance of text-based models and lack of an analytical model and methodology for studying extended stretches of spoken discourse.

Sociologists of science have observed that a line of research develops when problems become 'doable', that is, when investigators have available both a reasonably precise formulation of an interesting problem and an appropriate technology, or method, for addressing it. Gee's sociolinguistic model provides a way to represent narratives that focuses conceptually on their structure and its communicative functions, on the ways that different units are organized linguistically and thematically. By distinguishing among different elements and levels of a story, this framework gives us a way to track its development. In turn, as I have tried to demonstrate, this allows us to specify in detail how a particular story is produced through the interaction of speakers. I would not claim that this is the only useful model for research on the interactional production of narrative accounts, but it turns this into a 'doable' problem. And, if the sociologists of science are correct, this may lead to a wider application of the interactional perspective in narrative research.

NOTES

1. I would like to thank Jim Gee and Vicky Steinitz for their support and help in my work and the preparation of this chapter.
2. There is now a large corpus of narrative studies. In addition to sources cited in the text, some recent monographs and papers are listed here, with the primary disciplinary focus noted to suggest the diversity of current work. Anthropology and folklore: Bauman 1986; Behar 1992; Shuman 1986; Young 1987. Economics: McCloskey 1985. Education:

Grumet 1988; Witherell and Noddings 1991. History: Cronon 1992; H. White 1989. Law: Bennett and Feldman 1981; *Michigan Law Review* 1989; J. B. White 1984; Williams 1991. Medicine: Charon 1986, 1989; Gerhardt 1991; Hunter 1991; Kleinman 1989. Psychiatry and psychoanalysis: Schafer 1992; Slavney and McHugh 1984; Spence 1982. Psychology: Bruner 1986, 1990; Cohler 1982; McAdams and Ochberg 1988; Mishler 1986a, 1986b; Peterson and McCabe 1983: Polkinghorne 1988; Rosenwald and Ochberg 1992; Sarbin 1986. Sociolinguistics: Labov 1982; Polanyi 1985b. Sociology: Boje 1991; Riessman 1990, 1992. The new *Journal of Narrative and Life History* publishes research reports from a variety of perspectives and disciplines.

3. Emphasis on interactional processes is a central feature of ethnomethodology, conversation analysis, symbolic interactionism and other social constructivist lines of inquiry. However, analyses of discourse within these traditions, for example in conversation analysis, focus primarily on brief exchanges between speakers. And although there is no lack of attention to extended stretches of text or speech in sociolinguistics, anthropology and many other fields, these tend to be framed within text-based models of analysis and do not focus on interactional processes. Important exceptions to this last observation include studies by folklorists and ethnolinguists of the 'performance' of oral narratives; see, for example, Bauman 1986; Bauman and Briggs 1990; Hymes 1981. A principal aim of the study reported here is to show how the interactional perspective may be applied to the analysis of extended stretches of discourse, such as interviews and stories.
4. Transcription conventions for narrative units are borrowed from Gee (1991). Slashes (/) mark the ends of Idea Units; new Lines start at the left-hand margin and are indented on succeeding text lines; STANZA headings refer to groups of topically related Lines and STROPHE headings to thematically related STANZAS; PART headings refer to thematically related STROPHES and are the sections or episodes of the overall story; capitalized WORDS/PHRASES specify the thematic focus of Idea Units (not included in clinical interview transcripts). Pauses of one-tenth of a second are marked by a dot (.) and of one second by an asterisk (*); comments of one speaker inserted into the other's talk are enclosed in brackets ([ ]); overlaps between speakers are enclosed in curly brackets ({ }); stretching of a word or sound is shown by a colon (: , e.g. ah:m); unclear speech by three dots in parentheses ((...)); intake of breath as follows: .hh.
5. My discussion draws upon Marianne Paget's characterization of 'in-depth' interviews in terms of puzzlement and a search for understanding, and on her analysis of the ways that 'practices of questioning shape the evolving discourse' (Paget 1983: 78).

REFERENCES

Bauman, Richard (1986) *Story, Performance and Event: Contextual Studies of Oral Narrative*. Cambridge: Cambridge University Press.

Bauman, Richard and Briggs, Charles L. (1990) 'Poetics and Performance as Critical Perspectives on Language and Social Life', in B. J. Siegel, A. R. Beals, S. A. Tyler (eds) *Annual Review of Anthropology*. Palo Alto, CA: Annual Reviews, pp. 59–88.

Behar, Ruth (1992) *Translated Woman: Crossing the Border with Esperanza's Story*. Boston, MA: Beacon Press.

Bennett, W. Lance and Feldman, Martha S. (1981) *Reconstructing Reality in the Courtroom*. New Brunswick, NJ: Rutgers University Press.

Boje, David M. (1991) 'The Storytelling Organization: A Study of Story Performance in an Office-supply Firm', *Administrative Science Quarterly* **36**: 106–26.

Bruner, Jerome (1986) *Actual Minds, Possible Worlds*. Cambridge, MA: Harvard University Press.

Bruner, Jerome (1990) *Acts of Meaning*. Cambridge, MA: Harvard University Press.

Charon, Rita (1986) 'To Render the Lives of Patients', *Literature and Medicine* **5**, 58–74.

Charon, Rita (1989) 'Doctor–Patient/Reader–Writer: Learning to Find the Text', *Soundings* **72**, 1101–16.

Clark, Jack A. and Mishler, Elliot G. (1992) 'Attending to Patients' Stories: Reframing the Clinical Task', *Sociology of Health and Illness* **14**, 344–72.

Cohler, Bertram J. (1982) 'Personal Narrative and Life Course', in P. B. Baltes and O. G. Brim, Jr (eds) *Life-span Development and Behavior*. New York: Academic Press, pp. 205–41.

Cronon, William (1992) 'A Place for Stories: Nature, History and Narrative', *Journal of American History* **78**, 1347–76.

Gee, James P. (1985) 'The Narrativization of Experience in the Oral Style', *Journal of Education* **167**, 9–35.

Gee, James P. (1991) 'A Linguistic Approach to Narrative', *Journal of Narrative and Life History* **1**, 15–39.

Gerhardt, Ursulla (1991) 'Research Note: The Roles of the Wife and Marital Reality Construction in the Narrative Interview: Conceptual Models in Qualitative Data Interpretation', *Sociology of Health and Illness* **13**, 411–28.

Grumet, Madeline (1988) *Bitter Milk: Women and Teaching*. Amherst, MA: University of Massachusetts Press.

Hunter, Kathryn M. (1991) *Doctor's Stories: The Narrative Structure of Medical Knowledge*. Princeton, NJ: Princeton University Press.

Hymes, Dell (1981) *'In vain I tried to tell you': Essays in Native American Ethnopoetics*. Philadelphia, PA: University of Pennsylvania Press.

Kleinman, Arthur (1989) *The Illness Narratives: Suffering, Healing and the Human Condition*. New York: Basic Books.

Labov, William (1972) 'The Transformation of Experience in Narrative Syntax', in W. Labov (ed.) *Language in the Inner City: Studies in the Black English Vernacular*. Philadelphia, PA: University of Pennsylvania Press, pp. 354–96.

Labov, William (1982) 'Speech Actions and Reactions in Personal Narrative', in D. Tannen (ed.) *Analyzing Discourse: Text and Talk*. Washington, DC: Georgetown University Press, pp. 219–47.

Labov, William and Waletzky, Joshua (1967) 'Narrative Analysis: Oral Versions of Personal Experience', in J. Helm (ed.) *Essays on the Verbal and Visual Arts*. Seattle, WA: University of Washington Press, pp. 12–44.

McAdams, Dan P. and Ochberg, Richard L. (eds) (1988) *Psychobiography and Life Narratives*. Durham, NC: Duke University Press.

McCloskey, Donald N. (1985) *The Rhetoric of Economics*. Madison, WI: University of Wisconsin Press.

Michigan Law Review (Special Issue) (1989) *Legal Storytelling* **87**, 2073–494.

Mishler, Elliot G. (1984) *The Discourse of Medicine: Dialectics of Medical Interviews*. Norwood, NJ: Ablex.

Mishler, Elliot G. (1986a) *Research Interviewing: Context and Narrative*. Cambridge, MA: Harvard University Press.

Mishler, Elliot G. (1986b) 'The Analysis of Interview Narratives', in T. R. Sarbin (ed.) *Narrative Psychology: The Storied Nature of Human Conduct*. New York: Praeger, pp. 235–55.

Mishler, Elliot G., Clark, Jack A., Ingelfinger, Joseph and Simon, Michael (1989) 'The Language of Attentive Patient Care: A Comparison of Two Medical Interviews', *Journal of General Internal Medicine* **4**, 325–35.

Paget, Marianne A. (1983) 'On the Work of Talk: Studies in Misunderstandings', in S. Fisher and A. D. Todd (eds) *The Social Organization of Doctor–Patient Communication*. Washington, DC: Center for Applied Linguistics, pp. 55–74.

Peterson, Carole and McCabe, Allyssa (1983) *Developmental Psycholinguistics: Three Ways of Looking at a Child's Narrative*. New York: Plenum Press.

Polanyi, Livia (1985a) 'Conversational Storytelling', in T. A. van Dijk (ed.) *Handbook of Discourse Analysis*. London: Academic Press, pp. 183–201.

Polanyi, Livia (1985b) *The American Story*. Norwood, NJ: Ablex.

Polkinghorne, Donald E. (1988) *Narrative Knowing and the Human Sciences*. Albany, NY: SUNY Press.

Riessman, Catherine K. (1990) *Divorce Talk: Women and Men Make Sense of Personal Relationships*. New Brunswick, NJ: Rutgers University Press.

Riessman, Catherine K. (1992) 'Making Sense of Marital Violence: One Woman's Narrative', in G. C. Rosenwald and R. L. Ochberg (eds) *Storied Lives: The Cultural Politics of Self-understanding*. New Haven, CT: Yale University Press, pp. 231–49.

Rosenwald, George C. and Ochberg, Richard L. (eds) (1992) *Storied Lives:*

The Cultural Politics of Self-understanding. New Haven, CT: Yale University Press.

Sarbin, Theodore R. (ed.) (1986) *Narrative Psychology: The Storied Nature of Human Conduct*. New York: Praeger.

Schafer, Roy (1992) *Retelling a Life: Narration and Dialogue in Psychoanalysis*. New York: Basic Books.

Shuman, Amy (1986) *Storytelling Rights: The Uses of Oral and Written Texts by Urban Adolescents*. Cambridge: Cambridge University Press.

Slavney, Phillip R. and McHugh, Paul R. (1984) 'Life Stories and Meaningful Connections: Reflections on a Clinical Method in Psychiatry and Medicine', *Perspectives in Biology and Medicine* 27, 279–88.

Spence, Donald P. (1982) *Narrative Truth and Historical Truth: Meaning and Interpretation in Psychoanalysis*. New York: Norton.

White, Hayden (1973) *Metahistory: The Historical Imagination in Nineteenth-century Europe*. Baltimore, MD: Johns Hopkins University Press.

White, Hayden (1989) 'The Rhetoric of Interpretation', in P. Hernadi (ed.) *The Rhetoric of Interpretation and the Interpretation of Rhetoric*. Durham, NC: Duke University Press, pp. 1–22.

White, James B. (1984) *When Words Lose Their Meaning: Constitutions and Reconstitutions of Language, Character and Community*. Chicago, IL: University of Chicago Press.

Williams, Patricia J. (1991) *The Alchemy of Race and Rights: Diary of a Law Professor*. Cambridge, MA: Harvard University Press.

Witherell, Carol and Noddings, Nel (eds) (1991) *Stories Lives Tell: Narrative and Dialogue in Education*. New York: Teachers College Press.

Young, Katharine G. (1987) *Taleworlds and Storyrealms: The Phenomenology of Narrative*. Dortrecht: Martinus Nijhoff.

TWELVE

The institutional narrative as drama

Lars-Christer Hydén

1. INTRODUCTION

Narratives exist in cultural, social and institutional contexts which, to different degrees, allow, presuppose or restrict mutual communication about narratives. (For a historical note, see Stock 1984.) For instance, this concerns the right to listen to or read a story, the possibility to make comments about the story, to rewrite or retell parts or the whole narrative, or even to construct an entirely new narrative based on some other interpretation of the same set of events. Most modern fictional literature is based on the principle that everyone may become a reader and take part in a story, although only the author has the right to construct the story. Narratives told by a family member at a dinner table, on the other hand, may not only be commented on by other family members, but could even be co-constructed or re-constructed in a joint process involving several family members (Ochs et al. 1992).

One specific social and cultural context of narratives is the modern bureaucratic organization. In these settings, narratives may be constructed at several organizational levels and in different forms. One instance of this is the so-called atrocity stories (Dingwall 1977): clients use narratives about professionals in order to justify their own behaviour; or one professional group may use stories about another professional group in order to decrease the other one's social status. Another form is 'case stories' (Pithouse and Atkinson 1988), which are related by professionals about clients. A further example, which will be of concern in this chapter, is narratives written about clients or citizens by an institutional representative.

Typical of this latter kind of written narrative is the fact that formal and legal rules restrict both authorship and readership in a way that circumscribes the possibilities of a dialogue. The functions of the written narrative are determined by organizational factors and administrative traditions and routines. Examples of this kind of written, institutional narratives are investigatory reports by social workers (Hydén 1991), police reports (Jönsson 1988), medical reports (Cicourel 1975, 1985; Barrett 1988), and reports submitted to courts (Cicourel 1968; Spencer 1988). These texts all contain a 'story' about one or several persons, their actions and mutual relationships, and specifically about the possible relationship between the person/persons and the authority in question.

Written, institutional narratives are rarely appreciated as narratives, but are more commonly treated as instances of generic 'texts'. This is probably due to the fact that the narrative aspects of the texts are often not immediately evident to the reader or observer, because the focus is on factual, administrative or judicial content. When written, institutional texts – irrespective of whether they are of a narrative nature – have been studied by social scientists, two approaches have generally been used (Heath 1982).

The first way to study institutional texts is to focus on the functions of the text in a larger social or organizational context (Garfinkel 1967; Cicourel 1968; Smith 1974; Spencer 1988). These studies are based on observations either of how, for instance, the institutional text is used by juvenile officials in order to bring about certain desired effects (Cicourel 1968), or how the text ought to be read by competent readers in order to be fully appreciated and understood (Garfinkel 1967). But neither Cicourel nor Garfinkel raise the question of how a text has to be organized in order to serve some organizational function or to be read in a definite fashion.

The second way to study written institutional texts is to focus on how the interaction between client/citizen and institutional representative is *transformed* into a text. The interest is centred on the relation between organization, background knowledge, interaction and text. Several studies of this kind have been conducted by Cicourel (1975, 1985; see also Barrett 1988; Spencer 1988). An implicit assumption in most of these studies seems to be the idea of a more or less 'linear' transformation of the interactional properties into textual ones. But this 'transformational' process is apparently not uncomplicated, as Cicourel observes in the case of medical records:

> The medical summary text resembles a folk practice where stories are told in fairly uniform ways, irrespective of how the original experiences might have unfolded.
>
> (Cicourel 1975: 59)

Cicourel's remark indicates two circumstances. First, the written narrative is fairly autonomous in relation to the social interaction of doctor and patient in terms of the way events are identified and combined into a text and a story. That is, the narrative text cannot be reduced to and be treated as being identical with the social interaction although expressed in different terms. Secondly, the form of the institutional narrative is not arbitrary, but apparently draws on specific forms and ways of writing and expression, for instance 'folk practice'. This points to the necessity of investigating the composition of the narrative text itself, and not only its organizational functions or social context. I propose here an analysis of the institutional narrative as a *literary artifact*.

The study of institutional narratives and texts can benefit from the emerging field of narrative analysis in the social sciences (Labov 1972; Mishler 1986, this volume; Gee 1991; Riessman 1993). The main focus in this emerging field has been oral narratives and their analysis. For this reason, analysis of institutional textual narratives can probably also benefit from the theory of literature, and maybe especially from attempts by researchers and authors to analyse texts as parts of social contexts and practices: Bakhtin's (1986) conception of the novel as part of a social communication, Fish's (1980), Felman's (1983) and Pratt's (1977) application of Austin's speech-act concept to literary analysis or theories about the reader's aesthetic responses (Iser 1978) may all be examples of authors in whose writings the social and literary analyses intersect.

In the following, two kinds of written institutional text (see below) will be analysed with respect to their narrative structure. The aim is to identify and discuss how the narratives are constructed, which devices are employed, and by what means the stories progress. And the connection between the narrative structure and the institutional setting of the text is discerned.

Initially, the written, institutional narratives and their institutional contexts are introduced. The narratives are analysed with respect to their structure and technical devices employed. Lastly, the narrative structure is discussed in relation to specific institutional settings.

2. THE MATERIAL

Two kinds of written narratives have been used. The first is reports written by social workers for use as documents in the legal steps taken by the social authorities to remove children from the custody of their biological parents. These texts are submitted to local politicians and later to a special court which makes a formal decision after a judicial process. The second is reports written by psychiatrists in the process of the involuntary commitment of psychiatric patients to mental hospitals. In contrast to the social worker's reports, the commitment reports prepared by psychiatrists are submitted only to a group consisting of peer professionals and legal representatives acting as representatives of the community. The decision of this group, although non-judicial, is binding.

The material consists of all the reports by social workers concerning the removal of children from the custody of their biological parents and resulting in the placement of the children in 1983 in a certain major city in Sweden (31 cases). The psychiatric reports concerning the involuntary commitment of patients were selected from all the reports made at the psychiatric emergency clinic in that same city during the years 1985–90. The number of reports used in this study is 25, although, for practical reasons hard to establish, the actual total number of reports for the period is greater.

Keeping these limitations in mind, the material is comprehensive and may be regarded as representative of the way reports of this kind were written and constructed in the 1980s. The city studied has several local universities and for that reason has an over-representation of well-educated and experienced staff in both social welfare and psychiatry.

The social welfare reports are in general very long, consisting of between five and 15 typewritten pages. Very often one or several additional reports by psychiatrists or psychologists are added to the final report. The psychiatric reports are generally short and hand- or typewritten on preprinted forms.

These two kinds of written institutional narrative differ in one central aspect. The social welfare reports on children are structured as narratives: they have a beginning, a middle and an end, and are, in that respect, examples of strong narratives. The psychiatric commitment reports, on the other hand, have a weak narrative structure: the reports are composed on a pre-printed form, with headings and a given amount of space allotted for writing, thereby indicating not only the appropriate length of the written text but also the order of events.

In the following analysis two excerpts from the reports are used. The first excerpt consists of a selection from a larger text (ten typewritten pages) concerning the removal from parental custody and placement of a teenage girl – *Heroine*. The second excerpt consists of a full psychiatric report concerning a woman brought to the psychiatric emergency clinic.

Excerpt 1

(1) **Investigation regarding placement in accordance with the Care of Young Persons Act (LVU)**

[The prior history up to time of initial contact is not included.]
(2) Background: Conditions in the home have been continually
(3) disruptive since the fall of 19xx. The father has had a serious problem
(4) with alcohol for many years. He is a periodic drinker. In connection
(5) with his drinking, but on other occasions as well, there is a good deal
(6) of dissension between himself and his wife. During the time the
(7) family has been known to the investigator, the parents have
(8) separated and gotten back together again a number of times. This
(9) has created an insecure and anxious home environment for Heroine.
(10) When the father drinks, he becomes aggressive and violent. At such
(11) times he has often assaulted the mother. He has even on occasion
(12) struck Heroine. The investigator is of the opinion that the family's
(13) situation deteriorated in the fall of 19xx. The parents were unable to
(14) set boundaries for Heroine. There was fighting and dissension in the
(15) home. The parents felt unable to cope [...] The mother left her
(16) husband and daughter in the late fall.
[...]
(17) The investigator sees Heroine as a strong-minded and gifted girl.
(18) School reports indicate that she learns quickly when she applies
(19) herself. However, since the fall of 19xx, the school reports
(20) increasing concern about Heroine. She has missed school, is
(21) aggressive, and is unable to accept limits set by staff and classmates.
(22) She bit a teacher on one occasion, spat at adults, and another time
(23) bit a schoolmate. Heroine has been showing increasing anxiety
(24) in school culminating finally in violent behaviour.
[...]
(25) To all appearances, Heroine did not feel well during the late fall. She
(26) looked tired and pale. She has had to take care of herself and has
(27) changed night to day – has developed problems sleeping at night.
(28) She stopped attending class altogether. Her aggressive behaviour
(29) and anxiety have increased.
[The remarks of the parties concerned are not included here, nor the conclusions reached by the social workers.]

Excerpt 2

(1) **Certification issued at the psychiatric emergency ward at X-hospital April 19xx.**

(2) (Anamnesis) 50-year-old woman. On long-term sick leave for pain,

(3) back and shoulders. 2 grown-up children. No previous contact with
(4) psychiatry.
(5) At least one other period with similar but milder symptom profile in
(6) connection with the death of a close relative.
(7) No alcohol or pill abuse. Is described by a relative as sensitive and
(8) somewhat vulnerable but usually well adjusted psychologically.
(9) Reacted strongly however to illness and death in the family.
(10) (Current state) For the past 2 months increasing anxiety, problems
(11) with sleeping, euphoria and some confusion. Calls her sons in the
(12) middle of the night and speaks very fast and sometimes somewhat
(13) incoherently. Irritable and more aggressive than usual.
(14) Stayed with a son in XXX where two days ago she drove off in the
(15) car in the middle of the night. Was picked up by the police for
(16) drunken driving but scored 0 on the balloon test. Was driven home
(17) and her driving license revoked. Picked up again yesterday while
(18) wandering around in a confused state. Via XX hospital to ZZ mental
(19) hospital for 24-hours' observation.
(20) Pat.'s mother diagnosed for malignant tumour of the breast October
(21) 19xx. First appearance of symptoms in connection therewith.
(22) Acc. to daughters has had delusions of being chased by the army.
(23) (Somatic state) General state of health hot, sweaty, and some redness.
(24) Otherwise not affected.

[Lines 25–32 concerns the medical status of the patient.]

(33) (Psychological state) Normal dress. Appearance adequate for age.
(34) Oriented x 3. Behaves somewhat confused but gives appropriate
(35) answers to questions. Pat.'s own account fragmentary and
(36) incoherent. Clearly excitable with rapid vivid associations.
(37) Indications of paranoid ideas but no florid signs of psychosis.
(38) 0 hallucinations. 0 suicidal thoughts.
(39) (Summary) 50-year-old woman with no prior contact with
(40) psychiatry but at least one prior period with a similar, milder
(41) symptom profile. Excitable upon arrival, some confusion with
(42) indications of paranoid delusions and latent but divertable
(43) aggressivity.
(44) Underlying state, most probably deep sorrow and depression.
(45) Confused state with reactive components. Judged to be unable to
(46) take care of herself. Refuses admission to hospital and medication,
(47) for which reason treatment in accordance with section 5 of
(48) the Compulsory Mental Care Act [in Swedish LSPV], is an absolute
(49) requirement.
(50) [Signed] Dr. X

(Certain details in the two extracts have been altered to protect the parties concerned.)

3. ANALYTICAL MODEL

Three aspects in particular seem to be of importance in the study of written institutional narratives: the literary frames, the plot and the literary devices.

The *literary framework* or *genre* provides both the author and the reader with an indication of what kind of text or narrative to expect: a novel, a poem, a philosophical treatise or a scientific text. The genre determines the standards and norms of how the text and narrative ought to be written and conceived and understood by the reader (Bakhtin 1986; Fish 1980).

In much of the sociolinguistic literature on narratives, a story is generally considered to consist minimally of two event clauses joined by a status clause (see Labov 1972; Polanyi 1989). But although this may be an acceptable minimal characterization of what should qualify as a narrative, it is not a sufficient instrument with which to analyse written institutional narratives. These are generally highly stereotyped in terms of the language and wording used, the ways of describing persons and, especially, the structure of the story. This suggests the employment of the concept of '*plot*' in order to characterize the events reported in the stories, the set of characters and the relationships these have to each other. The concept of plot, as used in this chapter, could be defined as 'the intelligible whole that governs a succession of events in any story' (Ricoeur 1981 [quoted from Brooks 1984: 13]).

Of central concern in this context is also the study of the *events* and *characters* in the narrative: what kind of events are identified and how, and what set of characters are appearing and in what order do they enter the story?

The *literary devices* used in constructing a narrative may vary according to what kind of text is to be produced. In scientific texts, rhetorical devices are used in order to effect an impression of empirical accuracy and logical clarity, while metaphors may be used in poems.

3.1 The literary framework

Both the child welfare reports and psychiatric commitment reports are *written* by institutional representatives not only with a specific legal right to author this kind of text, but also with an obligation to do so under certain circumstances. Psychiatric commitment reports may be written only by a licensed medical doctor not working in private practice. A report on child welfare may be written only by a social worker employed by the municipal social welfare administration. Social workers and medical doctors write their reports not only as individual professionals, but also in their capacity as officials and *institutional representatives* legally responsible for their actions. This is further emphasized by the fact that most social reports are written by several social workers. In other words, the act of writing is not an individual undertaking. Both social workers and medical doctors are responsible for their reports as officials – not as individuals, as in the case of fictional writing. This means, first, that the actual individual writer has to be separated from the formal author, and secondly, that the actual physical writer has limited responsibility for the text since it is basically the formal author who is liable for the written text.

In a similar way, the texts can only be *read* by persons with a legal right to do so: certain fellow professionals and, in the case of social reports, lawyers and political appointees to the social welfare committees. These social circumscriptions result in a certain act of reading: the readers are not private persons reading for their own enjoyment or curiosity, but rather public representatives reading in order to be able to make formal decisions.

The patients or clients who are the subjects of the texts have no right to co-write the material. The psychiatric patients may even be excluded from the right to read the commitment report. If the clients or patients have comments on the text, they have to present these in formal or even legal forums.

This social and institutional context is part of the literary framework determining the writing and accessibility of the texts. (For the social reports, see Handleman 1983; Hacking 1991; Hydén 1991; Cedersund 1992; for a history of medical and psychiatric reports, see Stoeckle and Billings 1987; see also Hunter 1986; Long 1986; Brody 1987.) In a more specific sense, *the genre* of the texts are indicated in the physical format of the texts: both kinds of report use at least a pre-printed flyleaf which indicates the formal paragraphs of the Social Welfare or Health Act, according to which the report is written.

From excerpt 1

(1) Investigation regarding placement in accordance with the Care of Young Persons Act (LVU)

From excerpt 2
(1) Certification issued at the psychiatric emergency ward at X-hospital April 19xx.

The flyleaf also contains certain basic information about the formal authorship and about the citizens who are investigated.

These circumstances, taken together, offer clues as to what kind of text the author and reader have in front of them – its genre – and how it is to be constructed, read and understood (Fish 1980): namely, as a formal text which is part of the legal processing of a person and which justifies the proposed measures and the compulsory intervention of some authority in an individual's private sphere.

3.2 The plot

A story can only be told from the end, retrospectively, or as Sartre put it, from the point of view of an obituary: 'only the end can finally determine meaning, close the sentence as a signifying totality' (Brooks 1984: 22). The ending is the start.

The endings of the narratives studied here are always given beforehand: the commitment of a patient to a mental hospital or parents' loss of custody of their child. This is even the point of the narratives, as one of their functions is to justify this conclusion. The plot of both the social reports and the psychiatric commitment reports could be described as the 'logic' which inevitably forces the narrative characters into a situation where only one option seems viable: the proposed institutional action. This end is the starting point and gives all actions prior to this point their *significance*. They could be described as actions 'objectively' combined and leading to the unavoidable end irrespective of the awareness of the characters.

The plot combines and relates events to the characters and circumstances and gives them their significance. By this the plot defines what kinds of event are relevant to the story and how these events are to be conceived. In the same way, a finite set of characters are delimited as the characters having relevance for the narrative. If the plot constitutes the inner logic of the narrative, the actual unfolding of the narrative is the *story* as it is written and occurs in the reports.

3.2.1 The events and actions

In the social welfare narrative, the central events are actions that actually transgress or threaten to transgress the established social and moral order. This social and moral order is defined by the social and parental legislation, cultural tradition and norms – and the ideology of especially the middle class (Mills 1943).

The transgressive actions may be actions directed against children – generally small children – from primarily one or both parents. This is the case when one of the parents behaves in a fashion towards his or her child that is described as a transgression both of the moral and legal order.

From excerpt 1
(10) When the father drinks, he becomes aggressive and violent. At such
(11) times he has often assaulted the mother. He has even on occasion
(12) struck Heroine.

Alternately, these actions may have their origins in the child him/herself. This is generally the case if the child is under the age of 18. An example of this is when a teenager behaves in a way that is described as aggressive, dangerous and self-destructive, and in that way transgresses the morally acceptable norms.

From excerpt 1
(20) [Heroine]has missed school, is
(21) aggressive, and is unable to accept limits set by staff and classmates.
(22) She bit a teacher on one occasion, spat at adults, and another time
(23) bit a schoolmate.

In the psychiatric reports, the central element is actions, experiences or verbal behaviour that are described as 'inadequate' or deviant, actions that cannot be understood or explained according to the locally and situationally relevant norms and standards. For instance:

From excerpt 2
(22) Acc. to daughters has had delusions of being chased by the army.

To believe that the army is chasing you is identified as a relevant event because it transgresses norms of what is a commonly shared idea about what possibly can happen to a person. 'Inadequacy' may also concern the way a person talks, speaks or behaves in a conversation.

From excerpt 2

(10) (Current state) For the past 2 months increasing anxiety, problems
(11) with sleeping, euphoria and some confusion. Calls her sons in the
(12) middle of the night and speaks very fast and sometimes somewhat
(13) incoherently. Irritable and more aggressive than usual.

To be incoherent in speech or thinking, to have an increasing anxiety and to be somewhat confused are singled out as relevant behaviour and experiences which receive significance from the fact that the person has been submitted for commitment to mental hospital.

The boundary between the morally acceptable and unacceptable, and between the situationally adequate and inadequate, is the line to which all the actions of the characters in the narratives are related. The parents or teenagers in the social reports and the potential psychiatric patients in the psychiatric reports all approach and finally transgress this boundary. Then, after this first time, the transgression is repeated over and over again.

It is not only the actions of the clients and patients that receive their significance from their relation to the established moral and social order, but also the actions of social workers or psychiatrists. Their actions are defined as preservative in relation to the moral and social order. In both the social and psychiatric reports, the actions of the main characters always – sooner or later – transgress the moral and social order time and again, thereby driving home the point that a radical intervention from the representatives of the authorities is warranted.

From excerpt 2

(45) [...] Judged to be unable to
(46) take care of herself. Refuses admission to hospital and medication,
(47) for which reason treatment in accordance with section 5 of
(48) the Compulsory Mental Care Act [in Swedish LSPV], is an absolute
(49) requirement.

In this way, the plot lends significance to previous actions of the main characters: all actions are to be seen in the light of the inevitable propensity movement towards repeated transgressions of the moral and social order. By defining actions and relevant actions as transgressions of established norms, and of legal standards in particular, the narrative is linked to its social and institutional context.

3.2.2 The characters

All the studied narratives include a limited set of characters. In the social reports, four main characters appear: first, *Hero* – the main protagonist – who is either a small child, towards whom transgressive parental actions are directed, or a teenager; secondly, *the Unfit*, the person who directs transgressive actions towards Hero – often the father, or if Hero is a teenager, identical to Hero. The Unfit is the prime motor in the plot repeatedly committing transgressive actions; thirdly, *the Tragic*, generally a mother or some other adult, who attempts to protect Hero. The Tragic tries to shield Hero either from abusive assaults from the Unfit, or in the case of teenagers, from Hero's own transgressive actions. But the Tragic always tragically fails:

From excerpt 1
(11) [...] The investigator is of the opinion that the family's
(12) situation deteriorated in the fall of 19xx. The parents were unable to
(13) set boundaries for Heroine. There was fighting and dissension in the
(14) home. The parents felt unable to cope [...] The mother left her
(15) husband and daughter in the late fall.

Both the mother and the father tried to shield Heroine from her self-destructive actions, but both of them failed and the mother eventually left the family.

Lastly, there is *the Authority*, who is generally a social worker who steps into the shoes of the Tragic, pursuing the attempts to protect Hero from the Unfit or him/herself. In addition to these characters, secondary characters like teachers or neighbours sometimes make an appearance.

The number of characters in the psychiatric reports are more limited. *Hero* is the normal and sane person who is befallen by the second character, *the Pathological Process*, the prime motor of the approaching transgressions. Although the Pathological Process is not a physical person, in the narratives it is an autonomous and malign agent capable of causing signs of 'mental illness'. The third character is *the Implied Psychiatrist*, the arbitrator of transgressions and the interpreter of signs. The psychiatrist conducting the psychiatric interview in the narrative never – with few exceptions – appears directly in the narrative, but is visible only through his or her *effects* on Hero. In some cases this implied existence seems carefully elaborated in the account of the narrator:

From excerpt 2
(34) [...] Behaves somewhat confused but gives appropriate
(35) answers to questions.

The interviewing psychiatrist in this example is invisible – she is only present as an implicit effect: the fact that the patient's answers are considered as 'appropriate' (line 34) indicate the existence of questions from the psychiatrist.

As in the case of the social report, secondary characters sometimes appear: relatives, family members, psychiatric staff or other – referring – psychiatrists.

3.2.3 *The story*

Both narratives unfold in a fairly uniform way in both kinds of text: through a historical retrospect, over to a description of the transgression of the moral or social order, and the eventual appearance of a representative of some authority. These institutional representatives inevitably fail in their mission.

The social report unfolds in four successive phases. First, the latent risk: Hero is at risk of being subjected to transgressive actions from the Unfit (or from Hero him/herself). Secondly, the Unfit actually commits one or several transgressions which the Tragic is unable to prevent. Thirdly, the transgressions are reiterated and the Authority makes his presence on the scene felt by taking up the fallen mantle of the Tragic, although the Authority also fails in his mission. Fourthly, the Unfit commits a transgression which is unacceptable to the Authority and which, in that sense, ensures the vicissitude of Hero and the Unfit. As a result, the Authority proposes an action – commitment – which will save Hero from his/her fate once and for all.

Psychiatric reports unfold in three phases, similar to those in the social reports. In phase one, Hero is presented as an individual not yet subjected to the Pathological Process, although early signs are observed or may afterwards be identified. The exception is when Hero is well known as a psychiatric patient and is presented as a person who is totally identified with the Pathological Process. In phase two, the Pathological Process makes its appearance on the scene and befalls Hero:

From excerpt 2
(10) [...] For the past 2 months increasing anxiety, problems

(11) with sleeping, euphoria and some confusion. Calls her sons in the
(12) middle of the night and speaks very fast and sometimes somewhat
(13) incoherently. Irritable and more aggressive than usual.

In phase three, the Implied Psychiatrist meets with the Pathological Process and makes an assessment of the pathology. The Implied Psychiatrist is generally the voice of reason and mental health, investigating the Pathological Process through conversation and always finding that the Pathological Process has taken the upper hand.

From excerpt 2
(34) Oriented x 3. Behaves somewhat confused but gives appropriate
(35) answers to questions. Pat.'s own account fragmentary and
(36) incoherent.

Although the patient is oriented concerning location, time and situation, she is 'confused' and gives a 'fragmentary and incoherent' account of her whereabouts the last days.

Both kinds of stories end with the acknowledgement of the failure of all measures in the present situation. The only way to terminate the ongoing transgression is to propose a new, and this time, definite and final measure.

3.3 The literary devices

Both kinds of texts have a certain aura of 'objectivity' and formal correctness. This is effected, for instance, by seldom using personal (grammatical) subjects or by the use of a specialized language.

A central device used in the construction of the social reports is the use of both direct and indirect quotations. A closer look at the reports, and especially comparing several reports concerning the same person, shows that report texts are often included in the newer ones. Either the bulk of the older text is used, although this is never indicated, or some parts of it, such as the summary, are inserted into the new report. Sometimes short phrases or sentences from other special reports, such as medical or psychological reports or reports from a teacher, are used, especially as a way of making a characterization of Hero or some other character. In this, a perspective is indirectly built into the report. Hero is viewed from several different perspectives, by various professionals and laypersons, all of them expressing their points of view.

As the readers of the reports rarely have access to either the older reports or the reports by different specialists, the social report texts appear to be newly composed texts. As a consequence, the incorporation of older reports and sequences from other reports into a new social report results in a text which increasingly becomes part of a textual universe, which for every new report becomes enlarged and more and more closed on itself. Thus, social reports have a tendency, in this sense, to move within a textual universe which becomes more and more closed and self-perpetuating.

In contradistinction to this, the psychiatric commitment reports in my corpus are written in a kind of short-hand, somewhat staccato and apparently not constructed by the use of citation, although quotations from the person under scrutiny may be used. The main device used in the psychiatric reports is the use of a specific kind of perspective which could be called 'the view from nowhere' (to use the philosopher Thomas Nagel's expression). It is not the perspective of the omnipresent narrator of the nineteenth century novel, but rather a story told by an implicit narrator who is all-embracing and all-knowing. In this way, a specific effect is produced, namely, the impression of objectivity and impersonal professionalism.

Another frequently used device in the psychiatric commitment reports is the use of medical concepts, phrases and expressions, even for depicting fairly everyday phenomena.

From excerpt 2
(36) [...] Clearly excitable with rapid vivid associations.
(37) Indications of paranoid ideas but no florid signs of psychosis.
(38) 0 hallucinations. 0 suicidal thoughts.

By using concepts and expressions which are not part of the everyday vernacular, like 'florid signs of psychosis', '0' [no appearance], 'vivid associations', and hence excluding certain readers, an impression of professionalism is established and maintained. This professional image is further enhanced by the fact that personal nouns are used extremely rarely in the texts.

4. THE LITERARY WORLD

Through the narratives, events are *defined*, *depicted* and *ordered*. The definition of events has a relation to the institutional context of the narratives. Relevant events are defined in relation to existing legal frames or established conventions. The social reports define events in relation to the transgression of primarily the moral order, that is, what persons can and ought to do and what can be viewed as proper. The psychiatric reports focus on social norms, whether people seem to be acting in an adequate manner, that is, conforming to norms.

The events are depicted and ordered in relation to the institutional functions of the written narratives. It is the 'end', the suggested intervention and measure of the agency or authority, that not only is the reason for the story, but also confers a significance and order to the discrete moments.

With the written, institutional narratives, a new 'reality' is created: the social world is transformed into a 'literary/fictional world', at the same time as this literary/fictional world occupies an important place in the social world. This literary/fictional world is not only a narrative rendering of the social world, but also a transformation of the social world into a *written text*. Written texts have an autonomy in relation to both the author and the reader: the written narrative is an 'object', open to various readers' interpretations. Although the written narrative reports have a restricted group of readers, they still have a temporal permanence and are 'objects' with an autonomy in relation to the individuals involved. The concrete circumstances surrounding the actual writing of the report and the actual occurrence of the events depicted in the text, all fall into oblivion, whereas the written text abides and later can become the 'object' of renewed interpretations. The investigated person and the institutional representatives encounter themselves as characters in a written story with its own 'logic' – the plot – unfolding with uncertain references to their own lives. The focus is displaced from the social world interaction to the fictional world and the interaction of its inhabitants.

Although the institutional, written narrative is produced in a particular social context, and in that way is the 'product', 'function' or 'result' of this context, the narrative is, at the same time, a way to structure the institutional reality. Through the literary world, persons are positioned as characters in an unfolding story. What they do becomes part of a whole and is invested with moral and social significance. The behaviours of clients, patients, and representatives are not just piecemeal everyday actions lacking inner coherence and meaning, but rather are part of a broader moral and social project, as the fight against 'social wrongdoing' and 'illness'. In this way, the narrative plot confers significance not only on the fictional events but also on the institutional context.

5. DISCUSSION: INSTITUTIONAL NARRATIVES AND MORAL ORDER

To write a narrative is to exclude another potential story:

> ... every narrative, however seemingly 'full', is constructed on the basis of a set of events which might have been included but were left out; and this is as true of imaginary as it is of realistic narratives.
>
> (White 1980: 10)

This is perhaps not especially problematic as long as it concerns a dialogue through which other readings of a text or other perspectives of the events can be presented; that is, as long as the narrative is part of a communication process that has a mutual basis and aspires towards shared perspectives.

That a narrative always excludes another possible story seems to be especially true of the written, institutional narratives. They are part of an institutional setting that prohibits some of the persons involved in the story from reading it and commenting on it. The voice of the patients or clients goes unheard.

Institutional narratives are the result of a complex social process through which the clients and patients are socially constructed (Zimmerman 1969; Cedersund 1992). The narratives are produced as a part in a formal process and are constructed with respect to several different interests and readers. The narrative is composed by institutional representatives, although it may not be possible to single out any particular individual as the specific author, and it has a limited set of authorized readers. The written narratives do not, in this sense, constitute the world or certain events as perceived and experienced by any particular person. Rather, it is the depiction of events as conceived from the point of view of an impersonal institution upholding certain standards and norms and effectuating specific social interventions. A somewhat paradoxical implication of this is that the narratives even become estranged from the individual social workers or psychiatrists who become subjugated to their narrative characters.

Although the narratives get their significance through the institutional context, it is also possible to read the texts outside the institutional context and to consider them as biographical narratives or as sources of information and data on the life and ways of clients and patients (see, for instance, Platt 1981).

As biographical narrative, the texts have a peculiarity: they do not concern people in the life worlds, but rather actions and the internal relations and moral characters these actions express. In this sense, the institutional narratives studied here are more akin to the ancient Greek tragedies than to the psychological novels of the nineteenth century.

Apart from being part of a formal process, the narratives also help to create meaning for the professionals and their associates (politicians, legal staff, etc.) about their own actions and work, and the value of these in relation to the clients and patients (Pithouse and Atkinson 1988; Hall et al., this volume). This meaning is created with the help of the institutional narratives which re-constitute and confirm the prevalent moral order. The institutional narrative constitutes the social workers, psychiatrists, clients and patients as characters and their missions or destinies in an ongoing moral drama. Clients and patients are persons who succumb to their destiny because they have violated the moral order; the professionals are the representatives of the good, tragic, albeit still saviours, trying to prevent further violations. Hero, the Tragic, the Pathological Process, etc. are all more or less stereotyped moral characters into which the client or patient and the professionals are cast. The characters reflect and present recognizable cultural and social patterns of action and ways of handling problems.

In this way, the actions and conceptions of the professionals are confirmed and given a meaning beyond their immediate formal context: the professionals are confirmed as actors in an ongoing social, moral drama, supporting the good and just cause. But, as with all narratives, one narrative suppresses another, potential narrative – the narrative that has its beginning in the life world of clients and patients.

REFERENCES

Bakhtin, M. (1986) *Speech Genres and Other Late Essays*. Austin, TX: University of Texas Press.

Barrett, R. J. (1988) 'Clinical Writing and Documentary Construction of Schizophrenia', *Culture, Medicine, and Psychiatry* **12**, 265–99.

Brody, H. (1987) *Stories of Sickness*. New Haven, CT: Yale University Press.

Brooks, P. (1984) *Reading for the Plot. Design and Intention in Narrative*. New York: Vintage Books.

Cedersund, E. (1992) *Talk, Test and Institutional Order*. (Linköping Studies in Arts and Science, **78**) University of Linköping.

Cicourel, A. (1968) *The Social Organization of Juvenile Justice*. New York: Wiley.

Cicourel, A. (1975) 'Discourse and Text: Cognitive and Linguistic Processes in Studies of Social Structure', *Versus* **12**: 33–83.

Cicourel, A. (1985) 'Text and Discourse', *Annual Review of Anthropology* **14**, 159–85.

Dingwall, R. (1977) 'Atrocity Stories' and Professional Relationships', *Sociology of Work and Occupations* **4**, 371–96.

Felman, S. (1983) *The Literary Speech Act*. Ithaca, NY: Cornell University Press.

Fish, S. (1980) *Is There a Test in This Class? The Authority of Interpretative Communities*. Cambridge, MA: Harvard University Press.

Garfinkel, H. (1967) *Studies in Ethnomethodology*. New York: Prentice-Hall.

Gee, J. P. (1991) 'A Linguistic Approach to Narrative', *Journal of Narrative and Life History* **1**, 15–39.

Hacking, I. (1991) 'The Making and Molding of Child Abuse', *Critical Inquiry* **17**, 253–88.

Handleman, D. (1983) 'Shaping Phenomenal Reality: Dialectic and Disjunction in the Bureaucratic Synthesis of Child-abuse in Urban Newfoundland', *Social Analysis* **13**, 3–36.

Heath, C. (1982) 'Preserving the Consultation: Medical Record Cards and Professional Conduct', *Sociology of Health and Illness* **4**, 56–74.

Hunter, K. (1986) '"There Was This One Guy ..." The Uses of Anecdotes in Medicine', *Perspectives in Biology and Medicine* **29**, 619–30.

Hydén, L.-C. (1991) *Barnavårdsutredningen som identitet* [Swedish]. Social Welfare Administration, Stockholm, Research and Development Unit, Report, 6.

Iser, W. (1978) *The Act of Reading. A Theory of Aesthetic Response*. Baltimore, MD: Johns Hopkins University Press.

Jönsson, L. (1988) *On Being Heard in Court Trials and Police Interrogations*. (Linkōping Studies in Arts and Science, **25**.) University of Linkōping.

Labov, W. (1972) 'The Transformation of Experience in Narrative Syntax', in W. Labov (ed.) *Language in the Inner City*. Philadelphia, PA: University of Philadelphia Press.

Long, T. A. (1986) 'Narrative Unity and Clinical Judgement', *Theoretical Medicine* **7**, 75–92.

Mills, C. W. (1943) 'The Professional Ideology of Social Pathologists', *American Journal of Sociology* **49**, 165–80.

Mishler, E. G. (1986) *Research Interviewing: Context and Narrative*. Cambridge, MA: Harvard University Press.

Ochs, E., Taylor, C., Rudolph, D. and Smith, R. (1992) 'Storytelling as a Theory-building Activity', *Discourse Processes* **15**, 37–72.

Pithouse, A. and Atkinson, P. (1988) 'Telling the Case: Occupational Narrative in a Social Work Office', in N. Coupland (ed.) *Styles of Discourse*. Beckenham: Croom Helm.

Platt, J. (1981) 'Evidence and Proof in Documentary Research', Part I and II, *The Sociological Review* **29**, 31–66.

Polanyi, L. (1989) *Telling the American Story*. Cambridge, MA: MIT Press.
Pratt, M. L. (1977) *Toward a Speech-act Theory of Literary Discourse*. Bloomington, IN: Indiana University Press.
Riessman, C. K. (1993) *Narrative Analysis*. Newbury Park, CA: Sage.
Smith, D. E. (1974) 'The Social Construction of Documentary Reality', *Sociological Inquiry* **44**, 257–68.
Spencer, J. W. (1988) 'The Role of Text in the Processing People in Organizations', *Discourse Processes* **11**, 61–78.
Stock, B. (1984) 'Medieval Literacy, Linguistic Theory, and Social Organization', *New Literary History* **16**, 13–29.
Stoeckle, J. D. and Billings, J. A. (1987) 'A History of History-taking: The Medical Interview', *Journal of General Internal Medicine* **2**, 119–27.
White, H. (1980) 'The Value of Narrativity in the Representation of Reality', in W. J. T. Mitchell (ed.) *On Narrative*. Chicago, IL: The University of Chicago Press.
Zimmerman, Don H. (1969) 'Record-keeping and the Intake Process in a Public Welfare Agency', in S. Wheeler (ed.) *On Record: Files and Dossiers in American Life*. New York: Russel Sage Foundation.

THIRTEEN

Moral construction in social work discourse

Christopher Hall, Srikant Sarangi and Stefaan Slembrouck

1. INTRODUCTION

A view of professional activity as discourse practice is the subject of wide-ranging studies in the human sciences. When seen as developing historically through the interplay of relations of power and knowledge, professional activity can be approached as a form of social action which is accomplished through techniques of institutional gaze and surveillance (Foucault 1977). Social work, in particular, represents an array of discursive practices which are constituted by professional forms of knowledge and which are rooted in a range of surveillance practices with an aim to discipline and control groups and individuals in a society (Parton 1991; Rose 1990; Stenson 1989). In this chapter we explore such technologies of surveillance and control by grounding our discussion in a moral climate, as evidenced in the accounting practices of social workers. Our main claim is that in looking at cases of child abuse – failure to thrive – one notices how the scope of professional surveillance extends beyond the child as an object, as social workers get involved in scrutinizing and assessing parenthood.

2. CHILD ABUSE: THE SHIFTING FOCUS IN SOCIAL WORK

Child protection has become a major concern of social work activity and rhetoric since the 'discovery' of child abuse and neglect in the early 1970s (Parton 1985). While social work has always been concerned with the maltreatment of children by their parents, this discovery has moved the professional response away from voluntary, contractual involvement, that was oriented towards psychotherapy, to an investigative stance which is based on models of 'dangerous families' (Dale et al. 1986).

One can argue that the positioning of social work in the case of 'dangerous families' is a product of historical, institutional and political processes. For instance, the political climate in the United Kingdom in the 1980s stressed less state interference and more family responsibility. This raised issues about the realignment of the relations between the state and the family (also extending to those families which are considered to be 'too dangerous' or 'incapable of caring for or protecting their children'). As Parton comments:

> At its simplest, this [the relation between state agencies and the family in the 1980s] can be seen in terms of a move from concerns about child care and child abuse to ones about child protection, where the latter tries to combine attempts to protect children from the danger while protecting the privacy of the family from unwarrantable interventions.
>
> (Parton 1991: 3)

In the mid-1980s a series of highly publicized inquiries into the death of children, who were known by the welfare agencies to be at risk, suggested that state intervention was inadequate and lacked authority. On the other hand, the Cleveland affair in the United Kingdom in 1988 demonstrates that social workers and doctors can be over-zealous in removing children. Over a three-month period, 121 children were diagnosed as having been sexually abused on the basis of a controversial and unsubstantiated medical examination, and consequently were removed from their homes via 'dawn raids'. As Franklin and Parton (1991) note, social workers were characterized as either 'inept and passive' or 'intrusive and authoritarian'. One inquiry report even suggested that the social services should lose exclusive control over the child protection system (Carlile Report 1987: 140), thus highlighting the threat to their professional power.

Our aim is to examine how such developments bear upon the discourse practices of social workers, as the professional pressure is being felt to come up with accurate information, meticulous recording and decisive action, which would stand up as conclusive evidence.[1] We focus on interview data from an inner-city public welfare agency in the UK concerning a case of child abuse – failure to thrive.[2] In our analysis we will look at one particular case of child abuse/neglect, concentrating mainly on how the social worker's account of the events reads like a story of institutional facts about irresponsible parents. This story is instrumental in reproducing social relations and realities about child care and abuse in contemporary British society.

By looking at discourse as constitutive of social work practice, we bring together the view that moral conceptions are embedded in available discourse formations for talking about 'normal/deviant' family behaviour with the situational aspect of blame allocation in a particular case. The link between these is the performance of a social work story, which deploys moral guidelines as a basis for justifying institutional action, thus articulating 'pre-structured relations' in a way which is constitutive of social work 'practice' (see Bourdieu 1977). For us, it does not make sense to reduce performance to system. As Fairclough points out, 'the questionable assumption is that one can extrapolate from structure to practice, that one can arrive at conclusions about practice without directly analysing real instances of it' (1988: 33).

Discourse analysis offers the opportunity to consider how social work discourse is replete with moral activity, depending for its force on such contrasts and constructions. Much has been made of the moral element in social work decision-making, but frequently this is contrasted with a more objective, rational approach. In this context, narrative theory can inform the investigation of character construction and plot development (see Hydén, this volume). Characters, events, and actions are constituted using a wide range of rhetorical devices and some will be investigated in this chapter – notably moral characterizations attributed to clients and justifications ascribed to professionals.

3. ACCOUNTING PRACTICES IN SOCIAL WORK TALK

The central preoccupation of many institutional agencies – medical personnel, police, lawyers, welfare workers, journalists, to name a few – is with providing adequate descriptions of situations that require intervention (Heritage 1984). This entails going on record to provide reasons, causes, analyses and plans, thereby justifying and producing their professional *raison d'etre*.[3]

The search for causes is also intrinsic to social work discourse, since it is through accounting practices that social work is created and can become consequential. Pithouse and Atkinson are quite right in suggesting that a case is shaped and ordered through the account' (1988: 184). Social work involves a 'defensive discourse', in which accounts offer rebuttals to potential charges even before they are made (see Atkinson and Drew 1979: 106). In child protection work, in particular, the social worker is always rehearsing being before the judge.

Tied to the pressures on accounting practices are social workers' own attempts to establish professional power. As Abbott and Wallace point out, the caring professions are powerful

> through their power to command definitions of reality by which the lives of their clients are shaped. In other words, they create both the object of their intervention – the neglectful mother, the wayward teenager, the bad patient – and at the same time make these the targets of their intervention.
>
> (Abbott and Wallace 1990: 6)

In social work, therefore, for a situation to become a case, it is necessary that it is created as such by a responsible professional. This inevitably means that the key situations, through which social workers must negotiate their interventions, necessarily involve displays of professional competence which rest on the justifiableness of their accounts – in court, during case conferences, in discussions with superiors, in reports to others. As Pithouse and Atkinson (1988) maintain, social work is an invisible trade which involves displays of competence through good storytelling.

4. ACCOUNTING FOR A CASE OF FAILURE TO THRIVE

All types of child abuse and neglect, according to Dingwall et al., are 'the products of complex processes of identification, confirmation and disposal rather than something inherent in a child's presenting condition' (1983: 31). They further suggest that two types of evidence are used to accomplish the identification and labelling process: clinical evidence, which is based on the medical examination of the children, and social evidence about the child's environment, the household conditions and relationships.

The particular case we are examining is one of 'failure to thrive'. It concerns two 18-year-old parents and three young children in a metropolitan borough in Britain. Two of the children were considered not to be gaining the appropriate weight for their age and they were also experiencing periods of related illness. There were no marks or bruises that warranted explanation.

Unlike much of the work in the area of child protection, 'failure to thrive' cases do not involve the investigation of physical injury. On the surface it is an easily recognizable condition for health and welfare professionals, and yet it makes up a small proportion of the number of children officially recognized as having been subjected to or at risk of abuse – in the UK this is the child protection register. It is defined as where children's weight, height and head circumference is significantly below normal and the lowest three per cent is used as the benchmark. Batchelor and Kerslake (1990) show disagreements in definitions of failure to thrive among medical writers, and in particular the uncertain link between the condition and child neglect and abuse. However, many professionals appear to skate over these details and firmly identify a category of 'failure to thrive' which is directly associated with, in Maher's (1987) and Gilmore's (1988) terms, cases where medical and social assessment find evidence of persistent or severe neglect or rejection by the parents. Maher offers the following definition of 'failure to thrive':

> Children under 17 who have been medically diagnosed as suffering from severe non-organic failure to thrive or whose behavioural and emotional development have been severely affected, where medical and social assessments find evidence of either persistent or severe neglect or rejection.
>
> (Maher 1987: 25)

It follows, then, that the assessment of social conditions is all the more important (including the moral assessment of the parents).

Our analysis is based on interview data which was a part of an institutional review of certain decision-making processes (see Appendix 1 on pp. 281–5 for a transcript of the first part of the interview). The hearer was a researcher, but one who was known to the social worker as a former colleague. It can be expected that the interview required an account which fed on shared perceptions of what-we-all-know-about these types of case and process. The account would therefore need to be both situationally justifiable and professionally competent, i.e. appear as a good story using appropriate professional jargon.[4]

5. A STORY OF FACTS AND BLAME: NARRATIVE PERFORMANCE IN SOCIAL WORK TALK

In providing an account of his interventionist action, the social worker creates a story. This story begins when the researcher asks the social worker how he first became involved. At this point the social worker seizes the initiative (*well look I'll speak*) and continues to talk uninterruptedly for some ten minutes. As this monologue ends with the comment – *that in summary is the case*, it can be assumed that the social worker sees this as in some way a completed story. By telling a story uninterruptedly – 'don't ask me questions, my story will answer all your concerns' – the social worker accomplishes an account.

As we see it, the concept of storytelling is more embracing than the perspective of accounting. Although accounting is one inevitable aspect of a social workers' narrative, a social work story comprises more complex structures which involve narrative scenarios, multiple voices, narrator-actors, different readings and actions driven by moral preoccupations.[5] From the sociology of literature, we know that straightforward moral guidelines tend to go together with unproblematic plot development (Zima 1981). Hence, examining the impact of moral assessment in narrative scripts allows one to study the ways in which wider societal notions of 'normal/deviant' parenting interlock with the production of a situated narrative.[6] For instance, in the case we are looking at, reported actions are seen to be informed by moral classifications as the narrative deployment of a 'non-cooperative client' becomes a basis for justifying coercive, interventionist action.

Professional activity as a moral enterprise has been noted by Hydén (1994) and Jokinen and Juhila (1994). These studies show that the construction of facts and morals are interrelated. For instance, the factual status of eligibility for 'welfare benefit' or 'homelessness' is achieved through a moral assessment. In this case of 'failure to thrive', facts and blame are also interrelated, but the moral assessment appears to come after the establishment of the facts. 'Failure to thrive' requires first an 'objective' display of 'facts' – e.g being 'underweight' – but it also needs an account of how it could happen and who is to blame, so as to establish 'failure to thrive' as a category with disreputable connotations (as the Maher quote above already showed).

It is also worth bearing in mind that the interview with the researcher provides just one occasion for a situated construction of the case as one of child neglect. There are a number of other occasions where the *same* story will be told differently.[7] However, the construction of a social work case necessarily involves a number of arenas for performances, each building on to the next. The genre of court talk in particular appears throughout this text (as the case was to come before the court in a month's time). Hence, it does not make sense to attempt either to minimize the influence of the interview situation on the production of the account, or to assume naïvely that stories have an absolute fixidity which transcends the various performances. This narrative is doing social work (just as a chat over coffee with colleagues or a presentation at a case conference is). And, although empirically we might want to demonstrate the typicality of the examined features for social work discourse, this is really beside the point.

In our analysis, we proceed as follows: first, we look at the presence of institutionalized voices in the social worker's narrative which make the narrative hearable as a social work story. These help account for how this case is established as a case of 'failure to thrive' and why the parents are held responsible for this situation. But, more than this, the narrative seems to derive its internal coherence and consistency from taking the point of view of the social worker's action-logic. Therefore, in a second analysis, we point out the use of a three-stage device which is instrumental in producing the narrative account. Finally, we will return to the question of seeing this narrative as a form of social practice, which is instrumental in reproducing social relations and realities within child abuse.

5.1 The dialogic telling of a multi-voiced story

The case we are discussing begins with the child being taken to hospital by her mother.[8] One thing left for the social worker to explain is how the case came to be his. This explanation begins with the hospital visit (20ff.) but a temporal detour in the narrative follows, bringing in actors and entities who need introduction – the GP, the grandmother, the cohab (cohabitee), the accommodation, the youth, the weight scales. As stated above, the identification of a case as 'failure to thrive' involves clinical and social evidence as established by other professions such as the medics, the police, welfare workers, etc. It is worth considering where in the social worker's narrative the construction of facts is based on inter-institutional endorsement.

The first institutional voice we hear is a medical one. As far as identification is concerned, the social worker accepts and endorses the assessment done by the medics that the first child is underweight. The mention that the second child was gaining weight after having been admitted in hospital is used negatively as evidence corroborating the diagnosis. The medical evidence and concern is therefore immutable. If the medics are 'concerned' then something must be done.

But the medical voice is not simply brought in alongside a social voice. It stands in a dialogic relation to it. The first instance where this occurs is:

> she had lived with her mother who was then seventeen just turning eighteen at the grandmother's there was the maternal grandmother the mother had subsequently moved to her own [borough] provided accommodation in [this social work division] and had moved with a cohab so there was a young cohab aged eighteen there was a mother aged eighteen and a baby (pause)

> the hospital felt that this was a clear picture of failure to thrive the child was as I recall off the top of my head I think it was two and a half kilos under weight was very dehydrated and in fact had the situation been left further longer the child would have died.

These introductory comments immediately show the two voices as separate but dialogic couples. The 'social' talk in the first quote produces ingredients of a 'young, unmarried, recently created, unaccommodated family'. The 'medical' that follows immediately uses 'weights', symptoms like 'dehydrated' and 'underweight', and the ultimate medical concern with sustaining life. The initial description of the family in 'social' terms sets up notions of 'deficient parenting skills', whereas the medical talk converts the concern into measurable, *medico-scientific* entities. The 'medical' talk is brought in to continue the line of a social explanation – the medics would not professionally have been expected to make the sorts of links the social worker is making here (but only to consider the bio-physical steps that would be needed for removing the symptoms).

In other parts of the text, the 'legal' voice is paramount, but again it is appropriated by the social worker. For instance, in lines 74–89, the court and its available disposals are deployed as devices to negotiate available powers with the magistrates; the supervision order is discussed in terms of its potential for social work rather than as a legal disposal. Other voices which the social worker 'appropriates' can be identified in the narrative, including the grandparents, the foster parents, the voluntary organization.

Towards the end of the interview (not included in Appendix 1), when the social worker closes the story with *'that in summary is the case'*, he is asked to comment on how easy/difficult it was to work with the grandparents. The social worker recounts:

> oh they are very cooperative and no problem they are disgusted of the behaviour of the natural parents and they are very resentful because their position is they say why why that they bring these children into the world er if they cannot care for them and they are not interested in them that's their sort of erm sort of blinkered view they are not looking the wider perspective that they can hardly expect to there is lot of anger

What we see here is the construction of bad parenting, but this time the voice of grandparents is mobilized in support of the institutional viewpoint. Notice, however, the way in which the social worker distances himself and the social welfare institution from the 'blinkered view' of the grandparents.

However, as we see it, bringing in allied voices is not a mere strategic choice. Being a social worker involves daily conversing with these voices. Yet, the one voice which is not accessed directly is the mother's. Her involvement is mediated mainly through the voices of others (but see section 6 on the presence of an implicit 'carnivalesque' dimension of the story). This is, for instance, the case in the hospital scene, where the mother is for the first time portrayed as hostile:

> in fact had the situation been left further long the child would have died the child was admitted and what then happened was that the mother erm the staff found the mother very very difficult very hostile uncooperative erm and the the situation er caused so much anxiety that a place of safety was taken and the child was kept in the hospital'.

By contrast, where the medical world is criticized, the criticism is mitigated with an 'explanation' for the professionals' failure to act or see certain things. In this case, the medics' lack of action is explained as a 'breakdown in communication' and the story continues with an account of the medics' efficiency. Blame allocation here functions to safeguard the inter-institutional frameworks and occurs in the form of whose actions can be portrayed as crucially affecting the condition of the child.

Unlike in child abuse with physical injury, direct accusations are more complex in a case like this one. It is made available through the depictions of the parents by the social worker and other actors as unstable, immature and hostile. Blame allocation is also implicit in the report of interventions offered to the family as 'bending over backwards to accommodate them'. In addition, each offer is said to have been rebuffed by the mother with increasing violence (the allocation of the black social worker (lines 40–44), the involvement of the family welfare association (lines 63–69), the role of grandparents and foster parents providing a contrast (lines 55–59)). The parents' non-cooperation with the welfare network makes their situation eligible for being constructed in social work terms.[9]

Thus, accounting is taking place here at least at two levels: the moral character of the family members are being created and established in order to categorize their behaviour and explain the current state of affairs; at the same time, the justification for institutional and professional activity is taking place. Both are interdependent – the client is created in terms of institutional actions, and the social worker's activity is described in terms of the moral creation of the client. This 'prospective-retrospective' interpretation allows the social worker to re-interpret past events to suit current concerns – 'a parent was "really" an abuser all along – and to organize the unfolding present as yet further confirmation of the correctness of this ascription' (Dingwall et al. 1983: 80). Therefore, in a second analysis, we will focus on the specific structural characteristics of the narrative, in particular the accumulative use of a three-stage device in building up 'an extreme case' where 'last resort' decisions are being made.

5.2 The semantic-structural dimensions of the narrative

Recent studies of narrative have a large and small purview in the literature ('grand and petit recit', Lyotard 1984): narrative as a communicating device versus narrative as a legitimating and constituting discourse. Studies of professional storytelling have shown how narratives are constructed through the interaction of both levels, as social reality is displayed in terms of 'cases' and 'case talk' (Pithouse and Atkinson 1988) which itself appropriates and reinforces cultural formulations of motherhood, family life, etc. (Silverman 1987; Stenson 1989). Narratives are created which weave together events and characters, deviance and normality into professionally competent performances. Such narratives both construct professional discourse, and establish and reestablish professional legitimation and control.[10]

The strategic use of the narrative to produce a view that the social worker acted competently and that the client was responsible turns the story into a matter of 'competence' vs. 'culpability'. This is reflected in a step-by-step analysis of the recounted events which reveals the use of 'synecdoche' – the substitution of a part for the whole (Atkinson 1990). The following recursive pattern can be observed in the social worker's narrative account. As set out in the table in Appendix 2 (pp. 286–7), three stages can be distinguished, which refer to successive episodes in decision-making and action.

Thus we can see throughout the whole narrative a first stage, which sets out to construct the parents as responsible for a particular, undesirable situation, followed by a second stage in which concern is expressed about this situation. Finally, there is a third stage in which the social worker reports on the action which followed. This, in its turn, informs the first stage of the next episode. For instance, in the first horizontal row (episode 1), *'the hospital felt ... a clear picture of failure to thrive'* in column 1 gives the diagnostic aspect which justifies the conclusion drawn by the social worker as given in column 2 (*had the situation been left any further ... the child would have died*). This, in its turn, is followed by subsequent action/decision (*the child was admitted*) which is reported in column 3 and brings us into the first stage of the next episode, which is the second horizontal row (*the staff found the mother difficult*). Following Emerson (1981), Pomerantz (1986) and Best (1987), we have dubbed stages 2 and 3 'extreme case' and 'last resort' respectively.[11] By doing this, we want to capture the extent to which professional action is seen as unavoidable in response to parental negligence. In the narrative, the two competing constructions of competent professionals and blameworthy parents are not merely placed in opposition to one another, but systematically linked. 'Extreme case' and 'last resort' here are thought of as rhetorical devices, within which the conditions for the creation of a child abuse case and institutional activity is justified.

Now we will look at the recursive patterning in each or the three stages separately.

5.2.1 *Stage 1: Parental non-cooperation as a cause*

In cases where parental non-cooperation provides a justification for coercive intervention, it is perhaps necessary to dramatize the parents' behaviour as physically aggressive. This comes out more efficiently when the institutional representative is portrayed as physically subdued. What is striking about the items in the first column are the selection of lexico-grammatical structures which either stress the non-physical actions of the institutional representative by, for instance, combining an institutional agent with a mental process (e.g *the hospital felt ... , the staff found ... , the foster parent found ... , the assessment went very well*) to be contrasted with the combinations of the parents with agency in a material process of physical violence (*the black worker was kicked and punched, the mother was so hostile, I was threatened*) or with a mental/material process indicating closure of procedure, thus holding them responsible for the failure to apply certain institutional measures (*the parents refused to cooperate, they just stopped cooperating, parents failed to attend, the family were not cooperating with them either, the mother went off in temper before we could explain the recommendations*).

Generally, social workers, when first looking at a case, are reluctant to ascribe negative labels to it, until they have no alternative but to see these as proved. The two key features whereby this reluctant stance breaks down are what are called 'parental incorrigibility' and 'multi-agency pressure' (Dingwall et al. 1983: 92–8). Non-cooperation from this point of view is a complex formulation which requires a convincing degree of discredit.

Paradoxically, this also requires a phase of cooperation, if only to prove the competence of institutional intervention. A cooperative mother is conditional to the claim of a successful assessment. In episode 6, the thematic spiral of non-cooperation starts after the period of apparent cooperation which resulted in a reduced degree of legal control (*a lenient supervision order* and *the child going home*). The (emphasized) *'refused to cooperate'* which follows in episode 7 suggests this cooperation was not merely an illusion, but a devious act on the parents' part to get the baby home. The assessment *'went well'* but the lack of detail of success provides one cue for the listener not to expect that this period of 'cooperation' should be considered too seriously as having major implications for the rest of the story. *'Cutting a long story short'* (line 70) is equally strategic in playing down the mother's cooperation. There are other pointers to the fragile nature of the 'success' – for instance, an aside that the father was in a detention centre, and the mention that the supervision order gave no statutory powers – a narrative pointer which warns of the importance of this for the future.

5.2.2 *Stage 2: Extreme case formulations*

That the parents actively 'refused' to cooperate is shown as a deliberate action on their part and the second, intermediate stage now functions to stress that at a number of times this got into a critical stage (*had the situation been left any further, the situation caused much anxiety, it was really a serious matter, arrangement of access was a horrendous task, things became extremely difficult, our concern was … but not able to work on it, there was a rather climax, the situation got to the point, regrettably I was forced into a situation, I have no alternative but*). What we see here is that the social worker is relying on language forms which downtone his active involvement in the construction of the circumstances of the case: agency is disguised and the social worker becomes an entity affected by the situation.

Although it is the social worker who attempts to rationalize his own decisive actions, he goes through great pains to stress his non-involvement and distanced observation of the stage leading up to each intervention. Compare, in this respect, with expert witnesses in court who tend to feature as acting upon a reality thrust at them, whereas defendants, like the mother here, are talked of only in terms of active, voluntary involvement which allows responsibility to be cast. In summary, this case of social worker talk could be characterized as victim-of-circumstance talk in which anyone acting under the same circumstances would have come up with the same conclusion.

5.2.3 *Stage 3: Last resorts*

The extreme case formulations in column 2 form the first half of a two-slotted pattern for justifying the decisive character of the last resort intervention decisions/actions given in the third column. In this column the social worker (and other institutional representatives) occur as agents of various process types which stress either the competent, professional intervention of the social worker or the smooth interinstitutional cooperation (*we involved the FWA* [Family Welfare Association], *we attempted to review, I did a joint home visit …*

we went to cover three things, we tried very hard to liaise, not only had I to take places of safety that I had to apply section forty one allowing me to go with the police to get access).

The home visit reported in episode 9 constitutes a climax. Although the social worker describes it as motivated by a desire to know why the parents were not cooperating, it is not a polite inquiry. It is clearly a professional threat by which the social worker goes on record about the parents' uncooperativeness. The three threats that followed indicate that the social workers were beginning to use their heavy artillery. The parents responded with their own heavy artillery: threats, fright and danger of violence. It has passed through stages of passive non-cooperation, legal obligation to a climax of physical threat. The narrative pace changes to emphasize the climax of the home visit with the police. These coercive actions could be interpreted as showing the social worker's inefficiency. But obviously the social worker is trying to suggest that the course of action has more to do with the blameworthiness of the mother than with institutional failure.

6. AN ALTERNATIVE STORY: THE MOTHER'S VOICE

A social work story could have an explanation for the inadequacy of the parents in social work terms – for example, early childhood deprivation, poor social development, disrupted personal relationships, etc. That this story chooses to leave unexplained the parents' prognosis suggests that they are not really clients of the social services, rather the devices centre on the allocation of blame. One can talk of a vicious cycle here, in which the social worker's justification reinforces subsequent action which further reinforces the labelling process. But would an alternative account have been possible? If so, would it still be presentable as a case of 'failure to thrive'?

Throughout the story there are alternative versions lurking in the background which threaten to disrupt the balance of blame and responsibility. One alternative version lies in the mother's own account of what has happened. For any of the episodes which the social worker reports there is the possibility to construct an alternative, mother's version. For instance, in the hospital episode the mother is concluded to be 'uncooperative'. There can be little doubt that in those circumstances she must have shown traces of irritation or disapproval at some point. And this may have been caused by a variety of things, ranging from resistance to imposed institutional intervention to simple irritation about having to wait long hours and being kept in the dark about what was really going on. What is important, however, is that these signs of 'hostility' are used as indicators to assess her willingness to go along with institutional intervention, and, indirectly, her abilities to care for the child.

One important dimension here is the notion of available scripts which determine how institutional routines are reported. Scripts not only provide speakers with a particular way of sequencing a story in terms of chronology, action order, characters and forms of causality. They are essentially socially constructed entities (and have a reality-creating capacity) in that they also mould observations in terms of available scenarios with a limited number of outcomes and explanations. This is, for example, clear from the judge's ruling in court that there had been over-interference. This outcome would not have been possible without the essential Western ideology of the immunity of the nuclear family.

What is striking is the extent to which the narrative has been able to dismiss any doubts about the *facts* and who is to *blame*. One factor is the viewpoint in the storytelling which determines whose actions will be portrayed as lacking order and logic and as being random and anarchic. As only the social worker's and the institutional viewpoints are given, the mother's actions appear as loosely connected but apparently consistent acts of devious non-cooperation. As institutional actions provide the reference points for new developments and episodes in the story, the parents' actions are incorporated within this episodic structure, with the result that their activities outside these institutional encounters do not get reported. The chances therefore diminish that their actions appear as 'coherent' and 'logical' (nevertheless their voice is present to undermine the emergent interpretative coherence in the social worker's narrative).[12]

One reason for the onesidedness of this narrative is that it is functional in court, where no interpretative hiccups are allowed, else the evidence will be dismissed as inconclusive. Within the social work profession this onesidedness is unlikely to be challenged because the intervention process is seen as in the interest of the family (social work as a means to 'normalize' behaviour). However, the law only provides for minimal intervention in the family. The immunity of the family should only be given up when evidence is absolutely 'safe'.

One further dimension of the absence of an alternative, mother's version lies in the tendency to objectify the client in institutional interventions. This is reflected in the social worker's use of secondary evidence. He only selects other agencies' (e.g. the foster parents', the family welfare association's, etc.) negative assessments of the mother as secondary corroborating evidence. At no point does he report the mother's own account of the events.

The social worker thus has a defending role to play in the inter-institutional networks, hence the importance to appear to have made unavoidable, 'objective' observations and acted accordingly. Institutional procedures appear as the main route to guide the listener through the case. Referrals, case conferences and the use of legal sanctions are deployed as the main hooks on which to hang the story. This has the effect of highlighting institutional action as responsible, and as in accordance with the 'correct' procedures (Sarangi and Slembrouck 1996). To cast other institutions in non-cooperative terms is out of the question, although later the social worker admitted that there was some problem with coordinating work among the agencies. This illustrates that the position of the social work profession (relatively powerful in the parental context, but powerless in court) is a real factor which determines the nature of their professional talk.

As a narrator-actor, the social worker has control over the story. He may have been successful in painting 'a clear picture' of the case, framing the actors in their roles and himself stepping in and out of the frame (see the abundant use of visual and other metaphors like *'a clear picture'*, *'a blinkered view'*, *'taking a back seat'*, etc.). Not surprisingly, when the reader is informed about the police's discovery that the child is all right, this comes quite unexpected (the listener's *oh*, line 168). Until that point, the listener had been prepared for continuing discoveries of children not thriving. The storyteller here continues to build up the picture of the parents as uncooperative and the children as constantly at risk. At this point, however, the use of the most serious last resort (going in with the police) results in the discovery of the baby as *'developing perfectly acceptably'*. The listener is surprised. Indeed, it could be that doubt may now be cast on future uses of the three-stage device. And only by the disclaimer (*not to my surprise*, lines 165–166) is the storyteller able to rescue some credibility.

7. ROBUST STORIES WITH 'STRONG' MORALS

In our analysis we have treated social problem categories as rhetorical entities. This does not imply that we subscribe to a view of discourse practices as intentionally employed strategies. Instead, we believe that social work stories are constrained by the kind of discourse practices that are accessible to them and are currently used. They appear to gain authority and rigidity over time and context through a series of inter-institutional retellings (see also, Hall 1993). One could call a 'robust story' a story which has gained institutional credibility and patronage and can handle external threats. It is a story whose validity applies across the 'order of discourse'. We have tried to show that this is achieved by making use of a wide range of resources, in particular 'strong' conceptions of moral categorizations and attendant action scripts. Hence, as suggested by Thibault (1989), heteroglossic tendencies do not exclude the creation and maintenance of monoglossic formations which, as they interlock with dominant cultural notions, function to keep in place dominant cultural concepts. Or to use Latour's (1987) analogy, entities can be 'blackboxed' and protected as long as the allies lend their support. However, there are times when allies desert, the blackbox becomes reopened and a robust story can 'fail to thrive'.

APPENDIX 1

RI = research interviewer
SW = social worker

Rl: start when you took it on and I gather from what I could see you
took it on in about erm september eighty six
SW: that's right
Rl: and the kids were already in care is that right
SW: well look ***I'll*** speak to because I can I can
RI: I'll leave it to you [laughs]
SW: [unclear] I was allocated in to this case in september nineteen eighty
six the case erm had originally been allocated in area five erm for a
period of about six weeks prior to me taking it on the circumstances
were [...] that erm a child by the name of Catherine erm [...] had
been taken to Saint Hugo College Hospital by the child's mother in
july nineteen eighty six the circumstances were that Catherine had
been born in december nineteen eighty five she had lived with ***her***
mother who was then aged seventeen just turning eighteen erm at

the grandmother's maternal grandmother's home of and then the mother has subsequently moved to her own Littleton provided accommodation in area five and had moved in with erm a cohab so there was a young cohab about aged eighteen there was the mother who was eighteen and the baby [...]

Episode 1

now the baby was at some stage I think when she was about five months old erm taken to the GP who was *very* concerned about the child feeling that the child was under weight erm was not developing as it should and the referral was made to Saint Hugo College Hospital it would appear retrospectively that there was a breakdown in communication between the GP and the hospital the hospital perhaps not quite realising the erm the priority that this er situation should have so it turned out that was a further four weeks before the child was taken to the hospital for an appointment on being taken there erm the hospital felt that this was a clear picture of a failure to thrive the child was as I recall off the top of my head I think it was two and a half kilos under weight was very dehydrated and in fact had the situation been left further longer the child would have died the child was admitted

Episode 2

and what then happened was that the mother erm the the staff found the mother very very difficult very ***hostile*** uncooperative erm and the the situation er caused so much anxiety that a place of safety was taken and the child was kept in the hospital

Episode 3

there followed a number of case conferences the number of which I *cannot* recall that something in a region of three or four and one of those conferences the mother actually physically assaulted the chair [...] erm now a social worker from a hospital was appointed at that time the family is a er black family and the social worker at the hospital was a er black worker the that didn't seem to help at all in that the parents found it *very* difficult to cooperate with this man [...] the case was allocated in area five and I think it was in august nineteen eighty six because of course the family actually lived and again erm black social worker was allocated [...] there was an incident however involving this worker when he was assaulted he was kicked and punched and it was really a very serious matter on the basis that this worker would find it extremely difficult to proceed *I* was allocated which was in september now at that point various interim care orders had been granted but when I took on the case I took it on with a clear objective in mind and that was one of assessment [...]

Episode 4

now unfortunately the child had been placed with a foster parent and again because the mother was so ***hostile*** the foster parent found it impossible to work with her and this was actually ***in fear*** of having this mother come to her home and she in fact was so frightened that she asked for the child to be transferred [...]

Episode 5

when the child was transferred ***again*** we were in some difficulty because we felt that we couldn't arrange access in in the foster home as we normally would so what happened was that access had to be arranged in area office which was a horrendous task [...] to overcome this and to enable me to ***assess*** this family's ability to care for this child we involved the family welfare association in Bollington and we involved them with two erm objectives ***one*** was that they would assist in the assessment of the the parenting skills of these parents and secondly that they would they would provide a venue where access to the child could could happen [...]

Episode 6

erm cutting a long story short the assessment went very well and I managed to develop a relationship with the mother in particular the father unfortunately was in detention centre at that time and this caused some difficulties [...] but the the assessment did go well and by the november when the full care proceeding date was set I had called a further case conference and the case conference ***accepted*** my recommendation that we should go forward with care proceedings that that we should seek a supervision order rather than a full care order [...] we took it to court in november and this recommendation was accepted by the court all be it that we had reservations and the reservations were put very clear to the magistrates we were recommending the supervision that we wanted the court to know as indeed did the guardian ad litem our [...] erm that the supervision order gave us no erm statutory powers to remove the child or to do anything should the situation break down and that is the significant point for the future [...] anyway erm we came to a voluntary agreement which was agreed in court although again it couldn't be part of the order that mother was to continue erm her work with the family welfare association and that there was agreements made about her visits there and about my work with the family

Episode 7

what then happened was that as soon as the baby went home [...] very sadly the parents refused to cooperate and things became extremely difficult the situation was exacerbated by the birth of a second baby in the december of eighty six [...] we then had a double problem that [...] workwise we were putting in the family welfare association who were meant to be there to ***counsel*** the family and to offer them erm primary care which would involve them developing the parenting skills so they were heavily involved secondly there was myself who was the key worker thirdly there was a family aid from area five who was visiting twice a week

Episode 8

and it got to the point that by sort of january february nineteen eighty seven that ***none*** of us were actually able to work with the family at all and because they weren't allowed in us too and as I said they they just stopped cooperating erm [...] our concern was that here we have a statutory supervision order erm and we were not able to work on it at all we were not able to supervise [...] we attempted to hold case conferences where we could review this situation

Episode 9

and we did this unfortunately parents failed to attend and there was a rather climax and I can't remember the month but I think it was in march eighty seven erm when I did a home visit to the family a joint visit with the family welfare association and it was found that erm [...] it was [TEMPORARILY INTERRUPTED] we went to to cover three things one was that we wanted to let the family know that there was another case conference coming up and we wanted to tell them how important it was because clearly we were going to have to consider putting the new baby's name on the register [...] secondly we wanted to to see if we could investigate with the family ***why*** they were unwilling to cooperate erm and thirdly really to let them know that we were viewing the situation very seriously [...]

Episode 10

basically I was threatened at that interview it was a very frightening experience and both of us felt very lucky to get out without being physically assaulted erm [...] the situation got to the point where ah ***because*** no one was seeing the family we were getting second hand information that the new baby was also failing to thrive and we tried very hard to liaise with other agencies like the GP and the health visitor and we did this successfully

Episode 11

but the family were not cooperating with them either the baby was actually admitted to hospital in april for a short period and was diagnosed as having reflax which is a condition whereby erm the the the food erm is is is not or that the milk as it was the liquid is not retained it its just goes down so far and a valve then forces it out again and it's vomitted up and so of course the baby doesn't get nourishment ***that*** was diagnosed and mother was shown how to erm how to act how how to actually deal with that but after I think was a further three weeks erm three or four weeks having failed I may say to keep follow up appointments at the hospital the baby was again seen by the GP who felt further concerned and the baby was taken to Saint Toby where it was admitted and a diagnosis was made of a very erm clear failure to thrive in that from the time that it was admitted to the time ah sorry from the time of discharged

RI: yeah

SW: to the time of readmitting and had failed to put on much weight at all

Episode 12

and indeed by the time we had the next case conference which was at the end of april erm stroke beginning of may erm nineteen eighty seven the baby while at have been kept in hospital had actually put on weight having been fed under a normal regime indicating so the medics felt that clearly it was a question of the way the baby was being handled and fed [...] what the mother came to that case conference but went off in temper before we could explain the recommendations or the decisions and the decisions were that we should take in places of safety and on both the children one because we ***wanted*** to ensure that the baby was kept in hospital erm for further treatment and secondly that the second the first child Catherine who we were meant to be supervising because we have not managed to just ***see*** her we've been ***prevented*** in effect from seeing her erm we'd no way we we felt that the child was probably progressing quite well but we couldn't prove it and we felt we needed to see her to prove it [...] this was we tried to discuss this with mother but she wouldn't hear of it and regrettably I was forced into a situation where not only had I to take places of safety that I had to apply for a section forty one allowing me to to go with the police to gain access [...] we further tried to negotiate this with the parents but again getting no cooperation I have ***no*** erm alternative but to go with the police [...] both the the baby was already in hospital but the other child we've moved of course not to my surprise when she was removed and examined was found to be developing acceptably

RI: oh

SW: which is what we anticipated ***but*** we had to prove it and what then transpired was that we went of course for interim care proceedings and we got the interim care of the baby but not on Catherine the first child [...] however the parents took a decision erm to [...] erm leave or to place Catherine with the maternal grandmother and grandfather who had always kept in touch with the situation

APPENDIX 2

column 1	*column 2*	*column 3*
the hospital felt ... a clear picture of failure to thrive	had the situation been left further the child would have died	the child was admitted
the staff found the mother difficult	the situation caused much anxiety	a place of safety was taken
the family found it very difficult to cooperate with this man ... the black worker was kicked and punched	it was really a very serious matter and on that basis	I was allocated and I took it on with a clear objective
because the mother was so hostile the foster parent found it impossible to work	she asked for the child to be transferred	the child was transferred
because we felt that we couldn't arrange access in foster home as we normally would	arrangement of access in area office was a horrendous task	we involved the FWA [Family Welfare Association] with two objectives
cutting a long story short, the assessment went very well	I managed to develop a relationship with the mother in particular ... unfortunately the father was in d.c.	the case conference accepted my recommendation that we should seek a supervision order

column 1	*column 2*	*column 3*
as soon as the baby went home very sadly the parents refused to cooperate … with none of us	things became extremely difficult the situation was exacerbated by the birth of another child	we then had a double problem
none of us were actually able to work with the family at all because they just stopped cooperating	our concern was that here we have supervision order but not able to work on it	we attempted to hold case conferences where we could review this situation
unfortunately parents failed to attend	there was a rather climax	I did a joint home visit with the FWA [Family Welfare Association] … we went to cover three things
basically I was threatened at the interview lucky to get out unhurt	the situation got to the point … we got second hand information that the new baby was also failing to thrive	we tried very hard to liaise with other agencies and we did this successfully
but the family were not cooperating with them either … the mother shown to deal with feeding then having failed to keep follow-up appointments at the hospital	the GP felt further concerned	the (new) baby was admitted … and was diagnosed as failure to thrive
the mother came to that conference but went off in temper before we could explain the recommendations but she wouldn't hear of it	regrettably I was forced into a situation	where not only had I to take places of safety that I had to apply a section forty one allowing me to go with the police to gain access

NOTES

1. For a discussion of the social policy consquences of these developments, see Parton (1985, 1986) and Stevenson (1989).
2. All names in the data have been anonymized. Words in bold type are stressed by the speaker; dots in square brackets represent a short pause.
3. Garfinkel (1967) points out that all talk is accounting rather than this only being the case in situations experienced as 'accusations'.
4. As it was to form part of 'the scrutiny from the research section', the account would also function to convince the researcher that the social worker had performed according to institutional precepts.
5. As Latour and Bastide (1986) argue, one can approach scientific texts or, in this case, the social workers' account in the same way as a literary critic.
6. Among others, Pithouse and Atkinson (1988) and Dingwall et al. (1983) have examined social work discourse, but they have not concentrated on the processes of allocating blame and responsibility or on the importance of the display of moral appearance. However, 'blame' has emerged as an important theme in the study of talk in various contexts, e.g. cross-examination (Atkinson and Drew 1979), family disputes (Cuff 1980), doctor–patient interactions (Silverman 1987). Especially in studies of monologic accounts (cf. Watson 1978; Watson and Weinberg 1982), the allocation of blame and responsibility has emerged as central to the production of competent and accountable discourse.
7. As Linell and Jönsson (1991) point out, 'the professionally perspectivized narrative' in the case of police reports often amounts to the same story being told in different narratives, with discrepant relevances and rationalities.
8. At the point of contact with this social worker, the situation had been established as a case for about 18 months. The details of these initial processes were not available to the researchers (see lines 1–37 as to how the case came to this social worker).
9. Rather than concentrating on the form of the blaming through the sequence of conversation (Atkinson and Drew 1979; Watson 1978), we are interested in blame as a process of creating the parents as discredited moral characters.
10. See Hall, Sarangi and Slembrouck (forthcoming) on silent and silenced voices in social work narratives; Hydén (this volume) for a comparative account of psychiatric reports and social work reports; and Linell and Jönsson (1991) on perspective-setting in the context of police-suspect interaction.
11. The model used here resembles Toulmin's (1958) analysis of argumentation structures, where a claim appeals to facts but does so through a

'warrant' which authorizes the step taken.

12. Hall (1993) points out the influence of the 'unheard' story in social work discourse.

REFERENCES

Abbott, Pamela and Wallace, Claire (1990) *The Sociology of the Caring Professions*. London: Falmer Press.

Atkinson, Paul (1990) *The Ethnographic Imagination: Textual Constructions of Reality*. London: Routledge.

Atkinson, J. Maxwell and Drew, Paul (1979) *Order in Court: Verbal Interaction in Judicial Settings*. London: Macmillan.

Batchelor, Jane and Kerslake, Andrew (1990) *Failure to Find Failure to Thrive*. London: Whiting and Birch.

Best, Joel (1987) Rhetoric in Claims Making: Constructing the Missing Children Problem. *Social Problems* **34** (2), 101–21.

Bourdieu, Pierre (1977) *Outline of a Theory of Practice*. Cambridge: Cambridge University Press

Carlile Report (1987) *A Child in Mind: The Report of the Commission of Inquiry into the Circumstances Surrounding the Death of Kimberly Carlile*. London Borough of Greenwich.

Cleveland Report (1988) *Report of the Inquiry into Child Abuse in Cleveland*. London: HMSO.

Cuff, E. C. (1980) Some Issues in the Problem of Studying Versions in Everyday Situations. Department of Sociology. *Occasional Paper No. 3*, University of Manchester.

Dale, Peter, Davies, Murray, Morrison, Tony and Waters, Jim (1986) *Dangerous Families: Assessment and Treatment of Child Abuse*. London: Tavistock.

Dingwall, Robert, Eekelaar, John and Murray, Topsy (1983) *The Protection of Children: State Intervention and Family Life*. Oxford: Basil Blackwell.

Emerson, Robert M. (1981) On Last Resorts. *American Journal of Sociology*, **87** (1), 1–22.

Fairclough, Norman (1988) Michel Foucault and the Analysis of Discourse. *Research Papers of the Centre for Language in Social Life* **10**. Lancaster University.

Foucault, Michel (1977) *Discipline and Punish*. London: Allen and Lane.

Franklin, Bob and Parton, Nigel (eds) (1991) *Social Work, the Media and Public Relations*. London: Routledge.

Garfinkel, Harold (1967) *Studies in Ethnomethodology*. Engelwood Cliffs, NJ: Prentice-Hall.

Gilmore, Alan (1988) *Innocent Victims*. London: Michael Joseph.

Hall, Christopher (1993) Social Work as Narrative: An Investigation of the

Social and Literary Nature of Social Work Accounting. Unpublished PhD thesis. Brunel University.

Hall, Christopher, Sarangi, Srikant and Slembrouck, Stefaan (forthcoming) Silent and Silenced Voices: Interactional Construction of Audience in Social Work Talk in Jaworski, Adam (ed.) *Silence: Interdisciplinary Perspectives*. de Gruyter: Mouton.

Heritage, John (1984) *Garfinkel and Ethnomethodology*. Cambridge: Polity Press.

Hydén, Lars-Christer (1994) The Social Worker as Moral Worker, in Gunnarsson, Britt-Louise, Linell, Per and Nordberg, Bengt (eds) *Text and Talk in Professional Contexts*. Uppsala University. ASLA:s skriftserie 6.

Jokinen, Arja and Juhila, Kirsi (1994) The Discursive Construction of Homeless People's Identities. Paper presented at the *Sociolinguistics Symposium* 10, Lancaster University.

Latour, Bruno (1987) *Science in Action*. Milton Keynes: Open University Press.

Latour, Bruno and Bastide, Francois (1986) Writing Science – Fact and Fiction, in Callon, M., Law, J. and Rip, A. (eds) *Mapping the Dynamics of Science and Technology*. London: Macmillan.

Linell, Per and Jönsson, Linda (1991) Suspect Stories: Perspective-setting in an Asymmetrical Situation, in Marková, Ivana and Foppa, Klaus (eds) *Asymmetries in Dialogue*. Hemel Hempstead: Harvester Wheatsheaf, pp. 75–100.

Lyotard, Jean-Francois (1984) *The Postmodern Condition*. Manchester: Manchester University Press.

Maher, Peter (1987) *Child Abuse: The Educational Perspective*. London: Basil Blackwell.

Parton, Nigel (1985) *The Politics of Child Abuse*. London: Macmillan.

Parton, Nigel (1986) The Beckford Report: A Critical Appraisal. *British Journal of Social Work* **16** (5), 511–30.

Parton, Nigel (1991) *Governing the Family: Child Care, Child Protection and the State*. London: Macmillan.

Pithouse, Andrew and Atkinson, Paul (1988) Telling the Case: Occupational Narrative in a Social Work Office, in Coupland, N. (ed.) *Styles of Discourse*. London: Croom Helm.

Pomerantz, Anita (1986) Extreme Case Formulations: A Way of Legitimising Claims. *Human Studies* **9**, 219–29.

Rose, Nikolas (1990) *Governing the Soul: The Shaping of the Private Self*. London: Routledge.

Sarangi, Srikant and Slembrouck, Stefaan (1996) *Language, Bureaucracy and Social Control*. London: Longman.

Silverman, David (1987) *Communication and Medical Practice: Social Relations in the Clinic*. London: Sage.

Stenson, Kevin (1989) Social Work Discourse and the Social Work

Interview. Unpublished PhD thesis. Brunel University.

Stevenson, Olive (ed.) (1989) *Child Abuse: Public Policy and Professional Practice*. Hemel Hempstead: Harvester Wheatsheaf.

Thibault, Paul J. (1989) Semantic Variation, Social Heteroglossia, Intertextuality: Thematic and Axiological Meaning in Spoken Discourse. *Critical Studies* **1** (2), 181–209.

Toulmin, Stephen (1958) *The Uses of Argument*. Cambridge: Cambridge University Press.

Watson, Rod (1978) Categorization, Authorization and Blame – Negotiation in Conversation. *Sociology* **12** (1), 105–13.

Watson, Rod and Weinberg, Thomas (1982) Interviews and the Interactional Construction of Accounts of Homosexual Identity. *Social Analysis* **11**, 56–78.

Zima, Peter V. (1981) *Literatuur en Maatschappij*. Assen: Van Gorcum.

FOURTEEN

Contested vision: the discursive constitution of Rodney King

Charles Goodwin and Marjorie Harness Goodwin

On 3 March 1991 an amateur video photographer taped a group of Los Angeles policemen administering a very violent beating with metal clubs to an African-American motorist, Mr Rodney King, who had been stopped for a traffic violation. The 1992 trial of the four white policemen became a politically charged theatre for contested vision as opposing sides in the case used the same murky pixels to display to the jury incommensurate events (e.g., a brutal, savage beating of a man lying helpless on the ground versus careful police response to a dangerous 'PCP crazed giant' who was argued to be in control of the situation). By deploying an array of systematic discursive practices, including talk, ethnography, category systems articulated by expert witnesses, and various ways of highlighting the images provided by the tape, the lawyers for the policemen were able to restructure the complex perceptual field visible on the TV screen so that minute body movements of Mr King, rather than the actions of the policemen hitting him, became the focus of the jury's attention.

This chapter uses that trial to investigate the discursive practices used by members of a profession to shape events in the domain of professional scrutiny they focus their attention upon. The shaping process creates the objects of knowledge that become the insignia of a profession's craft: the theories, artifacts and bodies of expertise that are its special and distinctive domain of competence.[1] Analysis of the methods used by members of a community to build and contest the events that structure their lifeworld contributes to the development of a practice-based theory of knowledge and action.[2] The context of professional activity examined is legal argumentation. Three practices are investigated: (i) *coding schemes* used to transform the materials being attended to in a specific setting into the objects of knowledge that animate the discourse of a profession (Cicourel 1964, 1968); (ii) *highlighting*, making specific phenomena in a complex perceptual field salient by marking them in some fashion; and (iii) *the production and articulation of material representations*. By applying such practices to phenomena in the domain of scrutiny, participants build and contest *professional vision*, socially organized ways of seeing and understanding events that are answerable to the distinctive interests of a particular social group.

The Rodney King trial provides a vivid example of how the ability to see a meaningful event is not a transparent, psychological process, but is instead a socially situated activity accomplished through the deployment of a range of historically constituted discursive practices. An event being seen, a relevant *object of knowledge*, emerges through the interplay between a *domain of scrutiny* (the images made available by the King videotape) and a set of *discursive practices* (dividing the domain of scrutiny by highlighting a figure against a ground, applying specific coding schemes for the constitution and interpretation of relevant events, etc.) being deployed within a *specific activity* (arguing a legal case, etc.). Through use of such practices lawyers for both sides were able to structure, in ways that suited their own distinctive agendas, the complex perceptual field visible on the TV screen. All vision is perspectival and lodged within endogenous communities of practice. The unit being investigated is thus analogous to what Wittgenstein called a *language game*, a 'whole, consisting of language and the actions into which it is woven' (1958: §7).

PRACTICES FOR SHAPING VISION

The use of coding schemes, highlighting practices and the articulation of graphic representations to organize perception will now be examined in a specific professional setting: the courtroom. When the tape of Rodney King being beaten was broadcast, there was public outrage and four policeman were put on trial for excessive use of force. The principal piece of evidence against them was the videotape. The violence on it was so graphic that many people assumed that a conviction was almost automatic. However, the jury found the policemen innocent, a verdict that triggered the Los Angeles uprising. At a second Federal trial a year later, two of the officers were convicted of violating Mr King's civil rights, and two were acquitted.

Perhaps surprisingly, the main evidence used in the defense of the policemen was the tape showing them beating Mr King. Indeed, one of the officers convicted in the second trial, Sergeant Stacy Koon, spent much of his time between the two trials watching and rewatching the tape, seeing how it looked when projected on different walls of his house. Rather than wanting to minimize the events on the tape he told a reporter that

> If we had our way, we'd go down to Dodger Stadium and rip off that big-screen Mitsubishi and bring it into the courtroom and say, 'Hey, folks, you're in for the show of your life because when this tape gets blown up it's awesome.'
>
> (Mydans 1993d: A10)

For Rodney King the experience of looking at the tape was quite different: 'It's sickening to see it. It makes me sick to my stomach to watch it' (Newton 1993a: A16).

At the first trial the prosecution presented the tape of the beating as a selfexplicating, objective record. Thus the chief prosecutor said

> What more could you ask for? You have the videotape that shows objectively, without bias, impartially, what happened that night. The videotape shows conclusively what happened that night. It can't be rebutted.
>
> (Mydans 1993b: A7)

By way of contrast the lawyers defending the policemen did not treat the tape as a record that spoke for itself. Instead, they argued that it could be understood only by embedding the events visible on it within the work life of a profession. The defense proposed that the beating constituted an example of careful police craftwork, a form of professional discourse with the victim, in which he was a very active co-participant, indeed the party who controlled the interaction.

To make this claim successfully the defense provided the jury with both ethnography about police practices, and a coding scheme to analyse the events on the tape. The power of coding schemes to control perception in this fashion was central to the defense strategy. Basically the defense contended that if the police officers could legitimately see Mr King's actions as aggressive and a threat to them, then the police were entitled to use force to protect themselves and take him into custody.

EXPERT TESTIMONY

The central point debated within the trial was what the policemen who beat King perceived him to be doing. These perceptions were not treated as individual, psychological phenomena lodged within the minds of specific policemen, but instead as socially organized frameworks shared within the police profession. This had important consequences. In that such perceptions are not idiosyncratic phenomena restricted to individuals, but instead frameworks shared by a profession, *expert testimony* becomes possible. An expert, who was not present at the scene, can describe authoritatively what the policemen could legitimately see as they looked at the man they were beating.

Expert testimony is given a very distinctive shape within the adversarial system of the American courtroom (Drew 1992: 472–4; Shuy 1982). Each side hires its own experts, and attacks the credibility of its opponents' experts. Moreover, the use of expert witnesses intersects with rules establishing what counts as adequate proof. The jury is instructed to find the defendant innocent if there is reasonable doubt about his guilt. Reasonable doubt can be created by muddying the waters with a plausible alternative. In the words of the lawyer for defendant Briseño:

> Your experts really don't have to be better than their [the prosecution's] experts. All you've got to have are experts on both sides. I think [jurors] wonder: 'How could we as lay people know beyond a reasonable doubt, when the experts can't decide?'
>
> (Lieberman 1993b: A32)

Such a strategy can be quite successful. One of the jurors who acquitted the policemen in the first King trial said, 'Our instructions of how we could consider evidence stated … if there are two reasonable explanations for an event, we had to pick the one that points to innocence, not the one that points to guilt' (Lieberman 1993b: A32).

CODING AGGRESSION AS PROFESSIONAL PRACTICE

Allowing expert testimony on the use of force by the police had the effect of filtering the events visible on the tape through a police coding scheme, as articulated by an expert who instructed the jury how to see the body movements of the victim in terms of that system. What one finds in the trial is a dialogic framework encompassing the work of two different professions, as the discourse of the police with one of their suspects is embedded within the discourse of the courtroom.

In order to measure police perception a coding scheme for the escalation of force was applied to the tape: (i) if a suspect is aggressive, the proper police response is escalation of force in order to subdue him; (ii) when the suspect cooperates, then force is de-escalated. When an expert applies this coding scheme to the tape a new set of finely differentiated events, described through appropriate language drawn from the social sciences, is produced. In the words of one expert:[3]

Expert: There were,
ten distinct (1.0) uses of force.
rather than one single use of force.
...
In each of those, uses of force.
there was an escalation and a de-escalation, (0.8)
an assessment period, (1.5)
and then an escalation and a de-escalation again. (0.7)
And another assessment period.

The massive beating is now transformed into ten separate events, each with its own sequence of stages.

The use of this category system radically transforms the images visible on the tape by placing them within an expert frame of reference. Thus when Mr King is hit yet another blow, this is transformed from a moment of visible violence – what the prosecution in the second trial will instruct the jury to see as 'beating a suspect into submission' – into a display that the 'period of de-escalation has ceased':

Defense: Four oh five, oh one.
We see a blow being delivered. =
= Is that correct.
Expert: That's correct.
The – force has been again escalated (0.3)
to the level it had been previously, (0.4)
and the de-escalation has ceased.

...

Defense: And at–
At this point which is,
for the record four thirteen twenty nine, (0.4)
We see a blow being struck
and thus the end of the period of, de-escalation?
Is that correct Captain.

Expert: That's correct.
Force has now been elevated to the previous level, (0.6)
after this period of de-escalation.

A reader looking at this sequence might argue that what the expert is saying is a mere tautology: if someone is being hit again, then almost by definition any period of de-escalation of force (i.e. the moments when the suspect is not being hit) has ceased. However, much more than tautology is involved. By deploying the escalation–de-escalation framework the expert has provided a coding scheme that transforms the actions being coded into displays of careful, systematic police craftwork, e.g. a prototypical example of rational, rule-governed action. One of the defense lawyers said that what he wanted to show the jury was that 'What looks like uncontrolled uh brutality and random violence is indeed a very disciplined and controlled effort to take Mr King into custody' (Court TV 1992). A major resource for affecting such a perceptual transformation is the use of coding schemes such as the one articulated above by the defense's expert witness. Such schemes provide the jury with far from neutral templates for viewing and understanding in a particular way the events visible on the tape.

These structures also define the instruments of violence visible on the tape. When the escalation framework was first introduced the defense attorney showed the jury a chart of *tools* used by the police that included not only the batons that they were beating him with, but also the kicks that they gave him:

Defense: And this chart will show you the ***tools***
that Sergeant Koon had available to him on March third.

...

The next tool up, (1.9)
Is: (0.3) a side handle baton. (0.8)
a metal (0.3) baton. (1.0)
i:s a tool (0.8)
to protect yourself (0.9)

and to take people into custody. (1.0)
And in addition to that (0.3)
on the same level with this (0.5)
the experts will tell you as well as Sergeant Koon, (0.4)
that there are ***ki***cks,

A coding scheme, classifying phenomena visible on the tape as tools required for the work of a particular occupation, is deployed to transform what the prosecution described as brutal 'cowardly stomps' inflicted on a prone, beaten man, into a domain of professional craftwork.

The escalation–de-escalation framework was taught in the police academy as a guide for appropriate action when applying force. It generated a second coding scheme focused on the suspect's body. Central to the case made by the defense was the proposal that the policemen themselves were required to evaluate Mr King's actions as either *aggressive* or *cooperative* in order to decide whether to escalate or de-escalate force, that is whether they should hit him again. The key perceptual decision posed in the analysis of the tape thus becomes whether the policemen can legitimately see the suspect as aggressive, in which case, it is argued, they are justified in applying further force. The following is from the cross-examination of defendant Powell, the officer who landed the most blows on Mr King:

Prosecutor: You can't look at that video and say
that every one of those blows
is reasonable can you.
(1.0)
Powell: Oh I ***can*** if I put my perceptions in.

Crucially, the defense argues that an interpretive framework, focused on the suspect's actions, places control of the situation in the victim, since his actions control the response of the police:

Defense: Rodney ***King***
and Rodney King alone
was in control of the situation.

The net effect of buying into this category system as a framework for the interpretation of the tape is a most consequential structuring of the dense and complicated perceptual field provided by the tape, with the suspect/victim King, becoming the figure, the focus of minute scrutiny, while the officers performing the beating recede into the background.

EXPERT VISION: AN ETHNOGRAPHY OF SEEING

To analyse the tape in these terms the defense calls Sergeant Duke from the Los Angeles Police Department as an expert on the use of force by the police Fig. 14.1. Commentators on the first trial considered Sergeant Duke the most important and persuasive witness in the case.

Figure 14.1 Courtesy George Holliday © 1991. All rights reserved. NO REPRODUCTION OF THIS STILL MAY BE MADE WITHOUT THE PRIOR WRITTEN CONSENT OF GEORGE HOLLIDAY.

At the point where we enter the following sequence, the prosecutor has noted that Mr King appears to be moving into a position appropriate for handcuffing him, and that one officer is in fact reaching for his handcuffs, i.e. the suspect is being cooperative.

Prosecutor:	So uh would you,
	again consider this to be:
	a nonaggressive, movement by Mr King?
Sgt. Duke:	At this time no I wouldn't. (1.1)
Prosecutor:	It is aggressive.
Sgt. Duke:	Yes. It's starting to be. (0.9)
	This foot, is laying flat, (0.8)

8 There's [starting to be a ***bend***.] in uh (0.6)
9 this leg (0.4)
10 in his butt (0.4)
11 The buttocks area has [started to rise.] (0.7)
12 which would put us,
13 [at the beginning of our *spec*trum] again.

Here the process of coding events within a relevant perceptual field becomes an open contest as prosecution and defense use a range of discursive practices to debate whether body movements of Mr King visible on the videotape should be coded as cooperative or aggressive. By noting both submissive elements in Mr King's posture, and the fact that one of the officers is reaching for his handcuffs, the prosecutor has tried to make the case that the tape demonstrates that at this point the officers perceive King as cooperative. If he can establish this point, hitting Mr King again would be unjustified, and the officers should be found guilty of the crimes they are charged with. The contested vision being debated here has very high stakes.

To rebut the vision proposed by the prosecutor, Sergeant Duke uses the semantic resources provided by language to code as aggressive extremely subtle body movements of a man lying face down beneath the officers (lines 7–11). Note, for example, not only his explicit placement of King at the very edge, the beginning, of the aggressive spectrum (line 13), but also how very small movements are made much larger by situating them within a prospective horizon through repeated use of 'starting to' (lines 6, 8, 11). The events visible on the tape are enhanced and amplified by the language used to describe them.

This focusing of attention organizes the perceptual field provided by the videotape into a salient figure, the aggressive suspect, who is highlighted against an amorphous background containing nonfocal participants, the officers doing the beating. Such structuring of the materials provided by the image is accomplished not only through talk, but also through gesture. As Sergeant Duke speaks he brings his hand to the screen and points to the parts of Mr King's body that he is arguing display aggression (Fig. 14.2). Here a gesture and the perceptual field which it was articulating mutually elaborate each other, as the touchable events on the television screen provide visible *evidence* for the description constructed through talk. What emerges from Sergeant Duke's testimony is not

Figure 14.2 Courtesy George Holliday © 1991. All rights reserved. NO REPRODUCTION OF THIS STILL MAY BE MADE WITHOUT THE PRIOR WRITTEN CONSENT OF GEORGE HOLLIDAY.

just a *statement*, a static category, but a *demonstration* built through the active interplay between a coding scheme and the domain of scrutiny to which it is being applied. As talk and image mutually enhance each other, a demonstration that is greater than the sum of its parts emerges, while simultaneously, Mr King, rather than the officers, becomes the focus of attention as the expert's finger articulating the image delineates what is relevant within it.

By virtue of the category systems erected by the defense, the minute rise in Mr King's buttocks noted on the tape unleashes a cascade of perceptual inferences that have the effect of exonerating the officers. A rise in Mr King's body becomes interpreted as aggression, which in turn justifies an escalation of force. Like other parties faced with a coding task, the jury is led to engage in intense, minute cognitive scrutiny as they look at the tape of the beating to decide the issues at stake in the case. However, once the defense coding scheme is accepted as a relevant framework for looking at the tape, the operative perspective for viewing it is no longer a layperson's reaction to a man lying on the ground being beaten, but instead a micro-analysis of the movements being made by that man's body to see if it is exhibiting not pain, but aggression.

The expert witnesses for the defense simultaneously construct actions as both rational and without moral responsibility in the case of the police, and as mindlessly mechanical and morally responsible in the case of Rodney King.[4] Thus references to phenomena such as 'an assessment period' imply rational deliberation on the part of the police, without individual moral responsibility in terms other than the correctness of assessment (e.g. the agentless passive voice of 'We see a blow being delivered', 'The force has again been escalated', and 'kicks' as tools of the trade). On the other hand, Mr King is characterized both as an almost mindless, moving force (e.g. 'The buttocks area has started to rise ... ') and as being 'in control of the situation'. This is accomplished in part by the disassembly of King's body from a responsible agent into a bunch of moving parts. These become the triggering mechanism for a typified process which, it is argued, that the police are required to respond to in a disciplined, dispassionate way. Discourses of rationality, of mechanism and of moral responsibility are simultaneously, but strategically and selectively deployed.

In the first trial, though the prosecution disputed the analysis of specific body movements as displays of aggression, the relevance of looking at the tape in terms of such a category system was not challenged. Observers considered this to be a very serious mistake (Lieberman 1993a: A26). A key difference in the second trial, which led to the conviction of two of the officers, was that there the prosecution gave the jury alternative frameworks for interpreting the events on the tape. These included both a motive for the beating, namely that the policemen were teaching a man who'd been disrespectful to them a lesson (Mydans 1993c: A8), and ways of seeing the movements of Mr King's body that Sergeant Duke highlighted as normal muscular responses to a beating, rather than as displays of incipient aggression. Mr King 'cocks his leg', not in preparation for a charge, but because his leg naturally jerks after being hit with a metal club. The jury was instructed to look also at the body behaviour of the policemen who were not physically hitting Mr King, to see them as nonchalantly watching a beating rather than poised to subdue a still dangerous suspect. Instead of restricting focus to the body of Mr King, the second prosecutor drew the jury's attention to the slender stature of Officer Briseño, who was sent in alone at the end of the beating to handcuff the man that the defense was portraying as a dangerous giant. This prosecutor also emphasized to the jury inherent contradictions in the arguments being made by the defense: Mr King was being portrayed as both a cunning martial arts expert, scanning the scene to plot his next move, and as a deranged man crazed by drugs. Instead, the prosecution argued, he was simply a beaten man who fell helplessly to the ground.[5] Though most of the evidence used in the two trials was the same (most crucially the tape), the prosecutors in the second trial were able to build discursively their own interpretative frameworks to counter those that had been so effectively deployed by the defense, and thus provide the jury with ways of looking at the tape that were not made available to the first jury.

The perspectival framework provided by a professional coding scheme constitutes the objects in the domain of scrutiny that are the focus of attention. By using the coding scheme to animate the events being studied, the expert teaches the jury how to look at the tape, how to see relevant events within it (Shuy 1982: 125). He provides them with an ethnography of seeing that situates the events visible on the tape within the worklife and phenomenal world of a particular work community. Here, this ethnographer is not an outside anthropologist, but an actual member of the community whose work is being explicated. One of the very interesting things about expert testimony in court is the way in which it forces members of a discourse community to become metapragmatically aware of the communication practices that organize their work, including, in this case, violence as a systematic mode of discourse capable of being described scientifically as professional practice in minute detail.

In so far as the courtroom provides a dialogic framework encompassing the discourse of two different professions, scrutiny is occurring on a number of distinct levels: first, police scrutiny of the suspect's body as a guide for whether to beat him; secondly, scrutiny by those in court, including the jury and expert witnesses, as they assess the scrutiny of the police;[6] and thirdly, within the framework of this chapter there is yet another level of scrutiny as we examine how those in the courtroom scrutinize the police scrutinizing their victim.

HIGHLIGHTING

Coding schemes carry with them an array of cognitive operations, a structure of intentionality, an orientation towards the world being examined, that is lodged not within the mind of the individual, but instead within a domain of professional discourse. A person who agrees to use such a coding scheme to interpret the world that is relevant to his/her work, entrains his/her perceptions to a specific view of the world, even as he/she minutely examines it. By virtue of the coding schemes introduced by the defense, those in the courtroom, including the jury, are no longer focusing their attention on the blows of the police officers, but instead are analysing in minute detail the body behaviour of the victim in order to determine whether it counts as aggressive.

The perceptual field provided by the tape was manipulated and enhanced in other ways as well. At the very beginning of the tape, while the camera was still slightly out of focus, Mr King ran towards the officers. On the tape itself this event is hard to see; it happens very quickly and is difficult to discern in the midst of a dark but very complex perceptual field filled with other events, including numerous police officers, a police car and Mr King's own car. The images visible on the tape are made even more difficult to see by the movement of the zooming camera and its lack of focus.

One of the defense attorneys in the first trial had photographs made from individual tape frames. The photos were cropped, enlarged and pasted in sequence to form a display over a meter long that was placed in front of the jury on an easel. The salience of Mr King in these images was amplified through use of *highlighting*. As the defense attorney unveiled his display, he placed clear overlays with large white lines outlining Mr King's body on top of the photos (Fig. 14.3). The defense attorney enhances objects in the domain of scrutiny to call forth from the murky pixels on the video screen the discursive object that is the point of his argument: a large, violent, charging man who was so dangerous that hitting him

Figure 14.3 Courtesy George Holliday © 1991.

47 times with metal clubs was reasonable and justified. By virtue of the figure/ground relationship established through such highlighting, the policemen, all situated beyond the boundaries of the lines drawn by the lawyer, recede into the background.

When videotape is used as the medium for displaying Mr King's movements, a sense of what is happening as events unfold rapidly through time can be obtained only by replaying the tape repeatedly, while trying to select from the confusing images on the screen that subset of visible events that one is trying to concentrate upon. The work of the viewer is radically changed when these scenes are transformed into the photographic array. Movement through time becomes movement through space (i.e. the left to right progression of the cropped frames). Each image remains available to the viewer instead of disappearing when its successor arrives, so that both the sequence as a whole, and each event within it, can be contemplated and rescanned at leisure. Much of the visual clutter[7] in the original images is eliminated by cropping the photos.

In his analysis of similar representational practices in scientific discourse, Lynch (1988) wrote about them providing an *externalized retina*. The defense lawyer makes precisely the same argument, stating that by enhancing the image in this way he is able to structure the world being scrutinized so that it reveals what his client perceived (lines 5–8):

Defense: Rodney King, (0.4) in the very beginning, (1.0)
in the first six frames, (2.2)
of this incident, (2.4)
Went (4.7) from the grou:nd, (0.4) to a charge. (1.2)
And what Sergeant Koon will tell you =
= this is his rendi:tion, (0.4) of what he sa:w. (0.7)
((*Laying White Line Overlays on Top of Photos*))
This is how he perceived it. (3.6)
But once he saw Rodney King,
ri:se to his feet, (1.2) and attack at Powell, (1.4)
That in ***Koon***'s mind, (0.9) in charge of his officers (1.2)
that Rodney King has set the tone. (1.6)
Rodney King, (1.1) was trying to get in that position.

Once again talk and visual representation mutually amplify each other. Descriptors such as 'a charge' provide instructions for seeing the highlighted sequence on the easel, while that very same sequence provides seeable proof for the argument being made in the defense attorney's talk. (At the second trial Mr King testified that he ran after one of the officers who said 'We're going to kill you nigger. Run'). At line 13 the defense attorney points with his finger towards the last photograph in the series, the one where Mr King is actually making contact with Officer Powell. This deictic gesture establishes that image as the referent for 'that position' at the end of line 13, i.e. the attacking position that the defense is arguing Rodney King was repetitively trying to gain. Traditionally, work on gesture in interaction (and deixis in linguistics) has drawn a bubble around the perimeters of the participants' bodies. The body of the actor has not been connected to the built world within which it is situated. In these data the graphic display that receives the point is as much a constructed discursive object as the pointing finger or the utterance being spoken. All three mutually elaborate each other. Theoretical frameworks that partition the components of this process into separate fields of study cannot do justice to the reflexive relationship that exists between the talk, the gesture and the artifacts that have been built and put in place precisely to receive that pointing. It is necessary to view all of these phenomena as integrated components of a common activity.

THE POWER TO SPEAK AS A PROFESSIONAL

Expert witnesses, such as Sergeant Duke, are entitled to speak about events in the courtroom because of their membership in a relevant community of practitioners. Sergeant Duke's voice can be heard because he is a policeman, an expert on police use of force, and thus someone who can speak about what the policemen on the tape are perceiving as they look at Mr King writhing around on the ground. The structure of his expertise, which warrants his right to speak authoritatively, creates a situated perspective from which events on the tape are viewed.

	((*After demonstrating by playing the videotape that Mr King appears to be moving his right hand behind his back with the palm tip.*))
Prosecutor:	That would be the position you'd want him in.=
	= Is that correct. (0.6)
Sgt. Duke:	Not, (0.2) Not with uh:, (0.2) the way he is. (0.6)

	His uh:, (0.4) His leg is uh
	Is bent in this area. (0.6)
	Uh:, (0.2) Had he moved in this hand here being uh:
	(0.4) straight up and down.
	That causes me concern (0.7)
Prosecutor:	Uh does it also cause you concern
	that someone's ***step***ped on the back of his neck.
Sgt. Duke:	(0.6) No it does not.

Here, as in the data examined earlier, Sergeant Duke displays intense concern about very small movements of Mr King's leg and hand. However, when asked about the fact that an officer has stepped on the back of Mr King's neck, Sergeant Duke states, in effect, that violent actions performed by a police officer against their suspect cause him no concern at all. The events on the tape are being viewed and articulated by Sergeant Duke from a local, situated perspective, that of the police who are beating Mr King, and indeed this is precisely his domain of expertise.

In so far as the perceptual structures that organize interpretation of the tape are lodged within a profession and not an isolated individual, there is a tremendous asymmetry about who can speak as an expert about the events on the tape, and thus structure interpretation of it. Sergeant Duke's expertise is restricted to the police and he articulates *only* their perspective:

Sgt. Duke	They're taught to evaluate.
	And that's what they were doing in the last two frames.
	Or three frames.
Prosecutor:	Can you read their mind uh, (1.4) Sergeant Duke.
	(1.3)
Sgt. Duke:	I can, (0.4) form an opinion based on my training.
	and having trained people,
	what I can perceive that their perceptions are.
	(0.6)
Prosecutor:	Well what's Mr. King's perceptions at this time.
	(0.6)
Sgt. Duke:	I've never been a suspect.
	I don't know.

While administering a beating like this is recognized within the courtroom as the craftwork of a profession, no equivalent social group exists for the suspect. Victims do not constitute a profession. Thus no expert witnesses are available to interpret these events and animate the images on the tape from his perspective. In the second trial, Mr King was called as a witness. However, he could not testify about whether the policemen beating him were using unreasonable force since he lacked 'expertise on the constitution or the use of force' (Newton 1993a: A16).

The effect of all this is the production of a set of contradictory asymmetries.[8] Within the domain of discourse recorded on the videotape it is argued that Mr King is in control of the interaction and this is what the first jury found. However, within the discourse of the courtroom no one can speak for the suspect. His perception is not lodged within a profession and thus publicly available to others as a set of official discursive procedures. Within the discourse of the trial he is an object to be scrutinized, not an actor with a voice of his own. However, within the discourse visible on the tape he is constituted as the controlling actor.

The way in which professional coding schemes for constituting control and asymmetry in interaction are used by the police to justify the way that they beat someone alerts us to ethical problems that can arise when, as social scientists we put our professional skills at the service of another profession, and amplify its voice and the power it can enforce over those who become the objects of its scrutiny.

CONCLUSION

Central to the social and cognitive organization of a profession is its ability to shape events in the world it is focusing its attention upon into the phenomenal objects around which the discourse of the profession is organized, e.g. to locate legally consequential instances of aggression or cooperation in the visible movements of a man's body. This chapter has investigated three practices used to accomplish such professional vision: coding schemes, highlighting, and the production and articulation of graphic representations. Such work contributes to efforts by linguistic anthropologists, practice theorists and conversation analysts to develop anthropologically informed analyses of human action and cognition as socially situated phenomena, e.g. activities accomplished through ongoing, contingent work within the historically shaped settings of the lived social world.

The ability to see relevant entities is not lodged in the individual mind, but instead within a community of competent practitioners. This has a range of consequences. First, the power to see authoritatively and produce the range of phenomena that are consequential for the organization of a society is not homogeneously distributed. Different professions – medicine, law, the police – have the power to see legitimately, constitute and articulate alternative kinds of event. Professional vision is perspectival, lodged within specific social entities, and unevenly allocated. The consequences that this had for who was entitled to instruct the jury about what was happening on the Rodney King videotape supports Foucault's (1981) analysis of how the discursive procedures of a society structure what kinds of talk can and cannot be heard, who is qualified to speak the truth, and the conditions that establish the rationality of statements. However, rather than situating such phenomena entirely in a rather general notion of 'discourse', it is necessary to investigate in detail the situated practices through which socially relevant talk and vision are accomplished, something made possible by the resources of fields such as conversation analysis.

Secondly, such vision is not a purely mental process, but instead something accomplished through the competent deployment in a relevant setting of a complex of situated practices. An earlier generation of anthropologists, influenced by Saussure's notion of *langue*, brought precision and clarity to their analytical projects by focusing on the grammars of cultural phenomena such as category systems and myths, while ignoring the courses of practical action within which categories and stories were articulated in the endogenous scenes of a society's everyday activities. The procedures investigated in this chapter move beyond the mind of the actor to encompass features of the setting where action is occurring. Through practices such as highlighting, coding and articulating graphic representations, categories (such as aggression) are linked to specific phenomena in a relevant domain of scrutiny (e.g. the images provided by the videotape), creating a whole that is greater than the sum of its parts, e.g. a visible demonstration of aggression. As argued by Wittgenstein (1958), a category or rule cannot determine its own application; rules are lodged within practices. Seeing what can count as 'aggression' in a relevant domain of scrutiny is both a contingent accomplishment and a locus for contestation, indeed a central site for legal argument. Categories and the phenomena, to which they are being applied, mutually elaborate each other

(C. Goodwin, in press; Heritage 1984; Keller and Keller 1993), and indeed this is precisely one of the central processes that provides for ongoing change in legal and other category systems.

There are good reasons why the configuration of practices investigated in this chapter are generic, pervasive and consequential in human activity. First, processes of classification are central to human cognition, at times forming the basic subject matter of entire fields such as cognitive anthropology. Through the construction and use of coding schemes, relevant classification systems are socially organized as professional and bureaucratic knowledge structures, entraining in fine detail the cognitive activity of those who administer them, producing some of the objects of knowledge around which discourse in a profession is organized, and frequently constituting accountable loci of power for those whose actions are surveyed and coded. Secondly, though most theorizing about human cognition in the twentieth century has focused on mental events, e.g. internal representations, a number of activity theorists, students of scientific and everyday practice, ethnomethodologists and cognitive anthropologists have consistently insisted that the ability of human beings to modify the world around them, to structure settings for the activities that habitually occur within them, and to build tools and other representational artifacts is as central to human cognition as processes hidden inside the brain. The ability to build structures in the world that organize knowledge, shape perception and structure future action, is one way that human cognition is shaped through ongoing historical practices. Graphic representations constitute a prototypical example of how human beings build external cognitive artifacts for the organization and persuasive display of relevant knowledge. This chapter has investigated some of the ways a professional community organizes the production and understanding of such representations through the deployment of situated practices articulated within ongoing processes of human interaction (see also C. Goodwin 1995). Human activity characteristically occurs in environments that provide a very complicated perceptual field. A quite general class of cognitive practices consists of methods for highlighting that perceptual field so that phenomena relevant to the activity the participants are engaged in are made salient, a process that simultaneously helps classify those phenomena (e.g. as an aggressive movement). Practices such as highlighting link relevant features of a setting to the activity being performed in that setting.

In view of the generic character of the issues that these practices address, it is not surprising that they frequently work in concert with each other, e.g, Sergeant Duke's pointing finger linked a category in a coding scheme to specific phenomena visible in a graphic representation. The way in which such highlighting structures the perception of others by reshaping a domain of scrutiny so that some phenomena are made salient, while others fade into the background, has strong rhetorical and political consequences. By looking at how these practices work together within situated courses of action, it becomes possible to investigate quite diverse phenomena within a single analytical framework. As these practices are used within sequences of talk-in-interaction, members of a profession both hold each accountable for, and contest, the proper perception and constitution of the objects of knowledge around which their discourse is organized.[9]

NOTES

An earlier version of this chapter appeared in the *American Anthropologist* **96**(3), 606–33, September 1994. We gratefully acknowledge the permission granted by *American Anthropological Association* to print this chapter in the present volume. We owe a tremendous debt to Lucy Suchman for demonstrating to us just how important the way in which participants tailor and reshape objects in work settings, in order to accomplish local tasks, is for any understanding of human cognition and action. We wish to thank Lisa Capps, Aaron Cicourel, Janet Keller, John Heritage, Bernard Hibbits, Cathryn Houghton, Per Linell, Hugh Mehan, Curtis Renoe, Peggy Sanday, Lucy Suchman and Patty Jo Watson for helpful and insightful comments on an earlier version of this analysis. We thank Court TV for permission to use images from their broadcast of the Rodney King Trial.

1. Elsewhere we have extended this analysis to other professions, including archaeology (C. Goodwin 1994), airline operations (M. Goodwin 1995, 1996; C. Goodwin and Goodwin in press) and oceanography (C. Goodwin 1995). A more extended version of the present analysis can be found in C. Goodwin (1994).
2. See Bourdieu (1977), Chaiklin and Lave (1993), Hanks (1987) and Lave and Wenger (1991) for contemporary work on practice theory. Analysis of how cognition makes use of phenomena distributed in everyday settings can be found in Lave (1988), Rogoff (1990), Rogoff and Lave (1984) and Suchman (1987). Hutchins (1995) provides a very clear demonstration of how cognition is not located in the mind of a single individual, but instead is embedded within distributed systems, includ-

ing socially differentiated actors and external representations embodied in tools. Dougherty and Keller (1982) demonstrate how cognitive frameworks and material features of a setting mutually constitute each other. A collection of recent work by linguistic anthropologists on the discursive constitution of context can be found in Duranti and Goodwin (1992). Work on Activity Theory (Wertsch 1985; Engeström 1987), growing out of the pioneering work of Vygotsky (1978), has long stressed the mediated, historically shaped character of both cognition and social organization. Though focused on the organization of sequences of talk rather than tool-mediated cognition, the field of Conversation Analysis (Atkinson and Heritage 1984; Drew and Heritage 1992; Sachs 1992; Sachs, Schegloff and Jefferson 1974) has developed the most powerful resources currently available for the analysis of the interactive organization of emerging action within actual settings (C. Goodwin 1995), including the way in which each next action relies upon prior action for its proper interpretation while simultaneously reshaping the context that will provide the ground for subsequent action.

3. In the following examples data are transcribed using the system developed by Gail Jefferson (Sachs, Schegloff and Jefferson 1974, 731–3) for the analysis of conversation. The conventions most relevant to the analysis in the present chapter include the use of ***bold italics*** to indicate talk spoken with special emphasis, a left bracket [to mark the onset of overlapping talk and numbers in parentheses, e.g. (1.2), to note the length of silences in seconds and tenths of seconds. A dash marks the cut-off of the current sound. An equal sign indicates 'latching', that there is no interval between the end of one unit and the beginning of a next. Transcribers' comments are italicized in double parentheses; talk enclosed with single parentheses indicates a problematic hearing. Punctuation symbols are used to mark intonation changes rather than as grammatical symbols: a period indicates a falling contour, a question mark a rising contour, and a comma a falling-rising contour, as might be found in the midst of a list.
4. We are deeply indebted to Lucy Suchman for bringing the phenomena discussed in this paragraph to our attention.
5. The prosecution arguments at the second trial noted here are drawn from Charles Goodwin's notes, made at the closing argument, and newspaper reports.
6. The ability to record events on videotape and replay them in the court created baroque possibilities for layering and framing the perception of events. At the second trial one of the defendants, Officer Briseño, chose not to testify. However, the prosecution received permission to play for the jury videotape of his testimony at the first trial in which he criticized the actions of the other defendants. 'That placed jurors in the Federal trial in the unusual position of watching a defendant on one videotape

describe yet another videotape' (Newton 1993c: A25). The jury was able to watch 'as the taped Officer Briseño spoke from the monitor accompanied by the word 'Live', while the real Officer Briseño sat passively with the other defendants, following his own year-old words on a transcript' (Mydans 1993a: A8).

7. The notion of what events constitute 'clutter' to be eliminated is, of course, an important political decision being made by the party who reshapes the image for presentation to the jury.
8. For analysis of how asymmetries are consequential to the organization of discourse, see Linell and Luckmann (1991) and Drew (1991).
9. Professional settings provide a perspicuous site for the investigation of how objects of knowledge, controlled by and relevant to the defining work of a specific community, are socially constructed from within the settings that make up the lifeworld of that community, i.e. endogenously, through systematic discursive procedures. This should not, however, be taken to imply that such processes are limited to professional discourse. The way in which we reify our realities through practices such as highlighting and coding are pervasive features of human social and cognitive life.

REFERENCES

Atkinson, J. Maxwell and Heritage, John (eds) (1984) *Structures of Social Action*. Cambridge: Cambridge University Press.

Bourdieu, Pierre (1977) *Outline of a Theory of Practice*. Cambridge: Cambridge University Press (translated by Richard Nice).

Chaiklin, Seth and Lave, Jean (eds) (1993) *Understanding Practice: Perspectives on Activity and Context*. Cambridge: Cambridge University Press.

Cicourel, Aaron V. (1964) *Method and Measurement in Sociology*. New York: Free Press.

Cicourel, Aaron V. (1968) *The Social Organization of Juvenile Justice*. New York: Wiley.

Court TV (1992) *The 'Rodney King' Case: What the Jury Saw in* California v. Powell. New York: Court TV Video Library Service.

Dougherty, Janet W. D. and Keller, Charles (1982) Taskonomy: A Practical Approach to Knowledge Structures. *American Ethnologist*, **9** (4), 763–71.

Drew, Paul (1991) Asymmetries of Knowledge in Conversational Interactions. In Ivana Marková and Klaus Foppa (eds), *Asymmetries in Dialogue* (pp. 21–48). Hemel Hempstead: Harvester Wheatsheaf.

Drew, Paul (1992) Contested Evidence in Courtroom Examination: The Case of a Trial for Rape. In Paul Drew and John Heritage (eds), *Talk at Work: Interaction in Institutional Settings* (pp. 470–520). Cambridge: Cambridge University Press.

Drew, Paul and Heritage, John (eds) (1992) *Talk at Work: Interaction in Institutional Settings.* Cambridge: Cambridge University Press.

Duranti, Alessandro and Goodwin, Charles (eds) (1992) *Rethinking Context: Language as an Interactive Phenomenon.* Cambridge: Cambridge University Press.

Engeström, Yrjö (1987) *Learning by Expanding: An Activity-Theoretical Approach to Developmental Research.* Helsinki: Orienta-Konsultit Oy.

Foucault, Michel (1981) The Order of Discourse. In R. Young (ed), *Untying the Text: A Post-Structuralist Reader* (pp. 48–78). Boston: Routledge, Kegan, Paul.

Goodwin, Charles (1994) Professional Vision. *American Anthropologist* **96** (3), 606–33.

Goodwin, Charles (1995) Seeing in Depth. *Social Studies of Science* **25**, 237–274.

Goodwin, Charles (in press) Transparent Vision. In Elinor Ochs, Emanuel A. Schegloff and Sandra Thompson (eds) *Interaction and Grammar.* Cambridge: Cambridge University Press.

Goodwin, Charles and Goodwin, Marjorie Harness (in press) Seeing as a Situated Activity: Formulating Planes. In David Middleton and Yrjö Engestrom (eds), *Cognition and Communication at Work.* Cambridge: Cambridge University Press.

Goodwin, Marjorie Harness (1995) Assembling a Response: Setting and Collaboratively Constructed Work Talk. In Paul ten Have and George Psathas (eds) *Situated Order: Studies in the Social Organization of Talk and Embodied Activities* (pp. 173–86). Washington DC: University Press of America.

Goodwin, Marjorie Harness (1996) Informings and Announcements in Their Environment: Prosody within a Multi-Activity Work Setting. In Elizabeth Couper-Kuhlen and Margret Selting (eds), *Prosody in Conversation: Interactional Studies* (pp. 436–61). Cambridge: Cambridge University Press.

Hanks, William (1987) Discourse Genres in a Theory of Practice. *American Ethnologist* **14** (4), 668–92.

Heritage, John (1984) *Garfinkel and Ethnomethodology.* Cambridge: Polity Press.

Hutchins, Edwin (1995) *Cognition in the Wild.* Cambridge, MA: MIT Press.

Keller, Charles and Keller, Janet Dixon (1993) Thinking and Acting with Iron. In Seth Chaiklin and Jean Lave (eds), *Understanding Practice: Perspectives on Activity and Context* (pp. 125–43). Cambridge: Cambridge University Press.

Lave, Jean (1988) *Cognition in Practice.* Cambridge: Cambridge University Press.

Lave, Jean (1991) Situating Learning in Communities of Practice. In Lauren Resnick, John M. Levine and Stephanie D. Teasley (eds), *Perspectives on*

Socially Shared Cognition (pp. 63–84). Washington, DC: American Psychological Association.

Lave, Jean and Wenger, Etienne (1991) *Situated Learning: Legitimate Peripheral Participation*. Cambridge: Cambridge University Press.

Lieberman, Paul (1993a, 7 February) King Case Prosecutors Must Scale Hurdles of History. *The Los Angeles Times*, p. Al, A26.

Lieberman, Paul (1993b, 4 April) King Trial May Come Down to a Case of Expert vs. Expert. *The Los Angeles Times*, p. Al, A32.

Linell, Per and Luckmann, Thomas (1991) Asymmetries in Dialogue: Some Conceptual Preliminaries. In Ivana Marková and Klaus Foppa (eds), *Asymmetries in Dialogue* (pp. 1–20). Hemel Hempstead: Harvester Wheatsheaf.

Lynch, Michael (1988) The Externalized Retina: Selection and Mathematization in the Visual Documentation of Objects in the Life Sciences. *Human Studies* **11**, 201–34.

Mydans, Seth (1993a, 7 April) Defendant on Videotape Gives Trial an Odd Air. *The New York Times*, p. A8.

Mydans, Seth (1993b, 21 April) Prosecutor in Beating Case Urges Jury to Rely on Tape. *The New York Times*, p. A7.

Mydans, Seth (1993c, 9 April) Prosecutor in Officers' Case Ends With Focus on Beating. *The New York Times*, p. A8.

Mydans, Seth (1993d, 2 February) Their Lives Consumed, Los Angeles Officers Await Trial. *The New York Times*, p. A10.

Newton, Jim (1993a, 10 March) 'I Was Just Trying to Stay Alive,' King Tells Federal Jury. *Los Angeles Times*, p. Al, A16.

Newton, Jim (1993b, 11 March) King Admits Lies but Insists That He Didn't Hit Officers. *The Los Angeles Times*, p. Al, A18.

Newton, Jim (1993c, 7 April) King Jury Sees Key Videotape; Prosecutors Rest. *The Los Angeles Times*, p. Al, A25.

Rogoff, Barbara (1990) *Apprenticeship in Thinking*. New York: Oxford University Press.

Rogoff, Barbara and Lave, Jean (eds) (1984) *Everyday Cognition: Its Development in Social Context*. Cambridge, MA: Harvard University Press.

Sacks, Harvey (1992). *Lectures on Conversation: Volume I*. Edited by Gail Jefferson, with an Introduction by Emanuel A. Schegloff. Oxford: Basil Blackwell.

Sacks, Harvey, Schegloff, Emanuel A. and Jefferson, Gail (1974) A Simplest Systematics for the Organization of Turn-taking for Conversation. *Language* **50**, 696–735.

Shuy, Roger (1982) The Unit of Analysis in a Criminal Law Case. In Deborah Tannen (ed.), *Analyzing Discourse: Text and Talk* (pp. 113–26). Washington, DC: Georgetown University Press.

Suchman, Lucy A. (1987) *Plans and Situated Actions: The Problem of Human Machine Communication*. Cambridge: Cambridge University Press.

Vygotsky, L. S. (1978) *Mind in Society: The Development of Higher Psychological Processes.* Cambridge: Harvard University Press.

Wertsch, James (1985) *Culture, Communication and Cognition: Vygotskian Perspectives.* Cambridge: Cambridge University Press.

Wittgenstein, Ludwig (1958) *Philosophical Investigations.* Edited by G. E. M. Anscombe and R. Rhees, translated by G. E. M. Anscombe, 2nd edition, Oxford: Blackwell.

Name Index

Subject Index